W9-BDO-230

BARRON'S
FOREIGN LANGUAGE GUIDES

SPANISH
Verbs

THIRD EDITION

Christopher Kendris

B.S., M.S., Columbia University
M.A., Ph.D., Northwestern University

Former Assistant Professor
Department of French and Spanish
State University of New York at Albany

Theodore Kendris

Ph.D., Université Laval, Québec, Canada

Department of Languages and Cultures
Bloomsburg University of Pennsylvania
Bloomsburg, Pennsylvania

BARRON'S

To St. Sophia Greek Orthodox Church
of Albany, New York, our parish
and
to the eternal memory of our beloved
YOLANDA KENDRIS
who is always by our side.
With love

All inquiries should be addressed to:
Barron's Educational Series, Inc.
250 Wireless Boulevard
Hauppauge, New York 11788
www.barronseduc.com

Library of Congress Control Card No. 2011936595

ISBN: 978-0-7641-4776-0

PRINTED IN CHINA
9 8 7 6 5

Contents

Abbreviations

adj.   adjetivo (adjective)

ant.   anterior

comp.   compuesto (compound, perfect)

e.g.   for example

fut.   futuro (future)

i.e.   that is, that is to say

imp.   imperfecto (imperfect)

ind.   indicativo (indicative)

inf.   infinitivo (infinitive)

p.   page

part.   participio (participle)

part. pas.   participio de pasado, participio pasivo (past participle)

part. pr.   participio de presente, participio activo, gerundio
       (present participle)

pas.   pasado, pasivo (past, passive)

perf.   perfecto (perfect)

perf. ind.   perfecto de indicativo (present perfect indicative)

perf. subj.   perfecto de subjuntivo (present perfect or past subjunctive)

plpf.   pluscuamperfecto (pluperfect)

Introduction

Verb conjugations are usually found scattered in Spanish grammar books and they are difficult to find quickly when needed. Verbs have always been a major problem for students no matter what system or approach the teacher uses. You will master Spanish verb forms if you study this book a few minutes every day, especially the pages before and after the alphabetical listing of the 301 verbs.

The verbs included here are arranged alphabetically by infinitive at the top of each page. The book contains many common verbs of high frequency, both reflexive and non-reflexive, which you need to know. It also contains many other frequently used verbs that are irregular in some way. On page 310 we give you an additional 1,000 Spanish verbs that are conjugated in the same way as model verbs. If the verb you have in mind is not given, consult the list that begins on page 310.

The subject pronouns have been omitted from the conjugations in order to emphasize the verb forms. We give you the subject pronouns on page xlii. Turn to that page now and become acquainted with them.

The first thing to do when you use this book is to become familiar with it from cover to cover—turn to the table of contents at the beginning of this book as we guide you in the following way:

(a)   Beginning on page vii we show you how to form a present participle (e.g., **hablar/hablando**) regularly in Spanish, and we give you examples. We also give you the common irregular present participles and the many uses of the present participle.

(b)   On page ix we show you how to form a past participle regularly in Spanish, and we give you examples (e.g., **hablar/hablado**). We also give you the common irregular past participles and the many uses of the past participle (for example, **he hablado**/I have spoken).

(c)   On page xi you will find the principal parts (that is, the "building blocks" of the different forms of Spanish verbs) of some important Spanish verbs. This is useful because if you know these you are well on your way to mastering Spanish verb forms.

(d)   On page xii we give you a sample English verb conjugation so that you can get an idea of the way a verb is expressed in the English tenses. Many people do not know one tense from another because they have never learned the use of verb tenses in a systematic and organized way—not even in English! How can you know, for example, that you need the conditional form of a verb in Spanish when you want to say *"I would go"* to the movies if . . ." or the pluperfect tense in

Spanish if you want to say *"I had gone . . . ?"* The sample English verb conjugation with the names of the tenses and their numerical ranking will help you to distinguish one tense from another so that you will know what tense you need to express a verb in Spanish.

(e)   On page xiv we begin a summary of meanings and uses of Spanish verb tenses and moods as related to English verb tenses and moods. That section is very important and useful because we separate the seven simple tenses from the seven compound tenses. We give you the name of each tense in Spanish and English starting with the present indicative, which we call tense number one because it is the most frequently used tense. We assign a number to each tense name so that you can fix each one in your mind and associate the tense names and numbers in their logical order. We explain briefly what each tense is, when you use it, and we give examples using verbs in sentences in Spanish and English. At the end of each tense we show you how to form that tense for regular verbs (verbs that follow a regular, easily predictable conjugation pattern).

(f)   On page xxxii we explain the Imperative, which is a mood, not a tense, and we give numerous examples using it.

(g)   On page xxxv we explain briefly the progressive forms of tenses, and we give examples. On the following page we note the future subjunctive and the future perfect subjunctive. We explain how these two rarely used tenses are formed, and we give examples of what tenses are used in place of them in informal writing and in conversation.

(h)   On page xxxvii we give you a summary of all the fourteen tenses in Spanish with English equivalents, which we have divided into the seven simple tenses and the seven compound tenses. After referring to that summary frequently, you will soon know that tense number 1 is the present indicative, tense number 2 is the imperfect indicative, and so on. We also explain how each compound tense is based on each simple tense. Try to see these two divisions as two frames, two pictures, with the seven simple tenses in one frame and the seven compound tenses in another frame. Place them side by side in your mind, and you will see how tense number 8 is related to tense number 1, tense number 9 to tense number 2, and so on. If you study the numerical arrangement of each of the seven simple tenses and associate the tense number with the tense name, you will find it very easy to learn the names of the seven compound tenses, how they rank numerically according to use, how they are formed, and when they are used. Spend at least ten minutes every day studying these preliminary pages to help you understand better the fourteen tenses in Spanish.

Finally, in the back pages of this book there are useful indexes: an English-Spanish verb index, an index of common irregular Spanish verb forms identified by infinitive, and a list of over 1,000 Spanish verbs that are conjugated like model verbs among the 301.

We sincerely hope that this book will be of some help to you in learning and using Spanish verbs.

CHRISTOPHER KENDRIS, Ph.D.
THEODORE KENDRIS, Ph.D.

Formation of the Present and Past Participles in Spanish

Formation of the present participle in Spanish

A present participle is a verb form which, in English, ends in *-ing;* for example, *singing, eating, receiving.* In Spanish, a present participle is regularly formed as follows:

drop the **ar** of an **-ar** ending verb, like **cantar**, and add **ando**: **cantando**/singing

drop the **er** of an **-er** ending verb, like **comer**, and add **-iendo**: **comiendo**/eating

drop the **ir** of an **-ir** ending verb, like **recibir**, and add **iendo**: **recibiendo**/receiving

In English, a gerund also ends in **-ing**, but there is a distinct difference in use between a gerund and a present participle in English. In brief, it is this: in English, when a present participle is used as a noun it is called a gerund; for example, *Reading is good.* As a present participle in English, it would be used as follows: *While reading,* the boy fell asleep.

In the first example *(Reading is good), reading* is a gerund because it is the subject of the verb *is.* In Spanish, however, we do not use the present participle form as a noun to serve as a subject; we use the infinitive form of the verb: *Leer es bueno.*

Common irregular present participles

INFINITIVE	PRESENT PARTICIPLE
caer to fall	**cayendo** falling
conseguir to attain, to achieve	**consiguiendo** attaining, achieving
construir to construct	**construyendo** constructing
corregir to correct	**corrigiendo** correcting
creer to believe	**creyendo** believing
decir to say, to tell	**diciendo** saying, telling
despedirse to say good-bye	**despidiéndose** saying good-bye
destruir to destroy	**destruyendo** destroying
divertirse to enjoy oneself	**divirtiéndose** enjoying oneself
dormir to sleep	**durmiendo** sleeping
huir to flee	**huyendo** fleeing
ir to go	**yendo** going
leer to read	**leyendo** reading
mentir to lie (tell a falsehood)	**mintiendo** lying
morir to die	**muriendo** dying
oír to hear	**oyendo** hearing
pedir to ask (for), to request	**pidiendo** asking (for), requesting
poder to be able	**pudiendo** being able
reír to laugh	**riendo** laughing
repetir to repeat	**repitiendo** repeating
seguir to follow	**siguiendo** following
sentir to feel	**sintiendo** feeling
servir to serve	**sirviendo** serving
traer to bring	**trayendo** bringing
venir to come	**viniendo** coming
vestir to dress	**vistiendo** dressing
vestirse to dress oneself	**vistiéndose** dressing oneself

Uses of the present participle

1. To form the progressive tenses: **The Progressive Present** is formed by using **estar** in the present tense plus the present participle of the main verb you are using. **The Progressive Past** is formed by using **estar** in the imperfect indicative plus the present participle of the main verb you are using. (See page xxxv for a complete description of the uses and formation of the progressive tenses.)

2. To give vividness to an action that occurred (preterit + present participle): *El niño entró llorando en la casa*/The little boy came into the house crying.

3. To express the English use of *by* + present participle in Spanish, we use the gerund form, which has the same ending as a present participle explained above: *Trabajando, se gana dinero*/By working, one earns (a person earns) money; *Estudiando mucho, Pepe recibió buenas notas*/By studying hard, Joe received good grades.

   Note that no preposition is used in front of the present participle (the Spanish gerund) even though it is expressed in English as *by* + present participle.

   Note, too, that in Spanish we use **al** + inf. (not + present part.) to express *on* or *upon* + present part. in English: *Al entrar en la casa, el niño comenzó a llorar*/Upon entering the house, the little boy began to cry.

4. To form the Perfect Participle: **habiendo hablado**/having talked.

Formation of the past participle in Spanish

A past participle is a verb form which, in English, usually ends in *-ed:* for example, *worked, talked, arrived,* as in *I have worked, I have talked, I have arrived.* There are many irregular past participles in English; for example, *gone, sung,* as in *She has gone, We have sung.* In Spanish, a past participle is regularly formed as follows:

drop the **ar** of an **-ar** ending verb, like **cantar,** add **-ado**: **cantado**/sung

drop the **er** of an **-er** ending verb, like **comer,** add **-ido**: **comido**/eaten

drop the **ir** of an **-ir** ending verb, like **recibir,** add **-ido**: **recibido**/received

Common irregular past participles

INFINITIVE	PAST PARTICIPLE
abrir to open	**abierto** opened
caer to fall	**caído** fallen
creer to believe	**creído** believed
cubrir to cover	**cubierto** covered
decir to say, to tell	**dicho** said, told
descubrir to discover	**descubierto** discovered
deshacer to undo	**deshecho** undone
devolver to return (something)	**devuelto** returned (something)
escribir to write	**escrito** written
hacer to do, to make	**hecho** done, made
imponer to impose	**impuesto** imposed
imprimir to print	**impreso** printed
ir to go	**ido** gone
leer to read	**leído** read
morir to die	**muerto** died
oír to hear	**oído** heard
poner to put	**puesto** put
rehacer to redo, to remake	**rehecho** redone, remade
reír to laugh	**reído** laughed
resolver to resolve, to solve	**resuelto** resolved, solved
romper to break	**roto** broken
traer to bring	**traído** brought
ver to see	**visto** seen
volver to return	**vuelto** returned

Uses of the past participle

1. To form the seven compound tenses

2. To form the Perfect Infinitive: *haber hablado*/to have spoken

3. To form the Perfect Participle: *habiendo hablado*/having spoken

4. To serve as an adjective, which must agree in gender and number with the noun it modifies: *El señor Molina es muy respetado*/ Mr. Molina is very respected. *La señora González es muy conocida*/Mrs. González is very well known.

5. To express the result of an action with **estar** and sometimes with **quedar** or **quedarse**: *La puerta está abierta*/The door is open; *Las cartas están escritas*/The letters are written; *Los niños se quedaron asustados*/The children remained frightened.

6. To express the passive voice with **ser**: *La ventana fue abierta por el ladrón*/The window was opened by the robber.

Principal Parts of Some Important Spanish Verbs

INFINITIVE	PRESENT PARTICIPLE	PAST PARTICIPLE	PRESENT INDICATIVE	PRETERIT
abrir	abriendo	abierto	abro	abrí
andar	andando	andado	ando	anduve
caber	cabiendo	cabido	quepo	cupe
caer	cayendo	caído	caigo	caí
conseguir	consiguiendo	conseguido	consigo	conseguí
construir	construyendo	construido	construyo	construí
corregir	corrigiendo	corregido	corrijo	corregí
creer	creyendo	creído	creo	creí
cubrir	cubriendo	cubierto	cubro	cubrí
dar	dando	dado	doy	di
decir	diciendo	dicho	digo	dije
descubrir	descubriendo	descubierto	descubro	descubrí
deshacer	deshaciendo	deshecho	deshago	deshice
despedirse	despidiéndose	despedido	me despido	me despedí
destruir	destruyendo	destruido	destruyo	destruí
devolver	devolviendo	devuelto	devuelvo	devolví
divertirse	divirtiéndose	divertido	me divierto	me divertí
dormir	durmiendo	dormido	duermo	dormí
escribir	escribiendo	escrito	escribo	escribí
estar	estando	estado	estoy	estuve
haber	habiendo	habido	he	hube
hacer	haciendo	hecho	hago	hice
huir	huyendo	huido	huyo	huí
ir	yendo	ido	voy	fui
irse	yéndose	ido	me voy	me fui
leer	leyendo	leido	leo	leí

INFINITIVE	PRESENT PARTICIPLE	PAST PARTICIPLE	PRESENT INDICATIVE	PRETERIT
mentir	mintiendo	mentido	miento	mentí
morir	muriendo	muerto	muero	morí
oír	oyendo	oído	oigo	oí
oler	oliendo	olido	huelo	olí
pedir	pidiendo	pedido	pido	pedí
poder	pudiendo	podido	puedo	pude
poner	poniendo	puesto	pongo	puse
querer	queriendo	querido	quiero	quise
reír	riendo	reído	río	reí
repetir	repitiendo	repetido	repito	repetí
resolver	resolviendo	resuelto	resuelvo	resolví
romper	rompiendo	roto	rompo	rompí
saber	sabiendo	sabido	sé	supe
salir	saliendo	salido	salgo	salí
seguir	siguiendo	seguido	sigo	seguí
sentir	sintiendo	sentido	siento	sentí
ser	siendo	sido	soy	fui
servir	sirviendo	servido	sirvo	serví
tener	teniendo	tenido	tengo	tuve
traer	trayendo	traído	traigo	traje
venir	viniendo	venido	vengo	vine
ver	viendo	visto	veo	vi
vestir	vistiendo	vestido	visto	vestí
volver	volviendo	vuelto	vuelvo	volví

Sample English Verb Conjugation

INFINITIVE **to eat**
PRESENT PARTICIPLE eating   *PAST PARTICIPLE* eaten

Tense no.	The seven simple tenses
1 *Present Indicative*	I eat, you eat, he (she, it) eats; we eat, you eat, they eat
	or: I do eat, you do eat, he (she, it) does eat; we do eat, you do eat, they do eat
	or: I am eating, you are eating, he (she, it) is eating; we are eating, you are eating, they are eating

2 *Imperfect Indicative*		I was eating, you were eating, he (she, it) was eating; we were eating, you were eating, they were eating
	or:	I ate, you ate, he (she, it) ate; we ate, you ate, they ate
	or:	I used to eat, you used to eat, he (she, it) used to eat; we used to eat, you used to eat, they used to eat
3 *Preterit*		I ate, you ate, he (she, it) ate; we ate, you ate, they ate
	or:	I did eat, you did eat, he (she, it) did eat; we did eat, you did eat, they did eat
4 *Future*		I will (shall) eat, you will eat, he (she, it) will eat; we will (shall) eat, you will eat, they will eat
5 *Conditional*		I would eat, you would eat, he (she, it) would eat; we would eat, you would eat, they would eat
6 *Present Subjunctive*		that I may eat, that you may eat, that he (she, it) may eat; that we may eat, that you may eat, that they may eat
7 *Imperfect or Past Subjunctive*		that I might eat, that you might eat, that he (she, it) might eat; that we might eat, that you might eat, that they might eat
8 *Present Perfect or Past Indefinite*		I have eaten, you have eaten, he (she, it) has eaten; we have eaten, you have eaten, they have eaten
9 *Pluperfect Indic. or Past Perfect*		I had eaten, you had eaten, he (she, it) had eaten; we had eaten, you had eaten, they had eaten
10 *Past Anterior or Preterit Perfect*		I had eaten, you had eaten, he (she, it) had eaten; we had eaten, you had eaten, they had eaten
11 *Future Perfect or Future Anterior*		I will (shall) have eaten, you will have eaten, he (she, it) will have eaten; we will (shall) have eaten, you will have eaten, they will have eaten
12 *Conditional Perfect*		I would have eaten, you would have eaten, he (she, it) would have eaten; we would have eaten, you would have eaten, they would have eaten

13	*Present Perfect or Past Subjunctive*	that I may have eaten, that you may have eaten, that he (she, it) may have eaten; that we may have eaten, that you may have eaten that they may have eaten
14	*Pluperfect or Past Perfect Subjunctive*	that I might have eaten, that you might have eaten, that he (she, it) might have eaten; that we might have eaten, that you might have eaten, that they might have eaten
	Imperative or Command	— eat, let him (her) eat; let us eat, let them eat

A Summary of Meanings and Uses of Spanish Verb Tenses and Moods as Related to English Verb Tenses and Moods

A verb is where the action is! A verb is a word that expresses an action (like *go, eat, write*) or a state of being (like *think, believe, be*). Tense means time. Spanish and English verb tenses are divided into three main groups of time: past, present, and future. A verb tense shows if an action or state of being took place, is taking place, or will take place.

Spanish and English verbs are also used in four moods, or modes. (There is also the Infinitive Mood, but we are not concerned with that here.) Mood has to do with the *way* a person regards an action or a state that he expresses. For example, a person may merely make a statement or ask a question—this is the Indicative Mood, which we use most of the time in Spanish and English. A person may say that he *would do* something if something else were possible or that he *would have done* something if something else had been possible—this is the Conditional Mood. A person may use a verb *in such a way* that he indicates a wish, a fear, a regret, a joy, a request, a supposition, or something of this sort—this is the Subjunctive Mood. The Subjunctive Mood is used in Spanish much more than in English. Finally, a person may command someone to do something or demand that something be done—this is the Imperative Mood.

There are six tenses in English: Present, Past, Future, Present Perfect, Past Perfect, and Future Perfect. The first three are simple tenses. The other three are compound tenses and are based on the simple tenses. In Spanish, however, there are fourteen tenses, seven of which are simple and seven of which are compound (containing both the helping verb *haber* and the past participle ending in *-ado* or *-ido*). The seven compound tenses are based on the seven simple tenses. In Spanish and English a verb tense is simple if it consists of one verb form, e.g., *estudio*. A verb tense is compound if it consists of two parts—the auxiliary (or helping) verb plus the past participle, e.g., *he estudiado*. See the Summary of verb tenses and moods in Spanish with English equivalents on page xxxvii. We have numbered each tense name for easy reference and recognition.

In Spanish there is also another tense that is used to express an action in the present. It is called the Progressive Present. Please turn to page xxxv for more information about the progressive forms of verbs.

In the pages that follow, the tenses and moods are given in Spanish and the equivalent name or names in English are given in parentheses. Although some of the names given in English are not considered to be tenses (because there are only six), they are given for the purpose of identification as they are related to the Spanish names. The comparison includes only the essential points you need to know about the meanings and uses of Spanish verb tenses and moods as related to English usage. We shall use examples to illustrate their meanings and uses. This is not intended to be a detailed treatise. It is merely a summary. We hope you find it helpful.

THE SEVEN SIMPLE TENSES

Tense No. 1   Presente de Indicativo
                 (Present Indicative)

This tense is used most of the time in Spanish and English. It indicates:
  (a) An action or a state of being at the present time.
     EXAMPLES:
     1. **Hablo** español. *I speak* Spanish.
                          I am speaking Spanish.
                          I do speak Spanish.
     2. **Creo en** Dios. *I believe* in God.

  (b) Habitual action.
     EXAMPLES:
     Voy a la biblioteca todos los días.
     I go to the library every day.
     I do go to the library every day.

(c) A general truth, something that is permanently true.

EXAMPLES:

1. Seis menos dos **son** cuatro.
   Six minus two *are* four.
2. El ejercicio **hace** maestro al novicio.
   Practice *makes* perfect.

(d) Vividness when talking or writing about past events.

EXAMPLES:

El asesino **se pone** pálido. **Tiene** miedo. **Sale** de la casa y **corre** a lo largo del río. The murderer *turns* pale. *He is* afraid. *He goes out* of the house and *runs* along the river.

(e) A near future.

EXAMPLES:

1. Mi hermano **llega** mañana.
   My brother *arrives* tomorrow.
2. ¿**Miramos** la televisión ahora?
   Shall we watch television now?

(f) An action or state of being that occurred in the past and *continues up to the present.* In Spanish this is an idiomatic use of the present tense of a verb with **hace**, which is also in the present.

EXAMPLES:

Hace tres horas que **miro** la televisión.
I have been watching television for three hours.

(g) The meaning of *almost* or *nearly* when used with **por poco.**

EXAMPLES:

Por poco me **matan.**
They almost *killed* me.

This tense is regularly formed as follows:

Drop the -ar ending of an infinitive, like **hablar**, and add the following endings: o, as, a; amos, áis, an

You then get: **hablo, hablas, habla;**
　　　　　　　　 hablamos, habláis, hablan

Drop the -er ending of an infinitive, like **beber**, and add the following endings: o, es, e; emos, éis, en

You then get: **bebo, bebes, bebe;**
　　　　　　　　 bebemos, bebéis, beben

Drop the -ir ending of an infinitive, like **recibir**, and add the following endings: o, es, e; imos, ís, en

You then get: **recibo, recibes, recibe;**
                   recibimos, recibís, reciben

Tense No. 2 **Imperfecto de Indicativo** *past continuous*
                   (Imperfect Indicative)

This is a past tense. Imperfect suggests that the action is incomplete. The imperfect tense expresses an action or a state of being that was continuous in the past and its completion is not indicated. This tense is used, therefore, to express:

(a) An action that was going on in the past at the same time as another action.

> EXAMPLE:
> Mi hermano **leía** y mi padre **hablaba**.
> My brother *was reading* and my father *was talking.*

(b) An action that was going on in the past when another action occurred.

> EXAMPLE:
> Mi hermana **cantaba** cuando yo entré.
> My sister *was singing* when I came in.

(c) An action that a person did habitually in the past.

> EXAMPLE:
> 1. Cuando **estábamos** en Nueva York, **íbamos** al cine todos los sábados.
>   When *we were* in New York, *we went* to the movies every Saturday.
>   When *we were* in New York, *we used to go* to the movies every Saturday.
> 2. Cuando **vivíamos** en California, **íbamos** a la playa todos los días.
>   When *we used to live* in California, *we would go* to the beach every day.

> NOTE: In this last example, *we would go* looks like the conditional, but it is not. It is the imperfect tense in this sentence because habitual action in the past is expressed.

(d) A description of a mental, emotional, or physical condition in the past.

> EXAMPLES:
> 1. (mental condition) **Quería** ir al cine.
>   I *wanted* to go to the movies.
> Common verbs in this use are **creer, desear, pensar, poder, preferir, querer, saber, sentir.**

2. (emotional condition)   **Estaba** contento de verlo.
                                      I *was* happy to see him.
3. (physical condition)   Mi madre **era** hermosa cuando **era** pequeña.
                                      My mother *was* beautiful when she *was* young.

(e) The time of day in the past.
    EXAMPLES:
    1. ¿Qué hora **era?**
       What time *was* it?
    2. **Eran** las tres.
       It was three o'clock.

(f) An action or state of being that occurred in the past and *lasted for a certain length of time* prior to another past action. In English it is usually translated as a pluperfect tense. (The pluperfect is what happened *before* another action. Another way to look at it is that *perfect* means that the action is complete. *Plus* means that it is *more* than complete.) The pluperfect in English is formed with *had been* plus the present participle of the verb you are using. It is like the special use of the presente de indicativo explained in the above section in paragraph (f), except that the action or state of being no longer exists at the present time. This is an idiomatic use of the imperfect tense of a verb with **hacía**, which is also in the imperfect.
    EXAMPLE:
    Hacía tres horas que **miraba** la televisión cuando mi hermano entró.
    I had been watching television for three hours when my brother came in.

(g) An indirect quotation in the past.
    EXAMPLE:
    Present: Dice que **quiere** venir a mi casa.
                    He says *he wants to come to my house.*
    Past: Dijo que **quería** venir a mi casa.
                    He said *he wanted* to come to my house.

This tense is regularly formed as follows:
Drop the -ar ending of an infinitive, like **hablar**, and add the following endings: **aba, abas, aba; ábamos, abais, aban**
You then get: hablaba, hablabas, hablaba;
               hablábamos, hablabais, hablaban

The usual equivalent in English is: I was talking OR I used to talk OR I talked; you were talking OR you used to talk OR you talked, etc.

Drop the -er ending of an infinitive, like beber, or the -ir ending of an infinitive, like recibir, and add the following endings: ía, ías, ía; íamos, íais, ían

You then get: bebía, bebías, bebía;
                 bebíamos, bebíais, bebían
                 recibía, recibías, recibía;
                 recibíamos, recibíais, recibían

The usual equivalent in English is: I was drinking OR I used to drink OR I drank; you were drinking OR you used to drink OR you drank, etc.; I was receiving OR I used to receive OR I received; you were receiving OR you used to receive OR you received, etc.

Verbs that are irregular in the imperfect indicative:

ir/to go   iba, ibas, iba; (I was going, I used to go, etc.)
               íbamos, íbais, íban

ser/to be   era, eras, era; (I was, I used to be, etc.)
               éramos, erais, eran

ver/to see   veía, veías, veía; (I was seeing, I used to see, etc.)
               veíamos, veíais, veían

Tense No. 3   Pretérito
               (Preterit)

This tense expresses an action that was completed at some time in the past.
EXAMPLES:
   1. Mi padre llegó ayer.
      My father *arrived* yesterday.
      My father *did arrive* yesterday.
   2. María fue a la iglesia esta mañana.
      Mary *went* to church this morning.
      Mary *did go* to church this morning.
   3. ¿Qué pasó?
      What *happened?*
      What *did happen?*
   4. Tomé el desayuno a las siete.
      I *had* breakfast at seven o'clock.
      I *did have* breakfast at seven o'clock.
   5. Salí de casa, tomé el autobús y llegué a la escuela a las ocho.
      I left the house, *I took* the bus and *I arrived* at school at eight o'clock.

In Spanish, some verbs that express a mental state have a different meaning when used in the preterit.

EXAMPLES:

1. La **conocí** la semana pasada en el baile.
   I *met* her last week at the dance.
   (**Conocer,** which means *to know* or *be acquainted with,* means *met,* that is, is introduced to for the first time, when it is used in the preterit.)

2. **Pude** hacerlo.
   I *succeeded* in doing it.
   (**Poder,** which means *to be able,* means *succeeded* in the preterit.)

3. **No pude** hacerlo.
   I *failed* to do it.
   (**Poder,** when used in the negative in the preterit, means *failed* or *did not succeed.*)

4. **Quise** llamarle.
   I *tried* to call you.
   (**Querer,** which means *to wish* or *want,* means *tried* in the preterit.)

5. **No quise** hacerlo.
   I *refused* to do it.
   (**Querer,** when used in the negative in the preterit, means *refused.*)

6. **Supe** la verdad.
   I *found out* the truth.
   (**Saber,** which means *to know,* means *found out* in the preterit.)

7. **Tuve** una carta de mi amigo Roberto.
   I *received* a letter from my friend Robert.
   (**Tener,** which means *to have,* means *received* in the preterit.)

This tense is regularly formed as follows:

Drop the -ar ending of an infinitive, like hablar, and add the following endings: **é, aste, ó; amos, asteis, aron**

You then get: **hablé, hablaste, habló;**
                hablamos, hablasteis, hablaron

The usual equivalent in English is: I talked OR I did talk; you talked OR you did talk, etc. OR I spoke OR I did speak; you spoke OR you did speak, etc.

Drop the **-er** ending of an infinitive, like beber, or the **-ir** ending of an infinitive, like recibir, and add the following endings: **í, iste, ió; imos, isteis, ieron**

You then get: **bebí, bebiste, bebió;**
                bebimos, bebisteis, bebieron
                recibí, recibiste, recibió;
                recibimos, recibisteis, recibieron

The usual equivalent in English is: I drank OR I did drink; you drank OR you did drink, etc.; I received OR I did receive, etc.

Tense No. 4   Futuro
                (Future)

In Spanish and English, the future tense is used to express an action or a state of being that will take place at some time in the future.

EXAMPLES:

1. Lo **haré.**
   I shall do it.
   I will do it.

2. **Iremos** al campo la semana que viene.
   We shall go to the country next week.
   We will go to the country next week.

Note: You can also use **ir + a** in the present tense to talk about the future.
Mañana, **voy a comprar** una bicicleta.
Tomorrow, **I am going to buy** a bicycle.

Also, in Spanish the future tense is used to indicate:

(a) Conjecture regarding the present.

EXAMPLES:

1. ¿Qué hora **será?**
   I wonder what time it is.

2. ¿Quién **será** a la puerta?
   Who *can that be* at the door?
   I wonder who is at the door.

(b) Probability regarding the present.

EXAMPLES:

1. **Serán** las cinco.
   It is probably five o'clock.
   It must be five o'clock.

2. **Tendrá** muchos amigos.
   He probably has many friends.
   He must have many friends.

3. María **estará** enferma.
   Mary *is probably* sick.
   Mary *must be* sick.

(c) An indirect quotation.

EXAMPLE:

María dice que **vendrá** mañana.
Mary says that she *will come* tomorrow.

Finally, remember that the future is never used in Spanish after *si* when *si* means *if.*

This tense is regularly formed as follows:

Add the following endings to the whole infinitive: é, ás, á; emos, éis, án

Note that these Future endings happen to be the endings of haber in the present indicative: he, has, ha; hemos, habéis, han. Also note the accent marks on the Future endings, except for emos.

You then get: hablaré, hablarás, hablará;
hablaremos, hablaréis, hablarán
beberé, beberás, beberá;
beberemos, beberéis, beberán
recibiré, recibirás, recibirá;
recibiremos, recibiréis, recibirán

Tense No. 5   Potencial Simple
(Conditional)

The conditional is used in Spanish and in English to express:

(a) An action that you *would do* if something else were possible.
EXAMPLE:
Iría a España si tuviera dinero.
I would go to Spain if I had money.

(b) A conditional desire. This is a conditional of courtesy.
EXAMPLE:
Me **gustaría** tomar una limonada.
I would like (I should like) to have a lemonade . . . (What is implied is: if you are willing to let me have it.)

(c) An indirect quotation.
EXAMPLES:
1. María **dijo** que **vendría** mañana.
Mary *said* that she *would come* tomorrow.
2. María **decía** que **vendría** mañana.
Mary *was saying* that she *would come* tomorrow.
3. María **había dicho** que **vendría** mañana.
Mary *had said* that she *would come* tomorrow.

(d) Conjecture regarding the past.
EXAMPLE:
¿Quién **sería?**
I wonder who that was.

(e) Probability regarding the past.
EXAMPLE:
Serían las cinco cuando salieron.
It was probably five o'clock when they went out.

This tense is regularly formed as follows:

Add the following endings to the whole infinitive:

ía, ías, ía; íamos, íais, ían

> Note that these conditional endings are the same endings of the imperfect indicative for -er and -ir verbs.

You then get: **hablaría, hablarías, hablaría;**
hablaríamos, hablaríais, hablarían

bebería, beberías, bebería;
beberíamos, beberíais, beberían

recibiría, recibirías, recibiría;
recibiríamos, recibiríais, recibirían

The usual translation in English is: I would talk, you would talk, etc.; I would drink, you would drink, etc.; I would receive, you would receive, etc.

Tense No. 6   Presente de Subjuntivo
            (Present Subjunctive)

The subjunctive mood is used in Spanish much more than in English. In Spanish the present subjunctive is used:

(a) To express a command in the **usted** or **ustedes** form, either in the affirmative or negative.

EXAMPLES:

1. **Siéntese** Ud. *Sit down.*
2. **No se siente** Ud. *Don't sit down.*
3. **Cierren** Uds. la puerta. *Close* the door.
4. **No cierren** Uds. la puerta. *Don't close* the door.
5. **Dígame** Ud. la verdad. *Tell me* the truth.

(b) To express a negative command in the familiar form **(tú).**

EXAMPLES:

1. **No te sientes.** *Don't sit down.*   3. **No duermas.** *Don't sleep.*
2. **No entres.** *Don't come in.*   4. **No lo hagas.** *Don't do it.*

(c) To express a negative command in the second plural **(vosotros).**

EXAMPLES:

1. **No os sentéis.** *Don't sit down.*   3. **No durmáis.** *Don't sleep.*
2. **No entréis.** *Don't come in.*   4. **No lo hagáis.** *Don't do it.*

(d) To express a command in the first person plural, either in the affirmative or negative **(nosotros).**

EXAMPLES:

1. **Sentémonos.** *Let's sit down.*
2. **No entremos.** *Let's not go in.*

See also **Imperativo** (Imperative) farther on.

(e) After a verb that expresses some kind of wish, insistence, preference, suggestion, or request.

EXAMPLES:

1. *Quiero* que María lo **haga.**
   I want Mary to do it.

   NOTE: In this example, English uses the infinitive form, *to do.* In Spanish, however, a new clause is needed introduced by *que* because there is a new subject, María. The present subjunctive of *hacer* is used (haga) because the main verb is *Quiero,* which indicates a wish. If there were no change in subject, Spanish would use the infinitive form, as we do in English, for example, *Quiero hacerlo*/I want to do it.

2. *Insisto* en que María lo **haga.**
   I insist that Mary *do* it.

3. *Prefiero* que María lo **haga.**
   I prefer that Mary *do* it.

4. *Pido* que María lo **haga.**
   I ask that Mary *do* it.

   NOTE: In examples 2, 3, and 4 here, English also uses the subjunctive form *do.* However, this is not the case in example no. 1.

(f) After a verb that expresses doubt, fear, joy, hope, sorrow, or some other emotion. Notice in the following examples, however, that the subjunctive is not used in English.

EXAMPLES:

1. *Dudo* que María lo **haga.**
   I doubt that Mary *is doing* it.
   I doubt that Mary *will do* it.

2. *No creo* que María **venga.**
   I don't believe (I doubt) that Mary *is coming.*
   I don't believe (I doubt) that Mary *will come.*

3. *Temo* que María **esté** enferma.
   I fear that Mary *is* ill.

4. *Me alegro* de que **venga** María.
   I'm glad that Mary *is coming.*
   I'm glad that Mary *will come.*

5. *Espero* que María no **esté** enferma.
   I hope that Mary *is* not ill.

(g) After certain impersonal expressions that show necessity, doubt, regret, importance, urgency, or possibility. Notice, however, that the subjunctive is not used in English in some of the following examples.

EXAMPLES:

1. *Es necesario que* María lo **haga.**
   It is necessary for Mary to do it.
   It is necessary that Mary *do* it. (Subjunctive in English)
2. *No es cierto que* María **venga.**
   It is doubtful (not certain) that Mary *is coming.*
   It is doubtful (not certain) that Mary *will come.*
3. *Es lástima que* María **no venga.**
   It's too bad (a pity) that Mary *isn't coming.*
4. *Es importante que* María **venga.**
   It is important for Mary to come.
   It is important that Mary *come.* (Subjunctive in English)
5. *Es preciso que* María **venga.**
   It is necessary for Mary to come.
   It is necessary that Mary *come.* (Subjunctive in English)
6. *Es urgente que* María **venga.**
   It is urgent for Mary to come.
   It is urgent that Mary *come.* (Subjunctive in English)

(h) After certain conjunctions of time, such as, **antes (de) que, cuando, en cuanto, después (de) que, hasta que, mientras,** and the like. The subjunctive form of the verb is used when introduced by any of these time conjunctions if the time referred to is either indefinite or is expected to take place in the future. However, if the action was completed in the past, the indicative mood is used.

EXAMPLES:

1. Le hablaré a María cuando **venga.**
   I shall talk to Mary when she *comes.*
2. Vámonos antes (de) que **llueva.**
   Let's go before *it rains.*
3. En cuanto la **vea** yo, le hablaré.
   As soon as *I see her,* I will (shall) talk to her.
4. Me quedo aquí hasta que **vuelva.**
   I'm staying here until *he returns.*

NOTE: In the above examples, the subjunctive is not used in English.

(i) After certain conjunctions that express a condition, negation, or purpose, such as, **a menos que, con tal que, para que, a fin de que, sin que, en caso (de) que,** and the like. Notice, however, that the subjunctive is not used in English in the following examples.

EXAMPLES:

1. Démelo con tal que **sea** bueno.
   Give it to me provided that *it is* good.

2. Me voy a menos que **venga.**
   I'm leaving unless *he comes.*

(j) After certain adverbs, such as, **acaso, quizá,** and **tal vez.**
   EXAMPLE:
   Acaso **venga** mañana.
   Perhaps *he will come* tomorrow.
   Perhaps *he is coming* tomorrow.

(k) After **aunque** if the action has not yet occurred.
   EXAMPLE:
   Aunque María **venga** esta noche, no me quedo.
   Although Mary *may come* tonight, I'm not staying.
   Although Mary *is coming* tonight, I'm not staying.

(l) In an adjectival clause if the antecedent is something or someone that
   is indefinite, negative, vague, or nonexistent.
   EXAMPLES:
   1. Busco un libro que **sea** interesante.
      I'm looking for a book that *is* interesting.
      NOTE: In this example, *que* (which is the relative pronoun) refers
      to *un libro* (which is the antecedent). Since *un libro* is indefinite,
      the verb in the following clause must be in the subjunctive *(sea).*
      Notice, however, that the subjunctive is not used in English.
   2. ¿Hay alguien aquí que **hable** francés?
      Is there anyone here who *speaks* French?
      NOTE: In this example, *que* (which is the relative pronoun) refers
      to *alguien* (which is the antecedent). Since *alguien* is indefinite
      and somewhat vague—we do not know who this anyone might
      be—the verb in the following clause must be in the subjunctive
      (hable). Notice, however, that the subjunctive is not used in
      English.
   3. No hay nadie que **pueda** hacerlo.
      There is no one who *can* do it.
      NOTE: In this example, *que* (which is the relative pronoun) refers
      to *nadie* (which is the antecedent). Since *nadie* is nonexistent, the
      verb in the following clause must be in the subjunctive *(pueda).*
      Notice, however, that the subjunctive is not used in English.

(m) After **por más que** or **por mucho que**.
   EXAMPLES:
   1. **Por más que hable usted,** no quiero escuchar.
      No matter how much you talk, I don't want to listen.

2. **Por mucho que se alegre,** no me importa.
   No matter how glad he is, I don't care.

(n) After the expression **ojalá (que)**, which expresses a great desire. This interjection means *would to God!* or *may God grant!* . . . It is derived from the Arabic, *ya Allah!* (Oh, God!)
   EXAMPLE:
   ¡Ojalá que vengan mañana!
   Would to God that they come tomorrow!
   May God grant that they come tomorrow!
   How I wish that they would come tomorrow!
   If only they would come tomorrow!

Finally, remember that the present subjunctive is never used in Spanish after *si* when *si* means *if.*

The present subjunctive of regular verbs and many irregular verbs is normally formed as follows:
Go to the present indicative, 1st pers. sing., of the verb you have in mind, drop the ending **o,** and
   for an **-ar** ending type, add: **e, es, e; emos, éis, en**
   for an **-er** or **-ir** ending type, add: **a, as, a; amos, áis, an**

As you can see, the characteristic vowel in the present subjunctive endings for an **-ar** type verb is **e** in the six persons.

As you can see, the characteristic vowel in the present subjunctive endings for an **-er** or **-ir** type verb is **a** in all six persons.

Since the present subjunctive of some irregular verbs is not normally formed as stated above *(e.g.,* **dar, dormir, haber, ir, secar, sentir, ser, tocar)**, you must look up the verb you have in mind in the alphabetical listing in this book.

Tense No. 7   Imperfecto de Subjuntivo
               (Imperfect Subjunctive)

This past tense is used for the same reasons as the presente de subjuntivo—that is, after certain verbs, conjunctions, impersonal expressions, etc., which were explained and illustrated above in tense no. 6. The main difference between these two tenses is the time of the action.
   If the verb in the main clause is in the present indicative or future or present perfect indicative or imperative, the *present subjunctive* or the *present perfect subjunctive* is used in the dependent clause—as long as there is some element that requires the use of the subjunctive.

However, if the verb in the main clause is in the imperfect indicative, preterit, conditional, or pluperfect indicative, the *imperfect subjunctive* (this tense) or *pluperfect subjunctive* is ordinarily used in the dependent clause—as long as there is some element that requires the use of the subjunctive.

EXAMPLES:
1. *Insistí* en que María lo **hiciera**.
   I insisted that Mary *do it.*
2. Se lo *explicaba* a María **para que lo comprendiera.**
   I was explaining it to Mary *so that she might understand it.*

Note that the imperfect subjunctive is used after **como si** to express a condition contrary to fact.

EXAMPLE:
Me habla como si **fuera** un niño.
He speaks to me as if *I were* a child.

NOTE: In this last example, the subjunctive is used in English for the same reason.

Finally, note that **quisiera** (the imperfect subjunctive of **querer**) can be used as a polite way to express a wish or desire, as in *I should like:* **Quisiera hablar ahora/**I should like to speak now.

The imperfect subjunctive is regularly formed as follows:

For all verbs, drop the **ron** ending of the 3rd pers. pl. of the preterit and add the following endings:

ra, ras, ra; **ramos, rais, ran**	OR	**se, ses, se;** **semos, seis, sen**

The only accent mark on the forms of the imperfect subjunctive is on the 1st pers. pl. form (**nosotros**) and it is placed on the vowel that is right in front of the ending **ramos** or **semos**. This keeps the stress on the same syllable.

THE SEVEN COMPOUND TENSES

Tense No. 8   **Perfecto de Indicativo**
              (Present Perfect Indicative)

This is the first of the seven compound tenses. This tense expresses an action that took place at no definite time in the past. It is also called the past indefinite. It is a compound tense because it is formed with the present indicative of **haber** (the auxiliary or helping verb) plus the past participle of your main verb. Note the translation into English in the examples that follow. Then compare this tense with the **perfecto de subjuntivo**, which is tense no. 13. For the seven simple tenses of **haber** (which you need to know to form these seven compound tenses), see **haber** listed alphabetically among the 301 verbs in this book.

EXAMPLES:

1. (Yo) **he hablado.**
   I have spoken.
2. (Tú) no **has venido** a verme.
   You have not come to see me.
3. Elena **ha ganado** el premio.
   Helen *has won* the prize.

Tense No. 9   **Pluscuamperfecto de Indicativo**
                (Pluperfect *or* Past Perfect Indicative)

This is the second of the compound tenses. In Spanish and English, this past tense is used to express an action that happened in the past *before* another past action. Since it is used in relation to another past action, the other past action is ordinarily expressed in the preterit. However, it is not always necessary to have the other past action expressed, as in example 2 on the following page.

In English, this tense is formed with the past tense of *to have* (had) plus the past participle of your main verb. In Spanish, this tense is formed with the imperfect indicative of **haber** plus the past participle of the verb you have in mind. Note the translation into English in the examples that follow. Then compare this tense with the **pluscuamperfecto de subjuntivo**, which is tense no. 14. For the seven simple tenses of **haber** (which you need to know to form these seven compound tenses), see **haber** listed alphabetically among the 301 verbs in this book.

EXAMPLES:

1. Cuando **llegué a casa, mi hermano había salido.**
   When I *arrived* home, my brother *had gone out.*
   NOTE: *First,* my brother went out; *then,* I arrived home. Both actions happened in the past. The action that occurred in the past *before* the other past action is in the pluperfect, and in this example, it is *my brother had gone out* (**mi hermano había salido**).
   NOTE also that **llegué** (*I arrived*) is in the preterit because it is an action that happened in the past and it was completed.

2. Juan lo **había perdido** en la calle.
   John *had lost* it in the street.
   NOTE: In this example, the pluperfect indicative is used even
   though no other past action is expressed. It is assumed that John
   had lost something *before* some other past action.

Tense No. 10   **Pretérito Anterior** *or* **Pretérito Perfecto**
(Past Anterior *or* Preterit Perfect)

This is the third of the compound tenses. This past tense is compound
because it is formed with the preterit of **haber** plus the past participle of
the verb you are using. It is translated into English like the pluperfect
indicative, which is tense no. 9. This tense is not used much in spoken
Spanish. Ordinarily, the pluperfect indicative is used in spoken Spanish
(and sometimes even the simple preterit) in place of the past anterior.

   This tense is ordinarily used in formal writing, such as history and
literature. It is normally used after certain conjunctions of time, e.g.,
después que, cuando, apenas, luego que, en cuanto.
   EXAMPLE:
   Después que **hubo hablado,** salió.
   After *he had spoken,* he left.

Tense No. 11   **Futuro Perfecto**
(Future Perfect *or* Future Anterior)

This is the fourth of the compound tenses. This compound tense is formed
with the future of **haber** plus the past participle of the verb you have in
mind. In Spanish and in English, this tense is used to express an action that
will happen in the future *before* another future action. In English, this tense
is formed by using *shall have* or *will have* plus the past participle of the
verb you have in mind.
   EXAMPLE:
   María llegará mañana y **habré terminado** mi trabajo.
   Mary will arrive tomorrow and *I shall have finished* my work.
   NOTE: *First,* I shall finish my work; *then,* Mary will arrive. The
   action that will occur in the future *before* the other future action is in
   the **Futuro perfecto,** and in this example it is (yo) **habré terminado
   mi trabajo**.

Also, in Spanish the future perfect is used to indicate conjecture or
probability regarding recent past time.

EXAMPLES:

1. María **se habrá acostado.**
   Mary *has probably gone to bed.*
   Mary *must have gone to bed.*
2. José **habrá llegado.**
   Joseph *has probably arrived.*
   Joseph *must have arrived.*

Tense No. 12   Potencial Compuesto
(Conditional Perfect)

This is the fifth of the compound tenses. It is formed with the conditional of **haber** plus the past participle of your main verb. It is used in Spanish and English to express an action that you *would have done* if something else had been possible; that is, you would have done something *on condition* that something else had been possible.

In English it is formed by using *would have* plus the past participle of the verb you have in mind. Observe the difference between the following example and the one given for the use of the potencial simple.

EXAMPLE:

Habría ido a España si hubiera tenido dinero.
I would have gone to Spain if I had had money.

Also, in Spanish the conditional perfect is used to indicate probability or conjecture in the past.

EXAMPLES:

1. **Habrían sido** las cinco cuando salieron.
   It must have been five o'clock when they went out.
   (Compare this with the example given for the simple conditional.)
2. ¿Quién **habría sido?**
   Who *could that have been? (or* I wonder *who that could have been.)*
   (Compare this with the example that is given for the simple conditional.)

Tense No. 13   Perfecto de Subjuntivo
(Present Perfect *or* Past Subjunctive)

This is the sixth of the compound tenses. It is formed by using the present subjunctive of **haber** as the helping verb plus the past participle of the verb you have in mind.

If the verb in the main clause is in the present indicative, future, or present perfect tense, the present subjunctive is used *or* this tense is used in the dependent clause—provided, of course, that there is some element that requires the use of the subjunctive.

The present subjunctive is used if the action is not past. However, if the action is past, this tense (present perfect subjunctive) is used, as in the examples given below.

EXAMPLES:

1. María duda que yo le **haya hablado** al profesor.
   Mary doubts that *I have spoken* to the professor.
2. Siento que tú no **hayas venido** a verme.
   I am sorry that you *have not come* to see me.
3. Me alegro de que Elena **haya ganado** el premio.
   I am glad that Helen *has won* the prize.

In these three examples, the auxiliary verb **haber** is used in the present subjunctive because the main verb in the clause that precedes is one that requires the subjunctive mood of the verb in the dependent clause.

Tense No. 14   **Pluscuamperfecto de Subjuntivo**
                (Pluperfect *or* Past Perfect Subjunctive)

This is the seventh of the compound tenses. It is formed by using the imperfect subjunctive of **haber** as the helping verb plus the past participle of your main verb.

The translation of this tense into English is often like the pluperfect indicative.

If the verb in the main clause is in a past tense, this tense is used in the dependent clause—provided, of course, that there is some element that requires the use of the subjunctive.

EXAMPLES:

1. Sentí mucho que **no hubiera venido** María.
   I was very sorry that Mary *had not come.*
2. Me alegraba de que **hubiera venido** María.
   I was glad that Mary *had come.*
3. No creía que María **hubiera llegado.**
   I did not believe that Mary *had arrived.*

So much for the seven simple tenses and the seven compound tenses. Now, let's look at the Imperative Mood.

Imperativo
(Imperative *or* Command)

The imperative mood is used in Spanish and in English to express a command. We saw earlier that the subjunctive mood is used to express commands in the **Ud.** and **Uds.** forms, in addition to other uses of the subjunctive mood.

Here are other points you ought to know about the imperative.

(a) An indirect command or deep desire expressed in the third pers. sing. or pl. is in the subjunctive. Notice the use of *Let* or *May* in the English translations. **Que** introduces this kind of command.

EXAMPLES:

1. ¡Que lo **haga** Jorge!
   Let George do it!

2. ¡Que Dios se lo **pague**!
   May God reward you!

3. ¡Que **vengan** pronto!
   Let them come quickly!

4. ¡Que **entre** Roberto!
   Let Robert enter!

5. ¡Que **salgan**!
   Let them leave!

6. ¡Que **entren** las muchachas!
   Let the girls come in!

(b) In some indirect commands, **que** is omitted. Here, too, the subjunctive is used.

EXAMPLE:

¡**Viva** el presidente!
Long live the president!

(c) The verb form of the affirmative sing. familiar (**tú**) is the same as the 3rd pers. sing. of the present indicative when expressing a command.

EXAMPLES:

1. ¡**Entra** pronto!
   Come in quickly!

2. ¡**Sigue** leyendo!
   Keep on reading!
   Continue reading!

(d) There are some exceptions, however, to (c) above. The following verb forms are irregular in the affirmative sing. imperative (**tú** form only).

di (decir)

haz (hacer)

he (haber)

pon (poner)

sal (salir)

sé (ser)

ten (tener)

val (valer)

ve (ir)

ven (venir)

(e) In the affirmative command, 1st per. pl., instead of using the present subjunctive hortatory command, **vamos a** *(Let's* or *Let us)* + **inf.** may be used. (*Hortatory* is an odd word if you are new to language study. It's from the Latin word *hortari*, meaning *to exhort* or *to urge*.)

EXAMPLES:

1. **Vamos a** comer/Let's eat.
   or: **Comamos** (1st pers. pl., present subj., hortatory command)

2. **Vamos a** cantar/Let's sing.
   or: **Cantemos** (1st pers. pl., present subj., hortatory command)

(f) In the affirmative command, 1st pers. pl., **vamos** may be used to mean
Let's go: **Vamos** al cine/Let's go to the movies.

(g) However, if in the negative *(Let's not go)*, the present subjunctive of **ir** must be used: **No vayamos** al cine/Let's not go to the movies.

(h) Note that **vámonos** (1st pers. pl. of **irse**, imperative) means *Let's go,* or
Let's go away, or *Let's leave.* See (m) below.

(i) Also note that **no nos vayamos** (1st pers. pl. of **irse**, present subjunctive) means *Let's not go,* or *Let's not go away,* or *Let's not leave.*

(j) The imperative in the affirmative familiar plural (**vosotros, vosotras**) is formed by dropping the final **r** of the inf. and adding **d**.
EXAMPLES:
1. **¡Hablad!**/Speak!   3. **¡Id!**/Go!
2. **¡Comed!**/Eat!   4. **¡Venid!**/Come!

(k) When forming the affirmative familiar plural (**vosotros, vosotras**) imperative of a reflexive verb, the final **d** on the inf. must be dropped before the reflexive pronoun **os** is added, and both elements are joined to make one word.
EXAMPLES:
1. **¡Levantaos!**/Get up!   2. **¡Sentaos!**/Sit down!

(l) Referring to (k) above, when the final **d** is dropped in a reflexive verb ending in **-ir**, an accent mark must be written on the **i**.
EXAMPLES:
1. **¡Vestíos!**/Get dressed!   2. **¡Divertíos!**/Have a good time!

(m) When forming the 1st pers. pl. affirmative imperative of a reflexive verb, the final **s** must drop before the reflexive pronoun **os** is added, and both elements are joined to make one word. This requires an accent mark on the vowel of the syllable that was stressed before **os** was added.
EXAMPLE:
Vamos + nos changes to: **¡Vámonos!**/*Let's go!* or *Let's go away!* or *Let's leave!* See (h) above.

(n) All negative imperatives in the familiar 2nd pers. sing. (**tú**) and plural (**vosotros, vosotras**) are expressed in the present subjunctive.
EXAMPLES:
1. **¡No corras (tú)!**/Don't run!
2. **¡No corráis (vosotros** or **vosotras!)**/Don't run!
3. **¡No vengas (tú)!**/Don't come!
4. **¡No vengáis (vosotros** or **vosotras!)**/Don't come!

(o) Object pronouns (direct, indirect, or reflexive) with an imperative verb form in the **affirmative** are attached to the verb form.

EXAMPLES:

1. ¡Hágalo (Ud.)!/Do it!
2. ¡Díganoslo (Ud.)!/Tell it to us!
3. ¡Dímelo (tú)!/Tell it to me!
4. ¡Levántate (tú)!/Get up!
5. ¡Siéntese (Ud.)!/Sit down!
6. ¡Hacedlo (vosotros, vosotras)!/Do it!
7. ¡Démelo (Ud.)!/Give it to me!

(p) Object pronouns (direct, indirect, or reflexive) with an imperative verb form in the **negative** are placed in front of the verb form. Compare the following examples with those given in (o) above:

EXAMPLES:

1. ¡No lo haga (Ud.)!/Don't do it!
2. ¡No nos lo diga (Ud.)!/Don't tell it to us!
3. ¡No me lo digas (tú)!/Don't tell it to me!
4. ¡No te levantes (tú)!/Don't get up!
5. ¡No se siente (Ud.)!/Don't sit down!
6. ¡No lo hagáis (vosotros, vosotras)!/Don't do it!
7. ¡No me lo dé (Ud.)!/Don't give it to me!

(q) Note that in some Latin American countries the 2nd pers. pl. familiar (vosotros, vosotras) forms are avoided. In place of them, the 3rd pers. pl. Uds. forms are customarily used.

The Progressive forms of tenses: a note

(1) In Spanish, there are also progressive forms of tenses. They are the Progressive Present and the Progressive Past.

(2) The **Progressive Present** is formed by using *estar* in the present tense plus the present participle of your main verb; e.g., *Estoy hablando*/I am talking, i.e., I am (in the act of) talking (right now).

(3) The **Progressive Past** is formed by using *estar* in the imperfect indicative plus the present participle of your main verb; e.g., *Estaba hablando*/I was talking, i.e., I was (in the act of) talking (right then). This is useful when an action was in progress when another action took place: *Estaba leyendo cuando mi hermano entró*/ I was (in the act of) reading when my brother came in.

(4) The progressive forms are generally used when you want to emphasize or intensify an action; if you don't want to do that, then just use the simple present or simple imperfect; e.g., say *Hablo*, not *Estoy hablando*; or *Hablaba*, not *Estaba hablando*.

(5) Sometimes *ir* is used instead of *estar* to form the progressive tenses; e.g., *Va hablando*/He (she) keeps right on talking, *Iba hablando*/He (she) kept right on talking. Note that they do not have the exact same meaning as *Está hablando* and *Estaba hablando*. See (2) and (3) above.

(6) Also, at times *andar*, *continuar*, *seguir*, and *venir* are used as helping verbs in the present or imperfect indicative tenses plus the present participle to express the progressive forms: *Los muchachos andaban cantando*/The boys were walking along singing; *La maestra seguía leyendo a la clase*/The teacher kept right on reading to the class.

The Future Subjunctive and the Future Perfect Subjunctive: a note

The future subjunctive and the future perfect subjunctive exist in Spanish, but they are rarely used. Nowadays, instead of using the future subjunctive, one uses the present subjunctive or the present indicative. Instead of using the future perfect subjunctive, one uses the future perfect indicative or the present perfect subjunctive. However, if you are curious to know how to form the future subjunctive and the future perfect subjunctive in Spanish, read the following:

(1) To form the future subjunctive, take the third person plural of the preterit of any Spanish verb and change the ending **-ron** to **re**, **res**, **re**; **remos**, **reis**, **ren**. An accent mark is needed as shown below on the first person plural form to preserve the stress.

EXAMPLES:

amar	amare, amares, amare; amáremos, amareis, amaren
comer	comiere, comieres, comiere; comiéremos, comiereis, comieren
dar	diere, dieres, diere; diéremos, diereis, dieren
haber	hubiere, hubieres, hubiere; hubiéremos, hubiereis, hubieren
hablar	hablare, hablares, hablare; habláremos, hablareis, hablaren
ir *or* ser	fuere, fueres, fuere; fuéremos, fuereis, fueren

(2) Let's look at the forms of **amar** above to see what the English translation is of this tense:

(que) yo amare, (that) I love . . .
(que) tú amares, (that) you love . . .
(que) Ud. (él, ella) amare, (that) you (he, she) love . . .

(que) nosotros (-tras) amáremos, (that) we love . . .
(que) vosotros (-tras) amareis, (that) you love . . .
(que) Uds. (ellos ellas) amaren, (that) you (they) love . . .

(3) To form the future perfect subjunctive, use the future subjunctive form
of **haber** (shown above) as your auxiliary plus the past participle of the
verb you have in mind.

EXAMPLES:

(que) hubiere amado, hubieres amado, hubiere amado;
(que) hubiéremos amado, hubiereis amado, hubieren amado

English translation: (that) I have *or* I shall have loved, (that) you
have *or* will have loved, etc.

**Summary of verb tenses and moods in Spanish with English
equivalents**

	Los siete tiempos simples *The seven simple tenses*		Los siete tiempos compuestos *The seven compound tenses*
Tense No.	Tense Name	Tense No.	Tense Name
1	**Presente de indicativo** *Present indicative*	8	**Perfecto de indicativo** *Present perfect indicative*
2	**Imperfecto de indicativo** *Imperfect indicative*	9	**Pluscuamperfecto de indicativo** *Pluperfect or Past perfect indicative*
3	**Pretérito** *Preterit*	10	**Pretérito anterior (Pret. perfecto)** *Past anterior or Preterit perfect*
4	**Futuro** *Future*	11	**Futuro perfecto** *Future perfect or Future anterior*
5	**Potencial simple** *Conditional*	12	**Potencial compuesto** *Conditional perfect*
6	**Presente de subjuntivo** *Present subjunctive*	13	**Perfecto de subjuntivo** *Present perfect or Past subjunctive*
7	**Imperfecto de subjuntivo** *Imperfect subjunctive*	14	**Pluscuamperfecto de subjuntivo** *Pluperfect or Past perfect subjunctive*

The imperative is not a tense; it is a mood.

In Spanish, there are 7 simple tenses and 7 compound tenses. A simple tense means that the verb form consists of one word. A compound tense means that the verb form consists of two words (the auxiliary verb and the past participle). The auxiliary verb is also called a helping verb and in Spanish it is any of the 7 simple tenses of haber *(to have)*.

Each compound tense is based on each simple tense. The 14 tenses given on the previous page are arranged in the following logical order:

Tense number 8 is based on Tense number 1; in other words, you form the **Perfecto de indicativo** by using the auxiliary **haber** in the **Presente de indicativo** plus the past participle of the verb you are dealing with.

Tense number 9 is based on Tense number 2; in other words, you form the **Pluscuamperfecto de indicativo** by using the auxiliary **haber** in the **Imperfecto de indicativo** plus the past participle of the verb you are dealing with.

Tense number 10 is based on Tense number 3; in other words, you form the **Pretérito anterior** by using the auxiliary **haber** in the **Pretérito** plus the past participle of the verb you are dealing with.

Tense number 11 is based on Tense number 4; in other words, you form the **Futuro perfecto** by using the auxiliary **haber** in the **Futuro** plus the past participle of the verb you are dealing with.

Tense number 12 is based on Tense number 5; in other words, you form the **Potencial compuesto** by using the auxiliary **haber** in the **Potencial simple** plus the past participle of the verb you are dealing with.

Tense number 13 is based on Tense number 6; in other words, you form the **Perfecto de subjuntivo** by using the auxiliary **haber** in the **Presente de subjuntivo** plus the past participle of the verb you are dealing with.

Tense number 14 is based on Tense number 7; in other words, you form the **Pluscuamperfecto de subjuntivo** by using the auxiliary **haber** in the **Imperfecto de subjuntivo** plus the past participle of the verb you are dealing with.

What does all the above mean? This: If you ever expect to know or even recognize the meaning of any of the 7 compound tenses, you certainly have to know **haber** in the 7 simple tenses. If you do not, you cannot form the 7 compound tenses. This is one perfect example to illustrate that learning Spanish verb forms is a cumulative experience. Look up **haber** where it is listed alphabetically among the 301 verbs in this book and study the seven simple tenses.

An Easy Way to Form the Seven Compound Tenses in Spanish

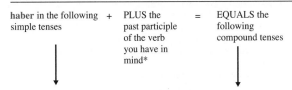

haber in the following + PLUS the = EQUALS the
simple tenses   past participle   following
                        of the verb   compound tenses
                        you have in
                        mind*

1. Presente de indicativo
2. Imperfecto de indicativo
3. Pretérito

4. Futuro
5. Potencial simple
6. Presente de subjuntivo
7. Imperfecto de subjuntivo

8. Perfecto de indicativo
9. Pluscuamperfecto de indicativo
10. Pretérito anterior (Pret. Perfecto)

11. Futuro perfecto
12. Potencial compuesto
13. Perfecto de subjuntivo
14. Pluscuamperfecto de subjuntivo

*To know how to form a past participle, see page ix.

Verbs Commonly Used With Indirect Object Pronouns

Some verbs are often used impersonally, with an indirect object pronoun. For example, *gustar* means to be pleasing to. While in English we say, I like ice cream, in Spanish we say **Me gusta el helado** (literally, To me, ice cream is pleasing).

So, in English the thing you like is the direct object, but in Spanish the thing you like is the subject of the sentence. For this reason, the verb *gustar* is used in the third person singular or plural when you talk about something you like. In other words, the verb agrees with the thing you like because it is the subject of the sentence: **Me gusta el café** / I like coffee. If you like more than one thing, *gustar* is in the plural: **Me gustan el café y la leche** / I like coffee and milk.

There is one other thing to keep in mind. If you are talking about the person (or persons) who likes (or like) the thing, don't forget the personal *a* before the person:

A Roberto le gusta el helado / Robert likes ice cream.
(Literally: To Robert, ice cream is pleasing to him.)

A las chicas les gustó la película / The girls liked the movie.
(Literally: To the girls, the movie was pleasing to them.)

Here are a few other verbs that are used this way: **encantar** (to delight, to love), **faltar** (to be lacking, to need), **importar** (to matter, to be important), **molestar** (to bother), **parecer** (to seem, to appear), and **quedar** (to remain, to be left).

EXAMPLES:

Nos encanta el chocolate. We love chocolate.
Me quedan sólo treinta dólares. I have only thirty dollars left (remaining).
A Pedro le falta un bolígrafo. Peter needs a pen.

See **faltar**, **importar**, **parecer**, and **quedarse** in the main verb section for more vocabulary related to these verbs.

Reflexive Verbs and Reflexive Pronouns

In English, a reflexive pronoun is a personal pronoun that contains *self* or *selves*. In Spanish and English, a reflexive pronoun causes the action of the verb to fall on the reflexive pronoun, which is in the same person and number as the subject. In Spanish, there is a required set of reflexive pronouns:

me	myself	nos	ourselves
te	yourself	os	yourselves
se	himself, herself, itself, yourself (Ud.)	se	themselves, yourselves (Uds.)

The reflexive infinitive can be recognized by the se added to the end of the verb: **lavar** to wash/**lavarse** to wash oneself.

Let's look at **lavarse** in the pretérito (tense 3):

Yo me lavé.	I washed myself.
Tú te lavaste.	You (sing. informal) washed yourself.
Él se lavó.	He washed himself.
Ella se lavó.	She washed herself.
Ud. se lavó.	You (sing. formal) washed yourself.
Nosotras nos lavamos.	We (f.) washed ourselves.
Nosotros nos lavamos.	We (m.) washed ourselves.
Vosotras os lavasteis.	You (f. pl. informal) washed yourselves.

Vosotros os lavasteis.	You (m. pl. informal) washed yourselves.
Ustedes se lavaron.	*You (pl. formal) washed yourselves.*
Ellas se lavaron.	They (f.) washed themselves.
Ellos se lavaron.	They (m.) washed themselves.

Note how the meaning of a verb changes when it is used reflexively:

Miguel lavó su coche. Michael washed his car.

Miguel se lavó las manos después de sacar la basura.
Michael washed his hands after taking out the trash.

Review and practice the reflexive verbs **irse, lavarse,** and **llamarse** among the verbs in this book to become familiar with the reflexive pronouns that go with the reflexive verbs.

The Spanish Alphabet and the New System of Alphabetizing

The Association of Spanish Language Academies met in Madrid for its 10th Annual Congress on April 27, 1994 and voted to eliminate **CH** and **LL** as separate letters of the Spanish alphabet.

Words beginning with **CH** will be listed alphabetically under the letter C. Words beginning with **LL** will be listed alphabetically under the letter L. The two separate letters historically have had separate headings in dictionaries and alphabetized word lists. Spanish words that contain the letter **ñ** are now alphabetized accordingly with words that do not contain the tilde over the **n**. For example, the Spanish system of alphabetizing used to place the word **andar** before **añadir** because the **ñ** would fall in after all words containing **n**. According to the new system, **añadir** is placed before **andar** because alphabetizing is now done letter by letter. The same applies to words containing **rr**.

The move was taken to simplify dictionaries, to make Spanish more compatible with English, and to aid translation and computer standardization. The vote was 17 in favor, 1 opposed, and 3 abstentions. Ecuador voted "no" and Panama, Nicaragua, and Uruguay abstained. (*The New York Times,* International Section, May 1, 1994, p. 16)

Subject Pronouns

(a) The subject pronouns for all verb forms on the following pages have been omitted in order to emphasize the verb forms, which is what this book is all about.

(b) The subject pronouns that have been omitted are as follows:

singular	plural
yo	nosotros (nosotras)
tú	vosotros (vosotras)
Ud. (él, ella)	Uds. (ellos, ellas)

Regular **-ir** verb endings with spelling   to open
change: irregular past participle

The Seven Simple Tenses		The Seven Compound Tenses	
Singular	Plural	Singular	Plural

1   presente de indicativo

abro	abrimos	
abres	abrís	
abre	abren	

8   perfecto de indicativo

he abierto	hemos abierto
has abierto	habéis abierto
ha abierto	han abierto

2   imperfecto de indicativo

abría	abríamos
abrías	abríais
abría	abrían

9   pluscuamperfecto de indicativo

había abierto	habíamos abierto
habías abierto	habíais abierto
había abierto	habían abierto

3   pretérito

abrí	abrimos
abriste	abristeis
abrió	abrieron

10   pretérito anterior

hube abierto	hubimos abierto
hubiste abierto	hubisteis abierto
hubo abierto	hubieron abierto

4   futuro

abriré	abriremos
abrirás	abriréis
abrirá	abrirán

11   futuro perfecto

habré abierto	habremos abierto
habrás abierto	habréis abierto
habrá abierto	habrán abierto

5   potencial simple

abriría	abriríamos
abrirías	abriríais
abriría	abrirían

12   potencial compuesto

habría abierto	habríamos abierto
habrías abierto	habríais abierto
habría abierto	habrían abierto

6   presente de subjuntivo

abra	abramos
abras	abráis
abra	abran

13   perfecto de subjuntivo

haya abierto	hayamos abierto
hayas abierto	hayáis abierto
haya abierto	hayan abierto

7   imperfecto de subjuntivo

abriera	abriéramos
abrieras	abrierais
abriera	abrieran
OR	
abriese	abriésemos
abrieses	abrieseis
abriese	abriesen

14   pluscuamperfecto de subjuntivo

hubiera abierto	hubiéramos abierto
hubieras abierto	hubierais abierto
hubiera abierto	hubieran abierto
OR	
hubiese abierto	hubiésemos abierto
hubieses abierto	hubieseis abierto
hubiese abierto	hubiesen abierto

imperativo

—	abramos
abre; no abras	abrid; no abráis
abra	abran

un abrimiento opening	en un abrir y cerrar de ojos in a wink
La puerta está abierta. The door is open.	**Todos los alumnos abrieron los libros.** All the students opened their books.
abrir paso to make way	
Los libros están abiertos. The books are open.	

absolver

Gerundio **absolviendo**   Part. pas. **absuelto**

to absolve, to acquit

Regular **-er** verb endings with spelling change: irregular past participle; stem change: Tenses 1, 6, Imperative

The Seven Simple Tenses		The Seven Compound Tenses	
Singular	Plural	Singular	Plural
1 presente de indicativo		8 perfecto de indicativo	
absuelvo	**absolvemos**	**he absuelto**	**hemos absuelto**
absuelves	**absolvéis**	**has absuelto**	**habéis absuelto**
absuelve	**absuelven**	**ha absuelto**	**han absuelto**
2 imperfecto de indicativo		9 pluscuamperfecto de indicativo	
absolvía	**absolvíamos**	**había absuelto**	**habíamos absuelto**
absolvías	**absolvíais**	**habías absuelto**	**habíais absuelto**
absolvía	**absolvían**	**había absuelto**	**habían absuelto**
3 pretérito		10 pretérito anterior	
absolví	**absolvimos**	**hube absuelto**	**hubimos absuelto**
absolviste	**absolvisteis**	**hubiste absuelto**	**hubisteis absuelto**
absolvió	**absolvieron**	**hubo absuelto**	**hubieron absuelto**
4 futuro		11 futuro perfecto	
absolveré	**absolveremos**	**habré absuelto**	**habremos absuelto**
absolverás	**absolveréis**	**habrás absuelto**	**habréis absuelto**
absolverá	**absolverán**	**habrá absuelto**	**habrán absuelto**
5 potencial simple		12 potencial compuesto	
absolvería	**absolveríamos**	**habría absuelto**	**habríamos absuelto**
absolverías	**absolveríais**	**habrías absuelto**	**habríais absuelto**
absolvería	**absolverían**	**habría absuelto**	**habrían absuelto**
6 presente de subjuntivo		13 perfecto de subjuntivo	
absuelva	**absolvamos**	**haya absuelto**	**hayamos absuelto**
absuelvas	**absolváis**	**hayas absuelto**	**hayáis absuelto**
absuelva	**absuelvan**	**haya absuelto**	**hayan absuelto**
7 imperfecto de subjuntivo		14 pluscuamperfecto de subjuntivo	
absolviera	**absolviéramos**	**hubiera absuelto**	**hubiéramos absuelto**
absolvieras	**absolvierais**	**hubieras absuelto**	**hubierais absuelto**
absolviera	**absolvieran**	**hubiera absuelto**	**hubieran absuelto**
OR		OR	
absolviese	**absolviésemos**	**hubiese absuelto**	**hubiésemos absuelto**
absolvieses	**absolvieseis**	**hubieses absuelto**	**hubieseis absuelto**
absolviese	**absolviesen**	**hubiese absuelto**	**hubiesen absuelto**

imperativo	
—	**absolvamos**
absuelve; no absuelvas	**absolved; no absolváis**
absuelva	**absuelvan**

la absolución   absolution, acquittal, pardon
absolutamente   absolutely
absoluto, absoluta   absolute, unconditional

en absoluto   absolutely
salir absuelto   to come out clear of any charges

Reflexive irregular verb   to abstain

The Seven Simple Tenses		The Seven Compound Tenses	
Singular	Plural	Singular	Plural

1   presente de indicativo

		8 perfecto de indicativo	
me abstengo	**nos abstenemos**	**me he**	**nos hemos**
te abstienes	**os abstenéis**	**te has**	**os habéis** + **abstenido**
se abstiene	**se abstienen**	**se ha**	**se han**

2   imperfecto de indicativo

		9 pluscuamperfecto de indicativo	
me abstenía	**nos absteníamos**	**me había**	**nos habíamos**
te abstenías	**os absteníais**	**te habías**	**os habíais** + **abstenido**
se abstenía	**se abstenían**	**se había**	**se habían**

3   pretérito

		10 pretérito anterior	
me abstuve	**nos abstuvimos**	**me hube**	**nos hubimos**
te abstuviste	**os abstuvisteis**	**te hubiste**	**os hubisteis** + **abstenido**
se abstuvo	**se abstuvieron**	**se hubo**	**se hubieron**

4   futuro

		11 futuro perfecto	
me abstendré	**nos abstendremos**	**me habré**	**nos habremos**
te abstendrás	**os abstendréis**	**te habrás**	**os habréis** + **abstenido**
se abstendrá	**se abstendrán**	**se habrá**	**se habrán**

5   potencial simple

		12 potencial compuesto	
me abstendría	**nos abstendríamos**	**me habría**	**nos habríamos**
te abstendrías	**os abstendríais**	**te habrías**	**os habríais** + **abstenido**
se abstendría	**se abstendrían**	**se habría**	**se habrían**

6   presente de subjuntivo

		13 perfecto de subjuntivo	
me abstenga	**nos abstengamos**	**me haya**	**nos hayamos**
te abstengas	**os abstengáis**	**te hayas**	**os hayáis** + **abstenido**
se abstenga	**se abstengan**	**se haya**	**se hayan**

7   imperfecto de subjuntivo

		14 pluscuamperfecto de subjuntivo	
me abstuviera	**nos abstuviéramos**	**me hubiera**	**nos hubiéramos**
te abstuvieras	**os abstuvierais**	**te hubieras**	**os hubierais** + **abstenido**
se abstuviera	**se abstuvieran**	**se hubiera**	**se hubieran**
OR		OR	
me abstuviese	**nos abstuviésemos**	**me hubiese**	**nos hubiésemos**
te abstuvieses	**os abstuvieseis**	**te hubieses**	**os hubieseis** + **abstenido**
se abstuviese	**se abstuviesen**	**se hubiese**	**se hubiesen**

imperativo

—	**abstengámonos**
abstente; no te abstengas	**absteneos; no os abstengáis**
absténgase	**absténganse**

la abstención	abstention, forbearance	**Me abstengo de participar en la**
abstenerse de	to abstain from, to	**discusión.** I'm abstaining from
refrain from		participating in the discussion.
la abstinencia	abstinence, fasting	**hacer abstinencia** to fast

aburrir

Gerundio **aburriendo**   Part. pas. **aburrido**

to annoy, to bore, to vex

Regular **-ir** verb

The Seven Simple Tenses		The Seven Compound Tenses	
Singular	Plural	Singular	Plural
1 presente de indicativo		8 perfecto de indicativo	
aburro	aburrimos	he aburrido	hemos aburrido
aburres	aburrís	has aburrido	habéis aburrido
aburre	aburren	ha aburrido	han aburrido
2 imperfecto de indicativo		9 pluscuamperfecto de indicativo	
aburría	aburríamos	había aburrido	habíamos aburrido
aburrías	aburríais	habías aburrido	habíais aburrido
aburría	aburrían	había aburrido	habían aburrido
3 pretérito		10 pretérito anterior	
aburrí	aburrimos	hube aburrido	hubimos aburrido
aburriste	aburristeis	hubiste aburrido	hubisteis aburrido
aburrió	aburrieron	hubo aburrido	hubieron aburrido
4 futuro		11 futuro perfecto	
aburriré	aburriremos	habré aburrido	habremos aburrido
aburrirás	aburriréis	habrás aburrido	habréis aburrido
aburrirá	aburrirán	habrá aburrido	habrán aburrido
5 potencial simple		12 potencial compuesto	
aburriría	aburriríamos	habría aburrido	habríamos aburrido
aburrirías	aburriríais	habrías aburrido	habríais aburrido
aburriría	aburrirían	habría aburrido	habrían aburrido
6 presente de subjuntivo		13 perfecto de subjuntivo	
aburra	aburramos	haya aburrido	hayamos aburrido
aburras	aburráis	hayas aburrido	hayáis aburrido
aburra	aburran	haya aburrido	hayan aburrido
7 imperfecto de subjuntivo		14 pluscuamperfecto de subjuntivo	
aburriera	aburriéramos	hubiera aburrido	hubiéramos aburrido
aburrieras	aburrierais	hubieras aburrido	hubierais aburrido
aburriera	aburrieran	hubiera aburrido	hubieran aburrido
OR		OR	
aburriese	aburriésemos	hubiese aburrido	hubiésemos aburrido
aburrieses	aburrieseis	hubieses aburrido	hubieseis aburrido
aburriese	aburriesen	hubiese aburrido	hubiesen aburrido

imperativo	
—	aburramos
aburre; no aburras	aburrid; no aburráis
aburra	aburran

El actor **aburrió** el auditorio con su monólogo monótono.   The actor bored the audience with his monotonous monologue.
aburrido, aburrida boring

un **aburrimiento** annoyance, weariness un **aburridor**, una **aburridora** boring person
See also **aburrirse**.

aburrirse

Reflexive regular **-ir** verb   to be bored, to grow tired, to grow weary

The Seven Simple Tenses		The Seven Compound Tenses	
Singular	Plural	Singular	Plural
1 presente de indicativo		**8 perfecto de indicativo**	
me aburro	nos aburrimos	me he aburrido	nos hemos aburrido
te aburres	os aburrís	te has aburrido	os habéis aburrido
se aburre	se aburren	se ha aburrido	se han aburrido
2 imperfecto de indicativo		**9 pluscuamperfecto de indicativo**	
me aburría	nos aburríamos	me había aburrido	nos habíamos aburrido
te aburrías	os aburríais	te habías aburrido	os habíais aburrido
se aburría	se aburrían	se había aburrido	se habían aburrido
3 pretérito		**10 pretérito anterior**	
me aburrí	nos aburrimos	me hube aburrido	nos hubimos aburrido
te aburriste	os aburristeis	te hubiste aburrido	os hubisteis aburrido
se aburrió	se aburrieron	se hubo aburrido	se hubieron aburrido
4 futuro		**11 futuro perfecto**	
me aburriré	nos aburriremos	me habré aburrido	nos habremos aburrido
te aburrirás	os aburriréis	te habrás aburrido	os habréis aburrido
se aburrirá	se aburrirán	se habrá aburrido	se habrán aburrido
5 potencial simple		**12 potencial compuesto**	
me aburriría	nos aburriríamos	me habría aburrido	nos habríamos aburrido
te aburrirías	os aburriríais	te habrías aburrido	os habríais aburrido
se aburriría	se aburrirían	se habría aburrido	se habrían aburrido
6 presente de subjuntivo		**13 perfecto de subjuntivo**	
me aburra	nos aburramos	me haya aburrido	nos hayamos aburrido
te aburras	os aburráis	te hayas aburrido	os hayáis aburrido
se aburra	se aburran	se haya aburrido	se hayan aburrido
7 imperfecto de subjuntivo		**14 pluscuamperfecto de subjuntivo**	
me aburriera	nos aburriéramos	me hubiera aburrido	nos hubiéramos aburrido
te aburrieras	os aburrierais	te hubieras aburrido	os hubierais aburrido
se aburriera	se aburrieran	se hubiera aburrido	se hubieran aburrido
OR		OR	
me aburriese	nos aburriésemos	me hubiese aburrido	nos hubiésemos aburrido
te aburrieses	os aburrieseis	te hubieses aburrido	os hubieseis aburrido
se aburriese	se aburriesen	se hubiese aburrido	se hubiesen aburrido

imperativo	
—	aburrámonos
abúrrete; no te aburras	aburríos; no os aburráis
abúrrase	abúrranse

Hace treinta años que el profesor de
  español enseña la lengua en la
  misma escuela, pero no se aburre.
  The Spanish teacher has been teaching
  the language in the same school for
  thirty years, but he is not bored.

¡Qué aburrimiento! What a bore!
un aburrimiento annoyance,
  weariness
aburridamente tediously
See also **aburrir**.

acabar

Gerundio **acabando**   Part. pas. **acabado**

to finish, to end, to complete

Regular **-ar** verb

The Seven Simple Tenses		The Seven Compound Tenses	
Singular	Plural	Singular	Plural
1 presente de indicativo		**8 perfecto de indicativo**	
acabo	acabamos	he acabado	hemos acabado
acabas	acabáis	has acabado	habéis acabado
acaba	acaban	ha acabado	han acabado
2 imperfecto de indicativo		**9 pluscuamperfecto de indicativo**	
acababa	acabábamos	había acabado	habíamos acabado
acababas	acababais	habías acabado	habíais acabado
acababa	acababan	había acabado	habían acabado
3 pretérito		**10 pretérito anterior**	
acabé	acabamos	hube acabado	hubimos acabado
acabaste	acabasteis	hubiste acabado	hubisteis acabado
acabó	acabaron	hubo acabado	hubieron acabado
4 futuro		**11 futuro perfecto**	
acabaré	acabaremos	habré acabado	habremos acabado
acabarás	acabaréis	habrás acabado	habréis acabado
acabará	acabarán	habrá acabado	habrán acabado
5 potencial simple		**12 potencial compuesto**	
acabaría	acabaríamos	habría acabado	habríamos acabado
acabarías	acabaríais	habrías acabado	habríais acabado
acabaría	acabarían	habría acabado	habrían acabado
6 presente de subjuntivo		**13 perfecto de subjuntivo**	
acabe	acabemos	haya acabado	hayamos acabado
acabes	acabéis	hayas acabado	hayáis acabado
acabe	acaben	haya acabado	hayan acabado
7 imperfecto de subjuntivo		**14 pluscuamperfecto de subjuntivo**	
acabara	acabáramos	hubiera acabado	hubiéramos acabado
acabaras	acabarais	hubieras acabado	hubierais acabado
acabara	acabaran	hubiera acabado	hubieran acabado
OR		OR	
acabase	acabásemos	hubiese acabado	hubiésemos acabado
acabases	acabaseis	hubieses acabado	hubieseis acabado
acabase	acabasen	hubiese acabado	hubiesen acabado

	imperativo	
—	acabemos
acaba; no acabes	acabad; no acabéis
acabe	acaben

Acabo de comer. I have just eaten.	**se acabó** It's all over. It's finished.
María acaba de llegar. Mary has just arrived.	**acabar de + inf.** to have just + past part.
Acabábamos de entrar cuando el teléfono sonó. We had just entered when the telephone rang.	**acabar en** to result in
el acabamiento completion	**acabar por** to end by
	acabar bien to terminate successfully

Regular **-ar** verb   to accept

The Seven Simple Tenses		The Seven Compound Tenses	
Singular	Plural	Singular	Plural
1 presente de indicativo		8 perfecto de indicativo	
acepto	**aceptamos**	**he aceptado**	**hemos aceptado**
aceptas	**aceptáis**	**has aceptado**	**habéis aceptado**
acepta	**aceptan**	**ha aceptado**	**han aceptado**
2 imperfecto de indicativo		9 pluscuamperfecto de indicativo	
aceptaba	**aceptábamos**	**había aceptado**	**habíamos aceptado**
aceptabas	**aceptabais**	**habías aceptado**	**habíais aceptado**
aceptaba	**aceptaban**	**había aceptado**	**habían aceptado**
3 pretérito		10 pretérito anterior	
acepté	**aceptamos**	**hube aceptado**	**hubimos aceptado**
aceptaste	**aceptasteis**	**hubiste aceptado**	**hubisteis aceptado**
aceptó	**aceptaron**	**hubo aceptado**	**hubieron aceptado**
4 futuro		11 futuro perfecto	
aceptaré	**aceptaremos**	**habré aceptado**	**habremos aceptado**
aceptarás	**aceptaréis**	**habrás aceptado**	**habréis aceptado**
aceptará	**aceptarán**	**habrá aceptado**	**habrán aceptado**
5 potencial simple		12 potencial compuesto	
aceptaría	**aceptaríamos**	**habría aceptado**	**habríamos aceptado**
aceptarías	**aceptaríais**	**habrías aceptado**	**habríais aceptado**
aceptaría	**aceptarían**	**habría aceptado**	**habrían aceptado**
6 presente de subjuntivo		13 perfecto de subjuntivo	
acepte	**aceptemos**	**haya aceptado**	**hayamos aceptado**
aceptes	**aceptéis**	**hayas aceptado**	**hayáis aceptado**
acepte	**acepten**	**haya aceptado**	**hayan aceptado**
7 imperfecto de subjuntivo		14 pluscuamperfecto de subjuntivo	
aceptara	**aceptáramos**	**hubiera aceptado**	**hubiéramos aceptado**
aceptaras	**aceptarais**	**hubieras aceptado**	**hubierais aceptado**
aceptara	**aceptaran**	**hubiera aceptado**	**hubieran aceptado**
OR		OR	
aceptase	**aceptásemos**	**hubiese aceptado**	**hubiésemos aceptado**
aceptases	**aceptaseis**	**hubieses aceptado**	**hubieseis aceptado**
aceptase	**aceptasen**	**hubiese aceptado**	**hubiesen aceptado**

	imperativo	
—	**aceptemos**	
acepta; no aceptes	**aceptad; no aceptéis**	
acepte	**acepten**	

la acepción acceptation, meaning (of a word)	el aceptador, la aceptadora acceptor
aceptar o rechazar una oferta to accept or reject an offer	aceptar empleo to take a job
	el aceptante, la aceptante accepter
aceptable acceptable	acepto, acepta acceptable
aceptar + inf. to agree + inf.	la aceptación acceptance, acceptation

7

acercar
Gerundio **acercando**   Part. pas. **acercado**

to bring near, to place near

Regular **-ar** verb endings with spelling change: **c** becomes **qu** before **e**

The Seven Simple Tenses		The Seven Compound Tenses	
Singular	Plural	Singular	Plural
1 presente de indicativo		8 perfecto de indicativo	
acerco	acercamos	he acercado	hemos acercado
acercas	acercáis	has acercado	habéis acercado
acerca	acercan	ha acercado	han acercado
2 imperfecto de indicativo		9 pluscuamperfecto de indicativo	
acercaba	acercábamos	había acercado	habíamos acercado
acercabas	acercabais	habías acercado	habíais acercado
acercaba	acercaban	había acercado	habían acercado
3 pretérito		10 pretérito anterior	
acerqué	acercamos	hube acercado	hubimos acercado
acercaste	acercasteis	hubiste acercado	hubisteis acercado
acercó	acercaron	hubo acercado	hubieron acercado
4 futuro		11 futuro perfecto	
acercaré	acercaremos	habré acercado	habremos acercado
acercarás	acercaréis	habrás acercado	habréis acercado
acercará	acercarán	habrá acercado	habrán acercado
5 potencial simple		12 potencial compuesto	
acercaría	acercaríamos	habría acercado	habríamos acercado
acercarías	acercaríais	habrías acercado	habríais acercado
acercaría	acercarían	habría acercado	habrían acercado
6 presente de subjuntivo		13 perfecto de subjuntivo	
acerque	acerquemos	haya acercado	hayamos acercado
acerques	acerquéis	hayas acercado	hayáis acercado
acerque	acerquen	haya acercado	hayan acercado
7 imperfecto de subjuntivo		14 pluscuamperfecto de subjuntivo	
acercara	acercáramos	hubiera acercado	hubiéramos acercado
acercaras	acercarais	hubieras acercado	hubierais acercado
acercara	acercaran	hubiera acercado	hubieran acercado
OR		OR	
acercase	acercásemos	hubiese acercado	hubiésemos acercado
acercases	acercaseis	hubieses acercado	hubieseis acercado
acercase	acercasen	hubiese acercado	hubiesen acercado

imperativo	
—	acerquemos
acerca; no acerques	acercad; no acerquéis
acerque	acerquen

acerca de about, regarding, with regard to	**cerca de** near
acerca de esto hereof	**el cercado** fenced in area
el acercamiento approaching, approximation	**de cerca** close at hand, closely
la cerca fence, hedge	**mis parientes cercanos** my close relatives
	See also **acercarse**.

Reflexive verb: regular **-ar** verb endings with spelling change: **c** becomes **qu** before **e**

to approach, to draw near

The Seven Simple Tenses		The Seven Compound Tenses	
Singular	Plural	Singular	Plural

1 presente de indicativo

		8 perfecto de indicativo	
me acerco	nos acercamos	me he acercado	nos hemos acercado
te acercas	os acercáis	te has acercado	os habéis acercado
se acerca	se acercan	se ha acercado	se han acercado

2 imperfecto de indicativo

		9 pluscuamperfecto de indicativo	
me acercaba	nos acercábamos	me había acercado	nos habíamos acercado
te acercabas	os acercabais	te habías acercado	os habíais acercado
se acercaba	se acercaban	se había acercado	se habían acercado

3 pretérito

		10 pretérito anterior	
me acerqué	nos acercamos	me hube acercado	nos hubimos acercado
te acercaste	os acercasteis	te hubiste acercado	os hubisteis acercado
se acercó	se acercaron	se hubo acercado	se hubieron acercado

4 futuro

		11 futuro perfecto	
me acercaré	nos acercaremos	me habré acercado	nos habremos acercado
te acercarás	os acercaréis	te habrás acercado	os habréis acercado
se acercará	se acercarán	se habrá acercado	se habrán acercado

5 potencial simple

		12 potencial compuesto	
me acercaría	nos acercaríamos	me habría acercado	nos habríamos acercado
te acercarías	os acercaríais	te habrías acercado	os habríais acercado
se acercaría	se acercarían	se habría acercado	se habrían acercado

6 presente de subjuntivo

		13 perfecto de subjuntivo	
me acerque	nos acerquemos	me haya acercado	nos hayamos acercado
te acerques	os acerquéis	te hayas acercado	os hayáis acercado
se acerque	se acerquen	se haya acercado	se hayan acercado

7 imperfecto de subjuntivo

		14 pluscuamperfecto de subjuntivo	
me acercara	nos acercáramos	me hubiera acercado	nos hubiéramos acercado
te acercaras	os acercarais	te hubieras acercado	os hubierais acercado
se acercara	se acercaran	se hubiera acercado	se hubieran acercado
OR		OR	
me acercase	nos acercásemos	me hubiese acercado	nos hubiésemos acercado
te acercases	os acercaseis	te hubieses acercado	os hubieseis acercado
se acercase	se acercasen	se hubiese acercado	se hubiesen acercado

imperativo	
—	acerquémonos
acércate; no te acerques	acercaos; no os acerquéis
acérquese	acérquense

acerca de about, regarding, with regard to	cerca de near
la cercadura fence	cercar to enclose, fence in
el acercamiento approaching, approximation	de cerca close at hand, closely
cercano, cercana near	las cercanías neighborhood
	See also acercar.

acertar

Gerundio **acertando**   Part. pas. **acertado**

to hit the mark, to hit upon, to do
(something) right, to succeed in

Regular **-ar** verb endings with stem
change: Tenses 1, 6, Imperative

The Seven Simple Tenses		The Seven Compound Tenses	
Singular	Plural	Singular	Plural
1 presente de indicativo		8 perfecto de indicativo	
acierto	acertamos	he acertado	hemos acertado
aciertas	acertáis	has acertado	habéis acertado
acierta	aciertan	ha acertado	han acertado
2 imperfecto de indicativo		9 pluscuamperfecto de indicativo	
acertaba	acertábamos	había acertado	habíamos acertado
acertabas	acertabais	habías acertado	habíais acertado
acertaba	acertaban	había acertado	habían acertado
3 pretérito		10 pretérito anterior	
acerté	acertamos	hube acertado	hubimos acertado
acertaste	acertasteis	hubiste acertado	hubisteis acertado
acertó	acertaron	hubo acertado	hubieron acertado
4 futuro		11 futuro perfecto	
acertaré	acertaremos	habré acertado	habremos acertado
acertarás	acertaréis	habrás acertado	habréis acertado
acertará	acertarán	habrá acertado	habrán acertado
5 potencial simple		12 potencial compuesto	
acertaría	acertaríamos	habría acertado	habríamos acertado
acertarías	acertaríais	habrías acertado	habríais acertado
acertaría	acertarían	habría acertado	habrían acertado
6 presente de subjuntivo		13 perfecto de subjuntivo	
acierte	acertemos	haya acertado	hayamos acertado
aciertes	acertéis	hayas acertado	hayáis acertado
acierte	acierten	haya acertado	hayan acertado
7 imperfecto de subjuntivo		14 pluscuamperfecto de subjuntivo	
acertara	acertáramos	hubiera acertado	hubiéramos acertado
acertaras	acertarais	hubieras acertado	hubierais acertado
acertara	acertaran	hubiera acertado	hubieran acertado
OR		OR	
acertase	acertásemos	hubiese acertado	hubiésemos acertado
acertases	acertaseis	hubieses acertado	hubieseis acertado
acertase	acertasen	hubiese acertado	hubiesen acertado

	imperativo	
—		acertemos
acierta; no aciertes		acertad; no acertéis
acierte		acierten

acertado, acertada proper, fit	acertar a to happen to + inf.
acertamiento tact, ability	acertadamente opportunely
el acertador, la acertadora good guesser	acertar con to come across, to find
el acertijo riddle	ciertamente certainly

Gerundio acompañando   Part. pas. acompañado **acompañar**

Regular **-ar** verb

to accompany, to escort,
to go with, to keep company

The Seven Simple Tenses		The Seven Compound Tenses	
Singular	Plural	Singular	Plural
1 presente de indicativo		**8 perfecto de indicativo**	
acompaño	acompañamos	he acompañado	hemos acompañado
acompañas	acompañáis	has acompañado	habéis acompañado
acompaña	acompañan	ha acompañado	han acompañado
2 imperfecto de indicativo		**9 pluscuamperfecto de indicativo**	
acompañaba	acompañábamos	había acompañado	habíamos acompañado
acompañabas	acompañabais	habías acompañado	habíais acompañado
acompañaba	acompañaban	había acompañado	habían acompañado
3 pretérito		**10 pretérito anterior**	
acompañé	acompañamos	hube acompañado	hubimos acompañado
acompañaste	acompañasteis	hubiste acompañado	hubisteis acompañado
acompañó	acompañaron	hubo acompañado	hubieron acompañado
4 futuro		**11 futuro perfecto**	
acompañaré	acompañaremos	habré acompañado	habremos acompañado
acompañarás	acompañaréis	habrás acompañado	habréis acompañado
acompañará	acompañarán	habrá acompañado	habrán acompañado
5 potencial simple		**12 potencial compuesto**	
acompañaría	acompañaríamos	habría acompañado	habríamos acompañado
acompañarías	acompañaríais	habrías acompañado	habríais acompañado
acompañaría	acompañarían	habría acompañado	habrían acompañado
6 presente de subjuntivo		**13 perfecto de subjuntivo**	
acompañe	acompañemos	haya acompañado	hayamos acompañado
acompañes	acompañéis	hayas acompañado	hayáis acompañado
acompañe	acompañen	haya acompañado	hayan acompañado
7 imperfecto de subjuntivo		**14 pluscuamperfecto de subjuntivo**	
acompañara	acompañáramos	hubiera acompañado	hubiéramos acompañado
acompañaras	acompañarais	hubieras acompañado	hubierais acompañado
acompañara	acompañaran	hubiera acompañado	hubieran acompañado
OR		OR	
acompañase	acompañásemos	hubiese acompañado	hubiésemos acompañado
acompañases	acompañaseis	hubieses acompañado	hubieseis acompañado
acompañase	acompañasen	hubiese acompañado	hubiesen acompañado

imperativo	
—	acompañemos
acompaña; no acompañes	acompañad; no acompañéis
acompañe	acompañen

el acompañador, la acompañadora
  companion, chaperon, accompanist
el acompañamiento accompaniment,
  attendance
el acompañado, la acompañada
  assistant

un compañero, una compañera
  friend, mate, companion; **compañero
  de cuarto** roommate; **compañero
  de juego** playmate

11

aconsejar

Gerundio **aconsejando**   Part. pas. **aconsejado**

to advise, to counsel

Regular **-ar** verb

The Seven Simple Tenses		The Seven Compound Tenses	
Singular	Plural	Singular	Plural
1 presente de indicativo		8 perfecto de indicativo	
aconsejo	aconsejamos	he aconsejado	hemos aconsejado
aconsejas	aconsejáis	has aconsejado	habéis aconsejado
aconseja	aconsejan	ha aconsejado	han aconsejado
2 imperfecto de indicativo		9 pluscuamperfecto de indicativo	
aconsejaba	aconsejábamos	había aconsejado	habíamos aconsejado
aconsejabas	aconsejabais	habías aconsejado	habíais aconsejado
aconsejaba	aconsejaban	había aconsejado	habían aconsejado
3 pretérito		10 pretérito anterior	
aconsejé	aconsejamos	hube aconsejado	hubimos aconsejado
aconsejaste	aconsejasteis	hubiste aconsejado	hubisteis aconsejado
aconsejó	aconsejaron	hubo aconsejado	hubieron aconsejado
4 futuro		11 futuro perfecto	
aconsejaré	aconsejaremos	habré aconsejado	habremos aconsejado
aconsejarás	aconsejaréis	habrás aconsejado	habréis aconsejado
aconsejará	aconsejarán	habrá aconsejado	habrán aconsejado
5 potencial simple		12 potencial compuesto	
aconsejaría	aconsejaríamos	habría aconsejado	habríamos aconsejado
aconsejarías	aconsejaríais	habrías aconsejado	habríais aconsejado
aconsejaría	aconsejarían	habría aconsejado	habrían aconsejado
6 presente de subjuntivo		13 perfecto de subjuntivo	
aconseje	aconsejemos	haya aconsejado	hayamos aconsejado
aconsejes	aconsejéis	hayas aconsejado	hayáis aconsejado
aconseje	aconsejen	haya aconsejado	hayan aconsejado
7 imperfecto de subjuntivo		14 pluscuamperfecto de subjuntivo	
aconsejara	aconsejáramos	hubiera aconsejado	hubiéramos aconsejado
aconsejaras	aconsejarais	hubieras aconsejado	hubierais aconsejado
aconsejara	aconsejaran	hubiera aconsejado	hubieran aconsejado
OR		OR	
aconsejase	aconsejásemos	hubiese aconsejado	hubiésemos aconsejado
aconsejases	aconsejaseis	hubieses aconsejado	hubieseis aconsejado
aconsejase	aconsejasen	hubiese aconsejado	hubiesen aconsejado

imperativo	
—	aconsejemos
aconseja; no aconsejes	aconsejad; aconsejéis
aconseje	aconsejen

el aconsejador, la aconsejadora adviser, counselor	El tiempo da buen consejo. Time will tell.
aconsejar con to consult	aconsejarse to seek advice
el consejo advice, counsel	el aconsejamiento counseling

acordar

Regular -ar verb endings with stem change:
Tenses 1, 6, Imperative

to agree (upon)

The Seven Simple Tenses		The Seven Compound Tenses	
Singular	Plural	Singular	Plural
1 presente de indicativo		8 perfecto de indicativo	
acuerdo	acordamos	he acordado	hemos acordado
acuerdas	acordáis	has acordado	habéis acordado
acuerda	acuerdan	ha acordado	han acordado
2 imperfecto de indicativo		9 pluscuamperfecto de indicativo	
acordaba	acordábamos	había acordado	habíamos acordado
acordabas	acordabais	habías acordado	habíais acordado
acordaba	acordaban	había acordado	habían acordado
3 pretérito		10 pretérito anterior	
acordé	acordamos	hube acordado	hubimos acordado
acordaste	acordasteis	hubiste acordado	hubisteis acordado
acordó	acordaron	hubo acordado	hubieron acordado
4 futuro		11 futuro perfecto	
acordaré	acordaremos	habré acordado	habremos acordado
acordarás	acordaréis	habrás acordado	habréis acordado
acordará	acordarán	habrá acordado	habrán acordado
5 potencial simple		12 potencial compuesto	
acordaría	acordaríamos	habría acordado	habríamos acordado
acordarías	acordaríais	habrías acordado	habríais acordado
acordaría	acordarían	habría acordado	habrían acordado
6 presente de subjuntivo		13 perfecto de subjuntivo	
acuerde	acordemos	haya acordado	hayamos acordado
acuerdes	acordéis	hayas acordado	hayáis acordado
acuerde	acuerden	haya acordado	hayan acordado
7 imperfecto de subjuntivo		14 pluscuamperfecto de subjuntivo	
acordara	acordáramos	hubiera acordado	hubiéramos acordado
acordaras	acordarais	hubieras acordado	hubierais acordado
acordara	acordaran	hubiera acordado	hubieran acordado
OR		OR	
acordase	acordásemos	hubiese acordado	hubiésemos acordado
acordases	acordaseis	hubieses acordado	hubieseis acordado
acordase	acordasen	hubiese acordado	hubiesen acordado

imperativo	
—	acordemos
acuerda; no acuerdes	acordad; no acordéis
acuerde	acuerden

la acordada decision, resolution	desacordado, desacordada out of
desacordar to put out of tune	tune (music)
acordadamente jointly, by common	de acuerdo in agreement
consent	estar de acuerdo con to be in
desacordante discordant	agreement with
un acuerdo agreement	See also acordarse.

acordarse

Gerundio **acordándose** Part. pas. **acordado**

to remember

Reflexive verb: regular **-ar** verb endings
with stem change: Tenses 1, 6, Imperative

The Seven Simple Tenses		The Seven Compound Tenses	
Singular	Plural	Singular	Plural
1 presente de indicativo		8 perfecto de indicativo	
me acuerdo	nos acordamos	me he acordado	nos hemos acordado
te acuerdas	os acordáis	te has acordado	os habéis acordado
se acuerda	se acuerdan	se ha acordado	se han acordado
2 imperfecto de indicativo		9 pluscuamperfecto de indicativo	
me acordaba	nos acordábamos	me había acordado	nos habíamos acordado
te acordabas	os acordabais	te habías acordado	os habíais acordado
se acordaba	se acordaban	se había acordado	se habían acordado
3 pretérito		10 pretérito anterior	
me acordé	nos acordamos	me hube acordado	nos hubimos acordado
te acordaste	os acordasteis	te hubiste acordado	os hubisteis acordado
se acordó	se acordaron	se hubo acordado	se hubieron acordado
4 futuro		11 futuro perfecto	
me acordaré	nos acordaremos	me habré acordado	nos habremos acordado
te acordarás	os acordaréis	te habrás acordado	os habréis acordado
se acordará	se acordarán	se habrá acordado	se habrán acordado
5 potencial simple		12 potencial compuesto	
me acordaría	nos acordaríamos	me habría acordado	nos habríamos acordado
te acordarías	os acordaríais	te habrías acordado	os habríais acordado
se acordaría	se acordarían	se habría acordado	se habrían acordado
6 presente de subjuntivo		13 perfecto de subjuntivo	
me acuerde	nos acordemos	me haya acordado	nos hayamos acordado
te acuerdes	os acordéis	te hayas acordado	os hayáis acordado
se acuerde	se acuerden	se haya acordado	se hayan acordado
7 imperfecto de subjuntivo		14 pluscuamperfecto de subjuntivo	
me acordara	nos acordáramos	me hubiera acordado	nos hubiéramos acordado
te acordaras	os acordarais	te hubieras acordado	os hubierais acordado
se acordara	se acordaran	se hubiera acordado	se hubieran acordado
OR		OR	
me acordase	nos acordásemos	me hubiese acordado	nos hubiésemos acordado
te acordases	os acordaseis	te hubieses acordado	os hubieseis acordado
se acordase	se acordasen	se hubiese acordado	se hubiesen acordado

imperativo	
—	acordémonos
acuérdate; no te acuerdes	acordaos; no os acordéis
acuérdese	acuérdense

Lo siento, pero no me acuerdo de su nombre. I'm sorry, but I don't remember your name.
si mal no me acuerdo if I remember correctly, if my memory does not fail me

desacordarse to become forgetful
de común acuerdo unanimously, by mutual agreement
See also acordar.

14

Reflexive verb: regular **-ar** verb endings
with stem change: Tenses 1, 6, Imperative   to go to bed, to lie down

The Seven Simple Tenses		The Seven Compound Tenses	
Singular	Plural	Singular	Plural
1 presente de indicativo		8 perfecto de indicativo	
me acuesto	nos acostamos	me he acostado	nos hemos acostado
te acuestas	os acostáis	te has acostado	os habéis acostado
se acuesta	se acuestan	se ha acostado	se han acostado
2 imperfecto de indicativo		9 pluscuamperfecto de indicativo	
me acostaba	nos acostábamos	me había acostado	nos habíamos acostado
te acostabas	os acostabais	te habías acostado	os habíais acostado
se acostaba	se acostaban	se había acostado	se habían acostado
3 pretérito		10 pretérito anterior	
me acosté	nos acostamos	me hube acostado	nos hubimos acostado
te acostaste	os acostasteis	te hubiste acostado	os hubisteis acostado
se acostó	se acostaron	se hubo acostado	se hubieron acostado
4 futuro		11 futuro perfecto	
me acostaré	nos acostaremos	me habré acostado	nos habremos acostado
te acostarás	os acostaréis	te habrás acostado	os habréis acostado
se acostará	se acostarán	se habrá acostado	se habrán acostado
5 potencial simple		12 potencial compuesto	
me acostaría	nos acostaríamos	me habría acostado	nos habríamos acostado
te acostarías	os acostaríais	te habrías acostado	os habríais acostado
se acostaría	se acostarían	se habría acostado	se habrían acostado
6 presente de subjuntivo		13 perfecto de subjuntivo	
me acueste	nos acostemos	me haya acostado	nos hayamos acostado
te acuestes	os acostéis	te hayas acostado	os hayáis acostado
se acueste	se acuesten	se haya acostado	se hayan acostado
7 imperfecto de subjuntivo		14 pluscuamperfecto de subjuntivo	
me acostara	nos acostáramos	me hubiera acostado	nos hubiéramos acostado
te acostaras	os acostarais	te hubieras acostado	os hubierais acostado
se acostara	se acostaran	se hubiera acostado	se hubieran acostado
OR		OR	
me acostase	nos acostásemos	me hubiese acostado	nos hubiésemos acostado
te acostases	os acostaseis	te hubieses acostado	os hubieseis acostado
se acostase	se acostasen	se hubiese acostado	se hubiesen acostado

imperative	
—	acostémonos; no nos acostemos
acuéstate; no te acuestes	acostaos; no os acostéis
acuéstese; no se acueste	acuéstense; no se acuesten

Todas las noches me acuesto a las diez,
    mi hermanito se acuesta a las ocho,
    y mis padres se acuestan a las once.
Every night I go to bed at ten, my little
    brother goes to bed at eight, and my
    parents go to bed at eleven.

acostado, acostada   in bed, lying down
acostarse con las gallinas   to go to bed
    very early (with the hens/chickens)
acostar   to put to bed

acostumbrar   Gerundio acostumbrando   Part. pas. acostumbrado

to be accustomed,
to be in the habit of

Regular -ar verb

The Seven Simple Tenses		The Seven Compound Tenses	
Singular	Plural	Singular	Plural
1 presente de indicativo		8 perfecto de indicativo	
acostumbro	acostumbramos	he	hemos
acostumbras	acostumbráis	has	habéis + acostumbrado
acostumbra	acostumbran	ha	han
2 imperfecto de indicativo		9 pluscuamperfecto de indicativo	
acostumbraba	acostumbrábamos	había	habíamos
acostumbrabas	acostumbrabais	habías	habíais + acostumbrado
acostumbraba	acostumbraban	había	habían
3 pretérito		10 pretérito anterior	
acostumbré	acostumbramos	hube	hubimos
acostumbraste	acostumbrasteis	hubiste	hubisteis + acostumbrado
acostumbró	acostumbraron	hubo	hubieron
4 futuro		11 futuro perfecto	
acostumbraré	acostumbraremos	habré	habremos
acostumbrarás	acostumbraréis	habrás	habréis + acostumbrado
acostumbrará	acostumbrarán	habrá	habrán
5 potencial simple		12 potencial compuesto	
acostumbraría	acostumbraríamos	habría	habríamos
acostumbrarías	acostumbraríais	habrías	habríais + acostumbrado
acostumbraría	acostumbrarían	habría	habrían
6 presente de subjuntivo		13 perfecto de subjuntivo	
acostumbre	acostumbremos	haya	hayamos
acostumbres	acostumbréis	hayas	hayáis + acostumbrado
acostumbre	acostumbren	haya	hayan
7 imperfecto de subjuntivo		14 pluscuamperfecto de subjuntivo	
acostumbrara	acostumbráramos	hubiera	hubiéramos
acostumbraras	acostumbrarais	hubieras	hubierais + acostumbrado
acostumbrara	acostumbraran	hubiera	hubieran
OR		OR	
acostumbrase	acostumbrásemos	hubiese	hubiésemos
acostumbrases	acostumbraseis	hubieses	hubieseis + acostumbrado
acostumbrase	acostumbrasen	hubiese	hubiesen

	imperativo	
—	acostumbremos
acostumbra; no acostumbres	acostumbrad; no acostumbréis
acostumbre	acostumbren

acostumbradamente customarily
de costumbre customary, usual
la costumbre custom, habit
tener por costumbre to be in the habit of

acostumbrarse to become accustomed, to get used to
acostumbrarse a algo to become accustomed to something

16

Regular **-ar** verb   to accuse

The Seven Simple Tenses		The Seven Compound Tenses	
Singular	Plural	Singular	Plural
1 presente de indicativo		8 perfecto de indicativo	
acuso	acusamos	he acusado	hemos acusado
acusas	acusáis	has acusado	habéis acusado
acusa	acusan	ha acusado	han acusado
2 imperfecto de indicativo		9 pluscuamperfecto de indicativo	
acusaba	acusábamos	había acusado	habíamos acusado
acusabas	acusabais	habías acusado	habíais acusado
acusaba	acusaban	había acusado	habían acusado
3 pretérito		10 pretérito anterior	
acusé	acusamos	hube acusado	hubimos acusado
acusaste	acusasteis	hubiste acusado	hubisteis acusado
acusó	acusaron	hubo acusado	hubieron acusado
4 futuro		11 futuro perfecto	
acusaré	acusaremos	habré acusado	habremos acusado
acusarás	acusaréis	habrás acusado	habréis acusado
acusará	acusarán	habrá acusado	habrán acusado
5 potencial simple		12 potencial compuesto	
acusaría	acusaríamos	habría acusado	habríamos acusado
acusarías	acusaríais	habrías acusado	habríais acusado
acusaría	acusarían	habría acusado	habrían acusado
6 presente de subjuntivo		13 perfecto de subjuntivo	
acuse	acusemos	haya acusado	hayamos acusado
acuses	acuséis	hayas acusado	hayáis acusado
acuse	acusen	haya acusado	hayan acusado
7 imperfecto de subjuntivo		14 pluscuamperfecto de subjuntivo	
acusara	acusáramos	hubiera acusado	hubiéramos acusado
acusaras	acusarais	hubieras acusado	hubierais acusado
acusara	acusaran	hubiera acusado	hubieran acusado
OR		OR	
acusase	acusásemos	hubiese acusado	hubiésemos acusado
acusases	acusaseis	hubieses acusado	hubieseis acusado
acusase	acusasen	hubiese acusado	hubiesen acusado

imperativo	
—	acusemos
acusa; no acuses	acusad; no acuséis
acuse	acusen

el acusado, la acusada defendant, accused	**La propia conciencia acusa.** A guilty conscience needs no accuser. (Lit: One's own conscience accuses.)
la acusación accusation	
acusar recibo to acknowledge receipt	acusarse de un pecado to confess a sin
el acusador, la acusadora accuser	

admirar

Gerundio **admirando**   Part. pas. **admirado**

to admire

Regular **-ar** verb

The Seven Simple Tenses		The Seven Compound Tenses	
Singular	Plural	Singular	Plural
1 presente de indicativo		8 perfecto de indicativo	
admiro	admiramos	he admirado	hemos admirado
admiras	admiráis	has admirado	habéis admirado
admira	admiran	ha admirado	han admirado
2 imperfecto de indicativo		9 pluscuamperfecto de indicativo	
admiraba	admirábamos	había admirado	habíamos admirado
admirabas	admirabais	habías admirado	habíais admirado
admiraba	admiraban	había admirado	habían admirado
3 pretérito		10 pretérito anterior	
admiré	admiramos	hube admirado	hubimos admirado
admiraste	admirasteis	hubiste admirado	hubisteis admirado
admiró	admiraron	hubo admirado	hubieron admirado
4 futuro		11 futuro perfecto	
admiraré	admiraremos	habré admirado	habremos admirado
admirarás	admiraréis	habrás admirado	habréis admirado
admirará	admirarán	habrá admirado	habrán admirado
5 potencial simple		12 potencial compuesto	
admiraría	admiraríamos	habría admirado	habríamos admirado
admirarías	admiraríais	habrías admirado	habríais admirado
admiraría	admirarían	habría admirado	habrían admirado
6 presente de subjuntivo		13 perfecto de subjuntivo	
admire	admiremos	haya admirado	hayamos admirado
admires	admiréis	hayas admirado	hayáis admirado
admire	admiren	haya admirado	hayan admirado
7 imperfecto de subjuntivo		14 pluscuamperfecto de subjuntivo	
admirara	admiráramos	hubiera admirado	hubiéramos admirado
admiraras	admirarais	hubieras admirado	hubierais admirado
admirara	admiraran	hubiera admirado	hubieran admirado
OR		OR	
admirase	admirásemos	hubiese admirado	hubiésemos admirado
admirases	admiraseis	hubieses admirado	hubieseis admirado
admirase	admirasen	hubiese admirado	hubiesen admirado

	imperativo	
—	admiremos	
admira; no admires	admirad; no admiréis	
admire	admiren	

el admirador, la admiradora admirer
admirable admirable
la admiración admiration
admirablemente admirably
sentir admiración por alguien to feel
  admiration for someone

hablar en tono admirativo to speak
  in an admiring tone
**Mi hija quiere ser cantante porque
admira a Shakira.** My daughter
  wants to be a singer because she
  admires Shakira.

18

Regular **-ir** verb   to admit, to grant, to permit

The Seven Simple Tenses		The Seven Compound Tenses	
Singular	Plural	Singular	Plural
1 presente de indicativo		8 perfecto de indicativo	
admito	**admitimos**	**he admitido**	**hemos admitido**
admites	**admitís**	**has admitido**	**habéis admitido**
admite	**admiten**	**ha admitido**	**han admitido**
2 imperfecto de indicativo		9 pluscuamperfecto de indicativo	
admitía	**admitíamos**	**había admitido**	**habíamos admitido**
admitías	**admitíais**	**habías admitido**	**habíais admitido**
admitía	**admitían**	**había admitido**	**habían admitido**
3 pretérito		10 pretérito anterior	
admití	**admitimos**	**hube admitido**	**hubimos admitido**
admitiste	**admitisteis**	**hubiste admitido**	**hubisteis admitido**
admitió	**admitieron**	**hubo admitido**	**hubieron admitido**
4 futuro		11 futuro perfecto	
admitiré	**admitiremos**	**habré admitido**	**habremos admitido**
admitirás	**admitiréis**	**habrás admitido**	**habréis admitido**
admitirá	**admitirán**	**habrá admitido**	**habrán admitido**
5 potencial simple		12 potencial compuesto	
admitiría	**admitiríamos**	**habría admitido**	**habríamos admitido**
admitirías	**admitiríais**	**habrías admitido**	**habríais admitido**
admitiría	**admitirían**	**habría admitido**	**habrían admitido**
6 presente de subjuntivo		13 perfecto de subjuntivo	
admita	**admitamos**	**haya admitido**	**hayamos admitido**
admitas	**admitáis**	**hayas admitido**	**hayáis admitido**
admita	**admitan**	**haya admitido**	**hayan admitido**
7 imperfecto de subjuntivo		14 pluscuamperfecto de subjuntivo	
admitiera	**admitiéramos**	**hubiera admitido**	**hubiéramos admitido**
admitieras	**admitierais**	**hubieras admitido**	**hubierais admitido**
admitiera	**admitieran**	**hubiera admitido**	**hubieran admitido**
OR		OR	
admitiese	**admitiésemos**	**hubiese admitido**	**hubiésemos admitido**
admitieses	**admitieseis**	**hubieses admitido**	**hubieseis admitido**
admitiese	**admitiesen**	**hubiese admitido**	**hubiesen admitido**

	imperativo	
—	**admitamos**	
admite; no admitas	**admitid; no admitáis**	
admita	**admitan**	

Es cosa admitida que es necesario
  trabajar para tener éxito.   It's
  generally admitted that it's necessary
  to work in order to succeed.
la admisión   acceptance, admission

admitido, admitida   admitted
admisible   admissible
un examen de admisión   entrance
  exam

adorar

Gerundio **adorando**   Part. pas. **adorado**

to adore, to worship

Regular **-ar** verb

The Seven Simple Tenses		The Seven Compound Tenses	
Singular	Plural	Singular	Plural
1 presente de indicativo		8 perfecto de indicativo	
adoro	adoramos	he adorado	hemos adorado
adoras	adoráis	has adorado	habéis adorado
adora	adoran	ha adorado	han adorado
2 imperfecto de indicativo		9 pluscuamperfecto de indicativo	
adoraba	adorábamos	había adorado	habíamos adorado
adorabas	adorabais	habías adorado	habíais adorado
adoraba	adoraban	había adorado	habían adorado
3 pretérito		10 pretérito anterior	
adoré	adoramos	hube adorado	hubimos adorado
adoraste	adorasteis	hubiste adorado	hubisteis adorado
adoró	adoraron	hubo adorado	hubieron adorado
4 futuro		11 futuro perfecto	
adoraré	adoraremos	habré adorado	habremos adorado
adorarás	adoraréis	habrás adorado	habréis adorado
adorará	adorarán	habrá adorado	habrán adorado
5 potencial simple		12 potencial compuesto	
adoraría	adoraríamos	habría adorado	habríamos adorado
adorarías	adoraríais	habrías adorado	habríais adorado
adoraría	adorarían	habría adorado	habrían adorado
6 presente de subjuntivo		13 perfecto de subjuntivo	
adore	adoremos	haya adorado	hayamos adorado
adores	adoréis	hayas adorado	hayáis adorado
adore	adoren	haya adorado	hayan adorado
7 imperfecto de subjuntivo		14 pluscuamperfecto de subjuntivo	
adorara	adoráramos	hubiera adorado	hubiéramos adorado
adoraras	adorarais	hubieras adorado	hubierais adorado
adorara	adoraran	hubiera adorado	hubieran adorado
OR		OR	
adorase	adorásemos	hubiese adorado	hubiésemos adorado
adorases	adoraseis	hubieses adorado	hubieseis adorado
adorase	adorasen	hubiese adorado	hubiesen adorado

imperativo	
—	adoremos
adora; no adores	adorad; no adoréis
adore	adoren

el adorador, la adoradora   adorer, worshipper
adorable   adorable
adorado, adorada   adored
la adoración   adoration
adorablemente   adorably, adoringly

Proverb: Con la boca adorando y con el mazo dando.   Speak softly but carry a big stick. (Lit.: Worshiping with one's mouth and striking with a mallet.)

Regular **-ir** verb endings with stem change: Tenses 1, 6, Imperative   to acquire, to get, to obtain

The Seven Simple Tenses		The Seven Compound Tenses	
Singular	Plural	Singular	Plural
1 presente de indicativo		8 perfecto de indicativo	
adquiero	adquirimos	he adquirido	hemos adquirido
adquieres	adquirís	has adquirido	habéis adquirido
adquiere	adquieren	ha adquirido	han adquirido
2 imperfecto de indicativo		9 pluscuamperfecto de indicativo	
adquiría	adquiríamos	había adquirido	habíamos adquirido
adquirías	adquiríais	habías adquirido	habíais adquirido
adquiría	adquirían	había adquirido	habían adquirido
3 pretérito		10 pretérito anterior	
adquirí	adquirimos	hube adquirido	hubimos adquirido
adquiriste	adquiristeis	hubiste adquirido	hubisteis adquirido
adquirió	adquirieron	hubo adquirido	hubieron adquirido
4 futuro		11 futuro perfecto	
adquiriré	adquiriremos	habré adquirido	habremos adquirido
adquirirás	adquiriréis	habrás adquirido	habréis adquirido
adquirirá	adquirirán	habrá adquirido	habrán adquirido
5 potencial simple		12 potencial compuesto	
adquiriría	adquiriríamos	habría adquirido	habríamos adquirido
adquirirías	adquiriríais	habrías adquirido	habríais adquirido
adquiriría	adquirirían	habría adquirido	habrían adquirido
6 presente de subjuntivo		13 perfecto de subjuntivo	
adquiera	adquiramos	haya adquirido	hayamos adquirido
adquieras	adquiráis	hayas adquirido	hayáis adquirido
adquiera	adquieran	haya adquirido	hayan adquirido
7 imperfecto de subjuntivo		14 pluscuamperfecto de subjuntivo	
adquiriera	adquiriéramos	hubiera adquirido	hubiéramos adquirido
adquirieras	adquirierais	hubieras adquirido	hubierais adquirido
adquiriera	adquirieran	hubiera adquirido	hubieran adquirido
OR		OR	
adquiriese	adquiriésemos	hubiese adquirido	hubiésemos adquirido
adquirieses	adquirieseis	hubieses adquirido	hubieseis adquirido
adquiriese	adquiriesen	hubiese adquirido	hubiesen adquirido

imperativo	
—	adquiramos
adquiere; no adquieras	adquirid; no adquiráis
adquiera	adquieran

el adquirido, la adquiridora acquirer	adquirir un derecho to acquire a right
el (la) adquirente, el (la) adquiriente acquirer	los bienes adquiridos acquired wealth
la adquisición acquisition, attainment	adquirir un hábito to acquire a habit

advertir

Gerundio **advirtiendo**   Part. pas. **advertido**

to advise, to give notice, to give
warning, to take notice of, to warn

Irregular verb

The Seven Simple Tenses		The Seven Compound Tenses	
Singular	Plural	Singular	Plural
1 presente de indicativo		8 perfecto de indicativo	
advierto	advertimos	he advertido	hemos advertido
adviertes	advertís	has advertido	habéis advertido
advierte	advierten	ha advertido	han advertido
2 imperfecto de indicativo		9 pluscuamperfecto de indicativo	
advertía	advertíamos	había advertido	habíamos advertido
advertías	advertíais	habías advertido	habíais advertido
advertía	advertían	había advertido	habían advertido
3 pretérito		10 pretérito anterior	
advertí	advertimos	hube advertido	hubimos advertido
advertiste	advertisteis	hubiste advertido	hubisteis advertido
advirtió	advirtieron	hubo advertido	hubieron advertido
4 futuro		11 futuro perfecto	
advertiré	advertiremos	habré advertido	habremos advertido
advertirás	advertiréis	habrás advertido	habréis advertido
advertirá	advertirán	habrá advertido	habrán advertido
5 potencial simple		12 potencial compuesto	
advertiría	advertiríamos	habría advertido	habríamos advertido
advertirías	advertiríais	habrías advertido	habríais advertido
advertiría	advertirían	habría advertido	habrían advertido
6 presente de subjuntivo		13 perfecto de subjuntivo	
advierta	advirtamos	haya advertido	hayamos advertido
adviertas	advirtáis	hayas advertido	hayáis advertido
advierta	adviertan	haya advertido	hayan advertido
7 imperfecto de subjuntivo		14 pluscuamperfecto de subjuntivo	
advirtiera	advirtiéramos	hubiera advertido	hubiéramos advertido
advirtieras	advirtierais	hubieras advertido	hubierais advertido
advirtiera	advirtieran	hubiera advertido	hubieran advertido
OR		OR	
advirtiese	advirtiésemos	hubiese advertido	hubiésemos advertido
advirtieses	advirtieseis	hubieses advertido	hubieseis advertido
advirtiese	advirtiesen	hubiese advertido	hubiesen advertido

imperativo	
—	advirtamos
advierte; no adviertas	advertid; no advirtáis
advierta	adviertan

advertido, advertida skillful, clever, advised	después de repetidas advertencias after repeated warnings
la advertencia warning, notice, foreword	hacer una advertencia a un niño to correct a child's inappropriate behavior
advertidamente advisedly	
advertir en to notice, to take into account	

22

afeitarse

Reflexive regular **-ar** verb

to shave oneself

The Seven Simple Tenses		The Seven Compound Tenses	
Singular	Plural	Singular	Plural
1 presente de indicativo		8 perfecto de indicativo	
me afeito	nos afeitamos	me he afeitado	nos hemos afeitado
te afeitas	os afeitáis	te has afeitado	os habéis afeitado
se afeita	se afeitan	se ha afeitado	se han afeitado
2 imperfecto de indicativo		9 pluscuamperfecto de indicativo	
me afeitaba	nos afeitábamos	me había afeitado	nos habíamos afeitado
te afeitabas	os afeitabais	te habías afeitado	os habíais afeitado
se afeitaba	se afeitaban	se había afeitado	se habían afeitado
3 pretérito		10 pretérito anterior	
me afeité	nos afeitamos	me hube afeitado	nos hubimos afeitado
te afeitaste	os afeitasteis	te hubiste afeitado	os hubisteis afeitado
se afeitó	se afeitaron	se hubo afeitado	se hubieron afeitado
4 futuro		11 futuro perfecto	
me afeitaré	nos afeitaremos	me habré afeitado	nos habremos afeitado
te afeitarás	os afeitaréis	te habrás afeitado	os habréis afeitado
se afeitará	se afeitarán	se habrá afeitado	se habrán afeitado
5 potencial simple		12 potencial compuesto	
me afeitaría	nos afeitaríamos	me habría afeitado	nos habríamos afeitado
te afeitarías	os afeitaríais	te habrías afeitado	os habríais afeitado
se afeitaría	se afeitarían	se habría afeitado	se habrían afeitado
6 presente de subjuntivo		13 perfecto de subjuntivo	
me afeite	nos afeitemos	me haya afeitado	nos hayamos afeitado
te afeites	os afeitéis	te hayas afeitado	os hayáis afeitado
se afeite	se afeiten	se haya afeitado	se hayan afeitado
7 imperfecto de subjuntivo		14 pluscuamperfecto de subjuntivo	
me afeitara	nos afeitáramos	me hubiera afeitado	nos hubiéramos afeitado
te afeitaras	os afeitarais	te hubieras afeitado	os hubierais afeitado
se afeitara	se afeitaran	se hubiera afeitado	se hubieran afeitado
OR		OR	
me afeitase	nos afeitásemos	me hubiese afeitado	nos hubiésemos afeitado
te afeitases	os afeitaseis	te hubieses afeitado	os hubieseis afeitado
se afeitase	se afeitasen	se hubiese afeitado	se hubiesen afeitado

imperativo	
—	afeitémonos
aféitate; no te afeites	afeitaos; no os afeitéis
aféitese	aféitense

afeitar to shave	el afeite cosmetic, makeup
una afeitada, un afeitado a shave	Esta mañana, me levanté, me afeité y
una maquinilla de afeitar razor,	me fui al trabajo. This morning
shaver; una maquinilla de afeitar	I got up, shaved, and went to work.
eléctrica electric razor/shaver	

agradar

Gerundio **agradando**   Part. pas. **agradado**

to please, to be pleasing

Regular **-ar** verb

The Seven Simple Tenses		The Seven Compound Tenses	
Singular	Plural	Singular	Plural
1 presente de indicativo		8 perfecto de indicativo	
agrado	agradamos	he agradado	hemos agradado
agradas	agradáis	has agradado	habéis agradado
agrada	agradan	ha agradado	han agradado
2 imperfecto de indicativo		9 pluscuamperfecto de indicativo	
agradaba	agradábamos	había agradado	habíamos agradado
agradabas	agradabais	habías agradado	habíais agradado
agradaba	agradaban	había agradado	habían agradado
3 pretérito		10 pretérito anterior	
agradé	agradamos	hube agradado	hubimos agradado
agradaste	agradasteis	hubiste agradado	hubisteis agradado
agradó	agradaron	hubo agradado	hubieron agradado
4 futuro		11 futuro perfecto	
agradaré	agradaremos	habré agradado	habremos agradado
agradarás	agradaréis	habrás agradado	habréis agradado
agradará	agradarán	habrá agradado	habrán agradado
5 potencial simple		12 potencial compuesto	
agradaría	agradaríamos	habría agradado	habríamos agradado
agradarías	agradaríais	habrías agradado	habríais agradado
agradaría	agradarían	habría agradado	habrían agradado
6 presente de subjuntivo		13 perfecto de subjuntivo	
agrade	agrademos	haya agradado	hayamos agradado
agrades	agradéis	hayas agradado	hayáis agradado
agrade	agraden	haya agradado	hayan agradado
7 imperfecto de subjuntivo		14 pluscuamperfecto de subjuntivo	
agradara	agradáramos	hubiera agradado	hubiéramos agradado
agradaras	agradarais	hubieras agradado	hubierais agradado
agradara	agradaran	hubiera agradado	hubieran agradado
OR		OR	
agradase	agradásemos	hubiese agradado	hubiésemos agradado
agradases	agradaseis	hubieses agradado	hubieseis agradado
agradase	agradasen	hubiese agradado	hubiesen agradado

	imperativo	
—	agrademos	
agrada; no agrades	agradad; no agradéis	
agrade	agraden	

agradable pleasing, pleasant, agreeable	ser del agrado de uno to be to one's taste (liking)
el agrado pleasure, liking	agradador, agradadora eager to please
agradablemente agreeably, pleasantly	
Es de mi agrado. It's to my liking.	desagradable unpleasant, disagreeable
de su agrado to one's liking	

agradecer

Regular **-er** verb endings with spelling
change: **e** becomes **zc** before **a** or **o**

to thank, to be thankful for

The Seven Simple Tenses		The Seven Compound Tenses	
Singular	Plural	Singular	Plural
1 presente de indicativo		8 perfecto de indicativo	
agradezco	**agradecemos**	**he agradecido**	**hemos agradecido**
agradeces	**agradecéis**	**has agradecido**	**habéis agradecido**
agradece	**agradecen**	**ha agradecido**	**han agradecido**
2 imperfecto de indicativo		9 pluscuamperfecto de indicativo	
agradecía	**agradecíamos**	**había agradecido**	**habíamos agradecido**
agraceías	**agradecíais**	**habías agradecido**	**habíais agradecido**
agradecía	**agradecían**	**había agradecido**	**habían agradecido**
3 pretérito		10 pretérito anterior	
agradecí	**agradecimos**	**hube agradecido**	**hubimos agradecido**
agradeciste	**agradecisteis**	**hubiste agradecido**	**hubisteis agradecido**
agradeció	**agradecieron**	**hubo agradecido**	**hubieron agradecido**
4 futuro		11 futuro perfecto	
agradeceré	**agradeceremos**	**habré agradecido**	**habremos agradecido**
agradecerás	**agradeceréis**	**habrás agradecido**	**habréis agradecido**
agradecerá	**agradecerán**	**habrá agradecido**	**habrán agradecido**
5 potencial simple		12 potencial compuesto	
agradecería	**agradeceríamos**	**habría agradecido**	**habríamos agradecido**
agradecerías	**agradeceríais**	**habrías agradecido**	**habríais agradecido**
agradecería	**agradecerían**	**habría agradecido**	**habrían agradecido**
6 presente de subjuntivo		13 perfecto de subjuntivo	
agradezca	**agradezcamos**	**haya agradecido**	**hayamos agradecido**
agradezcas	**agradezcáis**	**hayas agradecido**	**hayáis agradecido**
agradezca	**agradezcan**	**haya agradecido**	**hayan agradecido**
7 imperfecto de subjuntivo		14 pluscuamperfecto de subjuntivo	
agradeciera	**agradeciéramos**	**hubiera agradecido**	**hubiéramos agradecido**
agradecieras	**agradecierais**	**hubieras agradecido**	**hubierais agradecido**
agradeciera	**agradecieran**	**hubiera agradecido**	**hubieran agradecido**
OR		OR	
agradeciese	**agradeciésemos**	**hubiese agradecido**	**hubiésemos agradecido**
agradecieses	**agradecieseis**	**hubieses agradecido**	**hubieseis agradecido**
agradeciese	**agradeciesen**	**hubiese agradecido**	**hubiesen agradecido**

	imperativo	
—	**agradezcamos**	
agradece; no agradezcas	**agradeced; no agradezcáis**	
agradezca	**agradezcan**	

agradecido, agradecida thankful, grateful	**desagradecidamente** ungratefully
desagradecer to be ungrateful	**muy agradecido** much obliged
el agradecimiento gratitude, gratefulness	**Yo le agradezco el regalo.** I am grateful for the present.

aguardar

Gerundio **aguardando**   Part. pas. **aguardado**

to expect, to wait for

Regular **-ar** verb

The Seven Simple Tenses		The Seven Compound Tenses	
Singular	Plural	Singular	Plural
1 presente de indicativo		8 perfecto de indicativo	
aguardo	aguardamos	he aguardado	hemos aguardado
aguardas	aguardáis	has aguardado	habéis aguardado
aguarda	aguardan	ha aguardado	han aguardado
2 imperfecto de indicativo		9 pluscuamperfecto de indicativo	
aguardaba	aguardábamos	había aguardado	habíamos aguardado
aguardabas	aguardabais	habías aguardado	habíais aguardado
aguardaba	aguardaban	había aguardado	habían aguardado
3 pretérito		10 pretérito anterior	
aguardé	aguardamos	hube aguardado	hubimos aguardado
aguardaste	aguardasteis	hubiste aguardado	hubisteis aguardado
aguardó	aguardaron	hubo aguardado	hubieron aguardado
4 futuro		11 futuro perfecto	
aguardaré	aguardaremos	habré aguardado	habremos aguardado
aguardarás	aguardaréis	habrás aguardado	habréis aguardado
aguardará	aguardarán	habrá aguardado	habrán aguardado
5 potencial simple		12 potencial compuesto	
aguardaría	aguardaríamos	habría aguardado	habríamos aguardado
aguardarías	aguardaríais	habrías aguardado	habríais aguardado
aguardaría	aguardarían	habría aguardado	habrían aguardado
6 presente de subjuntivo		13 perfecto de subjuntivo	
aguarde	aguardemos	haya aguardado	hayamos aguardado
aguardes	aguardéis	hayas aguardado	hayáis aguardado
aguarde	aguarden	haya aguardado	hayan aguardado
7 imperfecto de subjuntivo		14 pluscuamperfecto de subjuntivo	
aguardara	aguardáramos	hubiera aguardado	hubiéramos aguardado
aguardaras	aguardarais	hubieras aguardado	hubierais aguardado
aguardara	aguardaran	hubiera aguardado	hubieran aguardado
OR		OR	
aguardase	aguardásemos	hubiese aguardado	hubiésemos aguardado
aguardases	aguardaseis	hubieses aguardado	hubieseis aguardado
aguardase	aguardasen	hubiese aguardado	hubiesen aguardado

imperativo	
—	aguardemos
aguarda; no aguardes	aguardad; no aguardéis
aguarde	aguarden

la aguardada expecting, waiting guardar silencio to keep silent guardar to guard, to watch (over) ¡Dios guarde al Rey! God save the King!	Proverb: A quien sabe guardar una peseta nunca le faltará un duro. A penny saved is a penny earned.

alcanzar

Regular **-ar** verb endings with spelling change: **z** become **c** before **e**

to reach, to overtake

The Seven Simple Tenses		The Seven Compound Tenses	
Singular	Plural	Singular	Plural
1 presente de indicativo		8 perfecto de indicativo	
alcanzo	alcanzamos	he alcanzado	hemos alcanzado
alcanzas	alcanzáis	has alcanzado	habéis alcanzado
alcanza	alcanzan	ha alcanzado	han alcanzado
2 imperfecto de indicativo		9 pluscuamperfecto de indicativo	
alcanzaba	alcanzábamos	había alcanzado	habíamos alcanzado
alcanzabas	alcanzabais	habías alcanzado	habíais alcanzado
alcanzaba	alcanzaban	había alcanzado	habían alcanzado
3 pretérito		10 pretérito anterior	
alcancé	alcanzamos	hube alcanzado	hubimos alcanzado
alcanzaste	alcanzasteis	hubiste alcanzado	hubisteis alcanzado
alcanzó	alcanzaron	hubo alcanzado	hubieron alcanzado
4 futuro		11 futuro perfecto	
alcanzaré	alcanzaremos	habré alcanzado	habremos alcanzado
alcanzarás	alcanzaréis	habrás alcanzado	habréis alcanzado
alcanzará	alcanzarán	habrá alcanzado	habrán alcanzado
5 potencial simple		12 potencial compuesto	
alcanzaría	alcanzaríamos	habría alcanzado	habríamos alcanzado
alcanzarías	alcanzaríais	habrías alcanzado	habríais alcanzado
alcanzaría	alcanzarían	habría alcanzado	habrían alcanzado
6 presente de subjuntivo		13 perfecto de subjuntivo	
alcance	alcancemos	haya alcanzado	hayamos alcanzado
alcances	alcancéis	hayas alcanzado	hayáis alcanzado
alcance	alcancen	haya alcanzado	hayan alcanzado
7 imperfecto de subjuntivo		14 pluscuamperfecto de subjuntivo	
alcanzara	alcanzáramos	hubiera alcanzado	hubiéramos alcanzado
alcanzaras	alcanzarais	hubieras alcanzado	hubierais alcanzado
alcanzara	alcanzaran	hubiera alcanzado	hubieran alcanzado
OR		OR	
alcanzase	alcanzásemos	hubiese alcanzado	hubiésemos alcanzado
alcanzases	alcanzaseis	hubieses alcanzado	hubieseis alcanzado
alcanzase	alcanzasen	hubiese alcanzado	hubiesen alcanzado

	imperativo	
—	alcancemos	
alcanza; no alcances	alcanzad; no alcancéis	
alcance	alcancen	

el alcance overtaking, reach	dar alcance a to overtake
alcanzar a + inf. to manage to + inf.	alcanzar el tren to catch the train
al alcance de within reach of	alcanzable attainable, reachable
alcanzar una cuota to fill a quota	al alcance del oído within earshot

alegrarse

Gerundio **alegrándose**   Part. pas. **alegrado**

to be glad, to rejoice

Reflexive regular **-ar** verb

The Seven Simple Tenses		The Seven Compound Tenses	
Singular	Plural	Singular	Plural
1 presente de indicativo		**8 perfecto de indicativo**	
me alegro	nos alegramos	me he alegrado	nos hemos alegrado
te alegras	os alegráis	te has alegrado	os habéis alegrado
se alegra	se alegran	se ha alegrado	se han alegrado
2 imperfecto de indicativo		**9 pluscuamperfecto de indicativo**	
me alegraba	nos alegrábamos	me había alegrado	nos habíamos alegrado
te alegrabas	os alegrabais	te habías alegrado	os habíais alegrado
se alegraba	se alegraban	se había alegrado	se habían alegrado
3 pretérito		**10 pretérito anterior**	
me alegré	nos alegramos	me hube alegrado	nos hubimos alegrado
te alegraste	os alegrasteis	te hubiste alegrado	os hubisteis alegrado
se alegró	se alegraron	se hubo alegrado	se hubieron alegrado
4 futuro		**11 futuro perfecto**	
me alegraré	nos alegraremos	me habré alegrado	nos habremos alegrado
te alegrarás	os alegraréis	te habrás alegrado	os habréis alegrado
se alegrará	se alegrarán	se habrá alegrado	se habrán alegrado
5 potencial simple		**12 potencial compuesto**	
me alegraría	nos alegraríamos	me habría alegrado	nos habríamos alegrado
te alegrarías	os alegraríais	te habrías alegrado	os habríais alegrado
se alegraría	se alegrarían	se habría alegrado	se habrían alegrado
6 presente de subjuntivo		**13 perfecto de subjuntivo**	
me alegre	nos alegremos	me haya alegrado	nos hayamos álegrado
te alegres	os alegréis	te hayas alegrado	os hayáis alegrado
se alegre	se alegren	se haya alegrado	se hayan alegrado
7 imperfecto de subjuntivo		**14 pluscuamperfecto de subjuntivo**	
me alegrara	nos alegráramos	me hubiera alegrado	nos hubiéramos alegrado
te alegraras	os alegrarais	te hubieras alegrado	os hubierais alegrado
se alegrara	se alegraran	se hubiera alegrado	se hubieran alegrado
OR		OR	
me alegrase	nos alegrásemos	me hubiese alegrado	nos hubiésemos alegrado
te alegrases	os alegraseis	te hubieses alegrado	os hubieseis alegrado
se alegrase	se alegrasen	se hubiese alegrado	se hubiesen alegrado

imperativo	
—	alegrémonos
alégrate; no te alegres	alegraos; no os alegréis
alégrese	alégrense

la alegría joy, rejoicing, mirth	**tener mucha alegría** to be very glad
alegremente gladly, cheerfully	**alegrar la fiesta** to liven up the party
alegro allegro	**saltar de alegría** to jump for joy
alegre happy, joyful, merry, bright (color)	**¡Qué alegría!** What joy!

Gerundio almorzando   Part. pas. almorzado   **almorzar**

Regular -ar verb endings with stem change: Tenses 1, 6,   to lunch, to have lunch
Imperative; spelling change: **z** becomes **c** before **e**

The Seven Simple Tenses		The Seven Compound Tenses	
Singular	Plural	Singular	Plural
1 presente de indicativo		**8 perfecto de indicativo**	
almuerzo	almorzamos	he almorzado	hemos almorzado
almuerzas	almorzáis	has almorzado	habéis almorzado
almuerza	almuerzan	ha almorzado	han almorzado
2 imperfecto de indicativo		**9 pluscuamperfecto de indicativo**	
almorzaba	almorzábamos	había almorzado	habíamos almorzado
almorzabas	almorzabais	habías almorzado	habíais almorzado
almorzaba	almorzaban	había almorzado	habían almorzado
3 pretérito		**10 pretérito anterior**	
almorcé	almorzamos	hube almorzado	hubimos almorzado
almorzaste	almorzasteis	hubiste almorzado	hubisteis almorzado
almorzó	almorzaron	hubo almorzado	hubieron almorzado
4 futuro		**11 futuro perfecto**	
almorzaré	almorzaremos	habré almorzado	habremos almorzado
almorzarás	almorzaréis	habrás almorzado	habréis almorzado
almorzará	almorzarán	habrá almorzado	habrán almorzado
5 potencial simple		**12 potencial compuesto**	
almorzaría	almorzaríamos	habría almorzado	habríamos almorzado
almorzarías	almorzaríais	habrías almorzado	habríais almorzado
almorzaría	almorzarían	habría almorzado	habrían almorzado
6 presente de subjuntivo		**13 perfecto de subjuntivo**	
almuerce	almorcemos	haya almorzado	hayamos almorzado
almuerces	almorcéis	hayas almorzado	hayáis almorzado
almuerce	almuercen	haya almorzado	hayan almorzado
7 imperfecto de subjuntivo		**14 pluscuamperfecto de subjuntivo**	
almorzara	almorzáramos	hubiera almorzado	hubiéramos almorzado
almorzaras	almorzarais	hubieras almorzado	hubierais almorzado
almorzara	almorzaran	hubiera almorzado	hubieran almorzado
OR		OR	
almorzase	almorzásemos	hubiese almorzado	hubiésemos almorzado
almorzases	almorzaseis	hubieses almorzado	hubieseis almorzado
almorzase	almorzasen	hubiese almorzado	hubiesen almorzado

	imperativo	
—	almorcemos
almuerza; no almuerces	almorzad; no almorcéis
almuerce	almuercen

el desayuno breakfast	Todos los días desayuno en casa,
le cena dinner, supper	almuerzo en la escuela y ceno con
el almuerzo lunch	mi familia. Every day I (have)
cenar to have dinner, supper	breakfast at home, (have) lunch at
	school, and have dinner with my
	family.

alquilar

Gerundio **alquilando**   Part. pas. **alquilado**

to hire, to rent

The Seven Simple Tenses		The Seven Compound Tenses	
Singular	Plural	Singular	Plural
1 presente de indicativo		8 perfecto de indicativo	
alquilo	alquilamos	he alquilado	hemos alquilado
alquilas	alquiláis	has alquilado	habéis alquilado
alquila	alquilan	ha alquilado	han alquilado
2 imperfecto de indicativo		9 pluscuamperfecto de indicativo	
alquilaba	alquilábamos	había alquilado	habíamos alquilado
alquilabas	alquilabais	habías alquilado	habíais alquilado
alquilaba	alquilaban	había alquilado	habían alquilado
3 pretérito		10 pretérito anterior	
alquilé	alquilamos	hube alquilado	hubimos alquilado
alquilaste	alquilasteis	hubiste alquilado	hubisteis alquilado
alquiló	alquilaron	hubo alquilado	hubieron alquilado
4 futuro		11 futuro perfecto	
alquilaré	alquilaremos	habré alquilado	habremos alquilado
alquilarás	alquilaréis	habrás alquilado	habréis alquilado
alquilará	alquilarán	habrá alquilado	habrán alquilado
5 potencial simple		12 potencial compuesto	
alquilaría	alquilaríamos	habría alquilado	habríamos alquilado
alquilarías	alquilaríais	habrías alquilado	habríais alquilado
alquilaría	alquilarían	habría alquilado	habrían alquilado
6 presente de subjuntivo		13 perfecto de subjuntivo	
alquile	alquilemos	haya alquilado	hayamos alquilado
alquiles	alquiléis	hayas alquilado	hayáis alquilado
alquile	alquilen	haya alquilado	hayan alquilado
7 imperfecto de subjuntivo		14 pluscuamperfecto de subjuntivo	
alquilara	alquiláramos	hubiera alquilado	hubiéramos alquilado
alquilaras	alquilarais	hubieras alquilado	hubierais alquilado
alquilara	alquilaran	hubiera alquilado	hubieran alquilado
OR		OR	
alquilase	alquilásemos	hubiese alquilado	hubiésemos alquilado
alquilases	alquilaseis	hubieses alquilado	hubieseis alquilado
alquilase	alquilasen	hubiese alquilado	hubiesen alquilado

imperativo	
—	alquilemos
alquila; no alquiles	alquilad; no alquiléis
alquile	alquilen

alquilable rentable	el alquiler mensual monthly rental
desalquilar to vacate, stop renting	¿Dónde se puede alquilar ...? Where
SE ALQUILA FOR RENT	can (some)one rent a ...?
ALQUILA AVAILABLE	

Regular -az verb endings with spelling
change: **z** becomes **c** before **e**

to heave, to lift, to pick up,
to raise (prices)

The Seven Simple Tenses		The Seven Compound Tenses	
Singular	Plural	Singular	Plural
1 presente de indicativo		8 perfecto de indicativo	
alzo	alzamos	he alzado	hemos alzado
alzas	alzáis	has alzado	habéis alzado
alza	alzan	ha alzado	han alzado
2 imperfecto de indicativo		9 pluscuamperfecto de indicativo	
alzaba	alzábamos	había alzado	habíamos alzado
alzabas	alzabais	habías alzado	habíais alzado
alzaba	alzaban	había alzado	habían alzado
3 pretérito		10 pretérito anterior	
alcé	alzamos	hube alzado	hubimos alzado
alzaste	alzasteis	hubiste alzado	hubisteis alzado
alzó	alzaron	hubo alzado	hubieron alzado
4 futuro		11 futuro perfecto	
alzaré	alzaremos	habré alzado	habremos alzado
alzarás	alzaréis	habrás alzado	habréis alzado
alzará	alzarán	habrá alzado	habrán alzado
5 potencial simple		12 potencial compuesto	
alzaría	alzaríamos	habría alzado	habríamos alzado
alzarías	alzaríais	habrías alzado	habríais alzado
alzaría	alzarían	habría alzado	habrían alzado
6 presente de subjuntivo		13 perfecto de subjuntivo	
alce	alcemos	haya alzado	hayamos alzado
alces	alcéis	hayas alzado	hayáis alzado
alce	alcen	haya alzado	hayan alzado
7 imperfecto de subjuntivo		14 pluscuamperfecto de subjuntivo	
alzara	alzáramos	hubiera alzado	hubiéramos alzado
alzaras	alzarais	hubieras alzado	hubierais alzado
alzara	alzaran	hubiera alzado	hubieran alzado
OR		OR	
alzase	alzásemos	hubiese alzado	hubiésemos alzado
alzases	alzaseis	hubieses alzado	hubieseis alzado
alzase	alzasen	hubiese alzado	hubiesen alzado

imperativo	
—	alcemos
alza; no alces	alzad; no alcéis
alce	alcen

alzar velas to set the sails	alzar la mano to threaten, to raise
la alzadura elevation	one's hand
alzar con to run off with, to steal	alzar el codo to drink to excess (to
el alzamiento raising, lifting	raise one's elbow)
alzar la voz to raise one's voice	

amar

Gerundio **amando**   Part. pas. **amado**

to love

Regular **-ar** verb

The Seven Simple Tenses		The Seven Compound Tenses	
Singular	Plural	Singular	Plural
1 presente de indicativo		**8 perfecto de indicativo**	
amo	amamos	he amado	hemos amado
amas	amáis	has amado	habéis amado
ama	aman	ha amado	han amado
2 imperfecto de indicativo		**9 pluscuamperfecto de indicativo**	
amaba	amábamos	había amado	habíamos amado
amabas	amabais	habías amado	habíais amado
amaba	amaban	había amado	habían amado
3 pretérito		**10 pretérito anterior**	
amé	amamos	hube amado	hubimos amado
amaste	amasteis	hubiste amado	hubisteis amado
amó	amaron	hubo amado	hubieron amado
4 futuro		**11 futuro perfecto**	
amaré	amaremos	habré amado	habremos amado
amarás	amaréis	habrás amado	habréis amado
amará	amarán	habrá amado	habrán amado
5 potencial simple		**12 potencial compuesto**	
amaría	amaríamos	habría amado	habríamos amado
amarías	amaríais	habrías amado	habríais amado
amaría	amarían	habría amado	habrían amado
6 presente de subjuntivo		**13 perfecto de subjuntivo**	
ame	amemos	haya amado	hayamos amado
ames	améis	hayas amado	hayáis amado
ame	amen	haya amado	hayan amado
7 imperfecto de subjuntivo		**14 pluscuamperfecto de subjuntivo**	
amara	amáramos	hubiera amado	hubiéramos amado
amaras	amarais	hubieras amado	hubierais amado
amara	amaran	hubiera amado	hubieran amado
OR		OR	
amase	amásemos	hubiese amado	hubiésemos amado
amases	amaseis	hubieses amado	hubieseis amado
amase	amasen	hubiese amado	hubiesen amado

	imperativo	
—		amemos
	ama; no ames	amad; no améis
	ame	amen

la amabilidad amiability, kindness		**Proverb:** Amar y no ser amado es un
amablemente amiably, kindly		tiempo mal empleado. To love and
amable amiable, kind, affable		not be loved is a bad use (waste) of
el amor love		time

añadir

to add

The Seven Simple Tenses		The Seven Compound Tenses	
Singular	Plural	Singular	Plural
1 presente de indicativo		**8 perfecto de indicativo**	
añado	añadimos	he añadido	hemos añadido
añades	añadís	has añadido	habéis añadido
añade	añaden	ha añadido	han añadido
2 imperfecto de indicativo		**9 pluscuamperfecto de indicativo**	
añadía	añadíamos	había añadido	habíamos añadido
añadías	añadíais	habías añadido	habíais añadido
añadía	añadían	había añadido	habían añadido
3 pretérito		**10 pretérito anterior**	
añadí	añadimos	hube añadido	hubimos añadido
añadiste	añadisteis	hubiste añadido	hubisteis añadido
añadió	añadieron	hubo añadido	hubieron añadido
4 futuro		**11 futuro perfecto**	
añadiré	añadiremos	habré añadido	habremos añadido
añadirás	añadiréis	habrás añadido	habréis añadido
añadirá	añadirán	habrá añadido	habrán añadido
5 potencial simple		**12 potencial compuesto**	
añadiría	añadiríamos	habría añadido	habríamos añadido
añadirías	añadiríais	habrías añadido	habríais añadido
añadiría	añadirían	habría añadido	habrían añadido
6 presente de subjuntivo		**13 perfecto de subjuntivo**	
añada	añadamos	haya añadido	hayamos añadido
añadas	añadáis	hayas añadido	hayáis añadido
añada	añadan	haya añadido	hayan añadido
7 imperfecto de subjuntivo		**14 pluscuamperfecto de subjuntivo**	
añadiera	añadiéramos	hubiera añadido	hubiéramos añadido
añadieras	añadierais	hubieras añadido	hubierais añadido
añadiera	añadieran	hubiera añadido	hubieran añadido
OR		OR	
añadiese	añadiésemos	hubiese añadido	hubiésemos añadido
añadieses	añadieseis	hubieses añadido	hubieseis añadido
añadiese	añadiesen	hubiese añadido	hubiesen añadido

imperativo	
—	añadamos
añade; no añadas	añadid; no añadáis
añada	añadan

la añadidura	increase, addition	por añadidura	in addition
el añadimiento	addition	añadido, añadida	added, additional

33

andar

Gerundio **andando**   Part. pas. **andado**

to walk

Irregular **-ar** verb: Tenses 3 and 7

The Seven Simple Tenses		The Seven Compound Tenses	
Singular	Plural	Singular	Plural
1 presente de indicativo		**8 perfecto de indicativo**	
ando	andamos	he andado	hemos andado
andas	andáis	has andado	habéis andado
anda	andan	ha andado	han andado
2 imperfecto de indicativo		**9 pluscuamperfecto de indicativo**	
andaba	andábamos	había andado	habíamos andado
andabas	andabais	habías andado	habíais andado
andaba	andaban	había andado	habían andado
3 pretérito		**10 pretérito anterior**	
anduve	anduvimos	hube andado	hubimos andado
anduviste	anduvisteis	hubiste andado	hubisteis andado
anduvo	anduvieron	hubo andado	hubieron andado
4 futuro		**11 futuro perfecto**	
andaré	andaremos	habré andado	habremos andado
andarás	andaréis	habrás andado	habréis andado
andará	andarán	habrá andado	habrán andado
5 potencial simple		**12 potencial compuesto**	
andaría	andaríamos	habría andado	habríamos andado
andarías	andaríais	habrías andado	habríais andado
andaría	andarían	habría andado	habrían andado
6 presente de subjuntivo		**13 perfecto de subjuntivo**	
ande	andemos	haya andado	hayamos andado
andes	andéis	hayas andado	hayáis andado
ande	anden	haya andado	hayan andado
7 imperfecto de subjuntivo		**14 pluscuamperfecto de subjuntivo**	
anduviera	anduviéramos	hubiera andado	hubiéramos andado
anduvieras	anduvierais	hubieras andado	hubierais andado
anduviera	anduvieran	hubiera andado	hubieran andado
OR		OR	
anduviese	anduviésemos	hubiese andado	hubiésemos andado
anduvieses	anduvieseis	hubieses andado	hubieseis andado
anduviese	anduviesen	hubiese andado	hubiesen andado

	imperativo	
—	andemos
anda; no andes	andad; no andéis
ande	anden

buena andanza	good fortune	andar a caballo to ride a horse
a todo andar	at full speed	¿Cómo andan los negocios? How's
mala andanza	bad fortune	business?
a largo andar	in the long run	**Dime con quién andas y te diré quién**
andar a gatas	to crawl, to walk/on	**eres.** Tell me who your friends are
all fours		and I will tell you who you are.

34

aparecer

Regular **-er** verb endings with spelling
change: **c** becomes **zc** before **a** or **o**

to appear, to show up

The Seven Simple Tenses		The Seven Compound Tenses	
Singular	Plural	Singular	Plural
1 presente de indicativo		**8 perfecto de indicativo**	
aparezco	aparecemos	he aparecido	hemos aparecido
apareces	aparecéis	has aparecido	habéis aparecido
aparece	aparecen	ha aparecido	han aparecido
2 imperfecto de indicativo		**9 pluscuamperfecto de indicativo**	
aparecía	aparecíamos	había aparecido	habíamos aparecido
aparecías	aparecíais	habías aparecido	habíais aparecido
aparecía	aparecían	había aparecido	habían aparecido
3 pretérito		**10 pretérito anterior**	
aparecí	aparecimos	hube aparecido	hubimos aparecido
apareciste	aparecisteis	hubiste aparecido	hubisteis aparecido
apareció	aparecieron	hubo aparecido	hubieron aparecido
4 futuro		**11 futuro perfecto**	
apareceré	apareceremos	habré aparecido	habremos aparecido
aparecerás	apareceréis	habrás aparecido	habréis aparecido
aparecerá	aparecerán	habrá aparecido	habrán aparecido
5 potencial simple		**12 potencial compuesto**	
aparecería	apareceríamos	habría aparecido	habríamos aparecido
aparecerías	apareceríais	habrías aparecido	habríais aparecido
aparecería	aparecerían	habría aparecido	habrían aparecido
6 presente de subjuntivo		**13 perfecto de subjuntivo**	
aparezca	aparezcamos	haya aparecido	hayamos aparecido
aparezcas	aparezcáis	hayas aparecido	hayáis aparecido
aparezca	aparezcan	haya aparecido	hayan aparecido
7 imperfecto de subjuntivo		**14 pluscuamperfecto de subjuntivo**	
apareciera	apareciéramos	hubiera aparecido	hubiéramos aparecido
aparecieras	aparecierais	hubieras aparecido	hubierais aparecido
apareciera	aparecieran	hubiera aparecido	hubieran aparecido
OR		OR	
apareciese	apareciésemos	hubiese aparecido	hubiésemos aparecido
aparecieses	aparecieseis	hubieses aparecido	hubieseis aparecido
apareciese	apareciesen	hubiese aparecido	hubiesen aparecido

	imperativo	
—	aparezcamos	
aparece; no aparezcas	apareced; no aparezcáis	
aparezca	aparezcan	

---

una **aparición**   apparition, appearance
aparecerse en casa   to arrive home
 unexpectedly
parecer   to seem, to appear
parecerse a   to look alike

aparecerse a alguno   to see a ghost
un **aparecimiento**   apparition
un **aparecido**   ghost
See also **parecer** and **parecerse**.

apoderarse

Gerundio **apoderándose**   Part. pas. **apoderado**

to take power, to take possession

Reflexive regular **-ar** verb

The Seven Simple Tenses		The Seven Compound Tenses	
Singular	Plural	Singular	Plural
1 presente de indicativo		8 perfecto de indicativo	
me apodero	nos apoderamos	me he	nos hemos
te apoderas	os apoderáis	te has	os habéis + apoderado
se apodera	se apoderan	se ha	se han
2 imperfecto de indicativo		9 pluscuamperfecto de indicativo	
me apoderaba	nos apoderábamos	me había	nos habíamos
te apoderabas	os apoderabais	te habías	os habíais + apoderado
se apoderaba	se apoderaban	se había	se habían
3 pretérito		10 pretérito anterior	
me apoderé	nos apoderamos	me hube	nos hubimos
te apoderaste	os apoderasteis	te hubiste	os hubisteis + apoderado
se apoderó	se apoderaron	se hubo	se hubieron
4 futuro		11 futuro perfecto	
me apoderaré	nos apoderaremos	me habré	nos habremos
te apoderarás	os apoderaréis	te habrás	os habréis + apoderado
se apoderará	se apoderarán	se habrá	se habrán
5 potencial simple		12 potencial compuesto	
me apoderaría	nos apoderaríamos	me habría	nos habríamos
te apoderarías	os apoderaríais	te habrías	os habríais + apoderado
se apoderaría	se apoderarían	se habría	se habrían
6 presente de subjuntivo		13 perfecto de subjuntivo	
me apodere	nos apoderemos	me haya	nos hayamos
te apoderes	os apoderéis	te hayas	os hayáis + apoderado
se apodere	se apoderen	se haya	se hayan
7 imperfecto de subjuntivo		14 pluscuamperfecto de subjuntivo	
me apoderara	nos apoderáramos	me hubiera	nos hubiéramos
te apoderaras	os apoderarais	te hubieras	os hubierais + apoderado
se apoderara	se apoderaran	se hubiera	se hubieran
OR		OR	
me apoderase	nos apoderásemos	me hubiese	nos hubiésemos
te apoderases	os apoderaseis	te hubieses	os hubieseis + apoderado
se apoderase	se apoderasen	se hubiese	se hubiesen

imperativo	
—	apoderémonos
apodérate; no te apoderes	apoderaos; no os apoderéis
apodérese	apodérense

poder to be able	**apoderado, apoderada** empowered
apoderarse de algo to take possession	**el apoderado** proxy
of something	**apoderar** to empower, to authorize
el poder power	

The Seven Simple Tenses		The Seven Compound Tenses	
Singular	Plural	Singular	Plural

1 presente de indicativo		8 perfecto de indicativo	
aprendo	aprendemos	he aprendido	hemos aprendido
aprendes	aprendéis	has aprendido	habéis aprendido
aprende	aprenden	ha aprendido	han aprendido

2 imperfecto de indicativo		9 pluscuamperfecto de indicativo	
aprendía	aprendíamos	había aprendido	habíamos aprendido
aprendías	aprendíais	habías aprendido	habíais aprendido
aprendía	aprendían	había aprendido	habían aprendido

3 pretérito		10 pretérito anterior	
aprendí	aprendimos	hube aprendido	hubimos aprendido
aprendiste	aprendisteis	hubiste aprendido	hubisteis aprendido
aprendió	aprendieron	hubo aprendido	hubieron aprendido

4 futuro		11 futuro perfecto	
aprenderé	aprenderemos	habré aprendido	habremos aprendido
aprenderás	aprenderéis	habrás aprendido	habréis aprendido
aprenderá	aprenderán	habrá aprendido	habrán aprendido

5 potencial simple		12 potencial compuesto	
aprendería	aprenderíamos	habría aprendido	habríamos aprendido
aprenderías	aprenderíais	habrías aprendido	habríais aprendido
aprendería	aprenderían	habría aprendido	habrían aprendido

6 presente de subjuntivo		13 perfecto de subjuntivo	
aprenda	aprendamos	haya aprendido	hayamos aprendido
aprendas	aprendáis	hayas aprendido	hayáis aprendido
aprenda	aprendan	haya aprendido	hayan aprendido

7 imperfecto de subjuntivo		14 pluscuamperfecto de subjuntivo	
aprendiera	aprendiéramos	hubiera aprendido	hubiéramos aprendido
aprendieras	aprendierais	hubieras aprendido	hubierais aprendido
aprendiera	aprendieran	hubiera aprendido	hubieran aprendido
OR		OR	
aprendiese	aprendiésemos	hubiese aprendido	hubiésemos aprendido
aprendieses	aprendieseis	hubieses aprendido	hubieseis aprendido
aprendiese	aprendiesen	hubiese aprendido	hubiesen aprendido

imperativo	
—	aprendamos
aprende; no aprendas	aprended; no aprendáis
aprenda	aprendan

Mi abuela aprendió a navegar en Internet.   My grandmother learned to surf the Internet.

Cada día se aprende algo nuevo.   You learn something new every day.

el aprendiz, la aprendiza   apprentice

aprendiz de todo (mucho), oficial de nada   Jack of all trades, master of none

aprender a + inf.   to learn + inf.

el aprendizaje   apprenticeship

aprender de memoria   to memorize

apresurarse

Gerundio **apresurándose**   Part. pas. **apresurado**

to hasten, to hurry, to rush

Reflexive regular **-ar** verb

The Seven Simple Tenses		The Seven Compound Tenses	
Singular	Plural	Singular	Plural
1 presente de indicativo		**8 perfecto de indicativo**	
me apresuro	nos apresuramos	me he	nos hemos
te apresuras	os apresuráis	te has	os habéis + apresurado
se apresura	se apresuran	se ha	se han
2 imperfecto de indicativo		**9 pluscuamperfecto de indicativo**	
me apresuraba	nos apresurábamos	me había	nos habíamos
te apresurabas	os apresurabais	te habías	os habíais + apresurado
se apresuraba	se apresuraban	se había	se habían
3 pretérito		**10 pretérito anterior**	
me apresuré	nos apresuramos	me hube	nos hubimos
te apresuraste	os apresurasteis	te hubiste	os hubisteis + apresurado
se apresuró	se apresuraron	se hubo	se hubieron
4 futuro		**11 futuro perfecto**	
me apresuraré	nos apresuraremos	me habré	nos habremos
te apresurarás	os apresuraréis	te habrás	os habréis + apresurado
se apresurará	se apresurarán	se habrá	se habrán
5 potencial simple		**12 potencial compuesto**	
me apresuraría	nos apresuraríamos	me habría	nos habríamos
te apresurarías	os apresuraríais	te habrías	os habríais + apresurado
se apresuraría	se apresurarían	se habría	se habrían
6 presente de subjuntivo		**13 perfecto de subjuntivo**	
me apresure	nos apresuremos	me haya	nos hayamos
te apresures	os apresuréis	te hayas	os hayáis + apresurado
se apresure	se apresuren	se haya	se hayan
7 imperfecto de subjuntivo		**14 pluscuamperfecto de subjuntivo**	
me apresurara	nos apresuráramos	me hubiera	nos hubiéramos
te apresuraras	os apresurarais	te hubieras	os hubierais + apresurado
se apresurara	se apresuraran	se hubiera	se hubieran
OR		OR	
me apresurase	nos apresurásemos	me hubiese	nos hubiésemos
te apresurases	os apresuraseis	te hubieses	os hubieseis + apresurado
se apresurase	se apresurasen	se hubiese	se hubiesen

imperativo	
—	apresurémonos
apresúrate; no te apresures	apresuraos; no os apresuréis
apresúrese	apresúrense

la apresuración haste	apresuradamente hastily
el apresuramiento hastiness	apresurarse a + inf. to hurry + inf.
apresurado, apresurada hasty, quick	la prisa haste
apresurar to accelerate	tener prisa to be in a hurry

Regular **-ar** verb   to take advantage, to avail oneself, to use

The Seven Simple Tenses		The Seven Compound Tenses	
Singular	Plural	Singular	Plural
1 presente de indicativo		8 perfecto de indicativo	
aprovecho	aprovechamos	he	hemos
aprovechas	aprovecháis	has	habéis + aprovechado
aprovecha	aprovechan	ha	han
2 imperfecto de indicativo		9 pluscuamperfecto de indicativo	
aprovechaba	aprovechábamos	había	habíamos
aprovechabas	aprovechabais	habías	habíais + aprovechado
aprovechaba	aprovechaban	había	habían
3 pretérito		10 pretérito anterior	
aproveché	aprovechamos	hube	hubimos
aprovechaste	aprovechasteis	hubiste	hubisteis + aprovechado
aprovechó	aprovecharon	hubo	hubieron
4 futuro		11 futuro perfecto	
aprovecharé	aprovecharemos	habré	habremos
aprovecharás	aprovecharéis	habrás	habréis + aprovechado
aprovechará	aprovecharán	habrá	habrán
5 potencial simple		12 potencial compuesto	
aprovecharía	aprovecharíamos	habría	habríamos
aprovecharías	aprovecharíais	habrías	habríais + aprovechado
aprovecharía	aprovecharían	habría	habrían
6 presente de subjuntivo		13 perfecto de subjuntivo	
aproveche	aprovechemos	haya	hayamos
aproveches	aprovechéis	hayas	hayáis + aprovechado
aproveche	aprovechen	haya	hayan
7 imperfecto de subjuntivo		14 pluscuamperfecto de subjuntivo	
aprovechara	aprovecháramos	hubiera	hubiéramos
aprovecharas	aprovecharais	hubieras	hubierais + aprovechado
aprovechara	aprovecharan	hubiera	hubieran
OR		OR	
aprovechase	aprovechásemos	hubiese	hubiésemos
aprovechases	aprovechaseis	hubieses	hubieseis + aprovechado
aprovechase	aprovechasen	hubiese	hubiesen

imperativo

—	aprovechemos
aprovecha; no aproveches	aprovechad; no aprovechéis
aproveche	aprovechen

aprovechado, aprovechada
  economical
aprovechar to make use of
aprovechable available, profitable
aprovechar la ocasión to take the
  opportunity

aprovechamiento use, utilization
aprovecharse de to take advantage of,
  to abuse

arrojar

Gerundio **arrojando**   Part. pas. **arrojado**

to fling, to hurl, to throw

Regular **-ar** verb

The Seven Simple Tenses		The Seven Compound Tenses	
Singular	Plural	Singular	Plural
1 presente de indicativo		8 perfecto de indicativo	
arrojo	arrojamos	he arrojado	hemos arrojado
arrojas	arrojáis	has arrojado	habéis arrojado
arroja	arrojan	ha arrojado	han arrojado
2 imperfecto de indicativo		9 pluscuamperfecto de indicativo	
arrojaba	arrojábamos	había arrojado	habíamos arrojado
arrojabas	arrojabais	habías arrojado	habíais arrojado
arrojaba	arrojaban	había arrojado	habían arrojado
3 pretérito		10 pretérito anterior	
arrojé	arrojamos	hube arrojado	hubimos arrojado
arrojaste	arrojasteis	hubiste arrojado	hubisteis arrojado
arrojó	arrojaron	hubo arrojado	hubieron arrojado
4 futuro		11 futuro perfecto	
arrojaré	arrojaremos	habré arrojado	habremos arrojado
arrojarás	arrojaréis	habrás arrojado	habréis arrojado
arrojará	arrojarán	habrá arrojado	habrán arrojado
5 potencial simple		12 potencial compuesto	
arrojaría	arrojaríamos	habría arrojado	habríamos arrojado
arrojarías	arrojaríais	habrías arrojado	habríais arrojado
arrojaría	arrojarían	habría arrojado	habrían arrojado
6 presente de subjuntivo		13 perfecto de subjuntivo	
arroje	arrojemos	haya arrojado	hayamos arrojado
arrojes	arrojéis	hayas arrojado	hayáis arrojado
arroje	arrojen	haya arrojado	hayan arrojado
7 imperfecto de subjuntivo		14 pluscuamperfecto de subjuntivo	
arrojara	arrojáramos	hubiera arrojado	hubiéramos arrojado
arrojaras	arrojarais	hubieras arrojado	hubierais arrojado
arrojara	arrojaran	hubiera arrojado	hubieran arrojado
OR		OR	
arrojase	arrojásemos	hubiese arrojado	hubiésemos arrojado
arrojases	arrojaseis	hubieses arrojado	hubieseis arrojado
arrojase	arrojasen	hubiese arrojado	hubiesen arrojado

	imperativo
—	arrojemos
arroja; no arrojes	arrojad; no arrojéis
arroje	arrojen

---

el arrojador, la arrojadora   thrower
arrojar la esponja   to throw in the
   towel (sponge)
arrojado, arrojada   fearless

el arrojo   fearlessness
el arrojallamas   flame thrower (also
   el lanzallamas)
See also **lanzar**.

Regular **-ar** verb   to assure, to affirm, to assert, to insure

The Seven Simple Tenses		The Seven Compound Tenses	
Singular	Plural	Singular	Plural
1 presente de indicativo		8 perfecto de indicativo	
aseguro	aseguramos	he asegurado	hemos asegurado
aseguras	aseguráis	has asegurado	habéis asegurado
asegura	aseguran	ha asegurado	han asegurado
2 imperfecto de indicativo		9 pluscuamperfecto de indicativo	
aseguraba	asegurábamos	había asegurado	habíamos asegurado
asegurabas	asegurabais	habías asegurado	habíais asegurado
aseguraba	aseguraban	había asegurado	habían asegurado
3 pretérito		10 pretérito anterior	
aseguré	aseguramos	hube asegurado	hubimos asegurado
aseguraste	asegurasteis	hubiste asegurado	hubisteis asegurado
aseguró	aseguraron	hubo asegurado	hubieron asegurado
4 futuro		11 futuro perfecto	
aseguraré	aseguraremos	habré asegurado	habremos asegurado
asegurarás	aseguraréis	habrás asegurado	habréis asegurado
asegurará	asegurarán	habrá asegurado	habrán asegurado
5 potencial simple		12 potencial compuesto	
aseguraría	aseguraríamos	habría asegurado	habríamos asegurado
asegurarías	aseguraríais	habrías asegurado	habríais asegurado
aseguraría	asegurarían	habría asegurado	habrían asegurado
6 presente de subjuntivo		13 perfecto de subjuntivo	
asegure	aseguremos	haya asegurado	hayamos asegurado
asegures	aseguréis	hayas asegurado	hayáis asegurado
asegure	aseguren	haya asegurado	hayan asegurado
7 imperfecto de subjuntivo		14 pluscuamperfecto de subjuntivo	
asegurara	aseguráramos	hubiera asegurado	hubiéramos asegurado
aseguraras	asegurarais	hubieras asegurado	hubierais asegurado
asegurara	aseguraran	hubiera asegurado	hubieran asegurado
OR		OR	
asegurase	asegurásemos	hubiese asegurado	hubiésemos asegurado
asegurases	aseguraseis	hubieses asegurado	hubieseis asegurado
asegurase	asegurasen	hubiese asegurado	hubiesen asegurado

	imperativo	
—	aseguremos	
asegura; no asegures	asegurad; no aseguréis	
asegure	aseguren	

la aseguración insurance	tener por seguro for sure
¡Ya puede usted asegurarlo! You can be sure of it!	la seguridad security, surety
asegurable insurable	de seguro surely
el asegurado, la asegurada insured person	seguramente surely, securely
	asegurarse to make sure

asir

Gerundio **asiendo**   Part. pas. **asido**

to seize, to grasp

Irregular **-ir** verb in Tenses 1, 6, and Imperative

The Seven Simple Tenses		The Seven Compound Tenses	
Singular	Plural	Singular	Plural
1 presente de indicativo		8 perfecto de indicativo	
asgo	**asimos**	**he asido**	**hemos asido**
ases	**asís**	**has asido**	**habéis asido**
ase	**asen**	**ha asido**	**han asido**
2 imperfecto de indicativo		9 pluscuamperfecto de indicativo	
asía	**asíamos**	**había asido**	**habíamos asido**
asías	**asíais**	**habías asido**	**habíais asido**
asía	**asían**	**había asido**	**habían asido**
3 pretérito		10 pretérito anterior	
así	**asimos**	**hube asido**	**hubimos asido**
asiste	**asisteis**	**hubiste asido**	**hubisteis asido**
asió	**asieron**	**hubo asido**	**hubieron asido**
4 futuro		11 futuro perfecto	
asiré	**asiremos**	**habré asido**	**habremos asido**
asirás	**asiréis**	**habrás asido**	**habréis asido**
asirá	**asirán**	**habrá asido**	**habrán asido**
5 potencial simple		12 potencial compuesto	
asiría	**asiríamos**	**habría asido**	**habríamos asido**
asirías	**asiríais**	**habrías asido**	**habríais asido**
asiría	**asirían**	**habría asido**	**habrían asido**
6 presente de subjuntivo		13 perfecto de subjuntivo	
asga	**asgamos**	**haya asido**	**hayamos asido**
asgas	**asgáis**	**hayas asido**	**hayáis asido**
asga	**asgan**	**haya asido**	**hayan asido**
7 imperfecto de subjuntivo		14 pluscuamperfecto de subjuntivo	
asiera	**asiéramos**	**hubiera asido**	**hubiéramos asido**
asieras	**asierais**	**hubieras asido**	**hubierais asido**
asiera	**asieran**	**hubiera asido**	**hubieran asido**
OR		OR	
asiese	**asiésemos**	**hubiese asido**	**hubiésemos asido**
asieses	**asieseis**	**hubieses asido**	**hubieseis asido**
asiese	**asiesen**	**hubiese asido**	**hubiesen asido**

imperativo	
—	**asgamos**
ase; no asgas	**asid; no asgáis**
asga	**asgan**

asir de los cabellos to grab by the hair	asidos del brazo arm in arm
asirse a (or de) to take hold of, to seize, grab	asirse to quarrel with each other
asirse con to grapple with	asir del brazo to get hold of by the arm

Regular **-ir** verb   to attend, to assist, to be present

The Seven Simple Tenses		The Seven Compound Tenses	
Singular	Plural	Singular	Plural
1 presente de indicativo		8 perfecto de indicativo	
asisto	**asistimos**	**he asistido**	**hemos asistido**
asistes	**asistís**	**has asistido**	**habéis asistido**
asiste	**asisten**	**ha asistido**	**han asistido**
2 imperfecto de indicativo		9 pluscuamperfecto de indicativo	
asistía	**asistíamos**	**había asistido**	**habíamos asistido**
asistías	**asistíais**	**habías asistido**	**habíais asistido**
asistía	**asistían**	**había asistido**	**habían asistido**
3 pretérito		10 pretérito anterior	
asistí	**asistimos**	**hube asistido**	**hubimos asistido**
asististe	**asististeis**	**hubiste asistido**	**hubisteis asistido**
asistió	**asistieron**	**hubo asistido**	**hubieron asistido**
4 futuro		11 futuro perfecto	
asistiré	**asistiremos**	**habré asistido**	**habremos asistido**
asistirás	**asistiréis**	**habrás asistido**	**habréis asistido**
asistirá	**asistirán**	**habrá asistido**	**habrán asistido**
5 potencial simple		12 potencial compuesto	
asistiría	**asistiríamos**	**habría asistido**	**habríamos asistido**
asistirías	**asistiríais**	**habrías asistido**	**habríais asistido**
asistiría	**asistirían**	**habría asistido**	**habrían asistido**
6 presente de subjuntivo		13 perfecto de subjuntivo	
asista	**asistamos**	**haya asistido**	**hayamos asistido**
asistas	**asistáis**	**hayas asistido**	**hayáis asistido**
asista	**asistan**	**haya asistido**	**hayan asistido**
7 imperfecto de subjuntivo		14 pluscuamperfecto de subjuntivo	
asistiera	**asistiéramos**	**hubiera asistido**	**hubiéramos asistido**
asistieras	**asistierais**	**hubieras asistido**	**hubierais asistido**
asistiera	**asistieran**	**hubiera asistido**	**hubieran asistido**
OR		OR	
asistiese	**asistiésemos**	**hubiese asistido**	**hubiésemos asistido**
asistieses	**asistieseis**	**hubieses asistido**	**hubieseis asistido**
asistiese	**asistiesen**	**hubiese asistido**	**hubiesen asistido**

imperativo

—	**asistamos**
asiste; no asistas	**asistid; no asistáis**
asista	**asistan**

---

asistir a   to attend, to be present at
la asistencia social   social welfare
la asistencia   attendance, presence
la asistencia técnica   technical
   assistance

el asistimiento   assistance
**Habríamos asistido a la boda si
   hubiéramos estado invitados.**   We
   would have attended the wedding if
   we had been invited.

asustarse

Gerundio **asustándose**   Part. pas. **asustado**

to be frightened, to be scared   Reflexive regular **-ar** verb

The Seven Simple Tenses		The Seven Compound Tenses	
Singular	Plural	Singular	Plural
1 presente de indicativo		8 perfecto de indicativo	
me asusto	nos asustamos	me he asustado	nos hemos asustado
te asustas	os asustáis	te has asustado	os habéis asustado
se asusta	se asustan	se ha asustado	se han asustado
2 imperfecto de indicativo		9 pluscuamperfecto de indicativo	
me asustaba	nos asustábamos	me había asustado	nos habíamos asustado
te asustabas	os asustabais	te habías asustado	os habíais asustado
se asustaba	se asustaban	se había asustado	se habían asustado
3 pretérito		10 pretérito anterior	
me asusté	nos asustamos	me hube asustado	nos hubimos asustado
te asustaste	os asustasteis	te hubiste asustado	os hubisteis asustado
se asustó	se asustaron	se hubo asustado	se hubieron asustado
4 futuro		11 futuro perfecto	
me asustaré	nos asustaremos	me habré asustado	nos habremos asustado
te asustarás	os asustaréis	te habrás asustado	os habréis asustado
se asustará	se asustarán	se habrá asustado	se habrán asustado
5 potencial simple		12 potencial compuesto	
me asustaría	nos asustaríamos	me habría asustado	nos habríamos asustado
te asustarías	os asustaríais	te habrías asustado	os habríais asustado
se asustaría	se asustarían	se habría asustado	se habrían asustado
6 presente de subjuntivo		13 perfecto de subjuntivo	
me asuste	nos asustemos	me haya asustado	nos hayamos asustado
te asustes	os asustéis	te hayas asustado	os hayáis asustado
se asuste	se asusten	se haya asustado	se hayan asustado
7 imperfecto de subjuntivo		14 pluscuamperfecto de subjuntivo	
me asustara	nos asustáramos	me hubiera asustado	nos hubiéramos asustado
te asustaras	os asustarais	te hubieras asustado	os hubierais asustado
se asustara	se asustaran	se hubiera asustado	se hubieran asustado
OR		OR	
me asustase	nos asustásemos	me hubiese asustado	nos hubiésemos asustado
te asustases	os asustaseis	te hubieses asustado	os hubieseis asustado
se asustase	se asustasen	se hubiese asustado	se hubiesen asustado

	imperativo	
—		asustémonos
asústate; no te asustes		asustaos; no os asustéis
asústese		asústense

asustado, asustada frightened, scared	asustador, asustadora frightening
asustar to frighten, to scare	asustarse por nada to be frightened
asustadizo, asustadiza easily	by the slightest thing
frightened	Me asusto de pensarlo. It frightens
asustarse de + inf. to be afraid + inf.	me to think about it.

Regular **-ar** verb endings wtih spelling change: **c** becomes **qu** before **e**

to attack

The Seven Simple Tenses		The Seven Compound Tenses	
Singular	Plural	Singular	Plural
1 presente de indicativo		8 perfecto de indicativo	
ataco	**atacamos**	**he atacado**	**hemos atacado**
atacas	**atacáis**	**has atacado**	**habéis atacado**
ataca	**atacan**	**ha atacado**	**han atacado**
2 imperfecto de indicativo		9 pluscuamperfecto de indicativo	
atacaba	**atacábamos**	**había atacado**	**habíamos atacado**
atacabas	**atacabais**	**habías atacado**	**habíais atacado**
atacaba	**atacaban**	**había atacado**	**habían atacado**
3 pretérito		10 pretérito anterior	
ataqué	**atacamos**	**hube atacado**	**hubimos atacado**
atacaste	**atacasteis**	**hubiste atacado**	**hubisteis atacado**
atacó	**atacaron**	**hubo atacado**	**hubieron atacado**
4 futuro		11 futuro perfecto	
atacaré	**atacaremos**	**habré atacado**	**habremos atacado**
atacarás	**atacaréis**	**habrás atacado**	**habréis atacado**
atacará	**atacarán**	**habrá atacado**	**habrán atacado**
5 potencial simple		12 potencial compuesto	
atacaría	**atacaríamos**	**habría atacado**	**habríamos atacado**
atacarías	**atacaríais**	**habrías atacado**	**habríais atacado**
atacaría	**atacarían**	**habría atacado**	**habrían atacado**
6 presente de subjuntivo		13 perfecto de subjuntivo	
ataque	**ataquemos**	**haya atacado**	**hayamos atacado**
ataques	**ataquéis**	**hayas atacado**	**hayáis atacado**
ataque	**ataquen**	**haya atacado**	**hayan atacado**
7 imperfecto de subjuntivo		14 pluscuamperfecto de subjuntivo	
atacara	**atacáramos**	**hubiera atacado**	**hubiéramos atacado**
atacaras	**atacarais**	**hubieras atacado**	**hubierais atacado**
atacara	**atacaran**	**hubiera atacado**	**hubieran atacado**
OR		OR	
atacase	**atacásemos**	**hubiese atacado**	**hubiésemos atacado**
atacases	**atacaseis**	**hubieses atacado**	**hubieseis atacado**
atacase	**atacasen**	**hubiese atacado**	**hubiesen atacado**

	imperativo	
—	**ataquemos**	
ataca; no ataques	**atacad; no ataquéis**	
ataque	**ataquen**	

el ataque   attack
el, la atacante   attacker
atacado, atacada   attacked

el atacador, la atacadora   aggressor
un ataque al corazón   a heart attack

atravesar

Gerundio **atravesando** Part. pas. **atravesado**

to cross, to go through,
to run through

Regular **-ar** verb endings with stem
change: Tenses 1, 6, Imperative

The Seven Simple Tenses		The Seven Compound Tenses	
Singular	Plural	Singular	Plural
1 presente de indicativo		8 perfecto de indicativo	
atravieso	**atravesamos**	he atravesado	hemos atravesado
atraviesas	**atravesáis**	has atravesado	habéis atravesado
atraviesa	**atraviesan**	ha atravesado	han atravesado
2 imperfecto de indicativo		9 pluscuamperfecto de indicativo	
atravesaba	**atravesábamos**	había atravesado	habíamos atravesado
atravesabas	**atravesabais**	habías atravesado	habíais atravesado
atravesaba	**atravesaban**	había atravesado	habían atravesado
3 pretérito		10 pretérito anterior	
atravesé	**atravesamos**	hube atravesado	hubimos atravesado
atravesaste	**atravesasteis**	hubiste atravesado	hubisteis atravesado
atravesó	**atravesaron**	hubo atravesado	hubieron atravesado
4 futuro		11 futuro perfecto	
atravesaré	**atravesaremos**	habré atravesado	habremos atravesado
atravesarás	**atravesaréis**	habrás atravesado	habréis atravesado
atravesará	**atravesarán**	habrá atravesado	habrán atravesado
5 potencial simple		12 potencial compuesto	
atravesaría	**atravesaríamos**	habría atravesado	habríamos atravesado
atravesarías	**atravesaríais**	habrías atravesado	habríais atravesado
atravesaría	**atravesarían**	habría atravesado	habrían atravesado
6 presente de subjuntivo		13 perfecto de subjuntivo	
atraviese	**atravesemos**	haya atravesado	hayamos atravesado
atravieses	**atraveséis**	hayas atravesado	hayáis atravesado
atraviese	**atraviesen**	haya atravesado	hayan atravesado
7 imperfecto de subjuntivo		14 pluscuamperfecto de subjuntivo	
atravesara	**atravesáramos**	hubiera atravesado	hubiéramos atravesado
atravesaras	**atravesarais**	hubieras atravesado	hubierais atravesado
atravesara	**atravesaran**	hubiera atravesado	hubieran atravesado
OR		OR	
atravesase	**atravesásemos**	hubiese atravesado	hubiésemos atravesado
atravesases	**atravesaseis**	hubieses atravesado	hubieseis atravesado
atravesase	**atravesasen**	hubiese atravesado	hubiesen atravesado

	imperativo	
—	**atravesemos**	
atraviesa; no atravieses	**atravesad; no atraveséis**	
atraviese	**atraviesen**	

---

atravesar con   to meet
travesar   to cross
mirar de través   to look out of the
   corner of one's eye

la travesía   crossing (sea)
atravesable   traversable
a través de   across, through

atreverse

Reflexive regular **-er** verb

to dare, to venture

The Seven Simple Tenses		The Seven Compound Tenses	
Singular	Plural	Singular	Plural
1 presente de indicativo		8 perfecto de indicativo	
me atrevo	nos atrevemos	me he atrevido	nos hemos atrevido
te atreves	os atrevéis	te has atrevido	os habéis atrevido
se atreve	se atreven	se ha atrevido	se han atrevido
2 imperfecto de indicativo		9 pluscuamperfecto de indicativo	
me atrevía	nos atrevíamos	me había atrevido	nos habíamos atrevido
te atrevías	os atrevíais	te habías atrevido	os habíais atrevido
se atrevía	se atrevían	se había atrevido	se habían atrevido
3 pretérito		10 pretérito anterior	
me atreví	nos atrevimos	me hube atrevido	nos hubimos atrevido
te atreviste	os atrevisteis	te hubiste atrevido	os hubisteis atrevido
se atrevió	se atrevieron	se hubo atrevido	se hubieron atrevido
4 futuro		11 futuro perfecto	
me atreveré	nos atreveremos	me habré atrevido	nos habremos atrevido
te atreverás	os atreveréis	te habrás atrevido	os habréis atrevido
se atreverá	se atreverán	se habrá atrevido	se habrán atrevido
5 potencial simple		12 potencial compuesto	
me atrevería	nos atreveríamos	me habría atrevido	nos habríamos atrevido
te atreverías	os atreveríais	te habrías atrevido	os habríais atrevido
se atrevería	se atreverían	se habría atrevido	se habrían atrevido
6 presente de subjuntivo		13 perfecto de subjuntivo	
me atreva	nos atrevamos	me haya atrevido	nos hayamos atrevido
te atrevas	os atreváis	te hayas atrevido	os hayáis atrevido
se atreva	se atrevan	se haya atrevido	se hayan atrevido
7 imperfecto de subjuntivo		14 pluscuamperfecto de subjuntivo	
me atreviera	nos atreviéramos	me hubiera atrevido	nos hubiéramos atrevido
te atrevieras	os atrevierais	te hubieras atrevido	os hubierais atrevido
se atreviera	se atrevieran	se hubiera atrevido	se hubieran atrevido
OR		OR	
me atreviese	nos atreviésemos	me hubiese atrevido	nos hubiésemos atrevido
te atrevieses	os atrevieseis	te hubieses atrevido	os hubieseis atrevido
se atreviese	se atreviesen	se hubiese atrevido	se hubiesen atrevido

imperativo	
—	atrevámonos
atrévete; no te atrevas	atreveos; no os atreváis
atrévase	atrévanse

---

atrevido, atrevida   daring, bold
el atrevimiento   audacity, boldness
atrevidamente   boldly, daringly
atreverse con *or* contra   to be insolent
  to, to be offensive toward

¡Atrévete!   You just dare!
Hazlo si te atreves.   Do it if you dare.

avanzar

Gerundio **avanzando**   Part. pas. **avanzado**

to advance

Regular **-ar** verb endings with spelling
change: **z** becomes **c** before **e**

The Seven Simple Tenses		The Seven Compound Tenses	
Singular	Plural	Singular	Plural
1 presente de indicativo		**8 perfecto de indicativo**	
avanzo	avanzamos	he avanzado	hemos avanzado
avanzas	avanzáis	has avanzado	habéis avanzado
avanza	avanzan	ha avanzado	han avanzado
2 imperfecto de indicativo		**9 pluscuamperfecto de indicativo**	
avanzaba	avanzábamos	había avanzado	habíamos avanzado
avanzabas	avanzabais	habías avanzado	habíais avanzado
avanzaba	avanzaban	había avanzado	habían avanzado
3 pretérito		**10 pretérito anterior**	
avancé	avanzamos	hube avanzado	hubimos avanzado
avanzaste	avanzasteis	hubiste avanzado	hubisteis avanzado
avanzó	avanzaron	hubo avanzado	hubieron avanzado
4 futuro		**11 futuro perfecto**	
avanzaré	avanzaremos	habré avanzado	habremos avanzado
avanzarás	avanzaréis	habrás avanzado	habréis avanzado
avanzará	avanzarán	habrá avanzado	habrán avanzado
5 potencial simple		**12 potencial compuesto**	
avanzaría	avanzaríamos	habría avanzado	habríamos avanzado
avanzarías	avanzaríais	habrías avanzado	habríais avanzado
avanzaría	avanzarían	habría avanzado	habrían avanzado
6 presente de subjuntivo		**13 perfecto de subjuntivo**	
avance	avancemos	haya avanzado	hayamos avanzado
avances	avancéis	hayas avanzado	hayáis avanzado
avance	avancen	haya avanzado	hayan avanzado
7 imperfecto de subjuntivo		**14 pluscuamperfecto de subjuntivo**	
avanzara	avanzáramos	hubiera avanzado	hubiéramos avanzado
avanzaras	avanzarais	hubieras avanzado	hubierais avanzado
avanzara	avanzaran	hubiera avanzado	hubieran avanzado
OR		OR	
avanzase	avanzásemos	hubiese avanzado	hubiésemos avanzado
avanzases	avanzaseis	hubieses avanzado	hubieseis avanzado
avanzase	avanzasen	hubiese avanzado	hubiesen avanzado

	imperativo	
—	avancemos
avanza; no avances	avanzad; no avancéis
avance	avancen

---

avanzado, avanzada   advanced; de
  edad avanzada   advanced in years
la avanzada   advance guard
avante   forward, ahead

salir avante   to succeed
los avances tecnológicos
  technological advances

averiguar

Regular **-ar** verb endings with spelling
change: **gu** becomes **gü** before **e**

to find out, to inquire,
to investigate

The Seven Simple Tenses		The Seven Compound Tenses	
Singular	Plural	Singular	Plural

1 presente de indicativo		8 perfecto de indicativo	
averiguo	averiguamos	he averiguado	hemos averiguado
averiguas	averiguáis	has averiguado	habéis averiguado
averigua	averiguan	ha averiguado	han averiguado

2 imperfecto de indicativo		9 pluscuamperfecto de indicativo	
averiguaba	averiguábamos	había averiguado	habíamos averiguado
averiguabas	averiguabais	habías averiguado	habíais averiguado
averiguaba	averiguaban	había averiguado	habían averiguado

3 pretérito		10 pretérito anterior	
averigüé	averiguamos	hube averiguado	hubimos averiguado
averiguaste	averiguasteis	hubiste averiguado	hubisteis averiguado
averiguó	averiguaron	hubo averiguado	hubieron averiguado

4 futuro		11 futuro perfecto	
averiguaré	averiguaremos	habré averiguado	habremos averiguado
averiguarás	averiguaréis	habrás averiguado	habréis averiguado
averiguará	averiguarán	habrá averiguado	habrán averiguado

5 potencial simple		12 potencial compuesto	
averiguaría	averiguaríamos	habría averiguado	habríamos averiguado
averiguarías	averiguaríais	habrías averiguado	habríais averiguado
averiguaría	averiguarían	habría averiguado	habrían averiguado

6 presente de subjuntivo		13 perfecto de subjuntivo	
averigüe	averigüemos	haya averiguado	hayamos averiguado
averigües	averigüéis	hayas averiguado	hayáis averiguado
averigüe	averigüen	haya averiguado	hayan averiguado

7 imperfecto de subjuntivo		14 pluscuamperfecto de subjuntivo	
averiguara	averiguáramos	hubiera averiguado	hubiéramos averiguado
averiguaras	averiguarais	hubieras averiguado	hubierais averiguado
averiguara	averiguaran	hubiera averiguado	hubieran averiguado
OR		OR	
averiguase	averiguásemos	hubiese averiguado	hubiésemos averiguado
averiguases	averiguaseis	hubieses averiguado	hubieseis averiguado
averiguase	averiguasen	hubiese averiguado	hubiesen averiguado

imperativo	
—	averigüemos
averigua; no averigües	averiguad; no averigüéis
averigüe	averigüen

---

el averiguador, la averiguadora
   investigator
la averiguación   inquiry, investigation
averiguable   investigable

averiguadamente   surely, certainly

ayudar

Gerundio **ayudando**   Part. pas. **ayudado**

to help, to aid, to assist

Regular **-ar** verb

The Seven Simple Tenses		The Seven Compound Tenses	
Singular	Plural	Singular	Plural
1 presente de indicativo		8 perfecto de indicativo	
ayudo	ayudamos	he ayudado	hemos ayudado
ayudas	ayudáis	has ayudado	habéis ayudado
ayuda	ayudan	ha ayudado	han ayudado
2 imperfecto de indicativo		9 pluscuamperfecto de indicativo	
ayudaba	ayudábamos	había ayudado	habíamos ayudado
ayudabas	ayudabais	habías ayudado	habíais ayudado
ayudaba	ayudaban	había ayudado	habían ayudado
3 pretérito		10 pretérito anterior	
ayudé	ayudamos	hube ayudado	hubimos ayudado
ayudaste	ayudasteis	hubiste ayudado	hubisteis ayudado
ayudó	ayudaron	hubo ayudado	hubieron ayudado
4 futuro		11 futuro perfecto	
ayudaré	ayudaremos	habré ayudado	habremos ayudado
ayudarás	ayudaréis	habrás ayudado	habréis ayudado
ayudará	ayudarán	habrá ayudado	habrán ayudado
5 potencial simple		12 potencial compuesto	
ayudaría	ayudaríamos	habría ayudado	habríamos ayudado
ayudarías	ayudaríais	habrías ayudado	habríais ayudado
ayudaría	ayudarían	habría ayudado	habrían ayudado
6 presente de subjuntivo		13 perfecto de subjuntivo	
ayude	ayudemos	haya ayudado	hayamos ayudado
ayudes	ayudéis	hayas ayudado	hayáis ayudado
ayude	ayuden	haya ayudado	hayan ayudado
7 imperfecto de subjuntivo		14 pluscuamperfecto de subjuntivo	
ayudara	ayudáramos	hubiera ayudado	hubiéramos ayudado
ayudaras	ayudarais	hubieras ayudado	hubierais ayudado
ayudara	ayudaran	hubiera ayudado	hubieran ayudado
OR		OR	
ayudase	ayudásemos	hubiese ayudado	hubiésemos ayudado
ayudases	ayudaseis	hubieses ayudado	hubieseis ayudado
ayudase	ayudasen	hubiese ayudado	hubiesen ayudado

imperativo	
—	ayudemos
ayuda; no ayudes	ayudad; no ayudéis
ayude	ayuden

la ayuda   aid, assistance, help
un ayudador, una ayudadora   helper
ayudante   assistant
la ayuda financiera   financial aid

Proverb: **A quien madruga, Dios le ayuda.**   The early bird catches the worm.

bailar

to dance

The Seven Simple Tenses		The Seven Compound Tenses	
Singular	Plural	Singular	Plural
1 presente de indicativo		**8 perfecto de indicativo**	
bailo	bailamos	he bailado	hemos bailado
bailas	bailáis	has bailado	habéis bailado
baila	bailan	ha bailado	han bailado
2 imperfecto de indicativo		**9 pluscuamperfecto de indicativo**	
bailaba	bailábamos	había bailado	habíamos bailado
bailabas	bailabais	habías bailado	habíais bailado
bailaba	bailaban	había bailado	habían bailado
3 pretérito		**10 pretérito anterior**	
bailé	bailamos	hube bailado	hubimos bailado
bailaste	bailasteis	hubiste bailado	hubisteis bailado
bailó	bailaron	hubo bailado	hubieron bailado
4 futuro		**11 futuro perfecto**	
bailaré	bailaremos	habré bailado	habremos bailado
bailarás	bailaréis	habrás bailado	habréis bailado
bailará	bailarán	habrá bailado	habrán bailado
5 potencial simple		**12 potencial compuesto**	
bailaría	bailaríamos	habría bailado	habríamos bailado
bailarías	bailaríais	habrías bailado	habríais bailado
bailaría	bailarían	habría bailado	habrían bailado
6 presente de subjuntivo		**13 perfecto de subjuntivo**	
baile	bailemos	haya bailado	hayamos bailado
bailes	bailéis	hayas bailado	hayáis bailado
baile	bailen	haya bailado	hayan bailado
7 imperfecto de subjuntivo		**14 pluscuamperfecto de subjuntivo**	
bailara	bailáramos	hubiera bailado	hubiéramos bailado
bailaras	bailarais	hubieras bailado	hubierais bailado
bailara	bailaran	hubiera bailado	hubieran bailado
OR		OR	
bailase	bailásemos	hubiese bailado	hubiésemos bailado
bailases	bailaseis	hubieses bailado	hubieseis bailado
bailase	bailasen	hubiese bailado	hubiesen bailado

imperativo	
—	bailemos
baila; no bailes	bailad; no bailéis
baile	bailen

Cuando el gato va a sus devociones,
  bailan los ratones.   When the cat is
  away, the mice will play.
un baile   dance

un bailarín, una bailarina   dancer
  (professional)
un bailador, una bailadora   dancer

bajar

Gerundio **bajando**   Part. pas. **bajado**

to lower, to let down, to come down,
to go down, to descend

Regular **-ar** verb

The Seven Simple Tenses		The Seven Compound Tenses	
Singular	Plural	Singular	Plural
1 presente de indicativo		8 perfecto de indicativo	
bajo	bajamos	he bajado	hemos bajado
bajas	bajáis	has bajado	habéis bajado
baja	bajan	ha bajado	han bajado
2 imperfecto de indicativo		9 pluscuamperfecto de indicativo	
bajaba	bajábamos	había bajado	habíamos bajado
bajabas	bajabais	habías bajado	habíais bajado
bajaba	bajaban	había bajado	habían bajado
3 pretérito		10 pretérito anterior	
bajé	bajamos	hube bajado	hubimos bajado
bajaste	bajasteis	hubiste bajado	hubisteis bajado
bajó	bajaron	hubo bajado	hubieron bajado
4 futuro		11 futuro perfecto	
bajaré	bajaremos	habré bajado	habremos bajado
bajarás	bajaréis	habrás bajado	habréis bajado
bajará	bajarán	habrá bajado	habrán bajado
5 potencial simple		12 potencial compuesto	
bajaría	bajaríamos	habría bajado	habríamos bajado
bajarías	bajaríais	habrías bajado	habríais bajado
bajaría	bajarían	habría bajado	habrían bajado
6 presente de subjuntivo		13 perfecto de subjuntivo	
baje	bajemos	haya bajado	hayamos bajado
bajes	bajéis	hayas bajado	hayáis bajado
baje	bajen	haya bajado	hayan bajado
7 imperfecto de subjuntivo		14 pluscuamperfecto de subjuntivo	
bajara	bajáramos	hubiera bajado	hubiéramos bajado
bajaras	bajarais	hubieras bajado	hubierais bajado
bajara	bajaran	hubiera bajado	hubieran bajado
OR		OR	
bajase	bajásemos	hubiese bajado	hubiésemos bajado
bajases	bajaseis	hubieses bajado	hubieseis bajado
bajase	bajasen	hubiese bajado	hubiesen bajado

imperativo	
—	bajemos
baja; no bajes	bajad; no bajéis
baje	bajen

la baja reduction (fall) in prices	el piso bajo ground floor
rebajar to reduce	bajo down, below
la bajada descent	una rebaja rebate, discount
bajar de to get off	bajar/bajarse el correo electrónico to
bajamente basely	download e-mail
bajar de valor to decline in value	¿En qué estación debo bajar? At
en voz baja in a low voice	what station do I need to get off?

Reflexive regular **-ar** verb   to bathe oneself, to take a bath

The Seven Simple Tenses		The Seven Compound Tenses	
Singular	Plural	Singular	Plural
1 presente de indicativo		8 perfecto de indicativo	
me baño	nos bañamos	me he bañado	nos hemos bañado
te bañas	os bañáis	te has bañado	os habéis bañado
se baña	se bañan	se ha bañado	se han bañado
2 imperfecto de indicativo		9 pluscuamperfecto de indicativo	
me bañaba	nos bañábamos	me había bañado	nos habíamos bañado
te bañabas	os bañabais	te habías bañado	os habíais bañado
se bañaba	se bañaban	se había bañado	se habían bañado
3 pretérito		10 pretérito anterior	
me bañé	nos bañamos	me hube bañado	nos hubimos bañado
te bañaste	os bañasteis	te hubiste bañado	os hubisteis bañado
se bañó	se bañaron	se hubo bañado	se hubieron bañado
4 futuro		11 futuro perfecto	
me bañaré	nos bañaremos	me habré bañado	nos habremos bañado
te bañarás	os bañaréis	te habrás bañado	os habréis bañado
se bañará	se bañarán	se habrá bañado	se habrán bañado
5 potencial simple		12 potencial compuesto	
me bañaría	nos bañaríamos	me habría bañado	nos habríamos bañado
te bañarías	os bañaríais	te habrías bañado	os habríais bañado
se bañaría	se bañarían	se habría bañado	se habrían bañado
6 presente de subjuntivo		13 perfecto de subjuntivo	
me bañe	nos bañemos	me haya bañado	nos hayamos bañado
te bañes	os bañéis	te hayas bañado	os hayáis bañado
se bañe	se bañen	se haya bañado	se hayan bañado
7 imperfecto de subjuntivo		14 pluscuamperfecto de subjuntivo	
me bañara	nos bañáramos	me hubiera bañado	nos hubiéramos bañado
te bañaras	os bañarais	te hubieras bañado	os hubierais bañado
se bañara	se bañaran	se hubiera bañado	se hubieran bañado
OR		OR	
me bañase	nos bañásemos	me hubiese bañado	nos hubiésemos bañado
te bañases	os bañaseis	te hubieses bañado	os hubieseis bañado
se bañase	se bañasen	se hubiese bañado	se hubiesen bañado

imperativo	
—	bañémonos
báñate; no te bañes	bañaos; no os bañéis
báñese	báñense

una bañera, una bañadera bathtub	un baño bath, bathing
bañar to bathe	un baño de vapor steam bath
un bañador, una bañadora bather	bañar a la luz to light up, to
bañar un papel de lágrimas to write	illuminate
a mournful letter	

bastar

Gerundio **bastando**   Part. pas. **bastado**

to be enough, to be sufficient,
to suffice

Regular **-ar** verb

The Seven Simple Tenses		The Seven Compound Tenses	
Singular	Plural	Singular	Plural
1 presente de indicativo		8 perfecto de indicativo	
basta	**bastan**	**ha bastado**	**han bastado**
2 imperfecto de indicativo		9 pluscuamperfecto de indicativo	
bastaba	**bastaban**	**había bastado**	**habían bastado**
3 pretérito		10 pretérito anterior	
bastó	**bastaron**	**hubo bastado**	**hubieron bastado**
4 futuro		11 futuro perfecto	
bastará	**bastarán**	**habrá bastado**	**habrán bastado**
5 potencial simple		12 potencial compuesto	
bastaría	**bastarían**	**habría bastado**	**habrían bastado**
6 presente de subjuntivo		13 perfecto de subjuntivo	
que baste	**que basten**	**haya bastado**	**hayan bastado**
7 imperfecto de subjuntivo		14 pluscuamperfecto de subjuntivo	
que bastara	**que bastaran**	**hubiera bastado**	**hubieran bastado**
OR		OR	
que bastase	**que bastasen**	**hubiese bastado**	**hubiesen bastado**

imperativo
¡Que baste!   ¡Que basten!

¡Basta!   Enough! That will do!
This is an impersonal verb and it is used
mainly in the third person singular
and plural.

It is a regular ar verb and can be
conjugated in all the persons.

54

bautizar

Regular **-ar** verb endings with spelling change: **z** becomes **c** before **e**

to baptize, to christen

The Seven Simple Tenses		The Seven Compound Tenses	
Singular	Plural	Singular	Plural
1 presente de indicativo		**8 perfecto de indicativo**	
bautizo	bautizamos	he bautizado	hemos bautizado
bautizas	bautizáis	has bautizado	habéis bautizado
bautiza	bautizan	ha bautizado	han bautizado
2 imperfecto de indicativo		**9 pluscuamperfecto de indicativo**	
bautizaba	bautizábamos	había bautizado	habíamos bautizado
bautizabas	bautizabais	habías bautizado	habíais bautizado
bautizaba	bautizaban	había bautizado	habían bautizado
3 pretérito		**10 pretérito anterior**	
bauticé	bautizamos	hube bautizado	hubimos bautizado
bautizaste	bautizasteis	hubiste bautizado	hubisteis bautizado
bautizó	bautizaron	hubo bautizado	hubieron bautizado
4 futuro		**11 futuro perfecto**	
bautizaré	bautizaremos	habré bautizado	habremos bautizado
bautizarás	bautizaréis	habrás bautizado	habréis bautizado
bautizará	bautizarán	habrá bautizado	habrán bautizado
5 potencial simple		**12 potencial compuesto**	
bautizaría	bautizaríamos	habría bautizado	habríamos bautizado
bautizarías	bautizaríais	habrías bautizado	habríais bautizado
bautizaría	bautizarían	habría bautizado	habrían bautizado
6 presente de subjuntivo		**13 perfecto de subjuntivo**	
bautice	bauticemos	haya bautizado	hayamos bautizado
bautices	bauticéis	hayas bautizado	hayáis bautizado
bautice	bauticen	haya bautizado	hayan bautizado
7 imperfecto de subjuntivo		**14 pluscuamperfecto de subjuntivo**	
bautizara	bautizáramos	hubiera bautizado	hubiéramos bautizado
bautizaras	bautizarais	hubieras bautizado	hubierais bautizado
bautizara	bautizaran	hubiera bautizado	hubieran bautizado
OR		OR	
bautizase	bautizásemos	hubiese bautizado	hubiésemos bautizado
bautizases	bautizaseis	hubieses bautizado	hubieseis bautizado
bautizase	bautizasen	hubiese bautizado	hubiesen bautizado

	imperativo	
—	bauticemos	
bautiza; no bautices	bautizad; no bauticéis	
bautice	bauticen	

el bautisterio baptistery	el, la bautista Baptist
el bautismo baptism, christening	bautizar una calle to name a street
bautismal baptismal	

beber

Gerundio **bebiendo**   Part. pas. **bebido**

to drink   Regular **-er** verb

The Seven Simple Tenses		The Seven Compound Tenses	
Singular	Plural	Singular	Plural
1 presente de indicativo		8 perfecto de indicativo	
bebo	bebemos	**he bebido**	**hemos bebido**
bebes	bebéis	**has bebido**	**habéis bebido**
bebe	beben	**ha bebido**	**han bebido**
2 imperfecto de indicativo		9 pluscuamperfecto de indicativo	
bebía	bebíamos	**había bebido**	**habíamos bebido**
bebías	bebíais	**habías bebido**	**habíais bebido**
bebía	bebían	**había bebido**	**habían bebido**
3 pretérito		10 pretérito anterior	
bebí	bebimos	**hube bebido**	**hubimos bebido**
bebiste	bebisteis	**hubiste bebido**	**hubisteis bebido**
bebió	bebieron	**hubo bebido**	**hubieron bebido**
4 futuro		11 futuro perfecto	
beberé	beberemos	**habré bebido**	**habremos bebido**
beberás	beberéis	**habrás bebido**	**habréis bebido**
beberá	beberán	**habrá bebido**	**habrán bebido**
5 potencial simple		12 potencial compuesto	
bebería	beberíamos	**habría bebido**	**habríamos bebido**
beberías	beberíais	**habrías bebido**	**habríais bebido**
bebería	beberían	**habría bebido**	**habrían bebido**
6 presente de subjuntivo		13 perfecto de subjuntivo	
beba	bebamos	**haya bebido**	**hayamos bebido**
bebas	bebáis	**hayas bebido**	**hayáis bebido**
beba	beban	**haya bebido**	**hayan bebido**
7 imperfecto de subjuntivo		14 pluscuamperfecto de subjuntivo	
bebiera	bebiéramos	**hubiera bebido**	**hubiéramos bebido**
bebieras	bebierais	**hubieras bebido**	**hubierais bebido**
bebiera	bebieran	**hubiera bebido**	**hubieran bebido**
OR		OR	
bebiese	bebiésemos	**hubiese bebido**	**hubiésemos bebido**
bebieses	bebieseis	**hubieses bebido**	**hubieseis bebido**
bebiese	bebiesen	**hubiese bebido**	**hubiesen bebido**

imperativo	
—	**bebamos**
bebe; no bebas	**bebed; no bebáis**
beba	**beban**

una bebida drink, beverage	**beber a la salud** to drink to health
beber como una cuba to drink like a fish	**beber a sorbos** to sip
beber de to drink from	**embeber** to soak in, soak up, imbibe
querer beber la sangre a otro to hate somebody bitterly	**embebedor, embebedora** absorbent

bendecir

Irregular verb (**bendito**, when used as an adj. with **estar**)

to bless, to consecrate

The Seven Simple Tenses		The Seven Compound Tenses	
Singular	Plural	Singular	Plural
1 presente de indicativo		8 perfecto de indicativo	
bendigo	**bendecimos**	**he bendecido**	**hemos bendecido**
bendices	**bendecís**	**has bendecido**	**habéis bendecido**
bendice	**bendicen**	**ha bendecido**	**han bendecido**
2 imperfecto de indicativo		9 pluscuamperfecto de indicativo	
bendecía	**bendecíamos**	**había bendecido**	**habíamos bendecido**
bendecías	**bendecíais**	**habías bendecido**	**habíais bendecido**
bendecía	**bendecían**	**había bendecido**	**habían bendecido**
3 pretérito		10 pretérito anterior	
bendije	**bendijimos**	**hube bendecido**	**hubimos bendecido**
bendijiste	**bendijisteis**	**hubiste bendecido**	**hubisteis bendecido**
bendijo	**bendijeron**	**hubo bendecido**	**hubieron bendecido**
4 futuro		11 futuro perfecto	
bendeciré	**bendeciremos**	**habré bendecido**	**habremos bendecido**
bendecirás	**bendeciréis**	**habrás bendecido**	**habréis bendecido**
bendecirá	**bendecirán**	**habrá bendecido**	**habrán bendecido**
5 potencial simple		12 potencial compuesto	
bendeciría	**bendeciríamos**	**habría bendecido**	**habríamos bendecido**
bendecirías	**bendeciríais**	**habrías bendecido**	**habríais bendecido**
bendeciría	**bendecirían**	**habría bendecido**	**habrían bendecido**
6 presente de subjuntivo		13 perfecto de subjuntivo	
bendiga	**bendigamos**	**haya bendecido**	**hayamos bendecido**
bendigas	**bendigáis**	**hayas bendecido**	**hayáis bendecido**
bendiga	**bendigan**	**haya bendecido**	**hayan bendecido**
7 imperfecto de subjuntivo		14 pluscuamperfecto de subjuntivo	
bendijera	**bendijéramos**	**hubiera bendecido**	**hubiéramos bendecido**
bendijeras	**bendijerais**	**hubieras bendecido**	**hubierais bendecido**
bendijera	**bendijeran**	**hubiera bendecido**	**hubieran bendecido**
OR		OR	
bendijese	**bendijésemos**	**hubiese bendecido**	**hubiésemos bendecido**
bendijeses	**bendijeseis**	**hubieses bendecido**	**hubieseis bendecido**
bendijese	**bendijesen**	**hubiese bendecido**	**hubiesen bendecido**

	imperativo
—	**bendigamos**
bendice; no bendigas	**bendecid; no bendigáis**
bendiga	**bendigan**

Dormí como un bendito.   I slept like a baby/like a log.
la bendición   benediction, blessing
las bendiciones nupciales   marriage ceremony

un bendecidor, una bendecidora   blesser

borrar

Gerundio **borrando**   Part. pas. **borrado**

to erase, to cross out

Regular **-ar** verb

The Seven Simple Tenses		The Seven Compound Tenses	
Singular	Plural	Singular	Plural
1 presente de indicativo		8 perfecto de indicativo	
borro	borramos	he borrado	hemos borrado
borras	borráis	has borrado	habéis borrado
borra	borran	ha borrado	han borrado
2 imperfecto de indicativo		9 pluscuamperfecto de indicativo	
borraba	borrábamos	había borrado	habíamos borrado
borrabas	borrabais	habías borrado	habíais borrado
borraba	borraban	había borrado	habían borrado
3 pretérito		10 pretérito anterior	
borré	borramos	hube borrado	hubimos borrado
borraste	borrasteis	hubiste borrado	hubisteis borrado
borró	borraron	hubo borrado	hubieron borrado
4 futuro		11 futuro perfecto	
borraré	borraremos	habré borrado	habremos borrado
borrarás	borraréis	habrás borrado	habréis borrado
borrará	borrarán	habrá borrado	habrán borrado
5 potencial simple		12 potencial compuesto	
borraría	borraríamos	habría borrado	habríamos borrado
borrarías	borraríais	habrías borrado	habríais borrado
borraría	borrarían	habría borrado	habrían borrado
6 presente de subjuntivo		13 perfecto de subjuntivo	
borre	borremos	haya borrado	hayamos borrado
borres	borréis	hayas borrado	hayáis borrado
borre	borren	haya borrado	hayan borrado
7 imperfecto de subjuntivo		14 pluscuamperfecto de subjuntivo	
borrara	borráramos	hubiera borrado	hubiéramos borrado
borraras	borrarais	hubieras borrado	hubierais borrado
borrara	borraran	hubiera borrado	hubieran borrado
OR		OR	
borrase	borrásemos	hubiese borrado	hubiésemos borrado
borrases	borraseis	hubieses borrado	hubieseis borrado
borrase	borrasen	hubiese borrado	hubiesen borrado

imperativo	
—	borremos
borra; no borres	borrad; no borréis
borre	borren

la goma de borrar rubber eraser	**el borrador** eraser (chalk), rough draft
desborrar to burl (to clean off the knots from cloth)	**la tecla de borrado** delete key (computer)
la borradura erasure	
emborrar to pad, to stuff, to wad; to gulp down food	

Irregular verb (Tenses 3 and 7)   to boil, to bustle,
                                                                    to hustle, to stir

The Seven Simple Tenses		The Seven Compound Tenses	
Singular	Plural	Singular	Plural
1 presente de indicativo		8 perfecto de indicativo	
bullo	**bullimos**	**he bullido**	**hemos bullido**
bulles	**bullís**	**has bullido**	**habéis bullido**
bulle	**bullen**	**ha bullido**	**han bullido**
2 imperfecto de indicativo		9 pluscuamperfecto de indicativo	
bullía	**bullíamos**	**había bullido**	**habíamos bullido**
bullías	**bullíais**	**habías bullido**	**habíais bullido**
bullía	**bullían**	**había bullido**	**habían bullido**
3 pretérito		10 pretérito anterior	
bullí	**bullimos**	**hube bullido**	**hubimos bullido**
bulliste	**bullisteis**	**hubiste bullido**	**hubisteis bullido**
bulló	**bulleron**	**hubo bullido**	**hubieron bullido**
4 futuro		11 futuro perfecto	
bulliré	**bulliremos**	**habré bullido**	**habremos bullido**
bullirás	**bulliréis**	**habrás bullido**	**habréis bullido**
bullirá	**bullirán**	**habrá bullido**	**habrán bullido**
5 potencial simple		12 potencial compuesto	
bulliría	**bulliríamos**	**habría bullido**	**habríamos bullido**
bullirías	**bulliríais**	**habrías bullido**	**habríais bullido**
bulliría	**bullirían**	**habría bullido**	**habrían bullido**
6 presente de subjuntivo		13 perfecto de subjuntivo	
bulla	**bullamos**	**haya bullido**	**hayamos bullido**
bullas	**bulláis**	**hayas bullido**	**hayáis bullido**
bulla	**bullan**	**haya bullido**	**hayan bullido**
7 imperfecto de subjuntivo		14 pluscuamperfecto de subjuntivo	
bullera	**bulléramos**	**hubiera bullido**	**hubiéramos bullido**
bulleras	**bullerais**	**hubieras bullido**	**hubierais bullido**
bullera	**bulleran**	**hubiera bullido**	**hubieran bullido**
OR		OR	
bullese	**bullésemos**	**hubiese bullido**	**hubiésemos bullido**
bulleses	**bulleseis**	**hubieses bullido**	**hubieseis bullido**
bullese	**bullesen**	**hubiese bullido**	**hubiesen bullido**

imperativo	
—	**bullamos**
bulle; no bullas	**bullid; no bulláis**
bulla	**bullan**

un, una bullebulle busybody	el bullicio noise, bustle
un bullaje noisy crowd	la bulla bustle, noise, mob
bullente bubbling	bulliciosamente noisily

burlarse

Gerundio **burlándose**   Part. pas. **burlado**

to make fun of, to poke fun at,
to ridicule

Reflexive regular **-ar** verb

The Seven Simple Tenses		The Seven Compound Tenses	
Singular	Plural	Singular	Plural
1 presente de indicativo		8 perfecto de indicativo	
me burlo	nos burlamos	me he burlado	nos hemos burlado
te burlas	os burláis	te has burlado	os habéis burlado
se burla	se burlan	se ha burlado	se han burlado
2 imperfecto de indicativo		9 pluscuamperfecto de indicativo	
me burlaba	nos burlábamos	me había burlado	nos habíamos burlado
te burlabas	os burlabais	te habías burlado	os habíais burlado
se burlaba	se burlaban	se había burlado	se habían burlado
3 pretérito		10 pretérito anterior	
me burlé	nos burlamos	me hube burlado	nos hubimos burlado
te burlaste	os burlasteis	te hubiste burlado	os hubisteis burlado
se burló	se burlaron	se hubo burlado	se hubieron burlado
4 futuro		11 futuro perfecto	
me burlaré	nos burlaremos	me habré burlado	nos habremos burlado
te burlarás	os burlaréis	te habrás burlado	os habréis burlado
se burlará	se burlarán	se habrá burlado	se habrán burlado
5 potencial simple		12 potencial compuesto	
me burlaría	nos burlaríamos	me habría burlado	nos habríamos burlado
te burlarías	os burlaríais	te habrías burlado	os habríais burlado
se burlaría	se burlarían	se habría burlado	se habrían burlado
6 presente de subjuntivo		13 perfecto de subjuntivo	
me burle	nos burlemos	me haya burlado	nos hayamos burlado
te burles	os burléis	te hayas burlado	os hayáis burlado
se burle	se burlen	se haya burlado	se hayan burlado
7 imperfecto de subjuntivo		14 pluscuamperfecto de subjuntivo	
me burlara	nos burláramos	me hubiera burlado	nos hubiéramos burlado
te burlaras	os burlarais	te hubieras burlado	os hubierais burlado
se burlara	se burlaran	se hubiera burlado	se hubieran burlado
OR		OR	
me burlase	nos burlásemos	me hubiese burlado	nos hubiésemos burlado
te burlases	os burlaseis	te hubieses burlado	os hubieseis burlado
se burlase	se burlasen	se hubiese burlado	se hubiesen burlado

	imperativo
—	burlémonos
búrlate; no te burles	burlaos; no os burléis
búrlese	búrlense

---

el burlador, la burladora   practical
  joker, jester, wag
burlesco, burlesca   burlesque
burlarse de alguien   to make fun of
  someone

burlescamente   comically
burlar a alguien   to deceive someone
la burlería   mockery
hacer burla de   to make fun of
de burlas   for fun

60

Regular **-ar** verb endings with spelling change: **c** becomes **qu** before **e**

to look for, to seek

The Seven Simple Tenses		The Seven Compound Tenses	
Singular	Plural	Singular	Plural
1 presente de indicativo		8 perfecto de indicativo	
busco	buscamos	he buscado	hemos buscado
buscas	buscáis	has buscado	habéis buscado
busca	buscan	ha buscado	han buscado
2 imperfecto de indicativo		9 pluscuamperfecto de indicativo	
buscaba	buscábamos	había buscado	habíamos buscado
buscabas	buscabais	habías buscado	habíais buscado
buscaba	buscaban	había buscado	habían buscado
3 pretérito		10 pretérito anterior	
busqué	buscamos	hube buscado	hubimos buscado
buscaste	buscasteis	hubiste buscado	hubisteis buscado
buscó	buscaron	hubo buscado	hubieron buscado
4 futuro		11 futuro perfecto	
buscaré	buscaremos	habré buscado	habremos buscado
buscarás	buscaréis	habrás buscado	habréis buscado
buscará	buscarán	habrá buscado	habrán buscado
5 potencial simple		12 potencial compuesto	
buscaría	buscaríamos	habría buscado	habríamos buscado
buscarías	buscaríais	habrías buscado	habríais buscado
buscaría	buscarían	habría buscado	habrían buscado
6 presente de subjuntivo		13 perfecto de subjuntivo	
busque	busquemos	haya buscado	hayamos buscado
busques	busquéis	hayas buscado	hayáis buscado
busque	busquen	haya buscado	hayan buscado
7 imperfecto de subjuntivo		14 pluscuamperfecto de subjuntivo	
buscara	buscáramos	hubiera buscado	hubiéramos buscado
buscaras	buscarais	hubieras buscado	hubierais buscado
buscara	buscaran	hubiera buscado	hubieran buscado
OR		OR	
buscase	buscásemos	hubiese buscado	hubiésemos buscado
buscases	buscaseis	hubieses buscado	hubieseis buscado
buscase	buscasen	hubiese buscado	hubiesen buscado

imperativo	
—	busquemos
busca; no busques	buscad; no busquéis
busque	busquen

¿Qué busca Ud.? What are you looking for?	rebuscar to search into
la búsqueda search	la busca, la buscada research, search
Busco mis libros. I'm looking for my books.	el rebuscamiento searching
	un buscador search engine (Internet)

caber

Gerundio **cabiendo**   Part. pas. **cabido**

to be contained, to fit into

Irregular verb

The Seven Simple Tenses		The Seven Compound Tenses	
Singular	Plural	Singular	Plural
1 presente de indicativo		8 perfecto de indicativo	
quepo	cabemos	he cabido	hemos cabido
cabes	cabéis	has cabido	habéis cabido
cabe	caben	ha cabido	han cabido
2 imperfecto de indicativo		9 pluscuamperfecto de indicativo	
cabía	cabíamos	había cabido	habíamos cabido
cabías	cabíais	habías cabido	habíais cabido
cabía	cabían	había cabido	habían cabido
3 pretérito		10 pretérito anterior	
cupe	cupimos	hube cabido	hubimos cabido
cupiste	cupisteis	hubiste cabido	hubisteis cabido
cupo	cupieron	hubo cabido	hubieron cabido
4 futuro		11 futuro perfecto	
cabré	cabremos	habré cabido	habremos cabido
cabrás	cabréis	habrás cabido	habréis cabido
cabrá	cabrán	habrá cabido	habrán cabido
5 potencial simple		12 potencial compuesto	
cabría	cabríamos	habría cabido	habríamos cabido
cabrías	cabríais	habrías cabido	habríais cabido
cabría	cabrían	habría cabido	habrían cabido
6 presente de subjuntivo		13 perfecto de subjuntivo	
quepa	quepamos	haya cabido	hayamos cabido
quepas	quepáis	hayas cabido	hayáis cabido
quepa	quepan	haya cabido	hayan cabido
7 imperfecto de subjuntivo		14 pluscuamperfecto de subjuntivo	
cupiera	cupiéramos	hubiera cabido	hubiéramos cabido
cupieras	cupierais	hubieras cabido	hubierais cabido
cupiera	cupieran	hubiera cabido	hubieran cabido
OR		OR	
cupiese	cupiésemos	hubiese cabido	hubiésemos cabido
cupieses	cupieseis	hubieses cabido	hubieseis cabido
cupiese	cupiesen	hubiese cabido	hubiesen cabido

imperativo	
—	quepamos
cabe; no quepas	cabed; no quepáis
quepa	quepan

Pablo no cabe en sí.   Paul has a swelled head.

No quepo aquí.   I don't have enough room here.

No cabe duda de que . . .   There is no doubt that . . .

No me cabe en la cabeza.   I don't get (understand) it.

Todo cabe.   All is possible. (It all fits.)

The Seven Simple Tenses		The Seven Compound Tenses	
Singular	Plural	Singular	Plural
1 presente de indicativo		8 perfecto de indicativo	
caigo	**caemos**	**he caído**	**hemos caído**
caes	**caéis**	**has caído**	**habéis caído**
cae	**caen**	**ha caído**	**han caído**
2 imperfecto de indicativo		9 pluscuamperfecto de indicativo	
caía	**caíamos**	**había caído**	**habíamos caído**
caías	**caíais**	**habías caído**	**habíais caído**
caía	**caían**	**había caído**	**habían caído**
3 pretérito		10 pretérito anterior	
caí	**caímos**	**hube caído**	**hubimos caído**
caíste	**caísteis**	**hubiste caído**	**hubisteis caído**
cayó	**cayeron**	**hubo caído**	**hubieron caído**
4 futuro		11 futuro perfecto	
caeré	**caeremos**	**habré caído**	**habremos caído**
caerás	**caeréis**	**habrás caído**	**habréis caído**
caerá	**caerán**	**habrá caído**	**habrán caído**
5 potencial simple		12 potencial compuesto	
caería	**caeríamos**	**habría caído**	**habríamos caído**
caerías	**caeríais**	**habrías caído**	**habríais caído**
caería	**caerían**	**habría caído**	**habrían caído**
6 presente de subjuntivo		13 perfecto de subjuntivo	
caiga	**caigamos**	**haya caído**	**hayamos caído**
caigas	**caigáis**	**hayas caído**	**hayáis caído**
caiga	**caigan**	**haya caído**	**hayan caído**
7 imperfecto de subjuntivo		14 pluscuamperfecto de subjuntivo	
cayera	**cayéramos**	**hubiera caído**	**hubiéramos caído**
cayeras	**cayerais**	**hubieras caído**	**hubierais caído**
cayera	**cayeran**	**hubiera caído**	**hubieran caído**
OR		OR	
cayese	**cayésemos**	**hubiese caído**	**hubiésemos caído**
cayeses	**cayeseis**	**hubieses caído**	**hubieseis caído**
cayese	**cayesen**	**hubiese caído**	**hubiesen caído**

	imperativo	
—	**caigamos**	
cae; no caigas	**caed; no caigáis**	
caiga	**caigan**	

la caída the fall	recaer to relapse, fall back
caer enfermo (enferma) to fall sick	dejar caer to drop
a la caída del sol at sunset	caerse to fall, to fall down, to tumble
decaer to decay, decline	**Mi madre cayó enferma en octubre.**
a la caída de la tarde at the end of the	My mother fell ill in October.
afternoon	

callarse

Gerundio **callándose**

Part. pas. **callado**

to be silent, to keep quiet

Reflexive regular **-ar** verb

The Seven Simple Tenses		The Seven Compound Tenses	
Singular	Plural	Singular	Plural
1 presente de indicativo		**8 perfecto de indicativo**	
me callo	nos callamos	me he callado	nos hemos callado
te callas	os calláis	te has callado	os habéis callado
se calla	se callan	se ha callado	se han callado
2 imperfecto de indicativo		**9 pluscuamperfecto de indicativo**	
me callaba	nos callábamos	me había callado	nos habíamos callado
te callabas	os callabais	te habías callado	os habíais callado
se callaba	se callaban	se había callado	se habían callado
3 pretérito		**10 pretérito anterior**	
me callé	nos callamos	me hube callado	nos hubimos callado
te callaste	os callasteis	te hubiste callado	os hubisteis callado
se calló	se callaron	se hubo callado	se hubieron callado
4 futuro		**11 futuro perfecto**	
me callaré	nos callaremos	me habré callado	nos habremos callado
te callarás	os callaréis	te habrás callado	os habréis callado
se callará	se callarán	se habrá callado	se habrán callado
5 potencial simple		**12 potencial compuesto**	
me callaría	nos callaríamos	me habría callado	nos habríamos callado
te callarías	os callaríais	te habrías callado	os habríais callado
se callaría	se callarían	se habría callado	se habrían callado
6 presente de subjuntivo		**13 perfecto de subjuntivo**	
me calle	nos callemos	me haya callado	nos hayamos callado
te calles	os calléis	te hayas callado	os hayáis callado
se calle	se callen	se haya callado	se hayan callado
7 imperfecto de subjuntivo		**14 pluscuamperfecto de subjuntivo**	
me callara	nos calláramos	me hubiera callado	nos hubiéramos callado
te callaras	os callarais	te hubieras callado	os hubierais callado
se callara	se callaran	se hubiera callado	se hubieran callado
OR		OR	
me callase	nos callásemos	me hubiese callado	nos hubiésemos callado
te callases	os callaseis	te hubieses callado	os hubieseis callado
se callase	se callasen	se hubiese callado	se hubiesen callado

imperativo	
—	callémonos
cállate; no te calles	callaos; no os calléis
cállese	cállense

Quien calla, otorga. Silence means consent. (**otorgar:** to grant, to consent)	**callar la boca** to hold one's tongue
	callarse la boca to shut up
¡Cállese Ud.! Keep quiet!	**callar** to silence

cambiar

Regular **-ar** verb

to change

The Seven Simple Tenses		The Seven Compound Tenses	
Singular	Plural	Singular	Plural
1 presente de indicativo		8 perfecto de indicativo	
cambio	cambiamos	he cambiado	hemos cambiado
cambias	cambiáis	has cambiado	habéis cambiado
cambia	cambian	ha cambiado	han cambiado
2 imperfecto de indicativo		9 pluscuamperfecto de indicativo	
cambiaba	cambiábamos	había cambiado	habíamos cambiado
cambiabas	cambiabais	habías cambiado	habíais cambiado
cambiaba	cambiaban	había cambiado	habían cambiado
3 pretérito		10 pretérito anterior	
cambié	cambiamos	hube cambiado	hubimos cambiado
cambiaste	cambiasteis	hubiste cambiado	hubisteis cambiado
cambió	cambiaron	hubo cambiado	hubieron cambiado
4 futuro		11 futuro perfecto	
cambiaré	cambiaremos	habré cambiado	habremos cambiado
cambiarás	cambiaréis	habrás cambiado	habréis cambiado
cambiará	cambiarán	habrá cambiado	habrán cambiado
5 potencial simple		12 potencial compuesto	
cambiaría	cambiaríamos	habría cambiado	habríamos cambiado
cambiarías	cambiaríais	habrías cambiado	habríais cambiado
cambiaría	cambiarían	habría cambiado	habrían cambiado
6 presente de subjuntivo		13 perfecto de subjuntivo	
cambie	cambiemos	haya cambiado	hayamos cambiado
cambies	cambiéis	hayas cambiado	hayáis cambiado
cambie	cambien	haya cambiado	hayan cambiado
7 imperfecto de subjuntivo		14 pluscuamperfecto de subjuntivo	
cambiara	cambiáramos	hubiera cambiado	hubiéramos cambiado
cambiaras	cambiarais	hubieras cambiado	hubierais cambiado
cambiara	cambiaran	hubiera cambiado	hubieran cambiado
OR		OR	
cambiase	cambiásemos	hubiese cambiado	hubiésemos cambiado
cambiases	cambiaseis	hubieses cambiado	hubieseis cambiado
cambiase	cambiasen	hubiese cambiado	hubiesen cambiado

	imperativo	
—	cambiemos	
cambia; no cambies	cambiad; no cambiéis	
cambie	cambien	

cambiar de traje, de ropa to change one's clothing	**cambio minuto** small change
cambiar de opinión to change one's mind	**cambiar una rueda/un neumático** to change a wheel/a tire
el cambio exchange	**cambiar de idea** to change one's mind

caminar

Gerundio **caminando** Part. pas. **caminado**

to walk, to move along

Regular **-ar** verb

The Seven Simple Tenses		The Seven Compound Tenses	
Singular	Plural	Singular	Plural
1 presente de indicativo		**8 perfecto de indicativo**	
camino	caminamos	he caminado	hemos caminado
caminas	camináis	has caminado	habéis caminado
camina	caminan	ha caminado	han caminado
2 imperfecto de indicativo		**9 pluscuamperfecto de indicativo**	
caminaba	caminábamos	había caminado	habíamos caminado
caminabas	caminabais	habías caminado	habíais caminado
caminaba	caminaban	había caminado	habían caminado
3 pretérito		**10 pretérito anterior**	
caminé	caminamos	hube caminado	hubimos caminado
caminaste	caminasteis	hubiste caminado	hubisteis caminado
caminó	caminaron	hubo caminado	hubieron caminado
4 futuro		**11 futuro perfecto**	
caminaré	caminaremos	habré caminado	habremos caminado
caminarás	caminaréis	habrás caminado	habréis caminado
caminará	caminarán	habrá caminado	habrán caminado
5 potencial simple		**12 potencial compuesto**	
caminaría	caminaríamos	habría caminado	habríamos caminado
caminarías	caminaríais	habrías caminado	habríais caminado
caminaría	caminarían	habría caminado	habrían caminado
6 presente de subjuntivo		**13 perfecto de subjuntivo**	
camine	caminemos	haya caminado	hayamos caminado
camines	caminéis	hayas caminado	hayáis caminado
camine	caminen	haya caminado	hayan caminado
7 imperfecto de subjuntivo		**14 pluscuamperfecto de subjuntivo**	
caminara	camináramos	hubiera caminado	hubiéramos caminado
caminaras	caminarais	hubieras caminado	hubierais caminado
caminara	caminaran	hubiera caminado	hubieran caminado
OR		OR	
caminase	caminásemos	hubiese caminado	hubiésemos caminado
caminases	caminaseis	hubieses caminado	hubieseis caminado
caminase	caminasen	hubiese caminado	hubiesen caminado

imperativo	
—	caminemos
camina; no camines	caminad; no caminéis
camine	caminen

el camino road, highway
el camino de hierro railroad
en camino de on the way to
una caminata a long walk

estar en camino to be on one's way
hacer de un camino dos mandados to
kill two birds with one stone

66

Regular **-ar** verb

to fatigue, to tire,
to weary

The Seven Simple Tenses		The Seven Compound Tenses	
Singular	Plural	Singular	Plural
1 presente de indicativo		8 perfecto de indicativo	
canso	cansamos	he cansado	hemos cansado
cansas	cansáis	has cansado	habéis cansado
cansa	cansan	ha cansado	han cansado
2 imperfecto de indicativo		9 pluscuamperfecto de indicativo	
cansaba	cansábamos	había cansado	habíamos cansado
cansabas	cansabais	habías cansado	habíais cansado
cansaba	cansaban	había cansado	habían cansado
3 pretérito		10 pretérito anterior	
cansé	cansamos	hube cansado	hubimos cansado
cansaste	cansasteis	hubiste cansado	hubisteis cansado
cansó	cansaron	hubo cansado	hubieron cansado
4 futuro		11 futuro perfecto	
cansaré	cansaremos	habré cansado	habremos cansado
cansarás	cansaréis	habrás cansado	habréis cansado
cansará	cansarán	habrá cansado	habrán cansado
5 potencial simple		12 potencial compuesto	
cansaría	cansaríamos	habría cansado	habríamos cansado
cansarías	cansaríais	habrías cansado	habríais cansado
cansaría	cansarían	habría cansado	habrían cansado
6 presente de subjuntivo		13 perfecto de subjuntivo	
canse	cansemos	haya cansado	hayamos cansado
canses	canséis	hayas cansado	hayáis cansado
canse	cansen	haya cansado	hayan cansado
7 imperfecto de subjuntivo		14 pluscuamperfecto de subjuntivo	
cansara	cansáramos	hubiera cansado	hubiéramos cansado
cansaras	cansarais	hubieras cansado	hubierais cansado
cansara	cansaran	hubiera cansado	hubieran cansado
OR		OR	
cansase	cansásemos	hubiese cansado	hubiésemos cansado
cansases	cansaseis	hubieses cansado	hubieseis cansado
cansase	cansasen	hubiese cansado	hubiesen cansado

imperativo	
—	cansemos
cansa; no canses	cansad; no canséis
canse	cansen

María está cansada, Pedro está cansado y yo estoy cansado.	el cansancio fatigue, weariness
Nosotros estamos cansados.	el descansadero resting place
la cansera fatigue	cansado, cansada tired, exhausted
el descanso rest, relief	See also cansarse.

cansarse

Gerundio **cansándose**   Part. pas. **cansado**

to become tired, to become
weary, to get tired

Reflexive regular **-ar** verb

The Seven Simple Tenses		The Seven Compound Tenses	
Singular	Plural	Singular	Plural
1 presente de indicativo		8 perfecto de indicativo	
me canso	nos cansamos	me he cansado	nos hemos cansado
te cansas	os cansáis	te has cansado	os habéis cansado
se cansa	se cansan	se ha cansado	se han cansado
2 imperfecto de indicativo		9 pluscuamperfecto de indicativo	
me cansaba	nos cansábamos	me había cansado	nos habíamos cansado
te cansabas	os cansabais	te habías cansado	os habíais cansado
se cansaba	se cansaban	se había cansado	se habían cansado
3 pretérito		10 pretérito anterior	
me cansé	nos cansamos	me hube cansado	nos hubimos cansado
te cansaste	os cansasteis	te hubiste cansado	os hubisteis cansado
se cansó	se cansaron	se hubo cansado	se hubieron cansado
4 futuro		11 futuro perfecto	
me cansaré	nos cansaremos	me habré cansado	nos habremos cansado
te cansarás	os cansaréis	te habrás cansado	os habréis cansado
se cansará	se cansarán	se habrá cansado	se habrán cansado
5 potencial simple		12 potencial compuesto	
me cansaría	nos cansaríamos	me habría cansado	nos habríamos cansado
te cansarías	os cansaríais	te habrías cansado	os habríais cansado
se cansaría	se cansarían	se habría cansado	se habrían cansado
6 presente de subjuntivo		13 perfecto de subjuntivo	
me canse	nos cansemos	me haya cansado	nos hayamos cansado
te canses	os canséis	te hayas cansado	os hayáis cansado
se canse	se cansen	se haya cansado	se hayan cansado
7 imperfecto de subjuntivo		14 pluscuamperfecto de subjuntivo	
me cansara	nos cansáramos	me hubiera cansado	nos hubiéramos cansado
te cansaras	os cansarais	te hubieras cansado	os hubierais cansado
se cansara	se cansaran	se hubiera cansado	se hubieran cansado
OR		OR	
me cansase	nos cansásemos	me hubiese cansado	nos hubiésemos cansado
te cansases	os cansaseis	te hubieses cansado	os hubieseis cansado
se cansase	se cansasen	se hubiese cansado	se hubiesen cansado

imperativo	
—	cansémonos
cánsate; no te canses	cansaos; no os canséis
cánsese	cánsense

María se cansa, Pedro se cansa y yo me canso. Nosotros nos cansamos.	cansarse de esperar to get tired of waiting
Mary is getting tired, Peter is getting tired and I am getting tired. We are getting tired.	cansarse fácilmente to get tired easily
	cansarse de algo to get tired of something

The Seven Simple Tenses		The Seven Compound Tenses	
Singular	Plural	Singular	Plural
1 presente de indicativo		8 perfecto de indicativo	
canto	cantamos	he cantado	hemos cantado
cantas	cantáis	has cantado	habéis cantado
canta	cantan	ha cantado	han cantado
2 imperfecto de indicativo		9 pluscuamperfecto de indicativo	
cantaba	cantábamos	había cantado	habíamos cantado
cantabas	cantabais	habías cantado	habíais cantado
cantaba	cantaban	había cantado	habían cantado
3 pretérito		10 pretérito anterior	
canté	cantamos	hube cantado	hubimos cantado
cantaste	cantasteis	hubiste cantado	hubisteis cantado
cantó	cantaron	hubo cantado	hubieron cantado
4 futuro		11 futuro perfecto	
cantaré	cantaremos	habré cantado	habremos cantado
cantarás	cantaréis	habrás cantado	habréis cantado
cantará	cantarán	habrá cantado	habrán cantado
5 potencial simple		12 potencial compuesto	
cantaría	cantaríamos	habría cantado	habríamos cantado
cantarías	cantaríais	habrías cantado	habríais cantado
cantaría	cantarían	habría cantado	habrían cantado
6 presente de subjuntivo		13 perfecto de subjuntivo	
cante	cantemos	haya cantado	hayamos cantado
cantes	cantéis	hayas cantado	hayáis cantado
cante	canten	haya cantado	hayan cantado
7 imperfecto de subjuntivo		14 pluscuamperfecto de subjuntivo	
cantara	cantáramos	hubiera cantado	hubiéramos cantado
cantaras	cantarais	hubieras cantado	hubierais cantado
cantara	cantaran	hubiera cantado	hubieran cantado
OR		OR	
cantase	cantásemos	hubiese cantado	hubiésemos cantado
cantases	cantaseis	hubieses cantado	hubieseis cantado
cantase	cantasen	hubiese cantado	hubiesen cantado

imperativo	
—	cantemos
canta; no cantes	cantad; no cantéis
cante	canten

Quien canta su mal espanta. When you sing you drive away your grief.	**una canción** song
Mi hermana canta muy bien. My sister sings very well.	**una cantatriz** woman singer
	una cantata cantata (music)
Éso es otro cantar. / Ésa es otra canción. That's another story.	**cantor, cantora, cantante** singer
	encantar to enchant
	encantado, encantada enchanted

69

cargar

Gerundio **cargando** Part. pas. **cargado**

to load, to burden, to charge
(a battery)

Regular **-ar** verb endings with spelling
change: **g** becomes **gu** before **e**

The Seven Simple Tenses		The Seven Compound Tenses	
Singular	Plural	Singular	Plural
1 presente de indicativo		8 perfecto de indicativo	
cargo	cargamos	he cargado	hemos cargado
cargas	cargáis	has cargado	habéis cargado
carga	cargan	ha cargado	han cargado
2 imperfecto de indicativo		9 pluscuamperfecto de indicativo	
cargaba	cargábamos	había cargado	habíamos cargado
cargabas	cargabais	habías cargado	habíais cargado
cargaba	cargaban	había cargado	habían cargado
3 pretérito		10 pretérito anterior	
cargué	cargamos	hube cargado	hubimos cargado
cargaste	cargasteis	hubiste cargado	hubisteis cargado
cargó	cargaron	hubo cargado	hubieron cargado
4 futuro		11 futuro perfecto	
cargaré	cargaremos	habré cargado	habremos cargado
cargarás	cargaréis	habrás cargado	habréis cargado
cargará	cargarán	habrá cargado	habrán cargado
5 potencial simple		12 potencial compuesto	
cargaría	cargaríamos	habría cargado	habríamos cargado
cargarías	cargaríais	habrías cargado	habríais cargado
cargaría	cargarían	habría cargado	habrían cargado
6 presente de subjuntivo		13 perfecto de subjuntivo	
cargue	carguemos	haya cargado	hayamos cargado
cargues	carguéis	hayas cargado	hayáis cargado
cargue	carguen	haya cargado	hayan cargado
7 imperfecto de subjuntivo		14 pluscuamperfecto de subjuntivo	
cargara	cargáramos	hubiera cargado	hubiéramos cargado
cargaras	cargarais	hubieras cargado	hubierais cargado
cargara	cargaran	hubiera cargado	hubieran cargado
OR		OR	
cargase	cargásemos	hubiese cargado	hubiésemos cargado
cargases	cargaseis	hubieses cargado	hubieseis cargado
cargase	cargasen	hubiese cargado	hubiesen cargado

imperativo	
—	carguemos
carga; no cargues	cargad; no carguéis
cargue	carguen

cargoso, cargosa burdensome	una carga load, responsibility
la cargazón cargo	la descarga download (computer)
una cargazón de cabeza heaviness of the head	descargar to unload, to download (Internet)
el cargamento shipment	telecargar to download (Internet)
el cargador shipper	

Reflexive regular **-ar** verb   to get married, to marry

The Seven Simple Tenses		The Seven Compound Tenses	
Singular	Plural	Singular	Plural
1 presente de indicativo		8 perfecto de indicativo	
me caso	nos casamos	me he casado	nos hemos casado
te casas	os casáis	te has casado	os habéis casado
se casa	se casan	se ha casado	se han casado
2 imperfecto de indicativo		9 pluscuamperfecto de indicativo	
me casaba	nos casábamos	me había casado	nos habíamos casado
te casabas	os casabais	te habías casado	os habíais casado
se casaba	se casaban	se había casado	se habían casado
3 pretérito		10 pretérito anterior	
me casé	nos casamos	me hube casado	nos hubimos casado
te casaste	os casasteis	te hubiste casado	os hubisteis casado
se casó	se casaron	se hubo casado	se hubieron casado
4 futuro		11 futuro perfecto	
me casaré	nos casaremos	me habré casado	nos habremos casado
te casarás	os casaréis	te habrás casado	os habréis casado
se casará	se casarán	se habrá casado	se habrán casado
5 potencial simple		12 potencial compuesto	
me casaría	nos casaríamos	me habría casado	nos habríamos casado
te casarías	os casaríais	te habrías casado	os habríais casado
se casaría	se casarían	se habría casado	se habrían casado
6 presente de subjuntivo		13 perfecto de subjuntivo	
me case	nos casemos	me haya casado	nos hayamos casado
te cases	os caséis	te hayas casado	os hayáis casado
se case	se casen	se haya casado	se hayan casado
7 imperfecto de subjuntivo		14 pluscuamperfecto de subjuntivo	
me casara	nos casáramos	me hubiera casado	nos hubiéramos casado
te casaras	os casarais	te hubieras casado	os hubierais casado
se casara	se casaran	se hubiera casado	se hubieran casado
OR		OR	
me casase	nos casásemos	me hubiese casado	nos hubiésemos casado
te casases	os casaseis	te hubieses casado	os hubieseis casado
se casase	se casasen	se hubiese casado	se hubiesen casado

imperativo	
—	casémonos
cásate; no te cases	casaos; no os caséis
cásese	cásense

Antes que te cases, mira lo que haces. Look before you leap. (Before you get married, look at what you're doing.) un casamiento por amor a marriage based on love	casarse con alguien to marry someone los recién casados newlyweds un casamiento ventajoso a marriage of convenience

celebrar

Gerundio **celebrando**   Part. pas. **celebrado**

to celebrate

Regular **-ar** verb

The Seven Simple Tenses		The Seven Compound Tenses	
Singular	Plural	Singular	Plural
1 presente de indicativo		8 perfecto de indicativo	
celebro	celebramos	he celebrado	hemos celebrado
celebras	celebráis	has celebrado	habéis celebrado
celebra	celebran	ha celebrado	han celebrado
2 imperfecto de indicativo		9 pluscuamperfecto de indicativo	
celebraba	celebrábamos	había celebrado	habíamos celebrado
celebrabas	celebrabais	habías celebrado	habíais celebrado
celebraba	celebraban	había celebrado	habían celebrado
3 pretérito		10 pretérito anterior	
celebré	celebramos	hube celebrado	hubimos celebrado
celebraste	celebrasteis	hubiste celebrado	hubisteis celebrado
celebró	celebraron	hubo celebrado	hubieron celebrado
4 futuro		11 futuro perfecto	
celebraré	celebraremos	habré celebrado	habremos celebrado
celebrarás	celebraréis	habrás celebrado	habréis celebrado
celebrará	celebrarán	habrá celebrado	habrán celebrado
5 potencial simple		12 potencial compuesto	
celebraría	celebraríamos	habría celebrado	habríamos celebrado
celebrarías	celebraríais	habrías celebrado	habríais celebrado
celebraría	celebrarían	habría celebrado	habrían celebrado
6 presente de subjuntivo		13 perfecto de subjuntivo	
celebre	celebremos	haya celebrado	hayamos celebrado
celebres	celebréis	hayas celebrado	hayáis celebrado
celebre	celebren	haya celebrado	hayan celebrado
7 imperfecto de subjuntivo		14 pluscuamperfecto de subjuntivo	
celebrara	celebráramos	hubiera celebrado	hubiéramos celebrado
celebraras	celebrarais	hubieras celebrado	hubierais celebrado
celebrara	celebraran	hubiera celebrado	hubieran celebrado
OR		OR	
celebrase	celebrásemos	hubiese celebrado	hubiésemos celebrado
celebrases	celebraseis	hubieses celebrado	hubieseis celebrado
celebrase	celebrasen	hubiese celebrado	hubiesen celebrado

	imperativo	
—	celebremos	
celebra; no celebres	celebrad; no celebréis	
celebre	celebren	

célebre famous, celebrated, renowned	**ganar celebridad** to win fame
la celebridad fame, celebrity	**una persona célebre, una celebridad**
la celebración celebration	a celebrity
celebrado, celebrada popular, celebrated	

Regular -ar verb

to have supper, to eat supper,
to dine, to have dinner

The Seven Simple Tenses		The Seven Compound Tenses	
Singular	Plural	Singular	Plural
1 presente de indicativo		8 perfecto de indicativo	
ceno	cenamos	he cenado	hemos cenado
cenas	cenáis	has cenado	habéis cenado
cena	cenan	ha cenado	han cenado
2 imperfecto de indicativo		9 pluscuamperfecto de indicativo	
cenaba	cenábamos	había cenado	habíamos cenado
cenabas	cenabais	habías cenado	habíais cenado
cenaba	cenaban	había cenado	habían cenado
3 pretérito		10 pretérito anterior	
cené	cenamos	hube cenado	hubimos cenado
cenaste	cenasteis	hubiste cenado	hubisteis cenado
cenó	cenaron	hubo cenado	hubieron cenado
4 futuro		11 futuro perfecto	
cenaré	cenaremos	habré cenado	habremos cenado
cenarás	cenaréis	habrás cenado	habréis cenado
cenará	cenarán	habrá cenado	habrán cenado
5 potencial simple		12 potencial compuesto	
cenaría	cenaríamos	habría cenado	habríamos cenado
cenarías	cenaríais	habrías cenado	habríais cenado
cenaría	cenarían	habría cenado	habrían cenado
6 presente de subjuntivo		13 perfecto de subjuntivo	
cene	cenemos	haya cenado	hayamos cenado
cenes	cenéis	hayas cenado	hayáis cenado
cene	cenen	haya cenado	hayan cenado
7 imperfecto de subjuntivo		14 pluscuamperfecto de subjuntivo	
cenara	cenáramos	hubiera cenado	hubiéramos cenado
cenaras	cenarais	hubieras cenado	hubierais cenado
cenara	cenaran	hubiera cenado	hubieran cenado
OR		OR	
cenase	cenásemos	hubiese cenado	hubiésemos cenado
cenases	cenaseis	hubieses cenado	hubieseis cenado
cenase	cenasen	hubiese cenado	hubiesen cenado

imperativo	
—	cenemos
cena; no cenes	cenad; no cenéis
cene	cenen

—Carlos, ¿a qué hora cenas?
Charles, at what time do you have
dinner?
—Ceno a las ocho con mi familia en
casa.   I have dinner at eight at home
with my family.
la cena   supper (dinner)

la hora de cenar   dinnertime,
suppertime
La última cena   (*The Last Supper,*
fresco by Leonardo da Vinci)
quedarse sin cenar   to go (remain)
without dinner

cerrar

Gerundio **cerrando**   Part. pas. **cerrado**

to close, to shut, to turn off

Regular **-ar** verb endings with stem
change: Tenses 1, 6, Imperative

The Seven Simple Tenses		The Seven Compound Tenses	
Singular	Plural	Singular	Plural
1 presente de indicativo		8 perfecto de indicativo	
cierro	cerramos	he cerrado	hemos cerrado
cierras	cerráis	has cerrado	habéis cerrado
cierra	cierran	ha cerrado	han cerrado
2 imperfecto de indicativo		9 pluscuamperfecto de indicativo	
cerraba	cerrábamos	había cerrado	habíamos cerrado
cerrabas	cerrabais	habías cerrado	habíais cerrado
cerraba	cerraban	había cerrado	habían cerrado
3 pretérito		10 pretérito anterior	
cerré	cerramos	hube cerrado	hubimos cerrado
cerraste	cerrasteis	hubiste cerrado	hubisteis cerrado
cerró	cerraron	hubo cerrado	hubieron cerrado
4 futuro		11 futuro perfecto	
cerraré	cerraremos	habré cerrado	habremos cerrado
cerrarás	cerraréis	habrás cerrado	habréis cerrado
cerrará	cerrarán	habrá cerrado	habrán cerrado
5 potencial simple		12 potencial compuesto	
cerraría	cerraríamos	habría cerrado	habríamos cerrado
cerrarías	cerraríais	habrías cerrado	habríais cerrado
cerraría	cerrarían	habría cerrado	habrían cerrado
6 presente de subjuntivo		13 perfecto de subjuntivo	
cierre	cerremos	haya cerrado	hayamos cerrado
cierres	cerréis	hayas cerrado	hayáis cerrado
cierre	cierren	haya cerrado	hayan cerrado
7 imperfecto de subjuntivo		14 pluscuamperfecto de subjuntivo	
cerrara	cerráramos	hubiera cerrado	hubiéramos cerrado
cerraras	cerrarais	hubieras cerrado	hubierais cerrado
cerrara	cerraran	hubiera cerrado	hubieran cerrado
OR		OR	
cerrase	cerrásemos	hubiese cerrado	hubiésemos cerrado
cerrases	cerraseis	hubieses cerrado	hubieseis cerrado
cerrase	cerrasen	hubiese cerrado	hubiesen cerrado

imperativo	
—	cerremos
cierra; no cierres	cerrad; no cerréis
cierre	cierren

La puerta está cerrada.   The door is
  closed.
cerrar los ojos   to close one's eyes
cerrar los oídos   to turn a deaf ear
cerrar la boca   to shut up, to keep silent
encerrar   to lock up, to confine

la cerradura   lock
encerrarse   to live in seclusion, to retire
cerrar con llave   to lock up (to close
  with a key)
cerrar una cuenta   to close an account
una cerradura de combinación
  combination lock

certificar

Regular -ar verb endings with spelling change: e becomes qu before e

to certify, to register (a letter), to attest

The Seven Simple Tenses		The Seven Compound Tenses	
Singular	Plural	Singular	Plural
1 presente de indicativo		8 perfecto de indicativo	
certifico	certificamos	he certificado	hemos certificado
certificas	certificáis	has certificado	habéis certificado
certifica	certifican	ha certificado	han certificado
2 imperfecto de indicativo		9 pluscuamperfecto de indicativo	
certificaba	certificábamos	había certificado	habíamos certificado
certificabas	certificabais	habías certificado	habíais certificado
certificaba	certificaban	había certificado	habían certificado
3 pretérito		10 pretérito anterior	
certifiqué	certificamos	hube certificado	hubimos certificado
certificaste	certificasteis	hubiste certificado	hubisteis certificado
certificó	certificaron	hubo certificado	hubieron certificado
4 futuro		11 futuro perfecto	
certificaré	certificaremos	habré certificado	habremos certificado
certificarás	certificaréis	habrás certificado	habréis certificado
certificará	certificarán	habrá certificado	habrán certificado
5 potencial simple		12 potencial compuesto	
certificaría	certificaríamos	habría certificado	habríamos certificado
certificarías	certificaríais	habrías certificado	habríais certificado
certificaría	certificarían	habría certificado	habrían certificado
6 presente de subjuntivo		13 perfecto de subjuntivo	
certifique	certifiquemos	haya certificado	hayamos certificado
certifiques	certifiquéis	hayas certificado	hayáis certificado
certifique	certifiquen	haya certificado	hayan certificado
7 imperfecto de subjuntivo		14 pluscuamperfecto de subjuntivo	
certificara	certificáramos	hubiera certificado	hubiéramos certificado
certificaras	certificarais	hubieras certificado	hubierais certificado
certificara	certificaran	hubiera certificado	hubieran certificado
OR		OR	
certificase	certificásemos	hubiese certificado	hubiésemos certificado
certificases	certificaseis	hubieses certificado	hubieseis certificado
certificase	certificasen	hubiese certificado	hubiesen certificado

imperativo	
—	certifiquemos
certifica; no certifiques	certificad; no certifiquéis
certifique	certifiquen

la certificación certificate, certification	la certidumbre certainty
certificador, certificadora certifier	tener la certeza de que... to be sure that...
la certinidad assurance, certainty	la certeza certainty

cocer

Gerundio **cociendo**   Part. pas. **cocido**

to cook, to bake, to boil

Regular **-er** verb endings with stem change: Tenses 1, 6,
Imperative; spelling change: **c** becomes **z** before **a** or **o**

The Seven Simple Tenses		The Seven Compound Tenses	
Singular	Plural	Singular	Plural
1 presente de indicativo		8 perfecto de indicativo	
cuezo	cocemos	he cocido	hemos cocido
cueces	cocéis	has cocido	habéis cocido
cuece	cuecen	ha cocido	han cocido
2 imperfecto de indicativo		9 pluscuamperfecto de indicativo	
cocía	cocíamos	había cocido	habíamos cocido
cocías	cocíais	habías cocido	habíais cocido
cocía	cocían	había cocido	habían cocido
3 pretérito		10 pretérito anterior	
cocí	cocimos	hube cocido	hubimos cocido
cociste	cocisteis	hubiste cocido	hubisteis cocido
coció	cocieron	hubo cocido	hubieron cocido
4 futuro		11 futuro perfecto	
coceré	coceremos	habré cocido	habremos cocido
cocerás	coceréis	habrás cocido	habréis cocido
cocerá	cocerán	habrá cocido	habrán cocido
5 potencial simple		12 potencial compuesto	
cocería	coceríamos	habría cocido	habríamos cocido
cocerías	coceríais	habrías cocido	habríais cocido
cocería	cocerían	habría cocido	habrían cocido
6 presente de subjuntivo		13 perfecto de subjuntivo	
cueza	cozamos	haya cocido	hayamos cocido
cuezas	cozáis	hayas cocido	hayáis cocido
cueza	cuezan	haya cocido	hayan cocido
7 imperfecto de subjuntivo		14 pluscuamperfecto de subjuntivo	
cociera	cociéramos	hubiera cocido	hubiéramos cocido
cocieras	cocierais	hubieras cocido	hubierais cocido
cociera	cocieran	hubiera cocido	hubieran cocido
OR		OR	
cociese	cociésemos	hubiese cocido	hubiésemos cocido
cocieses	cocieseis	hubieses cocido	hubieseis cocido
cociese	cociesen	hubiese cocido	hubiesen cocido

imperativo

—	cozamos
cuece; no cuezas	coced; no cozáis
cueza	cuezan

la cocina kitchen	cocinar to cook
el cocinero, la cocinera cook, chef	un libro de cocina a cookbook
el cocimiento cooking	
el cocido plate of boiled meat and vegetables; stew	

Regular **-er** verb endings with spelling
change: **g** becomes **j** before **a** or **o**

to seize, to take, to grasp, to grab,
to catch, to get (understand)

The Seven Simple Tenses		The Seven Compound Tenses	
Singular	Plural	Singular	Plural
1 presente de indicativo		8 perfecto de indicativo	
cojo	cogemos	he cogido	hemos cogido
coges	cogéis	has cogido	habéis cogido
coge	cogen	ha cogido	han cogido
2 imperfecto de indicativo		9 pluscuamperfecto de indicativo	
cogía	cogíamos	había cogido	habíamos cogido
cogías	cogíais	habías cogido	habíais cogido
cogía	cogían	había cogido	habían cogido
3 pretérito		10 pretérito anterior	
cogí	cogimos	hube cogido	hubimos cogido
cogiste	cogisteis	hubiste cogido	hubisteis cogido
cogió	cogieron	hubo cogido	hubieron cogido
4 futuro		11 futuro perfecto	
cogeré	cogeremos	habré cogido	habremos cogido
cogerás	cogeréis	habrás cogido	habréis cogido
cogerá	cogerán	habrá cogido	habrán cogido
5 potencial simple		12 potencial compuesto	
cogería	cogeríamos	habría cogido	habríamos cogido
cogerías	cogeríais	habrías cogido	habríais cogido
cogería	cogerían	habría cogido	habrían cogido
6 presente de subjuntivo		13 perfecto de subjuntivo	
coja	cojamos	haya cogido	hayamos cogido
cojas	cojáis	hayas cogido	hayáis cogido
coja	cojan	haya cogido	hayan cogido
7 imperfecto de subjuntivo		14 pluscuamperfecto de subjuntivo	
cogiera	cogiéramos	hubiera cogido	hubiéramos cogido
cogieras	cogierais	hubieras cogido	hubierais cogido
cogiera	cogieran	hubiera cogido	hubieran cogido
OR		OR	
cogiese	cogiésemos	hubiese cogido	hubiésemos cogido
cogieses	cogieseis	hubieses cogido	hubieseis cogido
cogiese	cogiesen	hubiese cogido	hubiesen cogido

imperativo	
—	cojamos
coge; no cojas	coged; no cojáis
coja	cojan

---

la cogida   gathering of fruits, a catch
recoger   to pick (up), to gather
el cogedor   collector, dustpan
acoger   to greet, to receive, to welcome
escoger   to choose, to select

encoger   to shorten, to shrink
coger catarro (o resfriado)   to catch
cold
descoger   to expand, to extend

colegir

Gerundio **coligiendo**   Part. pas. **colegido**

to collect

Regular **-ir** verb endings with stem change: Tenses 1, 6, 7,
Imperative, *Gerundio*; spelling change: **g** becomes **j** before **a** or **o**

The Seven Simple Tenses		The Seven Compound Tenses	
Singular	Plural	Singular	Plural
1 presente de indicativo		8 perfecto de indicativo	
colijo	**colegimos**	**he colegido**	**hemos colegido**
coliges	**colegís**	**has colegido**	**habéis colegido**
colige	**coligen**	**ha colegido**	**han colegido**
2 imperfecto de indicativo		9 pluscuamperfecto de indicativo	
colegía	**colegíamos**	**había colegido**	**habíamos colegido**
colegías	**colegíais**	**habías colegido**	**habíais colegido**
colegía	**colegían**	**había colegido**	**habían colegido**
3 pretérito		10 pretérito anterior	
colegí	**colegimos**	**hube colegido**	**hubimos colegido**
colegiste	**colegisteis**	**hubiste colegido**	**hubisteis colegido**
coligió	**coligieron**	**hubo colegido**	**hubieron colegido**
4 futuro		11 futuro perfecto	
colegiré	**colegiremos**	**habré colegido**	**habremos colegido**
colegirás	**colegiréis**	**habrás colegido**	**habréis colegido**
colegirá	**colegirán**	**habrá colegido**	**habrán colegido**
5 potencial simple		12 potencial compuesto	
colegiría	**colegiríamos**	**habría colegido**	**habríamos colegido**
colegirías	**colegiríais**	**habrías colegido**	**habríais colegido**
colegiría	**colegirían**	**habría colegido**	**habrían colegido**
6 presente de subjuntivo		13 perfecto de subjuntivo	
colija	**colijamos**	**haya colegido**	**hayamos colegido**
colijas	**colijáis**	**hayas colegido**	**hayáis colegido**
colija	**colijan**	**haya colegido**	**hayan colegido**
7 imperfecto de subjuntivo		14 pluscuamperfecto de subjuntivo	
coligiera	**coligiéramos**	**hubiera colegido**	**hubiéramos colegido**
coligieras	**coligierais**	**hubieras colegido**	**hubierais colegido**
coligiera	**coligieran**	**hubiera colegido**	**hubieran colegido**
OR		OR	
coligiese	**coligiésemos**	**hubiese colegido**	**hubiésemos colegido**
coligieses	**coligieseis**	**hubieses colegido**	**hubieseis colegido**
coligiese	**coligiesen**	**hubiese colegido**	**hubiesen colegido**

	imperativo	
—	**colijamos**
colige; no colijas	**colegid; no colijáis**
colija	**colijan**

el colegio college, school	la colección collection
colectivo, colectiva collective	el colegio electoral electoral college

colgar

to hang (up)

Regular -ar verb endings with spelling change: **g** becomes
gu before **e**; stem change: Tenses 1, 6, Imperative

The Seven Simple Tenses		The Seven Compound Tenses	
Singular	Plural	Singular	Plural
1 presente de indicativo		**8 perfecto de indicativo**	
cuelgo	colgamos	he colgado	hemos colgado
cuelgas	colgáis	has colgado	habéis colgado
cuelga	cuelgan	ha colgado	han colgado
2 imperfecto de indicativo		**9 pluscuamperfecto de indicativo**	
colgaba	colgábamos	había colgado	habíamos colgado
colgabas	colgabais	habías colgado	habíais colgado
colgaba	colgaban	había colgado	habían colgado
3 pretérito		**10 pretérito anterior**	
colgué	colgamos	hube colgado	hubimos colgado
colgaste	colgasteis	hubiste colgado	hubisteis colgado
colgó	colgaron	hubo colgado	hubieron colgado
4 futuro		**11 futuro perfecto**	
colgaré	colgaremos	habré colgado	habremos colgado
colgarás	colgaréis	habrás colgado	habréis colgado
colgará	colgarán	habrá colgado	habrán colgado
5 potencial simple		**12 potencial compuesto**	
colgaría	colgaríamos	habría colgado	habríamos colgado
colgarías	colgaríais	habrías colgado	habríais colgado
colgaría	colgarían	habría colgado	habrían colgado
6 presente de subjuntivo		**13 perfecto de subjuntivo**	
cuelgue	colguemos	haya colgado	hayamos colgado
cuelgues	colguéis	hayas colgado	hayáis colgado
cuelgue	cuelguen	haya colgado	hayan colgado
7 imperfecto de subjuntivo		**14 pluscuamperfecto de subjuntivo**	
colgara	colgáramos	hubiera colgado	hubiéramos colgado
colgaras	colgarais	hubieras colgado	hubierais colgado
colgara	colgaran	hubiera colgado	hubieran colgado
OR		OR	
colgase	colgásemos	hubiese colgado	hubiésemos colgado
colgases	colgaseis	hubieses colgado	hubieseis colgado
colgase	colgasen	hubiese colgado	hubiesen colgado

	imperativo	
—	colguemos	
cuelga; no cuelgues	colgad; no colguéis	
cuelgue	cuelguen	

el colgadero hanger, hook on which to hang things	**¡Cuelgue!** Hang up!
dejar colgado (colgada) to be left disappointed	**descolgar** to take down, to pick up (a telephone receiver)
la colgadura drapery, tapestry	**colgar el teléfono** to hang up the telephone

colocar

Gerundio **colocando**   Part. pas. **colocado**

to put, to place

Regular **-ar** verb endings with spelling
change: **c** becomes **qu** before **e**

The Seven Simple Tenses		The Seven Compound Tenses	
Singular	Plural	Singular	Plural
1 presente de indicativo		8 perfecto de indicativo	
coloco	colocamos	he colocado	hemos colocado
colocas	colocáis	has colocado	habéis colocado
coloca	colocan	ha colocado	han colocado
2 imperfecto de indicativo		9 pluscuamperfecto de indicativo	
colocaba	colocábamos	había colocado	habíamos colocado
colocabas	colocabais	habías colocado	habíais colocado
colocaba	colocaban	había colocado	habían colocado
3 pretérito		10 pretérito anterior	
coloqué	colocamos	hube colocado	hubimos colocado
colocaste	colocasteis	hubiste colocado	hubisteis colocado
colocó	colocaron	hubo colocado	hubieron colocado
4 futuro		11 futuro perfecto	
colocaré	colocaremos	habré colocado	habremos colocado
colocarás	colocaréis	habrás colocado	habréis colocado
colocará	colocarán	habrá colocado	habrán colocado
5 potencial simple		12 potencial compuesto	
colocaría	colocaríamos	habría colocado	habríamos colocado
colocarías	colocaríais	habrías colocado	habríais colocado
colocaría	colocarían	habría colocado	habrían colocado
6 presente de subjuntivo		13 perfecto de subjuntivo	
coloque	coloquemos	haya colocado	hayamos colocado
coloques	coloquéis	hayas colocado	hayáis colocado
coloque	coloquen	haya colocado	hayan colocado
7 imperfecto de subjuntivo		14 pluscuamperfecto de subjuntivo	
colocara	colocáramos	hubiera colocado	hubiéramos colocado
colocaras	colocarais	hubieras colocado	hubierais colocado
colocara	colocaran	hubiera colocado	hubieran colocado
OR		OR	
colocase	colocásemos	hubiese colocado	hubiésemos colocado
colocases	colocaseis	hubieses colocado	hubieseis colocado
colocase	colocasen	hubiese colocado	hubiesen colocado

imperativo	
—	coloquemos
coloca; no coloques	colocad; no coloquéis
coloque	coloquen

---

la colocación   job, employment,
   position
colocar dinero   to invest money
colocar un pedido   to place an order

la agencia de colocaciones   job
   placement agency

comenzar

Regular **-ar** verb endings with spelling change: **z** becomes
c before **e**; stem change: Tenses 1, 6, Imperative

to begin, to start,
to commence

The Seven Simple Tenses		The Seven Compound Tenses	
Singular	Plural	Singular	Plural
1 presente de indicativo		8 perfecto de indicativo	
comienzo	**comenzamos**	**he comenzado**	**hemos comenzado**
comienzas	**comenzáis**	**has comenzado**	**habéis comenzado**
comienza	**comienzan**	**ha comenzado**	**han comenzado**
2 imperfecto de indicativo		9 pluscuamperfecto de indicativo	
comenzaba	**comenzábamos**	**había comenzado**	**habíamos comenzado**
comenzabas	**comenzabais**	**habías comenzado**	**habíais comenzado**
comenzaba	**comenzaban**	**había comenzado**	**habían comenzado**
3 pretérito		10 pretérito anterior	
comencé	**comenzamos**	**hube comenzado**	**hubimos comenzado**
comenzaste	**comenzasteis**	**hubiste comenzado**	**hubisteis comenzado**
comenzó	**comenzaron**	**hubo comenzado**	**hubieron comenzado**
4 futuro		11 futuro perfecto	
comenzaré	**comenzaremos**	**habré comenzado**	**habremos comenzado**
comenzarás	**comenzaréis**	**habrás comenzado**	**habréis comenzado**
comenzará	**comenzarán**	**habrá comenzado**	**habrán comenzado**
5 potencial simple		12 potencial compuesto	
comenzaría	**comenzaríamos**	**habría comenzado**	**habríamos comenzado**
comenzarías	**comenzaríais**	**habrías comenzado**	**habríais comenzado**
comenzaría	**comenzarían**	**habría comenzado**	**habrían comenzado**
6 presente de subjuntivo		13 perfecto de subjuntivo	
comience	**comencemos**	**haya comenzado**	**hayamos comenzado**
comiences	**comencéis**	**hayas comenzado**	**hayáis comenzado**
comience	**comiencen**	**haya comenzado**	**hayan comenzado**
7 imperfecto de subjuntivo		14 pluscuamperfecto de subjuntivo	
comenzara	**comenzáramos**	**hubiera comenzado**	**hubiéramos comenzado**
comenzaras	**comenzarais**	**hubieras comenzado**	**hubierais comenzado**
comenzara	**comenzaran**	**hubiera comenzado**	**hubieran comenzado**
OR		OR	
comenzase	**comenzásemos**	**hubiese comenzado**	**hubiésemos comenzado**
comenzases	**comenzaseis**	**hubieses comenzado**	**hubieseis comenzado**
comenzase	**comenzasen**	**hubiese comenzado**	**hubiesen comenzado**

imperativo	
—	**comencemos**
comienza; no comiences	**comenzad; no comencéis**
comience	**comiencen**

¿Qué tiempo hace? What is the weather like?	el comienzo beginning
Comienza a llover. It's starting to rain.	comenzar a + inf. to begin + inf.
Quiero comenzar al comienzo I'd like to begin at the beginning.	comenzar por + inf. to begin by + pres. part
Lo que mal comienza, mal acaba. What starts badly, ends badly.	al comienzo at the beginning, at first

comer

Gerundio **comiendo** Part. pas. **comido**

to eat

Regular **-er** verb

The Seven Simple Tenses	
Singular	Plural

The Seven Compound Tenses	
Singular	Plural

1 presente de indicativo

como	comemos
comes	coméis
come	comen

8 perfecto de indicativo

he comido	hemos comido
has comido	habéis comido
ha comido	han comido

2 imperfecto de indicativo

comía	comíamos
comías	comíais
comía	comían

9 pluscuamperfecto de indicativo

había comido	habíamos comido
habías comido	habíais comido
había comido	habían comido

3 pretérito

comí	comimos
comiste	comisteis
comió	comieron

10 pretérito anterior

hube comido	hubimos comido
hubiste comido	hubisteis comido
hubo comido	hubieron comido

4 futuro

comeré	comeremos
comerás	comeréis
comerá	comerán

11 futuro perfecto

habré comido	habremos comido
habrás comido	habréis comido
habrá comido	habrán comido

5 potencial simple

comería	comeríamos
comerías	comeríais
comería	comerían

12 potencial compuesto

habría comido	habríamos comido
habrías comido	habríais comido
habría comido	habrían comido

6 presente de subjuntivo

coma	comamos
comas	comáis
coma	coman

13 perfecto de subjuntivo

haya comido	hayamos comido
hayas comido	hayáis comido
haya comido	hayan comido

7 imperfecto de subjuntivo

comiera	comiéramos
comieras	comierais
comiera	comieran
OR	
comiese	comiésemos
comieses	comieseis
comiese	comiesen

14 pluscuamperfecto de subjuntivo

hubiera comido	hubiéramos comido
hubieras comido	hubierais comido
hubiera comido	hubieran comido
OR	
hubiese comido	hubiésemos comido
hubieses comido	hubieseis comido
hubiese comido	hubiesen comido

imperativo

—	comamos
come; no comas	comed; no comáis
coma	coman

Miguel está comiendo su comida en el comedor. Michael is eating his meal in the dining room.

Proverb: Dime qué comes y te diré quien eres. Tell me what you eat and I'll tell you who you are.

ganar de comer to earn a living

comerse to eat up
la comida meal
comer con gana to eat heartily
comer fuera de casa to eat out; dine out
comer de todo to eat everything
el comedor dining room
comer como un pajarito to eat like a little bird

The Seven Simple Tenses		The Seven Compound Tenses	
Singular	Plural	Singular	Plural

1 presente de indicativo		8 perfecto de indicativo	
compongo	**componemos**	**he compuesto**	**hemos compuesto**
compones	**componéis**	**has compuesto**	**habéis compuesto**
compone	**componen**	**ha compuesto**	**han compuesto**

2 imperfecto de indicativo		9 pluscuamperfecto de indicativo	
componía	**componíamos**	**había compuesto**	**habíamos compuesto**
componías	**componíais**	**habías compuesto**	**habíais compuesto**
componía	**componían**	**había compuesto**	**habían compuesto**

3 pretérito		10 pretérito anterior	
compuse	**compusimos**	**hube compuesto**	**hubimos compuesto**
compusiste	**compusisteis**	**hubiste compuesto**	**hubisteis compuesto**
compuso	**compusieron**	**hubo compuesto**	**hubieron compuesto**

4 futuro		11 futuro perfecto	
compondré	**compondremos**	**habré compuesto**	**habremos compuesto**
compondrás	**compondréis**	**habrás compuesto**	**habréis compuesto**
compondrá	**compondrán**	**habrá compuesto**	**habrán compuesto**

5 potencial simple		12 potencial compuesto	
compondría	**compondríamos**	**habría compuesto**	**habríamos compuesto**
compondrías	**compondríais**	**habrías compuesto**	**habríais compuesto**
compondría	**compondrían**	**habría compuesto**	**habrían compuesto**

6 presente de subjuntivo		13 perfecto de subjuntivo	
compongo	**compongamos**	**haya compuesto**	**hayamos compuesto**
compongas	**compongáis**	**hayas compuesto**	**hayáis compuesto**
componga	**compongan**	**haya compuesto**	**hayan compuesto**

7 imperfecto de subjuntivo		14 pluscuamperfecto de subjuntivo	
compusiera	**compusiéramos**	**hubiera compuesto**	**hubiéramos compuesto**
compusieras	**compusierais**	**hubieras compuesto**	**hubierais compuesto**
compusiera	**compusieran**	**hubiera compuesto**	**hubieran compuesto**
OR		OR	
compusiese	**compusiésemos**	**hubiese compuesto**	**hubiésemos compuesto**
compusieses	**compusieseis**	**hubieses compuesto**	**hubieseis compuesto**
compusiese	**compusiesen**	**hubiese compuesto**	**hubiesen compuesto**

imperativo	
—	**compongamos**
compón; no compongas	**componed; no compongáis**
componga	**compongan**

el compuesto compound, mixture	deponer to depose
la composición composition	imponer to impose
compuestamente neatly, orderly	exponer to expose, to exhibit
el compositor, la compositora	indisponer to indispose
composer (music)	

comprar

Gerundio **comprando**   Part. pas. **comprado**

to buy, to purchase

Regular **-ar** verb

The Seven Simple Tenses		The Seven Compound Tenses	
Singular	Plural	Singular	Plural
1 presente de indicativo		8 perfecto de indicativo	
compro	compramos	he comprado	hemos comprado
compras	compráis	has comprado	habéis comprado
compra	compran	ha comprado	han comprado
2 imperfecto de indicativo		9 pluscuamperfecto de indicativo	
compraba	comprábamos	había comprado	habíamos comprado
comprabas	comprabais	habías comprado	habíais comprado
compraba	compraban	había comprado	habían comprado
3 pretérito		10 pretérito anterior	
compré	compramos	hube comprado	hubimos comprado
compraste	comprasteis	hubiste comprado	hubisteis comprado
compró	compraron	hubo comprado	hubieron comprado
4 futuro		11 futuro perfecto	
compraré	compraremos	habré comprado	habremos comprado
comprarás	compraréis	habrás comprado	habréis comprado
comprará	comprarán	habrá comprado	habrán comprado
5 potencial simple		12 potencial compuesto	
compraría	compraríamos	habría comprado	habríamos comprado
comprarías	compraríais	habrías comprado	habríais comprado
compraría	comprarían	habría comprado	habrían comprado
6 presente de subjuntivo		13 perfecto de subjuntivo	
compre	compremos	haya comprado	hayamos comprado
compres	compréis	hayas comprado	hayáis comprado
compre	compren	haya comprado	hayan comprado
7 imperfecto de subjuntivo		14 pluscuamperfecto de subjuntivo	
comprara	compráramos	hubiera comprado	hubiéramos comprado
compraras	comprarais	hubieras comprado	hubierais comprado
comprara	compraran	hubiera comprado	hubieran comprado
OR		OR	
comprase	comprásemos	hubiese comprado	hubiésemos comprado
comprases	compraseis	hubieses comprado	hubieseis comprado
comprase	comprasen	hubiese comprado	hubiesen comprado

imperativo		
—		compremos
compra; no compres		comprad; no compréis
compre		compren

Yo compré mis zapatos en el centro comercial. I bought my shoes at the shopping center.	comprar al fiado, comprar a crédito to buy on credit
La amistad no se compra. Friendship cannot be bought (has no price).	la compra purchase comprable purchasable
comprador, compradora buyer	comprar con rebaja to buy at a discount ir de compras to go shopping hacer compras to shop

84

Regular **-er** verb   to understand

The Seven Simple Tenses		The Seven Compound Tenses	
Singular	Plural	Singular	Plural
1 presente de indicativo		8 perfecto de indicativo	
comprendo	comprendemos	he	hemos
comprendes	comprendéis	has	habéis + comprendido
comprende	comprenden	ha	han
2 imperfecto de indicativo		9 pluscuamperfecto de indicativo	
comprendía	comprendíamos	había	habíamos
comprendías	comprendíais	habías	habíais + comprendido
comprendía	comprendían	había	habían
3 pretérito		10 pretérito anterior	
comprendí	comprendimos	hube	hubimos
comprendiste	comprendisteis	hubiste	hubisteis + comprendido
comprendió	comprendieron	hubo	hubieron
4 futuro		11 futuro perfecto	
comprenderé	comprenderemos	habré	habremos
comprenderás	comprenderéis	habrás	habréis + comprendido
comprenderá	comprenderán	habrá	habrán
5 potencial simple		12 potencial compuesto	
comprendería	comprenderíamos	habría	habríamos
comprenderías	comprenderíais	habrías	habríais + comprendido
comprendería	comprenderían	habría	habrían
6 presente de subjuntivo		13 perfecto de subjuntivo	
comprenda	comprendamos	haya	hayamos
comprendas	comprendáis	hayas	hayáis + comprendido
comprenda	comprendan	haya	hayan
7 imperfecto de subjuntivo		14 pluscuamperfecto de subjuntivo	
comprendiera	comprendiéramos	hubiera	hubiéramos
comprendieras	comprendierais	hubieras	hubierais + comprendido
comprendiera	comprendieran	hubiera	hubieran
OR		OR	
comprendiese	comprendiésemos	hubiese	hubiésemos
comprendieses	comprendieseis	hubieses	hubieseis + comprendido
comprendiese	comprendiesen	hubiese	hubiesen

imperativo	
—	comprendamos
comprende; no comprendas	comprended; no comprendáis
comprenda	comprendan

la comprensión comprehension, understanding	comprensible comprehensible, understandable
la comprensibilidad comprehensibility, intelligibility	comprenderse to understand one another
comprensivo, comprensiva comprehensive	No comprendo. I don't understand.
	Sí, comprendo. Yes, I understand.

85

conducir

Gerundio **conduciendo**　　Part. pas. **conducido**

to lead, to conduct,
to drive

Irregular in Tenses 3 and 7, regular **-ir** verb endings in
all others; spelling change: **c** becomes **zc** before **a** or **o**

The Seven Simple Tenses		The Seven Compound Tenses	
Singular	Plural	Singular	Plural
1　presente de indicativo		8　perfecto de indicativo	
conduzco	conducimos	he conducido	hemos conducido
conduces	conducís	has conducido	habéis conducido
conduce	conducen	ha conducido	han conducido
2　imperfecto de indicativo		9　pluscuamperfecto de indicativo	
conducía	conducíamos	había conducido	habíamos conducido
conducías	conducíais	habías conducido	habíais conducido
conducía	conducían	había conducido	habían conducido
3　pretérito		10　pretérito anterior	
conduje	condujimos	hube conducido	hubimos conducido
condujiste	condujisteis	hubiste conducido	hubisteis conducido
condujo	condujeron	hubo conducido	hubieron conducido
4　futuro		11　futuro perfecto	
conduciré	conduciremos	habré conducido	habremos conducido
conducirás	conduciréis	habrás conducido	habréis conducido
conducirá	conducirán	habrá conducido	habrán conducido
5　potencial simple		12　potencial compuesto	
conduciría	conduciríamos	habría conducido	habríamos conducido
conducirías	conduciríais	habrías conducido	habríais conducido
conduciría	conducirían	habría conducido	habrían conducido
6　presente de subjuntivo		13　perfecto de subjuntivo	
conduzca	conduzcamos	haya conducido	hayamos conducido
conduzcas	conduzcáis	hayas conducido	hayáis conducido
conduzca	conduzcan	haya conducido	hayan conducido
7　imperfecto de subjuntivo		14　pluscuamperfecto de subjuntivo	
condujera	condujéramos	hubiera conducido	hubiéramos conducido
condujeras	condujerais	hubieras conducido	hubierais conducido
condujera	condujeran	hubiera conducido	hubieran conducido
OR		OR	
condujese	condujésemos	hubiese conducido	hubiésemos conducido
condujeses	condujeseis	hubieses conducido	hubieseis conducido
condujese	condujesen	hubiese conducido	hubiesen conducido

imperativo	
—	conduzcamos
conduce; no conduzcas	conducid; no conduzcáis
conduzca	conduzcan

el conductor, la conductora	el conducto　conduit, duct
conductor, director	la conducta　conduct, behavior
¿Sabe Ud. conducir?　Do you know	conducente　conducive
how to drive?	un carné de conducir　a driver's
Sí, conduzco todos los días.　Yes,	license
I drive every day.	

Regular **-ar** verb endings with stem
change: Tenses 1, 6, Imperative

to confess

The Seven Simple Tenses		The Seven Compound Tenses	
Singular	Plural	Singular	Plural
1 presente de indicativo		**8 perfecto de indicativo**	
confieso	confesamos	he confesado	hemos confesado
confiesas	confesáis	has confesado	habéis confesado
confiesa	confiesan	ha confesado	han confesado
2 imperfecto de indicativo		**9 pluscuamperfecto de indicativo**	
confesaba	confesábamos	había confesado	habíamos confesado
confesabas	confesabais	habías confesado	habíais confesado
confesaba	confesaban	había confesado	habían confesado
3 pretérito		**10 pretérito anterior**	
confesé	confesamos	hube confesado	hubimos confesado
confesaste	confesasteis	hubiste confesado	hubisteis confesado
confesó	confesaron	hubo confesado	hubieron confesado
4 futuro		**11 futuro perfecto**	
confesaré	confesaremos	habré confesado	habremos confesado
confesarás	confesaréis	habrás confesado	habréis confesado
confesará	confesarán	habrá confesado	habrán confesado
5 potencial simple		**12 potencial compuesto**	
confesaría	confesaríamos	habría confesado	habríamos confesado
confesarías	confesaríais	habrías confesado	habríais confesado
confesaría	confesarían	habría confesado	habrían confesado
6 presente de subjuntivo		**13 perfecto de subjuntivo**	
confiese	confesemos	haya confesado	hayamos confesado
confieses	confeséis	hayas confesado	hayáis confesado
confiese	confiesen	haya confesado	hayan confesado
7 imperfecto de subjuntivo		**14 pluscuamperfecto de subjuntivo**	
confesara	confesáramos	hubiera confesado	hubiéramos confesado
confesaras	confesarais	hubieras confesado	hubierais confesado
confesara	confesaran	hubiera confesado	hubieran confesado
OR		OR	
confesase	confesásemos	hubiese confesado	hubiésemos confesado
confesases	confesaseis	hubieses confesado	hubieseis confesado
confesase	confesasen	hubiese confesado	hubiesen confesado

imperativo	
—	confesemos
confiesa; no confieses	confesad; no confeséis
confiese	confiesen

la confesión confession	**el confesor** confessor
confesar de plano to confess openly	**confesarse culpable** to admit one's
el confesionario confession box	guilt
un, una confesante confessor	

conocer

Gerundio **conociendo**   Part. pas. **conocido**

to know, to be acquainted with

Regular **-er** verb endings with spelling change: **c** becomes **zc** before **a** or **o**

The Seven Simple Tenses		The Seven Compound Tenses	
Singular	Plural	Singular	Plural
1 presente de indicativo		8 perfecto de indicativo	
conozco	conocemos	he conocido	hemos conocido
conoces	conocéis	has conocido	habéis conocido
conoce	conocen	ha conocido	han conocido
2 imperfecto de indicativo		9 pluscuamperfecto de indicativo	
conocía	conocíamos	había conocido	habíamos conocido
conocías	conocíais	habías conocido	habíais conocido
conocía	conocían	había conocido	habían conocido
3 pretérito		10 pretérito anterior	
conocí	conocimos	hube conocido	hubimos conocido
conociste	conocisteis	hubiste conocido	hubisteis conocido
conoció	conocieron	hubo conocido	hubieron conocido
4 futuro		11 futuro perfecto	
conoceré	conoceremos	habré conocido	habremos conocido
conocerás	conoceréis	habrás conocido	habréis conocido
conocerá	conocerán	habrá conocido	habrán conocido
5 potencial simple		12 potencial compuesto	
conocería	conoceríamos	habría conocido	habríamos conocido
conocerías	conoceríais	habrías conocido	habríais conocido
conocería	conocerían	habría conocido	habrían conocido
6 presente de subjuntivo		13 perfecto de subjuntivo	
conozca	conozcamos	haya conocido	hayamos conocido
conozcas	conozcáis	hayas conocido	hayáis conocido
conozca	conozcan	haya conocido	hayan conocido
7 imperfecto de subjuntivo		14 pluscuamperfecto de subjuntivo	
conociera	conociéramos	hubiera conocido	hubiéramos conocido
conocieras	conocierais	hubieras conocido	hubierais conocido
conociera	conocieran	hubiera conocido	hubieran conocido
OR		OR	
conociese	conociésemos	hubiese conocido	hubiésemos conocido
conocieses	conocieseis	hubieses conocido	hubieseis conocido
conociese	conociesen	hubiese conocido	hubiesen conocido

	imperativo
—	conozcamos
conoce; no conozcas	conoced; no conozcáis
conozca	conozcan

¿Conoce Ud. bien los Estados Unidos?
  Do you know the United States well?
—¿Conoce Ud. a esa mujer?
—Sí, la conozco.
el conocimiento   knowledge
reconocer   to recognize, to admit

un conocido, una conocida   an
  acquaintance
desconocer   to be ignorant of
poner en conocimiento de   to inform
  (about)
muy conocido   very well-known

conseguir

Regular -ir verb endings with spelling change: **gu** becomes **g**
before **a** or **o**; stem change: Tenses 1, 6, Imperative, *Gerundio*

to attain, to get,
to obtain

The Seven Simple Tenses		The Seven Compound Tenses	
Singular	Plural	Singular	Plural
1 presente de indicativo		8 perfecto de indicativo	
consigo	conseguimos	he conseguido	hemos conseguido
consigues	conseguís	has conseguido	habéis conseguido
consigue	consiguen	ha conseguido	han conseguido
2 imperfecto de indicativo		9 pluscuamperfecto de indicativo	
conseguía	conseguíamos	había conseguido	habíamos conseguido
conseguías	conseguíais	habías conseguido	habíais conseguido
conseguía	conseguían	había conseguido	habían conseguido
3 pretérito		10 pretérito anterior	
conseguí	conseguimos	hube conseguido	hubimos conseguido
conseguiste	conseguisteis	hubiste conseguido	hubisteis conseguido
consiguió	consiguieron	hubo conseguido	hubieron conseguido
4 futuro		11 futuro perfecto	
conseguiré	conseguiremos	habré conseguido	habremos conseguido
conseguirás	conseguiréis	habrás conseguido	habréis conseguido
conseguirá	conseguirán	habrá conseguido	habrán conseguido
5 potencial simple		12 potencial compuesto	
conseguiría	conseguiríamos	habría conseguido	habríamos conseguido
conseguirías	conseguiríais	habrías conseguido	habríais conseguido
conseguiría	conseguirían	habría conseguido	habrían conseguido
6 presente de subjuntivo		13 perfecto de subjuntivo	
consiga	consigamos	haya conseguido	hayamos conseguido
consigas	consigáis	hayas conseguido	hayáis conseguido
consiga	consigan	haya conseguido	hayan conseguido
7 imperfecto de subjuntivo		14 pluscuamperfecto de subjuntivo	
consiguiera	consiguiéramos	hubiera conseguido	hubiéramos conseguido
consiguieras	consiguierais	hubieras conseguido	hubierais conseguido
consiguiera	consiguieran	hubiera conseguido	hubieran conseguido
OR		OR	
consiguiese	consiguiésemos	hubiese conseguido	hubiésemos conseguido
consiguieses	consiguieseis	hubieses conseguido	hubieseis conseguido
consiguiese	consiguiesen	hubiese conseguido	hubiesen conseguido

imperativo	
—	consigamos
consigue; no consigas	consigamos; no consigáis
consiga	consigan

el conseguimiento attainment	de consiguiente, por consiguiente
consiguientemente consequently	consequently
el consiguiente consequence	See also seguir.

constituir

Gerundio **constituyendo**   Part. pas. **constituido**

to constitute, to make up

Regular **-ir** verb endings with spelling change: add **y** before **a, e,** or **o**

The Seven Simple Tenses		The Seven Compound Tenses	
Singular	Plural	Singular	Plural
1 presente de indicativo		**8 perfecto de indicativo**	
constituyo	constituimos	he constituido	hemos constituido
constituyes	constituís	has constituido	habéis constituido
constituye	constituyen	ha constituido	han constituido
2 imperfecto de indicativo		**9 pluscuamperfecto de indicativo**	
constituía	constituíamos	había constituido	habíamos constituido
constituías	constituíais	habías constituido	habíais constituido
constituía	constituían	había constituido	habían constituido
3 pretérito		**10 pretérito anterior**	
constituí	constituimos	hube constituido	hubimos constituido
constituiste	constituisteis	hubiste constituido	hubisteis constituido
constituyó	constituyeron	hubo constituido	hubieron constituido
4 futuro		**11 futuro perfecto**	
constituiré	constituiremos	habré constituido	habremos constituido
constituirás	constituiréis	habrás constituido	habréis constituido
constituirá	constituirán	habrá constituido	habrán constituido
5 potencial simple		**12 potencial compuesto**	
constituiría	constituiríamos	habría constituido	habríamos constituido
constituirías	constituiríais	habrías constituido	habríais constituido
constituiría	constituirían	habría constituido	habrían constituido
6 presente de subjuntivo		**13 perfecto de subjuntivo**	
constituya	constituyamos	haya constituido	hayamos constituido
constituyas	constituyáis	hayas constituido	hayáis constituido
constituya	constituyan	haya constituido	hayan constituido
7 imperfecto de subjuntivo		**14 pluscuamperfecto de subjuntivo**	
constituyera	constituyéramos	hubiera constituido	hubiéramos constituido
constituyeras	constituyerais	hubieras constituido	hubierais constituido
constituyera	constituyeran	hubiera constituido	hubieran constituido
OR		OR	
constituyese	constituyésemos	hubiese constituido	hubiésemos constituido
constituyeses	constituyeseis	hubieses constituido	hubieseis constituido
constituyese	constituyesen	hubiese constituido	hubiesen constituido

imperativo	
—	constituyamos
constituye; no constituyas	constituid; no constituyáis
constituya	constituyan

constitutivo, constitutiva constitutive, essential
instituir to institute, to instruct, to teach
la constitución constitution

restituir to restore, to give back
el constitucionalismo constitutionalism
constituyente constituent

Regular **-ir** verb endings with spelling change: add **y** before **a, e,** or **o**

to construct, to build

The Seven Simple Tenses		The Seven Compound Tenses	
Singular	Plural	Singular	Plural
1 presente de indicativo		8 perfecto de indicativo	
construyo	construimos	he construido	hemos construido
construyes	construís	has construido	habéis construido
construye	construyen	ha construido	han construido
2 imperfecto de indicativo		9 pluscuamperfecto de indicativo	
construía	construíamos	había construido	habíamos construido
construías	construíais	habías construido	habíais construido
construía	construían	había construido	habían construido
3 pretérito		10 pretérito anterior	
construí	construimos	hube construido	hubimos construido
construiste	construisteis	hubiste construido	hubisteis construido
construyó	construyeron	hubo construido	hubieron construido
4 futuro		11 futuro perfecto	
construiré	construiremos	habré construido	habremos construido
construirás	construiréis	habrás construido	habréis construido
construirá	construirán	habrá construido	habrán construido
5 potencial simple		12 potencial compuesto	
construiría	construiríamos	habría construido	habríamos construido
construirías	construiríais	habrías construido	habríais construido
construiría	construirían	habría construido	habrían construido
6 presente de subjuntivo		13 perfecto de subjuntivo	
construya	construyamos	haya construido	hayamos construido
construyas	construyáis	hayas construido	hayáis construido
construya	construyan	haya construido	hayan construido
7 imperfecto de subjuntivo		14 pluscuamperfecto de subjuntivo	
construyera	construyéramos	hubiera construido	hubiéramos construido
construyeras	construyerais	hubieras construido	hubierais construido
construyera	construyeran	hubiera construido	hubieran construido
OR		OR	
construyese	construyésemos	hubiese construido	hubiésemos construido
construyeses	construyeseis	hubieses construido	hubieseis construido
construyese	construyesen	hubiese construido	hubiesen construido

imperativo

—	construyamos
construye; no construyas	construid; no construyáis
construya	construyan

---

la construcción   construction
reconstruir   to reconstruct
el constructor, la constructora   builder
Mi casa fue construida en 1889.
  My house was built in 1889.

la construcción naval   shipbuilding
constructivo, constructiva   constructive
la crítica constructiva   constructive criticism

contar

Gerundio **contando**   Part. pas. **contado**

to count, to relate, to tell

Regular **-ar** verb endings with stem change: Tenses 1, 6, Imperative

The Seven Simple Tenses		The Seven Compound Tenses	
Singular	Plural	Singular	Plural
1 presente de indicativo		**8 perfecto de indicativo**	
cuento	contamos	he contado	hemos contado
cuentas	contáis	has contado	habéis contado
cuenta	cuentan	ha contado	han contado
2 imperfecto de indicativo		**9 pluscuamperfecto de indicativo**	
contaba	contábamos	había contado	habíamos contado
contabas	contabais	habías contado	habíais contado
contaba	contaban	había contado	habían contado
3 pretérito		**10 pretérito anterior**	
conté	contamos	hube contado	hubimos contado
contaste	contasteis	hubiste contado	hubisteis contado
contó	contaron	hubo contado	hubieron contado
4 futuro		**11 futuro perfecto**	
contaré	contaremos	habré contado	habremos contado
contarás	contaréis	habrás contado	habréis contado
contará	contarán	habrá contado	habrán contado
5 potencial simple		**12 potencial compuesto**	
contaría	contaríamos	habría contado	habríamos contado
contarías	contaríais	habrías contado	habríais contado
contaría	contarían	habría contado	habrían contado
6 presente de subjuntivo		**13 perfecto de subjuntivo**	
cuente	contemos	haya contado	hayamos contado
cuentes	contéis	hayas contado	hayáis contado
cuente	cuenten	haya contado	hayan contado
7 imperfecto de subjuntivo		**14 pluscuamperfecto de subjuntivo**	
contara	contáramos	hubiera contado	hubiéramos contado
contaras	contarais	hubieras contado	hubierais contado
contara	contaran	hubiera contado	hubieran contado
OR		OR	
contase	contásemos	hubiese contado	hubiésemos contado
contases	contaseis	hubieses contado	hubieseis contado
contase	contasen	hubiese contado	hubiesen contado

	imperativo	
—	contemos	
cuenta; no cuentes	contad; no contéis	
cuente	cuenten	

Siéntate. Te contaré una historia maravillosa. Sit down. I'll tell you a marvelous story.	**descontar** to discount, to deduct
un cuento story, tale	**contar con** to depend on, to count on, to rely on
recontar to recount	**la cuenta** bill, check
estar en el cuento to be informed	**una cuenta bancaria** bank account

Regular **-ar** verb   to answer, to reply (to)

The Seven Simple Tenses		The Seven Compound Tenses	
Singular	Plural	Singular	Plural
1 presente de indicativo		8 perfecto de indicativo	
contesto	**contestamos**	**he contestado**	**hemos contestado**
contestas	**contestáis**	**has contestado**	**habéis contestado**
contesta	**contestan**	**ha contestado**	**han contestado**
2 imperfecto de indicativo		9 pluscuamperfecto de indicativo	
contestaba	**contestábamos**	**había contestado**	**habíamos contestado**
contestabas	**contestabais**	**habías contestado**	**habíais contestado**
contestaba	**contestaban**	**había contestado**	**habían contestado**
3 pretérito		10 pretérito anterior	
contesté	**contestamos**	**hube contestado**	**hubimos contestado**
contestaste	**contestasteis**	**hubiste contestado**	**hubisteis contestado**
contestó	**contestaron**	**hubo contestado**	**hubieron contestado**
4 futuro		11 futuro perfecto	
contestaré	**contestaremos**	**habré contestado**	**habremos contestado**
contestarás	**contestaréis**	**habrás contestado**	**habréis contestado**
contestará	**contestarán**	**habrá contestado**	**habrán contestado**
5 potencial simple		12 potencial compuesto	
contestaría	**contestaríamos**	**habría contestado**	**habríamos contestado**
contestarías	**contestaríais**	**habrías contestado**	**habríais contestado**
contestaría	**contestarían**	**habría contestado**	**habrían contestado**
6 presente de subjuntivo		13 perfecto de subjuntivo	
conteste	**contestemos**	**haya contestado**	**hayamos contestado**
contestes	**contestéis**	**hayas contestado**	**hayáis contestado**
conteste	**contesten**	**haya contestado**	**hayan contestado**
7 imperfecto de subjuntivo		14 pluscuamperfecto de subjuntivo	
contestara	**contestáramos**	**hubiera contestado**	**hubiéramos contestado**
contestaras	**contestarais**	**hubieras contestado**	**hubierais contestado**
contestara	**contestaran**	**hubiera contestado**	**hubieran contestado**
OR		OR	
contestase	**contestásemos**	**hubiese contestado**	**hubiésemos contestado**
contestases	**contestaseis**	**hubieses contestado**	**hubieseis contestado**
contestase	**contestasen**	**hubiese contestado**	**hubiesen contestado**

imperativo	
—	**contestemos**
contesta; no contestes	**contestad; no contestéis**
conteste	**contesten**

la contestación answer, reply	**contestar el teléfono** to answer the
contestar una pregunta to answer a	telephone
question	**contestable** contestable

continuar

Gerundio **continuando**   Part. pas. **continuado**

to continue

Regular **-ar** verb endings with spelling change: **u** becomes **ú** on stressed syllable (Tenses 1, 6, Imperative)

The Seven Simple Tenses		The Seven Compound Tenses	
Singular	Plural	Singular	Plural
1 presente de indicativo		8 perfecto de indicativo	
continúo	continuamos	he continuado	hemos continuado
continúas	continuáis	has continuado	habéis continuado
continúa	continúan	ha continuado	han continuado
2 imperfecto de indicativo		9 pluscuamperfecto de indicativo	
continuaba	continuábamos	había continuado	habíamos continuado
continuabas	continuabais	habías continuado	habíais continuado
continuaba	continuaban	había continuado	habían continuado
3 pretérito		10 pretérito anterior	
continué	continuamos	hube continuado	hubimos continuado
continuaste	continuasteis	hubiste continuado	hubisteis continuado
continuó	continuaron	hubo continuado	hubieron continuado
4 futuro		11 futuro perfecto	
continuaré	continuaremos	habré continuado	habremos continuado
continuarás	continuaréis	habrás continuado	habréis continuado
continuará	continuarán	habrá continuado	habrán continuado
5 potencial simple		12 potencial compuesto	
continuaría	continuaríamos	habría continuado	habríamos continuado
continuarías	continuaríais	habrías continuado	habríais continuado
continuaría	continuarían	habría continuado	habrían continuado
6 presente de subjuntivo		13 perfecto de subjuntivo	
continúe	continuemos	haya continuado	hayamos continuado
continúes	continuéis	hayas continuado	hayáis continuado
continúe	continúen	haya continuado	hayan continuado
7 imperfecto de subjuntivo		14 pluscuamperfecto de subjuntivo	
continuara	continuáramos	hubiera continuado	hubiéramos continuado
continuaras	continuarais	hubieras continuado	hubierais continuado
continuara	continuaran	hubiera continuado	hubieran continuado
OR		OR	
continuase	continuásemos	hubiese continuado	hubiésemos continuado
continusases	continuaseis	hubieses continuado	hubieseis continuado
continuase	continuasen	hubiese continuado	hubiesen continuado

imperativo	
—	continuemos
continúa; no continúes	continuad; no continuéis
continúe	continúen

la continuación	continuation	a continuación	to be continued, next,
descontinuar	to discontinue		immediately after, below
continuamente	continually	continuadamente	continually
la descontinuación	discontinuation	continuo, continúa	continuous

94

The Seven Simple Tenses		The Seven Compound Tenses	
Singular	Plural	Singular	Plural
1 presente de indicativo		8 perfecto de indicativo	
contradigo	contradecimos	he contradicho	hemos contradicho
contradices	contradecís	has contradicho	habéis contradicho
contradice	contradicen	ha contradicho	han contradicho
2 imperfecto de indicativo		9 pluscuamperfecto de indicativo	
contradecía	contradecíamos	había contradicho	habíamos contradicho
contradecías	contradecíais	habías contradicho	habíais contradicho
contradecía	contradecían	había contradicho	habían contradicho
3 pretérito		10 pretérito anterior	
contradije	contradijimos	hube contradicho	hubimos contradicho
contradijiste	contradijisteis	hubiste contradicho	hubisteis contradicho
contradijo	contradijeron	hubo contradicho	hubieron contradicho
4 futuro		11 futuro perfecto	
contradiré	contradiremos	habré contradicho	habremos contradicho
contradirás	contradiréis	habrás contradicho	habréis contradicho
contradirá	contradirán	habrá contradicho	habrán contradicho
5 potencial simple		12 potencial compuesto	
contradiría	contradiríamos	habría contradicho	habríamos contradicho
contradirías	contradiríais	habrías contradicho	habríais contradicho
contradiría	contradirían	habría contradicho	habrían contradicho
6 presente de subjuntivo		13 perfecto de subjuntivo	
contradiga	contradigamos	haya contradicho	hayamos contradicho
contradigas	contradigáis	hayas contradicho	hayáis contradicho
contradiga	contradigan	haya contradicho	hayan contradicho
7 imperfecto de subjuntivo		14 pluscuamperfecto de subjuntivo	
contradijera	contradijéramos	hubiera contradicho	hubiéramos contradicho
contradijeras	contradijerais	hubieras contradicho	hubierais contradicho
contradijera	contradijeran	hubiera contradicho	hubieran contradicho
OR		OR	
contradijese	contradijésemos	hubiese contradicho	hubiésemos contradicho
contradijeses	contradijeseis	hubieses contradicho	hubieseis contradicho
contradijese	contradijesen	hubiese contradicho	hubiesen contradicho

	imperativo	
—	congradigamos	
contradí; no contradigas	contradecid; contradigáis	
contradiga	contradigan	

contradictorio, contradictoria	contradictoriamente contradictorily
contradictory	contradecirse to contradict oneself
contradictor, contradictora	estar en contradicción con to be
contradictor	contradictory to
la contradicción contradiction	

contribuir

Gerundio **contribuyendo**   Part. pas. **contribuido**

to contribute

Regular **-ir** verb endings with spelling
change: add **y** before **a, e,** or **o**

The Seven Simple Tenses		The Seven Compound Tenses	
Singular	Plural	Singular	Plural
1 presente de indicativo		8 perfecto de indicativo	
contribuyo	**contribuimos**	**he contribuido**	**hemos contribuido**
contribuyes	**contribuís**	**has contribuido**	**habéis contribuido**
contribuye	**contribuyen**	**ha contribuido**	**han contribuido**
2 imperfecto de indicativo		9 pluscuamperfecto de indicativo	
contribuía	**contribuíamos**	**había contribuido**	**habíamos contribuido**
contribuías	**contribuíais**	**habías contribuido**	**habíais contribuido**
contribuía	**contribuían**	**había contribuido**	**habían contribuido**
3 pretérito		10 pretérito anterior	
contribuí	**contribuimos**	**hube contribuido**	**hubimos contribuido**
contribuiste	**contribuisteis**	**hubiste contribuido**	**hubisteis contribuido**
contribuyó	**contribuyeron**	**hubo contribuido**	**hubieron contribuido**
4 futuro		11 futuro perfecto	
contribuiré	**contribuiremos**	**habré contribuido**	**habremos contribuido**
contribuirás	**contribuiréis**	**habrás contribuido**	**habréis contribuido**
contribuirá	**contribuirán**	**habrá contribuido**	**habrán contribuido**
5 potencial simple		12 potencial compuesto	
contribuiría	**contribuiríamos**	**habría contribuido**	**habríamos contribuido**
contribuirías	**contribuiríais**	**habrías contribuido**	**habríais contribuido**
contribuiría	**contribuirían**	**habría contribuido**	**habrían contribuido**
6 presente de subjuntivo		13 perfecto de subjuntivo	
contribuya	**contribuyamos**	**haya contribuido**	**hayamos contribuido**
contribuyas	**contribuyáis**	**hayas contribuido**	**hayáis contribuido**
contribuya	**contribuyan**	**haya contribuido**	**hayan contribuido**
7 imperfecto de subjuntivo		14 pluscuamperfecto de subjuntivo	
contribuyera	**contribuyéramos**	**hubiera contribuido**	**hubiéramos contribuido**
contribuyeras	**contribuyerais**	**hubieras contribuido**	**hubierais contribuido**
contribuyera	**contribuyeran**	**hubiera contribuido**	**hubieran contribuido**
OR		OR	
contribuyese	**contribuyésemos**	**hubiese contribuido**	**hubiésemos contribuido**
contribuyeses	**contribuyeseis**	**hubieses contribuido**	**hubieseis contribuido**
contribuyese	**contribuyesen**	**hubiese contribuido**	**hubiesen contribuido**

imperativo	
—	**contribuyamos**
contribuye; no contribuyas	**contribuid; no contribuyáis**
contribuya	**contribuyan**

contribuidor, contribuidora
  contributor
la contribución   contribution, tax

la contribución directa   direct tax
la contribución municipal   local tax

corregir

The Seven Simple Tenses		The Seven Compound Tenses	
Singular	Plural	Singular	Plural
1 presente de indicativo		8 perfecto de indicativo	
corrijo	**corregimos**	**he corregido**	**hemos corregido**
corriges	**corregís**	**has corregido**	**habéis corregido**
corrige	**corrigen**	**ha corregido**	**han corregido**
2 imperfecto de indicativo		9 pluscuamperfecto de indicativo	
corregía	**corregíamos**	**había corregido**	**habíamos corregido**
corregías	**corregíais**	**habías corregido**	**habíais corregido**
corregía	**corregían**	**había corregido**	**habían corregido**
3 pretérito		10 pretérito anterior	
corregí	**corregimos**	**hube corregido**	**hubimos corregido**
corregiste	**corregisteis**	**hubiste corregido**	**hubisteis corregido**
corrigió	**corrigieron**	**hubo corregido**	**hubieron corregido**
4 futuro		11 futuro perfecto	
corregiré	**corregiremos**	**habré corregido**	**habremos corregido**
corregirás	**corregiréis**	**habrás corregido**	**habréis corregido**
corregirá	**corregirán**	**habrá corregido**	**habrán corregido**
5 potencial simple		12 potencial compuesto	
corregiría	**corregiríamos**	**habría corregido**	**habríamos corregido**
corregirías	**corregiríais**	**habrías corregido**	**habríais corregido**
corregiría	**corregirían**	**habría corregido**	**habrían corregido**
6 presente de subjuntivo		13 perfecto de subjuntivo	
corrija	**corrijamos**	**haya corregido**	**hayamos corregido**
corrijas	**corrijáis**	**hayas corregido**	**hayáis corregido**
corrija	**corrijan**	**haya corregido**	**hayan corregido**
7 imperfecto de subjuntivo		14 pluscuamperfecto de subjuntivo	
corrigiera	**corrigiéramos**	**hubiera corregido**	**hubiéramos corregido**
corrigieras	**corrigierais**	**hubieras corregido**	**hubierais corregido**
corrigiera	**corrigieran**	**hubiera corregido**	**hubieran corregido**
OR		OR	
corrigiese	**corrigiésemos**	**hubiese corregido**	**hubiésemos corregido**
corrigieses	**corrigieseis**	**hubieses corregido**	**hubieseis corregido**
corrigiese	**corrigiesen**	**hubiese corregido**	**hubiesen corregido**

imperativo	
—	**corrijamos**
corrige; no corrijas	**corregid; no corrijáis**
corrija	**corrijan**

corregir pruebas to read proofs	**incorregible** incorrigible
correcto, correcta correct	**correccional** correctional
corregible corrigible	**la corrección** correction
correctamente correctly	**el correccional** reformatory

correr

Gerundio **corriendo**   Part. pas. **corrido**

to run, to race, to flow

Regular **-er** verb

The Seven Simple Tenses		The Seven Compound Tenses	
Singular	Plural	Singular	Plural
1 presente de indicativo		8 perfecto de indicativo	
corro	corremos	he corrido	hemos corrido
corres	corréis	has corrido	habéis corrido
corre	corren	ha corrido	han corrido
2 imperfecto de indicativo		9 pluscuamperfecto de indicativo	
corría	corríamos	había corrido	habíamos corrido
corrías	corríais	habías corrido	habíais corrido
corría	corrían	había corrido	habían corrido
3 pretérito		10 pretérito anterior	
corrí	corrimos	hube corrido	hubimos corrido
corriste	corristeis	hubiste corrido	hubisteis corrido
corrió	corrieron	hubo corrido	hubieron corrido
4 futuro		11 futuro perfecto	
correré	correremos	habré corrido	habremos corrido
correrás	correréis	habrás corrido	habréis corrido
correrá	correrán	habrá corrido	habrán corrido
5 potencial simple		12 potencial compuesto	
correría	correríamos	habría corrido	habríamos corrido
correrías	correríais	habrías corrido	habríais corrido
correría	correrían	habría corrido	habrían corrido
6 presente de subjuntivo		13 perfecto de subjuntivo	
corra	corramos	haya corrido	hayamos corrido
corras	corráis	hayas corrido	hayáis corrido
corra	corran	haya corrido	hayan corrido
7 imperfecto de subjuntivo		14 pluscuamperfecto de subjuntivo	
corriera	corriéramos	hubiera corrido	hubiéramos corrido
corrieras	corrierais	hubieras corrido	hubierais corrido
corriera	corrieran	hubiera corrido	hubieran corrido
OR		OR	
corriese	corriésemos	hubiese corrido	hubiésemos corrido
corrieses	corrieseis	hubieses corrido	hubieseis corrido
corriese	corriesen	hubiese corrido	hubiesen corrido

	imperativo	
—	corramos	
corre; no corras	corred; no corráis	
corra	corran	

---

el correo   mail, post
el correo electrónico   e-mail
la corrida   race
correo aéreo   air mail
de corrida   at full speed

echar una carta al correo   to mail (post) a letter
recorrer   to travel on, to go over
descorrer   to flow (liquids); to draw a curtain or drape
por correo aparte   under separate cover (mail)

Regular **-ar** verb endings with stem
change: Tenses 1, 6, Imperative

to cost

The Seven Simple Tenses		The Seven Compound Tenses	
Singular	Plural	Singular	Plural
1 presente de indicativo		8 perfecto de indicativo	
cuesta	**cuestan**	**ha costado**	**han costado**
2 imperfecto de indicativo		9 pluscuamperfecto de indicativo	
costaba	**costaban**	**había costado**	**habían costado**
3 pretérito		10 pretérito anterior	
costó	**costaron**	**hubo costado**	**hubieron costado**
4 futuro		11 futuro perfecto	
costará	**costarán**	**habrá costado**	**habrán costado**
5 potencial simple		12 potencial compuesto	
costaría	**costarían**	**habría costado**	**habrían costado**
6 presente de subjuntivo		13 perfecto de subjuntivo	
que cueste	**que cuesten**	**que haya costado**	**que hayan costado**
7 imperfecto de subjuntivo		14 pluscuamperfecto de subjuntivo	
que costara	**que costaran**	**que hubiera costado**	**que hubieran costado**
OR		OR	
que costase	**que costasen**	**que hubiese costado**	**que hubiesen costado**

imperativo
¡Que cueste!   **¡Que cuesten!**

---

el costo de la vida   the cost of living
Cuesta + inf.   It is difficult to...
Cuesta creerlo   It's difficult to believe
   it.
costoso, costosa   costly, expensive
costar un ojo de la cara   to be very
   expensive (to cost an arm and a leg)
el costo   price, cost

cueste lo que cueste   at any cost
This is an impersonal verb and it is used
   mainly in the third person singular and
   plural. To conjugate it in the other
   tenses, use regular **-ar** verb endings
   and make the stem change in tenses
   1 and 6 and in the imperative (cuesta,
   cueste, costemos, costad, cuesten).

crecer

Gerundio **creciendo**   Part. pas. **crecido**

to grow

Regular **-er** verb endings with spelling
change: **c** becomes **zc** before **a** or **o**

The Seven Simple Tenses		The Seven Compound Tenses	
Singular	Plural	Singular	Plural
1 presente de indicativo		8 perfecto de indicativo	
crezco	crecemos	he crecido	hemos crecido
creces	crecéis	has crecido	habéis crecido
crece	crecen	ha crecido	han crecido
2 imperfecto de indicativo		9 pluscuamperfecto de indicativo	
crecía	crecíamos	había crecido	habíamos crecido
crecías	crecíais	habías crecido	habíais crecido
crecía	crecían	había crecido	habían crecido
3 pretérito		10 pretérito anterior	
crecí	crecimos	hube crecido	hubimos crecido
creciste	crecisteis	hubiste crecido	hubisteis crecido
creció	crecieron	hubo crecido	hubieron crecido
4 futuro		11 futuro perfecto	
creceré	creceremos	habré crecido	habremos crecido
crecerás	creceréis	habrás crecido	habréis crecido
crecerá	crecerán	habrá crecido	habrán crecido
5 potencial simple		12 potencial compuesto	
crecería	creceríamos	habría crecido	habríamos crecido
crecerías	creceríais	habrías crecido	habríais crecido
crecería	crecerían	habría crecido	habrían crecido
6 presente de subjuntivo		13 perfecto de subjuntivo	
crezca	crezcamos	haya crecido	hayamos crecido
crezcas	crezcáis	hayas crecido	hayáis crecido
crezca	crezcan	haya crecido	hayan crecido
7 imperfecto de subjuntivo		14 pluscuamperfecto de subjuntivo	
creciera	creciéramos	hubiera crecido	hubiéramos crecido
crecieras	crecierais	hubieras crecido	hubierais crecido
creciera	crecieran	hubiera crecido	hubieran crecido
OR		OR	
creciese	creciésemos	hubiese crecido	hubiésemos crecido
crecieses	crecieseis	hubieses crecido	hubieseis crecido
creciese	creciesen	hubiese crecido	hubiesen crecido

imperativo	
—	crezcamos
crece; no crezcas	creced; no crezcáis
crezca	crezcan

crecer como la mala hierba to grow	el crescendo crescendo (music)
like a weed	creciente growing, increasing
crecidamente abundantly	la luna creciente crescent moon

Regular -er verb endings with spelling change: **i** becomes
y in Tense 3 (3rd person) and Tense 7 (all)

to believe

The Seven Simple Tenses		The Seven Compound Tenses	
Singular	Plural	Singular	Plural
1 presente de indicativo		8 perfecto de indicativo	
creo	creemos	he creído	hemos creído
crees	creéis	has creído	habéis creído
cree	creen	ha creído	han creído
2 imperfecto de indicativo		9 pluscuamperfecto de indicativo	
creía	creíamos	había creído	habíamos creído
creías	creíais	habías creído	habíais creído
creía	creían	había creído	habían creído
3 pretérito		10 pretérito anterior	
creí	creímos	hube creído	hubimos creído
creíste	creísteis	hubiste creído	hubisteis creído
creyó	creyeron	hubo creído	hubieron creído
4 futuro		11 futuro perfecto	
creeré	creeremos	habré creído	habremos creído
creerás	creeréis	habrás creído	habréis creído
creerá	creerán	habrá creído	habrán creído
5 potencial simple		12 potencial compuesto	
creería	creeríamos	habría creído	habríamos creído
creerías	creeríais	habrías creído	habríais creído
creería	creerían	habría creído	habrían creído
6 presente de subjuntivo		13 perfecto de subjuntivo	
crea	creamos	haya creído	hayamos creído
creas	creáis	hayas creído	hayáis creído
crea	crean	haya creído	hayan creído
7 imperfecto de subjuntivo		14 pluscuamperfecto de subjuntivo	
creyera	creyéramos	hubiera creído	hubiéramos creído
creyeras	creyerais	hubieras creído	hubierais creído
creyera	creyeran	hubiera creído	hubieran creído
OR		OR	
creyese	creyésemos	hubiese creído	hubiésemos creído
creyeses	creyeseis	hubieses creído	hubieseis creído
creyese	creyesen	hubiese creído	hubiesen creído

	imperativo	
	—	creamos
	cree; no creas	creed; no creáis
	crea	crean

Ver es creer. Seeing is believing.	dar crédito to believe
la credulidad credulity	descreer to disbelieve
¡Ya lo creo! Of course!	Creo que sí. I think so.
el credo creed	Creo que no. I don't think so.
crédulo, crédula credulous, gullible	

criar

Gerundio **criando** Part. pas. **criado**

to breed, to raise,
to bring up (rear)

Regular **-ar** verb endings with spelling change: **i** becomes
í on stressed syllable (Tenses 1, 6, Imperative)

The Seven Simple Tenses		The Seven Compound Tenses	
Singular	Plural	Singular	Plural
1 presente de indicativo		8 perfecto de indicativo	
crío	criamos	he criado	hemos criado
crías	criáis	has criado	habéis criado
cría	crían	ha criado	han criado
2 imperfecto de indicativo		9 pluscuamperfecto de indicativo	
criaba	criábamos	había criado	habíamos criado
criabas	criabais	habías criado	habíais criado
criaba	criaban	había criado	habían criado
3 pretérito		10 pretérito anterior	
crié	criamos	hube criado	hubimos criado
criaste	criasteis	hubiste criado	hubisteis criado
crió	criaron	hubo criado	hubieron criado
4 futuro		11 futuro perfecto	
criaré	criaremos	habré criado	habremos criado
criarás	criaréis	habrás criado	habréis criado
criará	criarán	habrá criado	habrán criado
5 potencial simple		12 potencial compuesto	
criaría	criaríamos	habría criado	habríamos criado
criarías	criaríais	habrías criado	habríais criado
criaría	criarían	habría criado	habrían criado
6 presente de subjuntivo		13 perfecto de subjuntivo	
críe	criemos	haya criado	hayamos criado
críes	criéis	hayas criado	hayáis criado
críe	críen	haya criado	hayan criado
7 imperfecto de subjuntivo		14 pluscuamperfecto de subjuntivo	
criara	criáramos	hubiera criado	hubiéramos criado
criaras	criarais	hubieras criado	hubierais criado
criara	criaran	hubiera criado	hubieran criado
OR		OR	
criase	criásemos	hubiese criado	hubiésemos criado
criases	criaseis	hubieses criado	hubieseis criado
criase	criasen	hubiese criado	hubiesen criado

imperativo	
—	criemos
cría; no críes	criad; no criéis
críe	críen

la criandera, la criadora wet nurse	Dios los cría y ellos se juntan Birds
mala crianza bad manners,	of a feather flock together.
impoliteness	la crianza upbringing, nursing (milk)
el criado, la criada servant	dar crianza to educate, to bring up

Regular **-ar** verb endings with spelling change: **z** becomes **c** before **e**   to cross

The Seven Simple Tenses		The Seven Compound Tenses	
Singular	Plural	Singular	Plural
1 presente de indicativo		8 perfecto de indicativo	
cruzo	**cruzamos**	**he cruzado**	**hemos cruzado**
cruzas	**cruzáis**	**has cruzado**	**habéis cruzado**
cruza	**cruzan**	**ha cruzado**	**han cruzado**
2 imperfecto de indicativo		9 pluscuamperfecto de indicativo	
cruzaba	**cruzábamos**	**había cruzado**	**habíamos cruzado**
cruzabas	**cruzabais**	**habías cruzado**	**habíais cruzado**
cruzaba	**cruzaban**	**había cruzado**	**habían cruzado**
3 pretérito		10 pretérito anterior	
crucé	**cruzamos**	**hube cruzado**	**hubimos cruzado**
cruzaste	**cruzasteis**	**hubiste cruzado**	**hubisteis cruzado**
cruzó	**cruzaron**	**hubo cruzado**	**hubieron cruzado**
4 futuro		11 futuro perfecto	
cruzaré	**cruzaremos**	**habré cruzado**	**habremos cruzado**
cruzarás	**cruzaréis**	**habrás cruzado**	**habréis cruzado**
cruzará	**cruzarán**	**habrá cruzado**	**habrán cruzado**
5 potencial simple		12 potencial compuesto	
cruzaría	**cruzaríamos**	**habría cruzado**	**habríamos cruzado**
cruzarías	**cruzaríais**	**habrías cruzado**	**habríais cruzado**
cruzaría	**cruzarían**	**habría cruzado**	**habrían cruzado**
6 presente de subjuntivo		13 perfecto de subjuntivo	
cruce	**crucemos**	**haya cruzado**	**hayamos cruzado**
cruces	**crucéis**	**hayas cruzado**	**hayáis cruzado**
cruce	**crucen**	**haya cruzado**	**hayan cruzado**
7 imperfecto de subjuntivo		14 pluscuamperfecto de subjuntivo	
cruzara	**cruzáramos**	**hubiera cruzado**	**hubiéramos cruzado**
cruzaras	**cruzarais**	**hubieras cruzado**	**hubierais cruzado**
cruzara	**cruzaran**	**hubiera cruzado**	**hubieran cruzado**
OR		OR	
cruzase	**cruzásemos**	**hubiese cruzado**	**hubiésemos cruzado**
cruzases	**cruzaseis**	**hubieses cruzado**	**hubieseis cruzado**
cruzase	**cruzasen**	**hubiese cruzado**	**hubiesen cruzado**

imperativo	
—	**crucemos**
cruza; no cruces	**cruzad; no crucéis**
cruce	**crucen**

El que no se aventura no cruza el mar.   la cruzada   crusade, crossroads
  Nothing ventured, nothing gained.   la cruz de Malta   Maltese cross
el cruzamiento   crossing   la Cruz Roja Americana   the
la cruz   cross   American Red Cross

cubrir

Gerundio **cubriendo**   Part. pas. **cubierto**

to cover

Regular **-ir** verb endings; note irregular spelling of past participle: **cubierto**

The Seven Simple Tenses		The Seven Compound Tenses	
Singular	Plural	Singular	Plural
1 presente de indicativo		8 perfecto de indicativo	
cubro	**cubrimos**	**he cubierto**	**hemos cubierto**
cubres	**cubrís**	**has cubierto**	**habéis cubierto**
cubre	**cubren**	**ha cubierto**	**han cubierto**
2 imperfecto de indicativo		9 pluscuamperfecto de indicativo	
cubría	**cubríamos**	**había cubierto**	**habíamos cubierto**
cubrías	**cubríais**	**habías cubierto**	**habíais cubierto**
cubría	**cubrían**	**había cubierto**	**habían cubierto**
3 pretérito		10 pretérito anterior	
cubrí	**cubrimos**	**hube cubierto**	**hubimos cubierto**
cubriste	**cubristeis**	**hubiste cubierto**	**hubisteis cubierto**
cubrió	**cubrieron**	**hubo cubierto**	**hubieron cubierto**
4 futuro		11 futuro perfecto	
cubriré	**cubriremos**	**habré cubierto**	**habremos cubierto**
cubrirás	**cubriréis**	**habrás cubierto**	**habréis cubierto**
cubrirá	**cubrirán**	**habrá cubierto**	**habrán cubierto**
5 potencial simple		12 potencial compuesto	
cubriría	**cubriríamos**	**habría cubierto**	**habríamos cubierto**
cubrirías	**cubriríais**	**habrías cubierto**	**habríais cubierto**
cubriría	**cubrirían**	**habría cubierto**	**habrían cubierto**
6 presente de subjuntivo		13 perfecto de subjuntivo	
cubra	**cubramos**	**haya cubierto**	**hayamos cubierto**
cubras	**cubráis**	**hayas cubierto**	**hayáis cubierto**
cubra	**cubran**	**haya cubierto**	**hayan cubierto**
7 imperfecto de subjuntivo		14 pluscuamperfecto de subjuntivo	
cubriera	**cubriéramos**	**hubiera cubierto**	**hubiéramos cubierto**
cubrieras	**cubrierais**	**hubieras cubierto**	**hubierais cubierto**
cubriera	**cubrieran**	**hubiera cubierto**	**hubieran cubierto**
OR		OR	
cubriese	**cubriésemos**	**hubiese cubierto**	**hubiésemos cubierto**
cubrieses	**cubrieseis**	**hubieses cubierto**	**hubieseis cubierto**
cubriese	**cubriesen**	**hubiese cubierto**	**hubiesen cubierto**

imperativo	
—	**cubramos**
cubre; no cubras	**cubrid; no cubráis**
cubra	**cubran**

la cubierta cover, wrapping	cubrir los gastos to pay expenses
descubrir to discover	el cubrimiento covering
la cubierta del motor hood of an automobile	cubiertamente under cover
cubrir la mesa to lay the table	encubrir to hide, to conceal, to mask
	el encubrimiento hiding, concealment

Regular **-ar** verb   to take care of, to care for, to look after

The Seven Simple Tenses		The Seven Compound Tenses	
Singular	Plural	Singular	Plural
1 presente de indicativo		8 perfecto de indicativo	
cuido	cuidamos	he cuidado	hemos cuidado
cuidas	cuidáis	has cuidado	habéis cuidado
cuida	cuidan	ha cuidado	han cuidado
2 imperfecto de indicativo		9 pluscuamperfecto de indicativo	
cuidaba	cuidábamos	había cuidado	habíamos cuidado
cuidabas	cuidabais	habías cuidado	habíais cuidado
cuidaba	cuidaban	había cuidado	habían cuidado
3 pretérito		10 pretérito anterior	
cuidé	cuidamos	hube cuidado	hubimos cuidado
cuidaste	cuidasteis	hubiste cuidado	hubisteis cuidado
cuidó	cuidaron	hubo cuidado	hubieron cuidado
4 futuro		11 futuro perfecto	
cuidaré	cuidaremos	habré cuidado	habremos cuidado
cuidarás	cuidaréis	habrás cuidado	habréis cuidado
cuidará	cuidarán	habrá cuidado	habrán cuidado
5 potencial simple		12 potencial compuesto	
cuidaría	cuidaríamos	habría cuidado	habríamos cuidado
cuidarías	cuidaríais	habrías cuidado	habríais cuidado
cuidaría	cuidarían	habría cuidado	habrían cuidado
6 presente de subjuntivo		13 perfecto de subjuntivo	
cuide	cuidemos	haya cuidado	hayamos cuidado
cuides	cuidéis	hayas cuidado	hayáis cuidado
cuide	cuiden	haya cuidado	hayan cuidado
7 imperfecto de subjuntivo		14 pluscuamperfecto de subjuntivo	
cuidara	cuidáramos	hubiera cuidado	hubiéramos cuidado
cuidaras	cuidarais	hubieras cuidado	hubierais cuidado
cuidara	cuidaran	hubiera cuidado	hubieran cuidado
OR		OR	
cuidase	cuidásemos	hubiese cuidado	hubiésemos cuidado
cuidases	cuidaseis	hubieses cuidado	hubieseis cuidado
cuidase	cuidasen	hubiese cuidado	hubiesen cuidado

imperativo	
—	cuidemos
cuida; no cuides	cuidad; no cuidéis
cuide	cuiden

¡Cuidado! Careful!
Mi padre cuidó a mi madre mientras
  ella estaba enferma. My father took
  care of my mother while she was ill.
cuidar a un enfermo to care for
  someone who is ill
cuidar de to look after, to care for

el cuidado care, concern
con cuidado with care
tener cuidado to be careful
cuidadoso, cuidadosa careful
descuidar to neglect, to overlook
el descuido negligence, neglect
cuidarse to take care of oneself

105

cumplir

Gerundio **cumpliendo**   Part. pas. **cumplido**

to fulfill, to keep (a promise), to
reach one's birthday (use with **años**)

Regular **-ir** verb

The Seven Simple Tenses		The Seven Compound Tenses	
Singular	Plural	Singular	Plural
1 presente de indicativo		8 perfecto de indicativo	
cumplo	cumplimos	he cumplido	hemos cumplido
cumples	cumplís	has cumplido	habéis cumplido
cumple	cumplen	ha cumplido	han cumplido
2 imperfecto de indicativo		9 pluscuamperfecto de indicativo	
cumplía	cumplíamos	había cumplido	habíamos cumplido
cumplías	cumplíais	habías cumplido	habíais cumplido
cumplía	cumplían	había cumplido	habían cumplido
3 pretérito		10 pretérito anterior	
cumplí	cumplimos	hube cumplido	hubimos cumplido
cumpliste	cumplisteis	hubiste cumplido	hubisteis cumplido
cumplió	cumplieron	hubo cumplido	hubieron cumplido
4 futuro		11 futuro perfecto	
cumpliré	cumpliremos	habré cumplido	habremos cumplido
cumplirás	cumpliréis	habrás cumplido	habréis cumplido
cumplirá	cumplirán	habrá cumplido	habrán cumplido
5 potencial simple		12 potencial compuesto	
cumpliría	cumpliríamos	habría cumplido	habríamos cumplido
cumplirías	cumpliríais	habrías cumplido	habríais cumplido
cumpliría	cumplirían	habría cumplido	habrían cumplido
6 presente de subjuntivo		13 perfecto de subjuntivo	
cumpla	cumplamos	haya cumplido	hayamos cumplido
cumplas	cumpláis	hayas cumplido	hayáis cumplido
cumpla	cumplan	haya cumplido	hayan cumplido
7 imperfecto de subjuntivo		14 pluscuamperfecto de subjuntivo	
cumpliera	cumpliéramos	hubiera cumplido	hubiéramos cumplido
cumplieras	cumplierais	hubieras cumplido	hubierais cumplido
cumpliera	cumplieran	hubiera cumplido	hubieran cumplido
OR		OR	
cumpliese	cumpliésemos	hubiese cumplido	hubiésemos cumplido
cumplieses	cumplieseis	hubieses cumplido	hubieseis cumplido
cumpliese	cumpliesen	hubiese cumplido	hubiesen cumplido

	imperativo	
—		cumplamos
cumple; no cumplas		cumplid; no cumpláis
cumpla		cumplan

---

el cumpleaños   birthday
cumplir . . . años   to reach the age
 of . . .
cumplidamente   completely
Hoy cumplo diez y siete años   Today
 I am seventeen years old.

el cumplimiento   completion
cumplir con   to fulfill
¡Feliz cumpleaños!   Happy birthday!

Irregular verb   to give

The Seven Simple Tenses		The Seven Compound Tenses	
Singular	Plural	Singular	Plural
1 presente de indicativo		8 perfecto de indicativo	
doy	damos	he dado	hemos dado
das	dais	has dado	habéis dado
da	dan	ha dado	han dado
2 imperfecto de indicativo		9 pluscuamperfecto de indicativo	
daba	dábamos	había dado	habíamos dado
dabas	dabais	habías dado	habíais dado
daba	daban	había dado	habían dado
3 pretérito		10 pretérito anterior	
di	dimos	hube dado	hubimos dado
diste	disteis	hubiste dado	hubisteis dado
dio	dieron	hubo dado	hubieron dado
4 futuro		11 futuro perfecto	
daré	daremos	habré dado	habremos dado
darás	daréis	habrás dado	habréis dado
dará	darán	habrá dado	habrán dado
5 potencial simple		12 potencial compuesto	
daría	daríamos	habría dado	habríamos dado
darías	daríais	habrías dado	habríais dado
daría	darían	habría dado	habrían dado
6 presente de subjuntivo		13 perfecto de subjuntivo	
dé	demos	haya dado	hayamos dado
des	deis	hayas dado	hayáis dado
dé	den	haya dado	hayan dado
7 imperfecto de subjuntivo		14 pluscuamperfecto de subjuntivo	
diera	diéramos	hubiera dado	hubiéramos dado
dieras	dierais	hubieras dado	hubierais dado
diera	dieran	hubiera dado	hubieran dado
OR		OR	
diese	diésemos	hubiese dado	hubiésemos dado
dieses	dieseis	hubieses dado	hubieseis dado
diese	diesen	hubiese dado	hubiesen dado

	imperativo	
—	demos	
da; no des	dad; no deis	
dé	den	

A Dios rogando y con el mazo dando.
  Put your faith in God and keep your
  powder dry.
El tiempo da buen consejo.   Time will
  tell.
dar la mano (las manos) a alguien   to
  shake hands with someone

dar de comer   to feed
darse   to give oneself up, to give in
El comedor da al jardín.   The dining
  room faces the garden.
dar a   to face, to look out on(to)

deber

Gerundio **debiendo**   Part. pas. **debido**

to owe, must, ought   Regular **-er** verb

The Seven Simple Tenses		The Seven Compound Tenses	
Singular	Plural	Singular	Plural
1 presente de indicativo		**8 perfecto de indicativo**	
debo	**debemos**	**he debido**	**hemos debido**
debes	**debéis**	**has debido**	**habéis debido**
debe	**deben**	**ha debido**	**han debido**
2 imperfecto de indicativo		**9 pluscuamperfecto de indicativo**	
debía	**debíamos**	**había debido**	**habíamos debido**
debías	**debíais**	**habías debido**	**habíais debido**
debía	**debían**	**había debido**	**habían debido**
3 pretérito		**10 pretérito anterior**	
debí	**debimos**	**hube debido**	**hubimos debido**
debiste	**debisteis**	**hubiste debido**	**hubisteis debido**
debió	**debieron**	**hubo debido**	**hubieron debido**
4 futuro		**11 futuro perfecto**	
deberé	**deberemos**	**habré debido**	**habremos debido**
deberás	**deberéis**	**habrás debido**	**habréis debido**
deberá	**deberán**	**habrá debido**	**habrán debido**
5 potencial simple		**12 potencial compuesto**	
debería	**deberíamos**	**habría debido**	**habríamos debido**
deberías	**deberíais**	**habrías debido**	**habríais debido**
debería	**deberían**	**habría debido**	**habrían debido**
6 presente de subjuntivo		**13 perfecto de subjuntivo**	
deba	**debamos**	**haya debido**	**hayamos debido**
debas	**debáis**	**hayas debido**	**hayáis debido**
deba	**deban**	**haya debido**	**hayan debido**
7 imperfecto de subjuntivo		**14 pluscuamperfecto de subjuntivo**	
debiera	**debiéramos**	**hubiera debido**	**hubiéramos debido**
debieras	**debierais**	**hubieras debido**	**hubierais debido**
debiera	**debieran**	**hubiera debido**	**hubieran debido**
OR		OR	
debiese	**debiésemos**	**hubiese debido**	**hubiésemos debido**
debieses	**debieseis**	**hubieses debido**	**hubieseis debido**
debiese	**debiesen**	**hubiese debido**	**hubiesen debido**

imperativo	
—	**debamos**
debe; no debas	**debed; no debáis**
deba	**deban**

¿Cuánto le debo?   How much do I
  owe you?
¿En qué estación debo bajar?   At
  what station do I need to get off?
el deber   duty, obligation
estar en deuda con   to be indebted to

debiente   debtor
José debe de haber llegado.   Joseph
  must have arrived.
la deuda   debt;
debido a   due to

108

The Seven Simple Tenses		The Seven Compound Tenses	
Singular	Plural	Singular	Plural
1 presente de indicativo		8 perfecto de indicativo	
decido	**decidimos**	**he decidido**	**hemos decidido**
decides	**decidís**	**has decidido**	**habéis decidido**
decide	**deciden**	**ha decidido**	**han decidido**
2 imperfecto de indicativo		9 pluscuamperfecto de indicativo	
decidía	**decidíamos**	**había decidido**	**habíamos decidido**
decidías	**decidíais**	**habías decidido**	**habíais decidido**
decidía	**decidían**	**había decidido**	**habían decidido**
3 pretérito		10 pretérito anterior	
decidí	**decidimos**	**hube decidido**	**hubimos decidido**
decidiste	**decidisteis**	**hubiste decidido**	**hubisteis decidido**
decidió	**decidieron**	**hubo decidido**	**hubieron decidido**
4 futuro		11 futuro perfecto	
decidiré	**decidiremos**	**habré decidido**	**habremos decidido**
decidirás	**decidiréis**	**habrás decidido**	**habréis decidido**
decidirá	**decidirán**	**habrá decidido**	**habrán decidido**
5 potencial simple		12 potencial compuesto	
decidiría	**decidiríamos**	**habría decidido**	**habríamos decidido**
decidirías	**decidiríais**	**habrías decidido**	**habríais decidido**
decidiría	**decidirían**	**habría decidido**	**habrían decidido**
6 presente de subjuntivo		13 perfecto de subjuntivo	
decida	**decidamos**	**haya decidido**	**hayamos decidido**
decidas	**decidáis**	**hayas decidido**	**hayáis decidido**
decida	**decidan**	**haya decidido**	**hayan decidido**
7 imperfecto de subjuntivo		14 pluscuamperfecto de subjuntivo	
decidiera	**decidiéramos**	**hubiera decidido**	**hubiéramos decidido**
decidieras	**decidierais**	**hubieras decidido**	**hubierais decidido**
decidiera	**decidieran**	**hubiera decidido**	**hubieran decidido**
OR		OR	
decidiese	**decidiésemos**	**hubiese decidido**	**hubiésemos decidido**
decidieses	**decidieseis**	**hubieses decidido**	**hubieseis decidido**
decidiese	**decidiesen**	**hubiese decidido**	**hubiesen decidido**

imperativo	
—	**decidamos**
decide; no decidas	**decidid; no decidáis**
decida	**decidan**

la decisión decision	**estar decidido (decidida)** to make up
decidirse to make up one's mind, to be	one's mind
determined	**decisivo, decisiva** decisive
decidamente decidedly	**decidir a + inf.** to persuade + inf.; to
decisivamente decisively	decide + inf.

decir

Gerundio **diciendo**   Part. pas. **dicho**

to say, to tell

Irregular verb

The Seven Simple Tenses		The Seven Compound Tenses	
Singular	Plural	Singular	Plural
1 presente de indicativo		8 perfecto de indicativo	
digo	**decimos**	**he dicho**	**hemos dicho**
dices	**decís**	**has dicho**	**habéis dicho**
dice	**dicen**	**ha dicho**	**han dicho**
2 imperfecto de indicativo		9 pluscuamperfecto de indicativo	
decía	**decíamos**	**había dicho**	**habíamos dicho**
decías	**decíais**	**habías dicho**	**habíais dicho**
decía	**decían**	**había dicho**	**habían dicho**
3 pretérito		10 pretérito anterior	
dije	**dijimos**	**hube dicho**	**hubimos dicho**
dijiste	**dijisteis**	**hubiste dicho**	**hubisteis dicho**
dijo	**dijeron**	**hubo dicho**	**hubieron dicho**
4 futuro		11 futuro perfecto	
diré	**diremos**	**habré dicho**	**habremos dicho**
dirás	**diréis**	**habrás dicho**	**habréis dicho**
dirá	**dirán**	**habrá dicho**	**habrán dicho**
5 potencial simple		12 potencial compuesto	
diría	**diríamos**	**habría dicho**	**habríamos dicho**
dirías	**diríais**	**habrías dicho**	**habríais dicho**
diría	**dirían**	**habría dicho**	**habrían dicho**
6 presente de subjuntivo		13 perfecto de subjuntivo	
diga	**digamos**	**haya dicho**	**hayamos dicho**
digas	**digáis**	**hayas dicho**	**hayáis dicho**
diga	**digan**	**haya dicho**	**hayan dicho**
7 imperfecto de subjuntivo		14 pluscuamperfecto de subjuntivo	
dijera	**dijéramos**	**hubiera dicho**	**hubiéramos dicho**
dijeras	**dijerais**	**hubieras dicho**	**hubierais dicho**
dijera	**dijeran**	**hubiera dicho**	**hubieran dicho**
OR		OR	
dijese	**dijésemos**	**hubiese dicho**	**hubiésemos dicho**
dijeses	**dijeseis**	**hubieses dicho**	**hubieseis dicho**
dijese	**dijesen**	**hubiese dicho**	**hubiesen dicho**

imperativo	
—	**digamos**
di; no digas	**decid; no digáis**
diga	**digan**

Dígame, por favor, ¿dónde está la sala de espera?   Tell me, please, where is the waiting room located?

Dicho y hecho.   No sooner said than done.

Dime con quien andas y te diré quien eres.   Tell me who your friends are and I will tell you who you are.

querer decir   to mean
un decir   a familiar saying
un dicho   a saying, expression
decir adiós   to say good-bye

110

Regular **-er** verb endings with stem
change: Tenses 1, 6, Imperative

to forbid, to defend, to prohibit

The Seven Simple Tenses		The Seven Compound Tenses	
Singular	Plural	Singular	Plural
1 presente de indicativo		8 perfecto de indicativo	
defiendo	**defendemos**	**he defendido**	**hemos defendido**
defiendes	**defendéis**	**has defendido**	**habéis defendido**
defiende	**defienden**	**ha defendido**	**han defendido**
2 imperfecto de indicativo		9 pluscuamperfecto de indicativo	
defendía	**defendíamos**	**había defendido**	**habíamos defendido**
defendías	**defendíais**	**habías defendido**	**habíais defendido**
defendía	**defendían**	**había defendido**	**habían defendido**
3 pretérito		10 pretérito anterior	
defendí	**defendimos**	**hube defendido**	**hubimos defendido**
defendiste	**defendisteis**	**hubiste defendido**	**hubisteis defendido**
defendió	**defendieron**	**hubo defendido**	**hubieron defendido**
4 futuro		11 futuro perfecto	
defenderé	**defenderemos**	**habré defendido**	**habremos defendido**
defenderás	**defenderéis**	**habrás defendido**	**habréis defendido**
defenderá	**defenderán**	**habrá defendido**	**habrán defendido**
5 potencial simple		12 potencial compuesto	
defendería	**defenderíamos**	**habría defendido**	**habríamos defendido**
defenderías	**defenderíais**	**habrías defendido**	**habríais defendido**
defendería	**defenderían**	**habría defendido**	**habrían defendido**
6 presente de subjuntivo		13 perfecto de subjuntivo	
defienda	**defendamos**	**haya defendido**	**hayamos defendido**
defiendas	**defendáis**	**hayas defendido**	**hayáis defendido**
defienda	**defiendan**	**haya defendido**	**hayan defendido**
7 imperfecto de subjuntivo		14 pluscuamperfecto de subjuntivo	
defendiera	**defendiéramos**	**hubiera defendido**	**hubiéramos defendido**
defendieras	**defendierais**	**hubieras defendido**	**hubierais defendido**
defendiera	**defendieran**	**hubiera defendido**	**hubieran defendido**
OR		OR	
defendiese	**defendiésemos**	**hubiese defendido**	**hubiésemos defendido**
defendieses	**defendieseis**	**hubieses defendido**	**hubieseis defendido**
defendiese	**defendiesen**	**hubiese defendido**	**hubiesen defendido**

	imperativo	
—	**defendamos**
defiende; no defiendas	**defended; no defendáis**
defienda	**defiendan**

defendible defensible	defensor, defensora defender,
el defensorio defense, plea	supporter, protector
la defensa defense	estar a la defensiva to be on the
defensivo, defensiva defensive	defensive

dejar

Gerundio **dejando**   Part. pas. **dejado**

to let, to permit,
to allow, to leave

Regular **-ar** verb

The Seven Simple Tenses		The Seven Compound Tenses	
Singular	Plural	Singular	Plural
1 presente de indicativo		8 perfecto de indicativo	
dejo	dejamos	he dejado	hemos dejado
dejas	dejáis	has dejado	habéis dejado
deja	dejan	ha dejado	han dejado
2 imperfecto de indicativo		9 pluscuamperfecto de indicativo	
dejaba	dejábamos	había dejado	habíamos dejado
dejabas	dejabais	habías dejado	habíais dejado
dejaba	dejaban	había dejado	habían dejado
3 pretérito		10 pretérito anterior	
dejé	dejamos	hube dejado	hubimos dejado
dejaste	dejasteis	hubiste dejado	hubisteis dejado
dejó	dejaron	hubo dejado	hubieron dejado
4 futuro		11 futuro perfecto	
dejaré	dejaremos	habré dejado	habremos dejado
dejarás	dejaréis	habrás dejado	habréis dejado
dejará	dejarán	habrá dejado	habrán dejado
5 potencial simple		12 potencial compuesto	
dejaría	dejaríamos	habría dejado	habríamos dejado
dejarías	dejaríais	habrías dejado	habríais dejado
dejaría	dejarían	habría dejado	habrían dejado
6 presente de subjuntivo		13 perfecto de subjuntivo	
deje	dejemos	haya dejado	hayamos dejado
dejes	dejéis	hayas dejado	hayáis dejado
deje	dejen	haya dejado	hayan dejado
7 imperfecto de subjuntivo		14 pluscuamperfecto de subjuntivo	
dejara	dejáramos	hubiera dejado	hubiéramos dejado
dejaras	dejarais	hubieras dejado	hubierais dejado
dejara	dejaran	hubiera dejado	hubieran dejado
OR		OR	
dejase	dejásemos	hubiese dejado	hubiésemos dejado
dejases	dejaseis	hubieses dejado	hubieseis dejado
dejase	dejasen	hubiese dejado	hubiesen dejado

	imperativo
—	dejemos
deja; no dejes	dejad; no dejéis
deje	dejen

El alumno dejó sus libros en la sala de
  clase.   The pupil left his books in the
  classroom.
dejar caer   to drop (to let fall)
dejarse   to abandon (neglect) oneself

el dejo   abandonment
dejar atrás   to leave behind
dejado, dejada   dejected
dejar de + inf.   to stop + pres. part.

delinquir

Regular **-ir** verb endings with spelling
change: **qu** becomes **c** before **a** or **o**

to break the law,
to be guilty, to commit an offense

The Seven Simple Tenses		The Seven Compound Tenses	
Singular	Plural	Singular	Plural
1 presente de indicativo		8 perfecto de indicativo	
delinco	delinquimos	he delinquido	hemos delinquido
delinques	delinquís	has delinquido	habéis delinquido
delinque	delinquen	ha delinquido	han delinquido
2 imperfecto de indicativo		9 pluscuamperfecto de indicativo	
delinquía	delinquíamos	había delinquido	habíamos delinquido
delinquías	delinquíais	habías delinquido	habíais delinquido
delinquía	delinquían	había delinquido	habían delinquido
3 pretérito		10 pretérito anterior	
delinquí	delinquimos	hube delinquido	hubimos delinquido
delinquiste	delinquisteis	hubiste delinquido	hubisteis delinquido
delinquió	delinquieron	hubo delinquido	hubieron delinquido
4 futuro		11 futuro perfecto	
delinquiré	delinquiremos	habré delinquido	habremos delinquido
delinquirás	delinquiréis	habrás delinquido	habréis delinquido
delinquirá	delinquirán	habrá delinquido	habrán delinquido
5 potencial simple		12 potencial compuesto	
delinquiría	delinquiríamos	habría delinquido	habríamos delinquido
delinquirías	delinquiríais	habrías delinquido	habríais delinquido
delinquiría	delinquirían	habría delinquido	habrían delinquido
6 presente de subjuntivo		13 perfecto de subjuntivo	
delinca	delincamos	haya delinquido	hayamos delinquido
delincas	delincáis	hayas delinquido	hayáis delinquido
delinca	delincan	haya delinquido	hayan delinquido
7 imperfecto de subjuntivo		14 pluscuamperfecto de subjuntivo	
delinquiera	delinquiéramos	hubiera delinquido	hubiéramos delinquido
delinquieras	delinquierais	hubieras delinquido	hubierais delinquido
delinquiera	delinquieran	hubiera delinquido	hubieran delinquido
OR		OR	
delinquiese	delinquiésemos	hubiese delinquido	hubiésemos delinquido
delinquieses	delinquieseis	hubieses delinquido	hubieseis delinquido
delinquiese	delinquiesen	hubiese delinquido	hubiesen delinquido

imperativo	
—	delincamos
delinque; no delincas	delinquid; no delincáis
delinca	delincan

el delinquimiento, la delincuencia delinquency	un delincuente habitual an habitual offender
delincuente delinquent	

demostrar

Gerundio **demostrando**   Part. pas. **demostrado**

to demonstrate, to prove

Regular **-ar** verb endings with stem change: Tenses 1, 6, Imperative

The Seven Simple Tenses		The Seven Compound Tenses	
Singular	Plural	Singular	Plural
1 presente de indicativo		8 perfecto de indicativo	
demuestro	demostramos	he demostrado	hemos demostrado
demuestras	demostráis	has demostrado	habéis demostrado
demuestra	demuestran	ha demostrado	han demostrado
2 imperfecto de indicativo		9 pluscuamperfecto de indicativo	
demostraba	demostrábamos	había demostrado	habíamos demostrado
demostrabas	demostrabais	habías demostrado	habíais demostrado
demostraba	demostraban	había demostrado	habían demostrado
3 pretérito		10 pretérito anterior	
demostré	demostramos	hube demostrado	hubimos demostrado
demostraste	demostrasteis	hubiste demostrado	hubisteis demostrado
demostró	demostraron	hubo demostrado	hubieron demostrado
4 futuro		11 futuro perfecto	
demostraré	demostraremos	habré demostrado	habremos demostrado
demostrarás	demostraréis	habrás demostrado	habréis demostrado
demostrará	demostrarán	habrá demostrado	habrán demostrado
5 potencial simple		12 potencial compuesto	
demostraría	demostraríamos	habría demostrado	habríamos demostrado
demostrarías	demostraríais	habrías demostrado	habríais demostrado
demostraría	demostrarían	habría demostrado	habrían demostrado
6 presente de subjuntivo		13 perfecto de subjuntivo	
demuestre	demostremos	haya demostrado	hayamos demostrado
demuestres	demostréis	hayas demostrado	hayáis demostrado
demuestre	demuestren	haya demostrado	hayan demostrado
7 imperfecto de subjuntivo		14 pluscuamperfecto de subjuntivo	
demostrara	demostráramos	hubiera demostrado	hubiéramos demostrado
demostraras	demostrarais	hubieras demostrado	hubierais demostrado
demostrara	demostraran	hubiera demostrado	hubieran demostrado
OR		OR	
demostrase	demostrásemos	hubiese demostrado	hubiésemos demostrado
demostrases	demostraseis	hubieses demostrado	hubieseis demostrado
demostrase	demostrasen	hubiese demostrado	hubiesen demostrado

imperativo	
—	demostremos
demuestra; no demuestres	demostrad; no demostréis
demuestre	demuestren

demostrativo, demostrativa
  demonstrative
demostrable demonstrable
la demostración demonstration, proof
mostrar to show, to exhibit

demostrador, demostradora
  demonstrator
la demostración de cariño show of
  affection

Reflexive regular **-ar** verb   to breakfast, to have breakfast

The Seven Simple Tenses		The Seven Compound Tenses	
Singular	Plural	Singular	Plural

1   presente de indicativo

me desayuno	nos desayunamos
te desayunas	os desayunáis
se desayuna	se desayunan

8   perfecto de indicativo

me he	nos hemos	
te has	os habéis	+ desayunado
se ha	se han	

2   imperfecto de indicativo

me desayunaba	nos desayunábamos
te desayunabas	os desayunabais
se desayunaba	se desayunaban

9   pluscuamperfecto de indicativo

me había	nos habíamos	
te habías	os habíais	+ desayunado
se había	se habían	

3   pretérito

me desayuné	nos desayunamos
te desayunaste	os desayunasteis
se desayunó	se desayunaron

10   pretérito anterior

me hube	nos hubimos	
te hubiste	os hubisteis	+ desayunado
se hubo	se hubieron	

4   futuro

me desayunaré	nos desayunaremos
te desayunarás	os desayunaréis
se desayunará	se desayunarán

11   futuro perfecto

me habré	nos habremos	
te habrás	os habréis	+ desayunado
se habrá	se habrán	

5   potencial simple

me desayunaría	nos desayunaríamos
te desayunarías	os desayunaríais
se desayunaría	se desayunarían

12   potencial compuesto

me habría	nos habríamos	
te habrías	os habríais	+ desayunado
se habría	se habrían	

6   presente de subjuntivo

me desayune	nos desayunemos
te desayunes	os desayunéis
se desayune	se desayunen

13   perfecto de subjuntivo

me haya	nos hayamos	
te hayas	os hayáis	+ desayunado
se haya	se hayan	

7   imperfecto de subjuntivo

me desayunara	nos desayunáramos
te desayunaras	os desayunarais
se desayunara	se desayunaran
OR	
me desayunase	nos desayunásemos
te desayunases	os desayunaseis
se desayunase	se desayunasen

14   pluscuamperfecto de subjuntivo

me hubiera	nos hubiéramos	
te hubieras	os hubierais	+ desayunado
se hubiera	se hubieran	
OR		
me hubiese	nos hubiésemos	
te hubieses	os hubieseis	+ desayunado
se hubiese	se hubiesen	

imperativo

—	desayunémonos
desayúnate; no te desayunes	desayunaos; no os desayunéis
desayúnese	desayúnense

—¿Qué toma Ud. en el desayuno
 todas la mañanas?   What do
 you have for breakfast every
 morning?

desayunar   to breakfast
ayunar   to fast (not to eat)

—Tomo jugo de naranja, café con
 leche, pan tostado y un huevo.   I
 have orange juice, coffee with milk,
 toast and an egg.

el desayuno   breakfast
el ayuno   fast, fasting

descansar

Gerundio **descansando** Part. pas. **descansado**

to rest

Regular **-ar** verb

The Seven Simple Tenses		The Seven Compound Tenses	
Singular	Plural	Singular	Plural
1 presente de indicativo		**8 perfecto de indicativo**	
descanso	descansamos	he descansado	hemos descansado
descansas	descansáis	has descansado	habéis descansado
descansa	descansan	ha descansado	han descansado
2 imperfecto de indicativo		**9 pluscuamperfecto de indicativo**	
descansaba	descansábamos	había descansado	habíamos descansado
descansabas	descansabais	habías descansado	habíais descansado
descansaba	descansaban	había descansado	habían descansado
3 pretérito		**10 pretérito anterior**	
descansé	descansamos	hube descansado	hubimos descansado
descansaste	descansasteis	hubiste descansado	hubisteis descansado
descansó	descansaron	hubo descansado	hubieron descansado
4 futuro		**11 futuro perfecto**	
descansaré	descansaremos	habré descansado	habremos descansado
descansarás	descansaréis	habrás descansado	habréis descansado
descansará	descansarán	habrá descansado	habrán descansado
5 potencial simple		**12 potencial compuesto**	
descansaría	descansaríamos	habría descansado	habríamos descansado
descansarías	descansaríais	habrías descansado	habríais descansado
descansaría	descansarían	habría descansado	habrían descansado
6 presente de subjuntivo		**13 perfecto de subjuntivo**	
descanse	descansemos	haya descansado	hayamos descansado
descanses	descanséis	hayas descansado	hayáis descansado
descanse	descansen	haya descansado	hayan descansado
7 imperfecto de subjuntivo		**14 pluscuamperfecto de subjuntivo**	
descansara	descansáramos	hubiera descansado	hubiéramos descansado
descansaras	descansarais	hubieras descansado	hubierais descansado
descansara	descansaran	hubiera descansado	hubieran descansado
OR		OR	
descansase	descansásemos	hubiese descansado	hubiésemos descansado
descansases	descansaseis	hubieses descansado	hubieseis descansado
descansase	descansasen	hubiese descansado	hubiesen descansado

imperativo	
—	descansemos
descansa; no descanses	descansad; no descanséis
descanse	descansen

el descanso rest, relief	cansar de esperar to be tired of
el descansillo landing on a staircase	waiting
el descansadero resting place	cansar to fatigue, to tire, to weary
el descanso a discreción at ease	el descanso por enfermedad sick
(military)	leave
la cansera fatigue	

Regular **-ir** verb endings, note irregular
spelling of past participle: **descrito**

to describe,
to sketch, to delineate

The Seven Simple Tenses		The Seven Compound Tenses	
Singular	Plural	Singular	Plural
1 presente de indicativo		8 perfecto de indicativo	
describo	**describimos**	**he descrito**	**hemos descrito**
describes	**describís**	**has descrito**	**habéis descrito**
describe	**describen**	**ha descrito**	**han descrito**
2 imperfecto de indicativo		9 pluscuamperfecto de indicativo	
describía	**describíamos**	**había descrito**	**habíamos descrito**
describías	**describíais**	**habías descrito**	**habíais descrito**
describía	**describían**	**había descrito**	**habían descrito**
3 pretérito		10 pretérito anterior	
describí	**describimos**	**hube descrito**	**hubimos descrito**
describiste	**describisteis**	**hubiste descrito**	**hubisteis descrito**
describió	**describieron**	**hubo descrito**	**hubieron descrito**
4 futuro		11 futuro perfecto	
describiré	**describiremos**	**habré descrito**	**habremos descrito**
describirás	**describiréis**	**habrás descrito**	**habréis descrito**
describirá	**describirán**	**habrá descrito**	**habrán descrito**
5 potencial simple		12 potencial compuesto	
describiría	**describiríamos**	**habría descrito**	**habríamos descrito**
describirías	**describiríais**	**habrías descrito**	**habríais descrito**
describiría	**describirían**	**habría descrito**	**habrían descrito**
6 presente de subjuntivo		13 perfecto de subjuntivo	
describa	**describamos**	**haya descrito**	**hayamos descrito**
describas	**describáis**	**hayas descrito**	**hayáis descrito**
describa	**describan**	**haya descrito**	**hayan descrito**
7 imperfecto de subjuntivo		14 pluscuamperfecto de subjuntivo	
describiera	**describiéramos**	**hubiera descrito**	**hubiéramos descrito**
describieras	**describierais**	**hubieras descrito**	**hubierais descrito**
describiera	**describieran**	**hubiera descrito**	**hubieran descrito**
OR		OR	
describiese	**describiésemos**	**hubiese descrito**	**hubiésemos descrito**
describieses	**describieseis**	**hubieses descrito**	**hubieseis descrito**
describiese	**describiesen**	**hubiese descrito**	**hubiesen descrito**

imperativo

—	**describamos**
describe; no describas	**describid; no describáis**
describa	**describan**

la descripción description	descriptivo, descriptiva descriptive
escribir to write	escribir a máquina to typewrite
descriptor, descriptora describer	descripto, descripta described *(adj.)*
escribir a mano to write by hand	See also escribir.

descubrir

Gerundio **descubriendo**   Part. pas. **descubierto**

to discover

Regular **-ir** verb endings; note irregular
spelling of past participle: **descubierto**

The Seven Simple Tenses		The Seven Compound Tenses	
Singular	Plural	Singular	Plural
1 presente de indicativo		8 perfecto de indicativo	
descubro	descubrimos	he descubierto	hemos descubierto
descubres	descubrís	has descubierto	habéis descubierto
descubre	descubren	ha descubierto	han descubierto
2 imperfecto de indicativo		9 pluscuamperfecto de indicativo	
descubría	descubríamos	había descubierto	habíamos descubierto
descubrías	descubríais	habías descubierto	habíais descubierto
descubría	descubrían	había descubierto	habían descubierto
3 pretérito		10 pretérito anterior	
descubrí	descubrimos	hube descubierto	hubimos descubierto
descubriste	descubristeis	hubiste descubierto	hubisteis descubierto
descubrió	descubrieron	hubo descubierto	hubieron descubierto
4 futuro		11 futuro perfecto	
descubriré	descubriremos	habré descubierto	habremos descubierto
descubrirás	descubriréis	habrás descubierto	habréis descubierto
descubrirá	descubrirán	habrá descubierto	habrán descubierto
5 potencial simple		12 potencial compuesto	
descubriría	descubriríamos	habría descubierto	habríamos descubierto
descubrirías	descubriríais	habrías descubierto	habríais descubierto
descubriría	descubrirían	habría descubierto	habrían descubierto
6 presente de subjuntivo		13 perfecto de subjuntivo	
descubra	descubramos	haya descubierto	hayamos descubierto
descubras	descubráis	hayas descubierto	hayáis descubierto
descubra	descubran	haya descubierto	hayan descubierto
7 imperfecto de subjuntivo		14 pluscuamperfecto de subjuntivo	
descubriera	descubriéramos	hubiera descubierto	hubiéramos descubierto
descubrieras	descubrierais	hubieras descubierto	hubierais descubierto
descubriera	descubrieran	hubiera descubierto	hubieran descubierto
OR		OR	
descubriese	descubriésemos	hubiese descubierto	hubiésemos descubierto
descubrieses	descubrieseis	hubieses descubierto	hubieseis descubierto
descubriese	descubriesen	hubiese descubierto	hubiesen descubierto

imperativo	
—	descubramos
descubre; no descubras	descubrid; no descubráis
descubra	descubran

descubrirse to take off one's hat	descubridor, descubridora discoverer
cubrir to cover	cubrir la mesa to cover the table
el descubrimiento discovery	a la descubierta clearly, openly
cubrir el costo to cover the cost	

Regular **-ar** verb   to desire, to wish, to want

The Seven Simple Tenses		The Seven Compound Tenses	
Singular	Plural	Singular	Plural
1 presente de indicativo		8 perfecto de indicativo	
deseo	deseamos	he deseado	hemos deseado
deseas	deseáis	has deseado	habéis deseado
desea	desean	ha deseado	han deseado
2 imperfecto de indicativo		9 pluscuamperfecto de indicativo	
deseaba	deseábamos	había deseado	habíamos deseado
deseabas	deseabais	habías deseado	habíais deseado
deseaba	deseaban	había deseado	habían deseado
3 pretérito		10 pretérito anterior	
deseé	deseamos	hube deseado	hubimos deseado
deseaste	deseasteis	hubiste deseado	hubisteis deseado
deseó	desearon	hubo deseado	hubieron deseado
4 futuro		11 futuro perfecto	
desearé	desearemos	habré deseado	habremos deseado
desearás	desearéis	habrás deseado	habréis deseado
deseará	desearán	habrá deseado	habrán deseado
5 potencial simple		12 potencial compuesto	
desearía	desearíamos	habría deseado	habríamos deseado
desearías	desearíais	habrías deseado	habríais deseado
desearía	desearían	habría deseado	habrían deseado
6 presente de subjuntivo		13 perfecto de subjuntivo	
desee	deseemos	haya deseado	hayamos deseado
desees	deseéis	hayas deseado	hayáis deseado
desee	deseen	haya deseado	hayan deseado
7 imperfecto de subjuntivo		14 pluscuamperfecto de subjuntivo	
deseara	deseáramos	hubiera deseado	hubiéramos deseado
desearas	desearais	hubieras deseado	hubierais deseado
deseara	desearan	hubiera deseado	hubieran deseado
OR		OR	
desease	deseásemos	hubiese deseado	hubiésemos deseado
deseases	deseaseis	hubieses deseado	hubieseis deseado
desease	deseasen	hubiese deseado	hubiesen deseado

imperativo	
—	deseemos
desea; no desees	desead; no deseéis
desee	deseen

el deseo desire	**deseablemente** desirably
el deseador, la deseadora desirer, wisher	**deseable** desirable
deseoso, deseosa desirous	**dejar mucho que desear** to leave much to be desired
tener deseo de + inf. to be eager + inf.	

despedir

Gerundio **despidiendo**   Part. pas. **despedido**

to dismiss

Regular **-ir** verb endings with stem change:
Tenses 1, 3, 6, 7, Imperative, *Gerundio*

The Seven Simple Tenses		The Seven Compound Tenses	
Singular	Plural	Singular	Plural
1 presente de indicativo		**8 perfecto de indicativo**	
despido	despedimos	he despedido	hemos despedido
despides	despedís	has despedido	habéis despedido
despide	despiden	ha despedido	han despedido
2 imperfecto de indicativo		**9 pluscuamperfecto de indicativo**	
despedía	despedíamos	había despedido	habíamos despedido
despedías	despedíais	habías despedido	habíais despedido
despedía	despedían	había despedido	habían despedido
3 pretérito		**10 pretérito anterior**	
despedí	despedimos	hube despedido	hubimos despedido
despediste	despedisteis	hubiste despedido	hubisteis despedido
despidió	despidieron	hubo despedido	hubieron despedido
4 futuro		**11 futuro perfecto**	
despediré	despediremos	habré despedido	habremos despedido
despedirás	despediréis	habrás despedido	habréis despedido
despedirá	despedirán	habrá despedido	habrán despedido
5 potencial simple		**12 potencial compuesto**	
despediría	despediríamos	habría despedido	habríamos despedido
despedirías	despediríais	habrías despedido	habríais despedido
despediría	despedirían	habría despedido	habrían despedido
6 presente de subjuntivo		**13 perfecto de subjuntivo**	
despida	despidamos	haya despedido	hayamos despedido
despidas	despidáis	hayas despedido	hayáis despedido
despida	despidan	haya despedido	hayan despedido
7 imperfecto de subjuntivo		**14 pluscuamperfecto de subjuntivo**	
despidiera	despidiéramos	hubiera despedido	hubiéramos despedido
despidieras	despidierais	hubieras despedido	hubierais despedido
despidiera	despidieran	hubiera despedido	hubieran despedido
OR		OR	
despidiese	despidiésemos	hubiese despedido	hubiésemos despedido
despidieses	despidieseis	hubieses despedido	hubieseis despedido
despidiese	despidiesen	hubiese despedido	hubiesen despedido

imperativo	
—	despidamos
despide; no despidas	despedid; no despidáis
despida	despidan

---

un despedimiento, una despedida
 dismissal, discharge, farewell
despedirse to take leave of, to say
 good-bye to

despedirse a la francesa to take
 French leave

120

despedirse

Reflexive verb; regular **-ir** verb endings with stem
change: Tenses 1, 3, 6, 7, Imperative, *Gerundio*

to take leave of,
to say good-bye to

The Seven Simple Tenses		The Seven Compound Tenses	
Singular	Plural	Singular	Plural
1 presente de indicativo		**8 perfecto de indicativo**	
me despido	nos despedimos	me he	nos hemos
te despides	os despedís	te has	os habéis + despedido
se despide	se despiden	se ha	se han
2 imperfecto de indicativo		**9 pluscuamperfecto de indicativo**	
me despedía	nos despedíamos	me había	nos habíamos
te despedías	os despedíais	te habías	os habíais + despedido
se despedía	se despedían	se había	se habían
3 pretérito		**10 pretérito anterior**	
me despedí	nos despedimos	me hube	nos hubimos
te despediste	os despedisteis	te hubiste	os hubisteis + despedido
se despidió	se despidieron	se hubo	se hubieron
4 futuro		**11 futuro perfecto**	
me despediré	nos despediremos	me habré	nos habremos
te despedirás	os despediréis	te habrás	os habréis + despedido
se despedirá	se despedirán	se habrá	se habrán
5 potencial simple		**12 potencial compuesto**	
me despediría	nos despediríamos	me habría	nos habríamos
te despedirías	os despediríais	te habrías	os habríais + despedido
se despediría	se despedirían	se habría	se habrían
6 presente de subjuntivo		**13 perfecto de subjuntivo**	
me despida	nos despidamos	me haya	nos hayamos
te despidas	os despidáis	te hayas	os hayáis + despedido
se despida	se despidan	se haya	se hayan
7 imperfecto de subjuntivo		**14 pluscuamperfecto de subjuntivo**	
me despidiera	nos despidiéramos	me hubiera	nos hubiéramos
te despidieras	os despidierais	te hubieras	os hubierais + despedido
se despidiera	se despidieran	se hubiera	se hubieran
OR		OR	
me despidiese	nos despidiésemos	me hubiese	nos hubiésemos
te despidieses	os despidieseis	te hubieses	os hubieseis + despedido
se despidiese	se despidiesen	se hubiese	se hubiesen

imperativo	
—	despidámonos
despídete; no te despidas	despedíos; no os despidáis
despídase	despídanse

despedirse a la francesa to take French leave	**despedirse de** to take leave of, to say good-bye to
despedir to dismiss	
un despedimiento, una despedida dismissal, discharge, farewell	

despertar

Gerundio **despertando**   Part. pas. **despertado**

to enliven,
to awaken (someone)

Regular **-ar** verb endings with stem
change: Tenses 1, 6, Imperative

The Seven Simple Tenses		The Seven Compound Tenses	
Singular	Plural	Singular	Plural
1 presente de indicativo		8 perfecto de indicativo	
despierto	despertamos	he despertado	hemos despertado
despiertas	despertáis	has despertado	habéis despertado
despierta	despiertan	ha despertado	han despertado
2 imperfecto de indicativo		9 pluscuamperfecto de indicativo	
despertaba	despertábamos	había despertado	habíamos despertado
despertabas	despertabais	habías despertado	habíais despertado
despertaba	despertaban	había despertado	habían despertado
3 pretérito		10 pretérito anterior	
desperté	despertamos	hube despertado	hubimos despertado
despertaste	despertasteis	hubiste despertado	hubisteis despertado
despertó	despertaron	hubo despertado	hubieron despertado
4 futuro		11 futuro perfecto	
despertaré	despertaremos	habré despertado	habremos despertado
despertarás	despertaréis	habrás despertado	habréis despertado
despertará	despertarán	habrá despertado	habrán despertado
5 potencial simple		12 potencial compuesto	
despertaría	despertaríamos	habría despertado	habríamos despertado
despertarías	despertaríais	habrías despertado	habríais despertado
despertaría	despertarían	habría despertado	habrían despertado
6 presente de subjuntivo		13 perfecto de subjuntivo	
despierte	despertemos	haya despertado	hayamos despertado
despiertes	despertéis	hayas despertado	hayáis despertado
despierte	despierten	haya despertado	hayan despertado
7 imperfecto de subjuntivo		14 pluscuamperfecto de subjuntivo	
despertara	despertáramos	hubiera despertado	hubiéramos despertado
despertaras	despertarais	hubieras despertado	hubierais despertado
despertara	despertaran	hubiera despertado	hubieran despertado
OR		OR	
despertase	despertásemos	hubiese despertado	hubiésemos despertado
despertases	despertaseis	hubieses despertado	hubieseis despertado
despertase	despertasen	hubiese despertado	hubiesen despertado

imperativo	
—	despertemos
despierta; no despiertes	despertad; no despertéis
despierte	despierten

un despertador alarm clock	despierto, despierta wide awake, alert
el despertamiento awakening	See also despertarse.

122

despertarse

Reflexive verb; regular **-ar** verb endings
with stem change: Tenses 1, 6, Imperative

to wake up oneself

The Seven Simple Tenses		The Seven Compound Tenses		
Singular	Plural	Singular	Plural	
1 presente de indicativo		**8 perfecto de indicativo**		
me despierto	**nos despertamos**	**me he**	**nos hemos**	
te despiertas	**os despertáis**	**te has**	**os habéis**	+ despertado
se despierta	**se despiertan**	**se ha**	**se han**	
2 imperfecto de indicativo		**9 pluscuamperfecto de indicativo**		
me despertaba	**nos despertábamos**	**me había**	**nos habíamos**	
te despertabas	**os despertabais**	**te habías**	**os habíais**	+ despertado
se despertaba	**se despertaban**	**se había**	**se habían**	
3 pretérito		**10 pretérito anterior**		
me desperté	**nos despertamos**	**me hube**	**nos hubimos**	
te despertaste	**os despertasteis**	**te hubiste**	**os hubisteis**	+ despertado
se despertó	**se despertaron**	**se hubo**	**se hubieron**	
4 futuro		**11 futuro perfecto**		
me despertaré	**nos despertaremos**	**me habré**	**nos habremos**	
te despertarás	**os despertaréis**	**te habrás**	**os habréis**	+ despertado
se despertará	**se despertarán**	**se habrá**	**se habrán**	
5 potencial simple		**12 potencial compuesto**		
me despertaría	**nos despertaríamos**	**me habría**	**nos habríamos**	
te despertarías	**os despertaríais**	**te habrías**	**os habríais**	+ despertado
se despertaría	**se despertarían**	**se habría**	**se habrían**	
6 presente de subjuntivo		**13 perfecto de subjuntivo**		
me despierte	**nos despertemos**	**me haya**	**nos hayamos**	
te despiertes	**os despertéis**	**te hayas**	**os hayáis**	+ despertado
se despierte	**se despierten**	**se haya**	**se hayan**	
7 imperfecto de subjuntivo		**14 pluscuamperfecto de subjuntivo**		
me despertara	**nos despertáramos**	**me hubiera**	**nos hubiéramos**	
te despertaras	**os despertarais**	**te hubieras**	**os hubierais**	+ despertado
se despertara	**se despertaran**	**se hubiera**	**se hubieran**	
OR		OR		
me despertase	**nos despertásemos**	**me hubiese**	**nos hubiésemos**	
te despertases	**os despertaseis**	**te hubieses**	**os hubieseis**	+ despertado
se despertase	**se despertasen**	**se hubiese**	**se hubiesen**	

imperativo	
—	**despertémonos**
despiértate; no te despiertes	**despertaos; no os despertéis**
despiértese	**despiértense**

el despertamiento awakening	despertarse a las siete de la mañana
María sueña despierta. Mary	to wake up at seven in the morning
daydreams.	See also **despertar**.

destruir

Gerundio **destruyendo** Part. pas. **destruido**

to destroy

Regular -ir verb endings with spelling change: add **y** before **a**, **e**, or **o**

The Seven Simple Tenses		The Seven Compound Tenses	
Singular	Plural	Singular	Plural
1 presente de indicativo		**8 perfecto de indicativo**	
destruyo	destruimos	he destruido	hemos destruido
destruyes	destruís	has destruido	habéis destruido
destruye	destruyen	ha destruido	han destruido
2 imperfecto de indicativo		**9 pluscuamperfecto de indicativo**	
destruía	destruíamos	había destruido	habíamos destruido
destruías	destruíais	habías destruido	habíais destruido
destruía	destruían	había destruido	habían destruido
3 pretérito		**10 pretérito anterior**	
destruí	destruimos	hube destruido	hubimos destruido
destruiste	destruisteis	hubiste destruido	hubisteis destruido
destruyó	destruyeron	hubo destruido	hubieron destruido
4 futuro		**11 futuro perfecto**	
destruiré	destruiremos	habré destruido	habremos destruido
destruirás	destruiréis	habrás destruido	habréis destruido
destruirá	destruirán	habrá destruido	habrán destruido
5 potencial simple		**12 potencial compuesto**	
destruiría	destruiríamos	habría destruido	habríamos destruido
destruirías	destruiríais	habrías destruido	habríais destruido
destruiría	destruirían	habría destruido	habrían destruido
6 presente de subjuntivo		**13 perfecto de subjuntivo**	
destruya	destruyamos	haya destruido	hayamos destruido
destruyas	destruyáis	hayas destruido	hayáis destruido
destruya	destruyan	haya destruido	hayan destruido
7 imperfecto de subjuntivo		**14 pluscuamperfecto de subjuntivo**	
destruyera	destruyéramos	hubiera destruido	hubiéramos destruido
destruyeras	destruyerais	hubieras destruido	hubierais destruido
destruyera	destruyeran	hubiera destruido	hubieran destruido
OR		OR	
destruyese	destruyésemos	hubiese destruido	hubiésemos destruido
destruyeses	destruyeseis	hubieses destruido	hubieseis destruido
destruyese	destruyesen	hubiese destruido	hubiesen destruido

imperativo	
—	destruyamos
destruye; no destruyas	destruid; no destruyáis
destruya	destruyan

destructor, destructora destructor, destroyer	destruible destructible
destructivo, destructiva destructive	destructivamente destructively
la destrucción destruction	
destruidor, destruidora destroyer	

desvestirse

Regular **-ir** verb endings with stem change:
Tenses 1, 3, 6, 7, Imperative, *Gerundio*

to undress oneself,
to get undressed

The Seven Simple Tenses		The Seven Compound Tenses	
Singular	Plural	Singular	Plural

1 presente de indicativo		8 perfecto de indicativo		
me desvisto	nos desvestimos	me he	nos hemos	
te desvistes	os desvestís	te has	os habéis	+ desvestido
se desviste	se desvisten	se ha	se han	

2 imperfecto de indicativo		9 pluscuamperfecto de indicativo		
me desvestía	nos desvestíamos	me había	nos habíamos	
te desvestías	os desvestíais	te habías	os habíais	+ desvestido
se desvestía	se desvestían	se había	se habían	

3 pretérito		10 pretérito anterior		
me desvestí	nos desvestimos	me hube	nos hubimos	
te desvestiste	os desvestisteis	te hubiste	os hubisteis	+ desvestido
se desvistió	se desvistieron	se hubo	se hubieron	

4 futuro		11 futuro perfecto		
me desvestiré	nos desvestiremos	me habré	nos habremos	
te desvestirás	os desvestiréis	te habrás	os habréis	+ desvestido
se desvestirá	se desvestirán	se habrá	se habrán	

5 potencial simple		12 potencial compuesto		
me desvestiría	nos desvestiríamos	me habría	nos habríamos	
te desvestirías	os desvestiríais	te habrías	os habríais	+ desvestido
se desvestiría	se desvestirían	se habría	se habrían	

6 presente de subjuntivo		13 perfecto de subjuntivo		
me desvista	nos desvistamos	me haya	nos hayamos	
te desvistas	os desvistáis	te hayas	os hayáis	+ desvestido
se desvista	se desvistan	se haya	se hayan	

7 imperfecto de subjuntivo		14 pluscuamperfecto de subjuntivo		
me desvistiera	nos desvistiéramos	me hubiera	nos hubiéramos	
te desvistieras	os desvistierais	te hubieras	os hubierais	+ desvestido
se desvistiera	se desvistieran	se hubiera	se hubieran	
OR		OR		
me desvistiese	nos desvistiésemos	me hubiese	nos hubiésemos	
te desvistieses	os desvistieseis	te hubieses	os hubieseis	+ desvestido
se desvistiese	se desvistiesen	se hubiese	se hubiesen	

imperativo	
—	desvistámonos
desvístete; no te desvistas	desvestíos; no os desvistáis
desvístase	desvístanse

vestir to clothe, to dress	**el vestido** clothing, clothes, dress
vestirse to clothe oneself, to dress oneself	**vestidos usados** secondhand clothing
	See also **vestirse.**

detenerse

Gerundio **deteniéndose**

Part. pas. **detenido**

to stop (oneself)

Reflexive irregular verb

The Seven Simple Tenses		The Seven Compound Tenses	
Singular	Plural	Singular	Plural
1 presente de indicativo		8 perfecto de indicativo	
me detengo	nos detenemos	me he detenido	nos hemos detenido
te detienes	os detenéis	te has detenido	os habéis detenido
se detiene	se detienen	se ha detenido	se han detenido
2 imperfecto de indicativo		9 pluscuamperfecto de indicativo	
me detenía	nos deteníamos	me había detenido	nos habíamos detenido
te detenías	os deteníais	te habías detenido	os habíais detenido
se detenía	se detenían	se había detenido	se habían detenido
3 pretérito		10 pretérito anterior	
me detuve	nos detuvimos	me hube detenido	nos hubimos detenido
te detuviste	os detuvisteis	te hubiste detenido	os hubisteis detenido
se detuvo	se detuvieron	se hubo detenido	se hubieron detenido
4 futuro		11 futuro perfecto	
me detendré	nos detendremos	me habré detenido	nos habremos detenido
te detendrás	os detendréis	te habrás detenido	os habréis detenido
se detendrá	se detendrán	se habrá detenido	se habrán detenido
5 potencial simple		12 potencial compuesto	
me detendría	nos detendríamos	me habría detenido	nos habríamos detenido
te detendrías	os detendríais	te habrías detenido	os habríais detenido
se detendría	se detendrían	se habría detenido	se habrían detenido
6 presente de subjuntivo		13 perfecto de subjuntivo	
me detenga	nos detengamos	me haya detenido	nos hayamos detenido
te detengas	os detengáis	te hayas detenido	os hayáis detenido
se detenga	se detengan	se haya detenido	se hayan detenido
7 imperfecto de subjuntivo		14 pluscuamperfecto de subjuntivo	
me detuviera	nos detuviéramos	me hubiera detenido	nos hubiéramos detenido
te detuvieras	os detuvierais	te hubieras detenido	os hubierais detenido
se detuviera	se detuvieran	se hubiera detenido	se hubieran detenido
OR		OR	
me detuviese	nos detuviésemos	me hubiese detenido	nos hubiésemos detenido
te detuvieses	os detuvieseis	te hubieses detenido	os hubieseis detenido
se detuviese	se detuviesen	se hubiese detenido	se hubiesen detenido

imperativo	
—	detengámonos
detente; no te detengas	deteneos; no os detengáis
deténgase	deténganse

---

detener   to stop (someone or something), to detain
detenedor, detenedora   detainer
detenido, detenida   arrested
un detenido, una detenida   someone who has been arrested

la detención ilegal   false imprisonment
detenerse en una idea   to dwell on an idea

Regular **-er** verb endings with stem change: Tenses 1, 6, Imperative, Past Participle

to return (an object), to refund, to give back

The Seven Simple Tenses		The Seven Compound Tenses	
Singular	Plural	Singular	Plural
1 presente de indicativo		8 perfecto de indicativo	
devuelvo	**devolvemos**	**he devuelto**	**hemos devuelto**
devuelves	**devolvéis**	**has devuelto**	**habéis devuelto**
devuelve	**devuelven**	**ha devuelto**	**han devuelto**
2 imperfecto de indicativo		9 pluscuamperfecto de indicativo	
devolvía	**devolvíamos**	**había devuelto**	**habíamos devuelto**
devolvías	**devolvíais**	**habías devuelto**	**habíais devuelto**
devolvía	**devolvían**	**había devuelto**	**habían devuelto**
3 pretérito		10 pretérito anterior	
devolví	**devolvimos**	**hube devuelto**	**hubimos devuelto**
devolviste	**devolvisteis**	**hubiste devuelto**	**hubisteis devuelto**
devolvió	**devolvieron**	**hubo devuelto**	**hubieron devuelto**
4 futuro		11 futuro perfecto	
devolveré	**devolveremos**	**habré devuelto**	**habremos devuelto**
devolverás	**devolveréis**	**habrás devuelto**	**habréis devuelto**
devolverá	**devolverán**	**habrá devuelto**	**habrán devuelto**
5 potencial simple		12 potencial compuesto	
devolvería	**devolveríamos**	**habría devuelto**	**habríamos devuelto**
devolverías	**devolveríais**	**habrías devuelto**	**habríais devuelto**
devolvería	**devolverían**	**habría devuelto**	**habrían devuelto**
6 presente de subjuntivo		13 perfecto de subjuntivo	
devuelva	**devolvamos**	**haya devuelto**	**hayamos devuelto**
devuelvas	**devolváis**	**hayas devuelto**	**hayáis devuelto**
devuelva	**devuelvan**	**haya devuelto**	**hayan devuelto**
7 imperfecto de subjuntivo		14 pluscuamperfecto de subjuntivo	
devolviera	**devolviéramos**	**hubiera devuelto**	**hubiéramos devuelto**
devolvieras	**devolvierais**	**hubieras devuelto**	**hubierais devuelto**
devolviera	**devolvieran**	**hubiera devuelto**	**hubieran devuelto**
OR		OR	
devolviese	**devolviésemos**	**hubiese devuelto**	**hubiésemos devuelto**
devolvieses	**devolvieseis**	**hubieses devuelto**	**hubieseis devuelto**
devolviese	**devolviesen**	**hubiese devuelto**	**hubiesen devuelto**

imperativo	
—	**devolvamos**
devuelve; no devuelvas	**devolved; no devolváis**
devuelva	**devuelvan**

—¿Ha devuelto Ud. los libros a la biblioteca?   Have you returned the books to the library?
—Sí, señora, los devolví ayer.   Yes, ma'am, I returned them yesterday.

devolutivo, devolutiva returnable
devolver to vomit
volver to return, to go back
la devolución restitution, return

dirigir

Gerundio **dirigiendo**   Part. pas. **dirigido**

to direct

Regular **-ir** verb endings with spelling change: **g** becomes **j** before **a** or **o**

The Seven Simple Tenses		The Seven Compound Tenses	
Singular	Plural	Singular	Plural
1 presente de indicativo		8 perfecto de indicativo	
dirijo	dirigimos	he dirigido	hemos dirigido
diriges	dirigís	has dirigido	habéis dirigido
dirige	dirigen	ha dirigido	han dirigido
2 imperfecto de indicativo		9 pluscuamperfecto de indicativo	
dirigía	dirigíamos	había dirigido	habíamos dirigido
dirigías	dirigíais	habías dirigido	habíais dirigido
dirigía	dirigían	había dirigido	habían dirigido
3 pretérito		10 pretérito anterior	
dirigí	dirigimos	hube dirigido	hubimos dirigido
dirigiste	dirigisteis	hubiste dirigido	hubisteis dirigido
dirigió	dirigieron	hubo dirigido	hubieron dirigido
4 futuro		11 futuro perfecto	
dirigiré	dirigiremos	habré dirigido	habremos dirigido
dirigirás	dirigiréis	habrás dirigido	habréis dirigido
dirigirá	dirigirán	habrá dirigido	habrán dirigido
5 potencial simple		12 potencial compuesto	
dirigiría	dirigiríamos	habría dirigido	habríamos dirigido
dirigirías	dirigiríais	habrías dirigido	habríais dirigido
dirigiría	dirigirían	habría dirigido	habrían dirigido
6 presente de subjuntivo		13 perfecto de subjuntivo	
dirija	dirijamos	haya dirigido	hayamos dirigido
dirijas	dirijáis	hayas dirigido	hayáis dirigido
dirija	dirijan	haya dirigido	hayan dirigido
7 imperfecto de subjuntivo		14 pluscuamperfecto de subjuntivo	
dirigiera	dirigiéramos	hubiera dirigido	hubiéramos dirigido
dirigieras	dirigierais	hubieras dirigido	hubierais dirigido
dirigiera	dirigieran	hubiera dirigido	hubieran dirigido
OR		OR	
dirigiese	dirigiésemos	hubiese dirigido	hubiésemos dirigido
dirigieses	dirigieseis	hubieses dirigido	hubieseis dirigido
dirigiese	dirigiesen	hubiese dirigido	hubiesen dirigido

imperativo	
—	dirijamos
dirige; no dirijas	dirigid; no dirijáis
dirija	dirijan

el director, la directora director	**dirigible** manageable
director de orquesta orchestra conductor	**el dirigible** dirigible, blimp (aviation)
el dirigente, la dirigente leader	**dirigirse a** to make one's way to, to go to
dirigir la palabra a to address, to speak to	

Regular **-ar** verb

to excuse, to dispense,
to distribute, to exempt

The Seven Simple Tenses		The Seven Compound Tenses	
Singular	Plural	Singular	Plural
1 presente de indicativo		8 perfecto de indicativo	
dispenso	dispensamos	he dispensado	hemos dispensado
dispensas	dispensáis	has dispensado	habéis dispensado
dispensa	dispensan	ha dispensado	han dispensado
2 imperfecto de indicativo		9 pluscuamperfecto de indicativo	
dispensaba	dispensábamos	había dispensado	habíamos dispensado
dispensabas	dispensabais	habías dispensado	habíais dispensado
dispensaba	dispensaban	había dispensado	habían dispensado
3 pretérito		10 pretérito anterior	
dispensé	dispensamos	hube dispensado	hubimos dispensado
dispensaste	dispensasteis	hubiste dispensado	hubisteis dispensado
dispensó	dispensaron	hubo dispensado	hubieron dispensado
4 futuro		11 futuro perfecto	
dispensaré	dispensaremos	habré dispensado	habremos dispensado
dispensarás	dispensaréis	habrás dispensado	habréis dispensado
dispensará	dispensarán	habrá dispensado	habrán dispensado
5 potencial simple		12 potencial compuesto	
dispensaría	dispensaríamos	habría dispensado	habríamos dispensado
dispensarías	dispensaríais	habrías dispensado	habríais dispensado
dispensaría	dispensarían	habría dispensado	habrían dispensado
6 presente de subjuntivo		13 perfecto de subjuntivo	
dispense	dispensemos	haya dispensado	hayamos dispensado
dispenses	dispenséis	hayas dispensado	hayáis dispensado
dispense	dispensen	haya dispensado	hayan dispensado
7 imperfecto de subjuntivo		14 pluscuamperfecto de subjuntivo	
dispensara	dispensáramos	hubiera dispensado	hubiéramos dispensado
dispensaras	dispensarais	hubieras dispensado	hubierais dispensado
dispensara	dispensaran	hubiera dispensado	hubieran dispensado
OR		OR	
dispensase	dispensásemos	hubiese dispensado	hubiésemos dispensado
dispensases	dispensaseis	hubieses dispensado	hubieseis dispensado
dispensase	dispensasen	hubiese dispensado	hubiesen dispensado

imperativo	
—	dispensemos
dispensa; no dispenses	dispensad; no dispenséis
dispense	dispensen

¡Dispénseme! Excuse me!	dispensar de + inf. to excuse from
la dispensación dispensation	+ pres. part.
el dispensario dispensary, clinic	la dispensa privilege

distinguir

Gerundio **distinguiendo**   Part. pas. **distinguido**

to distinguish

Regular -**ir** verb endings with spelling change: **gu** becomes **g** before **a** or **o**

The Seven Simple Tenses		The Seven Compound Tenses	
Singular	Plural	Singular	Plural
1 presente de indicativo		8 perfecto de indicativo	
distingo	distinguimos	he distinguido	hemos distinguido
distingues	distinguís	has distinguido	habéis distinguido
distingue	distinguen	ha distinguido	han distinguido
2 imperfecto de indicativo		9 pluscuamperfecto de indicativo	
distinguía	distinguíamos	había distinguido	habíamos distinguido
distinguías	distinguíais	habías distinguido	habíais distinguido
distinguía	distinguían	había distinguido	habían distinguido
3 pretérito		10 pretérito anterior	
distinguí	distinguimos	hube distinguido	hubimos distinguido
distinguiste	distinguisteis	hubiste distinguido	hubisteis distinguido
distinguió	distinguieron	hubo distinguido	hubieron distinguido
4 futuro		11 futuro perfecto	
distinguiré	distinguiremos	habré distinguido	habremos distinguido
distinguirás	distinguiréis	habrás distinguido	habréis distinguido
distinguirá	distinguirán	habrá distinguido	habrán distinguido
5 potencial simple		12 potencial compuesto	
distinguiría	distinguiríamos	habría distinguido	habríamos distinguido
distinguirías	distinguiríais	habrías distinguido	habríais distinguido
distinguiría	distinguirían	habría distinguido	habrían distinguido
6 presente de subjuntivo		13 perfecto de subjuntivo	
distinga	distingamos	haya distinguido	hayamos distinguido
distingas	distingáis	hayas distinguido	hayáis distinguido
distinga	distingan	haya distinguido	hayan distinguido
7 imperfecto de subjuntivo		14 pluscuamperfecto de subjuntivo	
distinguiera	distinguiéramos	hubiera distinguido	hubiéramos distinguido
distinguieras	distinguierais	hubieras distinguido	hubierais distinguido
distinguiera	distinguieran	hubiera distinguido	hubieran distinguido
OR		OR	
distinguiese	distinguiésemos	hubiese distinguido	hubiésemos distinguido
distinguieses	distinguieseis	hubieses distinguido	hubieseis distinguido
distinguiese	distinguiesen	hubiese distinguido	hubiesen distinguido

imperativo		
—	distingamos	
distingue; no distingas	distinguid; no distingáis	
distinga	distingan	

distinguirse to distinguish oneself	**a distinción de** as distinct from
distintivo, distintiva distinctive	**distinto, distinta** different, distinct,
el distingo restriction	clear
la distinción distinction	

Reflexive verb; regular **-ir** verb endings with stem
change: Tenses 1, 3, 6, 7, Imperative, *Gerundio*

to have a good time,
to enjoy oneself

The Seven Simple Tenses		The Seven Compound Tenses	
Singular	Plural	Singular	Plural
1 presente de indicativo		8 perfecto de indicativo	
me divierto	**nos divertimos**	**me he divertido**	**nos hemos divertido**
te diviertes	**os divertís**	**te has divertido**	**os habéis divertido**
se divierte	**se divierten**	**se ha divertido**	**se han divertido**
2 imperfecto de indicativo		9 pluscuamperfecto de indicativo	
me divertía	**nos divertíamos**	**me había divertido**	**nos habíamos divertido**
te divertías	**os divertíais**	**te habías divertido**	**os habíais divertido**
se divertía	**se divertían**	**se había divertido**	**se habían divertido**
3 pretérito		10 pretérito anterior	
me divertí	**nos divertimos**	**me hube divertido**	**nos hubimos divertido**
te divertiste	**os divertisteis**	**te hubiste divertido**	**os hubisteis divertido**
se divirtió	**se divirtieron**	**se hubo divertido**	**se hubieron divertido**
4 futuro		11 futuro perfecto	
me divertiré	**nos divertiremos**	**me habré divertido**	**nos habremos divertido**
te divertirás	**os divertiréis**	**te habrás divertido**	**os habréis divertido**
se divertirá	**se divertirán**	**se habrá divertido**	**se habrán divertido**
5 potencial simple		12 potencial compuesto	
me divertiría	**nos divertiríamos**	**me habría divertido**	**nos habríamos divertido**
te divertirías	**os divertiríais**	**te habrías divertido**	**os habríais divertido**
se divertiría	**se divertirían**	**se habría divertido**	**se habrían divertido**
6 presente de subjuntivo		13 perfecto de subjuntivo	
me divierta	**nos divirtamos**	**me haya divertido**	**nos hayamos divertido**
te diviertas	**os divirtáis**	**te hayas divertido**	**os hayáis divertido**
se divierta	**se diviertan**	**se haya divertido**	**se hayan divertido**
7 imperfecto de subjuntivo		14 pluscuamperfecto de subjuntivo	
me divirtiera	**nos divirtiéramos**	**me hubiera divertido**	**nos hubiéramos divertido**
te divirtieras	**os divirtierais**	**te hubieras divertido**	**os hubierais divertido**
se divirtiera	**se divirtieran**	**se hubiera divertido**	**se hubieran divertido**
OR		OR	
me divirtiese	**nos divirtiésemos**	**me hubiese divertido**	**nos hubiésemos divertido**
te divirtieses	**os divirtieseis**	**te hubieses divertido**	**os hubieseis divertido**
se divirtiese	**se divirtiesen**	**se hubiese divertido**	**se hubiesen divertido**

	imperativo
—	**divirtámonos; no nos divirtamos**
diviértete; no te diviertas	**divertíos; no os divirtáis**
diviértase; no se divierta	**diviértanse; no se diviertan**

el divertimiento   amusement,
  diversion
diverso, diversa   diverse, different
la diversión   entertainment
divertir   to entertain
divertido, divertida   amusing,
  entertaining

una película divertida   an entertaining
  film
**Nos divertimos mucho en tu fiesta de
  cumpleaños.**   We enjoyed ourselves
  a lot at your birthday party.

dormir

Gerundio **durmiendo**   Part. pas. **dormido**

to sleep

Regular **-ir** verb endings with stem change:
Tenses 1, 3, 6, 7, Imperative, *Gerundio*

The Seven Simple Tenses		The Seven Compound Tenses	
Singular	Plural	Singular	Plural
1 presente de indicativo		8 perfecto de indicativo	
duermo	**dormimos**	**he dormido**	**hemos dormido**
duermes	**dormís**	**has dormido**	**habéis dormido**
duerme	**duermen**	**ha dormido**	**han dormido**
2 imperfecto de indicativo		9 pluscuamperfecto de indicativo	
dormía	**dormíamos**	**había dormido**	**habíamos dormido**
dormías	**dormíais**	**habías dormido**	**habíais dormido**
dormía	**dormían**	**había dormido**	**habían dormido**
3 pretérito		10 pretérito anterior	
dormí	**dormimos**	**hube dormido**	**hubimos dormido**
dormiste	**dormisteis**	**hubiste dormido**	**hubisteis dormido**
durmió	**durmieron**	**hubo dormido**	**hubieron dormido**
4 futuro		11 futuro perfecto	
dormiré	**dormiremos**	**habré dormido**	**habremos dormido**
dormirás	**dormiréis**	**habrás dormido**	**habréis dormido**
dormirá	**dormirán**	**habrá dormido**	**habrán dormido**
5 potencial simple		12 potencial compuesto	
dormiría	**dormiríamos**	**habría dormido**	**habríamos dormido**
dormirías	**dormiríais**	**habrías dormido**	**habríais dormido**
dormiría	**dormirían**	**habría dormido**	**habrían dormido**
6 presente de subjuntivo		13 perfecto de subjuntivo	
duerma	**durmamos**	**haya dormido**	**hayamos dormido**
duermas	**durmáis**	**hayas dormido**	**hayáis dormido**
duerma	**duerman**	**haya dormido**	**hayan dormido**
7 imperfecto de subjuntivo		14 pluscuamperfecto de subjuntivo	
durmiera	**durmiéramos**	**hubiera dormido**	**hubiéramos dormido**
durmieras	**durmierais**	**hubieras dormido**	**hubierais dormido**
durmiera	**durmieran**	**hubiera dormido**	**hubieran dormido**
OR		OR	
durmiese	**durmiésemos**	**hubiese dormido**	**hubiésemos dormido**
durmieses	**durmieseis**	**hubieses dormido**	**hubieseis dormido**
durmiese	**durmiesen**	**hubiese dormido**	**hubiesen dormido**

imperativo	
—	**durmamos**
duerme; no duermas	**dormid; no durmáis**
duerma	**duerman**

Gato que duerme no caza ratones.
  A sleeping cat doesn't catch mice.
dormir to doze
dormirse to fall asleep; (pres. part.:
  durmiéndose)
dormir a pierna suelta to sleep
  soundly

dormitar to doze
el dormitorio bedroom, dormitory
un dormilón, una dormilona
  sleepyhead
See also **dormirse**.

dormirse

Reflexive regular **-ir** verb endings with stem
change: Tenses 1, 3, 6, 7, Imperative, *Gerundio*

The Seven Simple Tenses		The Seven Compound Tenses	
Singular	Plural	Singular	Plural
1 presente de indicativo		8 perfecto de indicativo	
me duermo	**nos dormimos**	**me he dormido**	**nos hemos dormido**
te duermes	**os dormís**	**te has dormido**	**os habéis dormido**
se duerme	**se duermen**	**se ha dormido**	**se han dormido**
2 imperfecto de indicativo		9 pluscuamperfecto de indicativo	
me dormía	**nos dormíamos**	**me había dormido**	**nos habíamos dormido**
te dormías	**os dormíais**	**te habías dormido**	**os habíais dormido**
se dormía	**se dormían**	**se había dormido**	**se habían dormido**
3 pretérito		10 pretérito anterior	
me dormí	**nos dormimos**	**me hube dormido**	**nos hubimos dormido**
te dormiste	**os dormisteis**	**te hubiste dormido**	**os hubisteis dormido**
se durmió	**se durmieron**	**se hubo dormido**	**se hubieron dormido**
4 futuro		11 futuro perfecto	
me dormiré	**nos dormiremos**	**me habré dormido**	**nos habremos dormido**
te dormirás	**os dormiréis**	**te habrás dormido**	**os habréis dormido**
se dormirá	**se dormirán**	**se habrá dormido**	**se habrán dormido**
5 potencial simple		12 potencial compuesto	
me dormiría	**nos dormiríamos**	**me habría dormido**	**nos habríamos dormido**
te dormirías	**os dormiríais**	**te habrías dormido**	**os habríais dormido**
se dormiría	**se dormirían**	**se habría dormido**	**se habrían dormido**
6 presente de subjuntivo		13 perfecto de subjuntivo	
me duerma	**nos durmamos**	**me haya dormido**	**nos hayamos dormido**
te duermas	**os durmáis**	**te hayas dormido**	**os hayáis dormido**
se duerma	**se duerman**	**se haya dormido**	**se hayan dormido**
7 imperfecto de subjuntivo		14 pluscuamperfecto de subjuntivo	
me durmiera	**nos durmiéramos**	**me hubiera dormido**	**nos hubiéramos dormido**
te durmieras	**os durmierais**	**te hubieras dormido**	**os hubierais dormido**
se durmiera	**se durmieran**	**se hubiera dormido**	**se hubieran dormido**
OR		OR	
me durmiese	**nos durmiésemos**	**me hubiese dormido**	**nos hubiésemos dormido**
te durmieses	**os durmieseis**	**te hubieses dormido**	**os hubieseis dormido**
se durmiese	**se durmiesen**	**se hubiese dormido**	**se hubiesen dormido**

imperativo	
—	**durmámonos**
duérmete; no te duermas	**dormíos; no os durmáis**
duérmase	**duérmanse**

dormir to sleep	**el dormitorio** bedroom, dormitory
dormir a pierna suelta to sleep	See also **dormir**.
soundly	
dormitar to doze	

dudar

Gerundio **dudando**   Part. pas. **dudado**

to doubt

Regular **-ar** verb

The Seven Simple Tenses		The Seven Compound Tenses	
Singular	Plural	Singular	Plural
1 presente de indicativo		**8 perfecto de indicativo**	
dudo	dudamos	he dudado	hemos dudado
dudas	dudáis	has dudado	habéis dudado
duda	dudan	ha dudado	han dudado
2 imperfecto de indicativo		**9 pluscuamperfecto de indicativo**	
dudaba	dudábamos	había dudado	habíamos dudado
dudabas	dudabais	habías dudado	habíais dudado
dudaba	dudaban	había dudado	habían dudado
3 pretérito		**10 pretérito anterior**	
dudé	dudamos	hube dudado	hubimos dudado
dudaste	dudasteis	hubiste dudado	hubisteis dudado
dudó	dudaron	hubo dudado	hubieron dudado
4 futuro		**11 futuro perfecto**	
dudaré	dudaremos	habré dudado	habremos dudado
dudarás	dudaréis	habrás dudado	habréis dudado
dudará	dudarán	habrá dudado	habrán dudado
5 potencial simple		**12 potencial compuesto**	
dudaría	dudaríamos	habría dudado	habríamos dudado
dudarías	dudaríais	habrías dudado	habríais dudado
dudaría	dudarían	habría dudado	habrían dudado
6 presente de subjuntivo		**13 perfecto de subjuntivo**	
dude	dudemos	haya dudado	hayamos dudado
dudes	dudéis	hayas dudado	hayáis dudado
dude	duden	haya dudado	hayan dudado
7 imperfecto de subjuntivo		**14 pluscuamperfecto de subjuntivo**	
dudara	dudáramos	hubiera dudado	hubiéramos dudado
dudaras	dudarais	hubieras dudado	hubierais dudado
dudara	dudaran	hubiera dudado	hubieran dudado
OR		OR	
dudase	dudásemos	hubiese dudado	hubiésemos dudado
dudases	dudaseis	hubieses dudado	hubieseis dudado
dudase	dudasen	hubiese dudado	hubiesen dudado

imperativo	
—	dudemos
duda; no dudes	dudad; no dudéis
dude	duden

No lo dudo. I don't doubt it.	**sin duda** undoubtedly, without a doubt
Quien nada sabe, de nada duda.	**No cabe duda.** There is no doubt.
Whoever knows nothing doubts	**dudoso, dudosa** doubtful
nothing.	**dudosamente** doubtfully
la duda doubt	**dudar de algo** to doubt something
poner en duda to doubt, to question	

Regular -ar verb

to cast, to fling, to hurl,
to pitch, to throw

The Seven Simple Tenses		The Seven Compound Tenses	
Singular	Plural	Singular	Plural
1 presente de indicativo		8 perfecto de indicativo	
echo	echamos	he echado	hemos echado
echas	echáis	has echado	habéis echado
echa	echan	ha echado	han echado
2 imperfecto de indicativo		9 pluscuamperfecto de indicativo	
echaba	echábamos	había echado	habíamos echado
echabas	echabais	habías echado	habíais echado
echaba	echaban	había echado	habían echado
3 pretérito		10 pretérito anterior	
eché	echamos	hube echado	hubimos echado
echaste	echasteis	hubiste echado	hubisteis echado
echó	echaron	hubo echado	hubieron echado
4 futuro		11 futuro perfecto	
echaré	echaremos	habré echado	habremos echado
echarás	echaréis	habrás echado	habréis echado
echará	echarán	habrá echado	habrán echado
5 potencial simple		12 potencial compuesto	
echaría	echaríamos	habría echado	habríamos echado
echarías	echaríais	habrías echado	habríais echado
echaría	echarían	habría echado	habrían echado
6 presente de subjuntivo		13 perfecto de subjuntivo	
eche	echemos	haya echado	hayamos echado
eches	echéis	hayas echado	hayáis echado
eche	echen	haya echado	hayan echado
7 imperfecto de subjuntivo		14 pluscuamperfecto de subjuntivo	
echara	echáramos	hubiera echado	hubiéramos echado
echaras	echarais	hubieras echado	hubierais echado
echara	echaran	hubiera echado	hubieran echado
OR		OR	
echase	echásemos	hubiese echado	hubiésemos echado
echases	echaseis	hubieses echado	hubieseis echado
echase	echasen	hubiese echado	hubiesen echado

	imperativo	
—		echemos
echa; no eches		echad; no echéis
eche		echen

echar mano a   to grab
echar de menos a una persona   to
   miss a person
echar una carta al correo   to mail (post)
   a letter; echar raíces   to take root
una echada, un echamiento   cast,
   throw, casting, throwing

echarse   to lie down, rest, stretch out
   (oneself)
desechar   to reject
echar un vistazo   to have a look, take
   a glance

ejercer

Gerundio **ejerciendo**   Part. pas. **ejercido**

to exert, to exercise,
to practice (a profession)

Regular **-er** verb endings with spelling
change: **c** becomes **z** before **a** or **o**

The Seven Simple Tenses		The Seven Compound Tenses	
Singular	Plural	Singular	Plural
1 presente de indicativo		**8 perfecto de indicativo**	
ejerzo	ejercemos	he ejercido	hemos ejercido
ejerces	ejercéis	has ejercido	habéis ejercido
ejerce	ejercen	ha ejercido	han ejercido
2 imperfecto de indicativo		**9 pluscuamperfecto de indicativo**	
ejercía	ejercíamos	había ejercido	habíamos ejercido
ejercías	ejercíais	habías ejercido	habíais ejercido
ejercía	ejercían	había ejercido	habían ejercido
3 pretérito		**10 pretérito anterior**	
ejercí	ejercimos	hube ejercido	hubimos ejercido
ejerciste	ejercisteis	hubiste ejercido	hubisteis ejercido
ejerció	ejercieron	hubo ejercido	hubieron ejercido
4 futuro		**11 futuro perfecto**	
ejerceré	ejerceremos	habré ejercido	habremos ejercido
ejercerás	ejerceréis	habrás ejercido	habréis ejercido
ejercerá	ejercerán	habrá ejercido	habrán ejercido
5 potencial simple		**12 potencial compuesto**	
ejercería	ejerceríamos	habría ejercido	habríamos ejercido
ejercerías	ejerceríais	habrías ejercido	habríais ejercido
ejercería	ejercerían	habría ejercido	habrían ejercido
6 presente de subjuntivo		**13 perfecto de subjuntivo**	
ejerza	ejerzamos	haya ejercido	hayamos ejercido
ejerzas	ejerzáis	hayas ejercido	hayáis ejercido
ejerza	ejerzan	haya ejercido	hayan ejercido
7 imperfecto de subjuntivo		**14 pluscuamperfecto de subjuntivo**	
ejerciera	ejerciéramos	hubiera ejercido	hubiéramos ejercido
ejercieras	ejercierais	hubieras ejercido	hubierais ejercido
ejerciera	ejercieran	hubiera ejercido	hubieran ejercido
OR		OR	
ejerciese	ejerciésemos	hubiese ejercido	hubiésemos ejercido
ejercieses	ejercieseis	hubieses ejercido	hubieseis ejercido
ejerciese	ejerciesen	hubiese ejercido	hubiesen ejercido

	imperativo	
—		ejerzamos
ejerce; no ejerzas		ejerced; no ejerzáis
ejerza		ejerzan

¿Ejerce Ud. el derecho de voto? Es
muy importante. Do you exercise
your right to vote? It's very important.
el ejercicio exercise; El ejercicio hace
al maestro. Practice makes perfect.

hacer ejercicio to drill, to exercise
el ejército army
ejercitar to drill, to exercise, to train
ejercer la medicina to practice
   medicine

Regular **-ir** verb endings with spelling change: **g** becomes **j**
before **a** or **o**; stem change: Tenses 1, 6, Imperative, *Gerundio*

to elect, to select,
to choose

The Seven Simple Tenses		The Seven Compound Tenses	
Singular	Plural	Singular	Plural
1 presente de indicativo		8 perfecto de indicativo	
elijo	elegimos	he elegido	hemos elegido
eliges	elegís	has elegido	habéis elegido
elige	eligen	ha elegido	han elegido
2 imperfecto de indicativo		9 pluscuamperfecto de indicativo	
elegía	elegíamos	había elegido	habíamos elegido
elegías	elegíais	habías elegido	habíais elegido
elegía	elegían	había elegido	habían elegido
3 pretérito		10 pretérito anterior	
elegí	elegimos	hube elegido	hubimos elegido
elegiste	elegisteis	hubiste elegido	hubisteis elegido
eligió	eligieron	hubo elegido	hubieron elegido
4 futuro		11 futuro perfecto	
elegiré	elegiremos	habré elegido	habremos elegido
elegirás	elegiréis	habrás elegido	habréis elegido
elegirá	elegirán	habrá elegido	habrán elegido
5 potencial simple		12 potencial compuesto	
elegiría	elegiríamos	habría elegido	habríamos elegido
elegirías	elegiríais	habrías elegido	habríais elegido
elegiría	elegirían	habría elegido	habrían elegido
6 presente de subjuntivo		13 perfecto de subjuntivo	
elija	elijamos	haya elegido	hayamos elegido
elijas	elijáis	hayas elegido	hayáis elegido
elija	elijan	haya elegido	hayan elegido
7 imperfecto de subjuntivo		14 pluscuamperfecto de subjuntivo	
eligiera	eligiéramos	hubiera elegido	hubiéramos elegido
eligieras	eligierais	hubieras elegido	hubierais elegido
eligiera	eligieran	hubiera elegido	hubieran elegido
OR		OR	
eligiese	eligiésemos	hubiese elegido	hubiésemos elegido
eligieses	eligieseis	hubieses elegido	hubieseis elegido
eligiese	eligiesen	hubiese elegido	hubiesen elegido

imperativo

—	elijamos
elige; no elijas	elegid; no elijáis
elija	elijan

elegible eligible	la elección election
elegir + inf. to choose + inf.	el elector, la electora elector
la elegibilidad eligibility	
reelegir to reelect	

empezar

Gerundio **empezando**   Part. pas. **empezado**

to begin, to start

Regular **-ar** verb endings with spelling change: **z** becomes
c before **e**; stem change: Tenses 1, 6, Imperative

The Seven Simple Tenses		The Seven Compound Tenses	
Singular	Plural	Singular	Plural
1 presente de indicativo		8 perfecto de indicativo	
empiezo	**empezamos**	**he empezado**	**hemos empezado**
empiezas	**empezáis**	**has empezado**	**habéis empezado**
empieza	**empiezan**	**ha empezado**	**han empezado**
2 imperfecto de indicativo		9 pluscuamperfecto de indicativo	
empezaba	**empezábamos**	**había empezado**	**habíamos empezado**
empezabas	**empezabais**	**habías empezado**	**habíais empezado**
empezaba	**empezaban**	**había empezado**	**habían empezado**
3 pretérito		10 pretérito anterior	
empecé	**empezamos**	**hube empezado**	**hubimos empezado**
empezaste	**empezasteis**	**hubiste empezado**	**hubisteis empezado**
empezó	**empezaron**	**hubo empezado**	**hubieron empezado**
4 futuro		11 futuro perfecto	
empezaré	**empezaremos**	**habré empezado**	**habremos empezado**
empezarás	**empezaréis**	**habrás empezado**	**habréis empezado**
empezará	**empezarán**	**habrá empezado**	**habrán empezado**
5 potencial simple		12 potencial compuesto	
empezaría	**empezaríamos**	**habría empezado**	**habríamos empezado**
empezarías	**empezaríais**	**habrías empezado**	**habríais empezado**
empezaría	**empezarían**	**habría empezado**	**habrían empezado**
6 presente de subjuntivo		13 perfecto de subjuntivo	
empiece	**empecemos**	**haya empezado**	**hayamos empezado**
empieces	**empecéis**	**hayas empezado**	**hayáis empezado**
empiece	**empiecen**	**haya empezado**	**hayan empezado**
7 imperfecto de subjuntivo		14 pluscuamperfecto de subjuntivo	
empezara	**empezáramos**	**hubiera empezado**	**hubiéramos empezado**
empezaras	**empezarais**	**hubieras empezado**	**hubierais empezado**
empezara	**empezaran**	**hubiera empezado**	**hubieran empezado**
OR		OR	
empezase	**empezásemos**	**hubiese empezado**	**hubiésemos empezado**
empezases	**empezaseis**	**hubieses empezado**	**hubieseis empezado**
empezase	**empezasen**	**hubiese empezado**	**hubiesen empezado**

imperativo		
—		**empecemos**
empieza; no empieces		**empezad; no empecéis**
empiece		**empiecen**

empezar por + inf.   to begin by + pres.
  part.
empezar a + inf.   to begin + inf.
Ricardo empieza a escribir en inglés.
  Richard is beginning to write in
  English.

para empezar   to begin with, first of
all

emplear

to employ, to use

The Seven Simple Tenses		The Seven Compound Tenses	
Singular	Plural	Singular	Plural
1 presente de indicativo		8 perfecto de indicativo	
empleo	empleamos	he empleado	hemos empleado
empleas	empleáis	has empleado	habéis empleado
emplea	emplean	ha empleado	han empleado
2 imperfecto de indicativo		9 pluscuamperfecto de indicativo	
empleaba	empleábamos	había empleado	habíamos empleado
empleabas	empleabais	habías empleado	habíais empleado
empleaba	empleaban	había empleado	habían empleado
3 pretérito		10 pretérito anterior	
empleé	empleamos	hube empleado	hubimos empleado
empleaste	empleasteis	hubiste empleado	hubisteis empleado
empleó	emplearon	hubo empleado	hubieron empleado
4 futuro		11 futuro perfecto	
emplearé	emplearemos	habré empleado	habremos empleado
emplearás	emplearéis	habrás empleado	habréis empleado
empleará	emplearán	habrá empleado	habrán empleado
5 potencial simple		12 potencial compuesto	
emplearía	emplearíamos	habría empleado	habríamos empleado
emplearías	emplearíais	habrías empleado	habríais empleado
emplearía	emplearían	habría empleado	habrían empleado
6 presente de subjuntivo		13 perfecto de subjuntivo	
emplee	empleemos	haya empleado	hayamos empleado
emplees	empleéis	hayas empleado	hayáis empleado
emplee	empleen	haya empleado	hayan empleado
7 imperfecto de subjuntivo		14 pluscuamperfecto de subjuntivo	
empleara	empleáramos	hubiera empleado	hubiéramos empleado
emplearas	emplearais	hubieras empleado	hubierais empleado
empleara	emplearan	hubiera empleado	hubieran empleado
OR		OR	
emplease	empleásemos	hubiese empleado	hubiésemos empleado
empleases	empleaseis	hubieses empleado	hubieseis empleado
emplease	empleasen	hubiese empleado	hubiesen empleado

imperativo	
—	empleemos
emplea; no emplees	emplead; no empleéis
emplee	empleen

un empleado, una empleada employee	EMPLEO SOLICITADO POSITION WANTED
el empleo job, employment, occupation, use	emplearse to be used
un empleador, una empleadora employer	

encontrar

Gerundio **encontrando**   Part. pas. **encontrado**

to meet, to encounter, to find

Regular **-ar** verb endings with stem change: Tenses 1, 6, Imperative

The Seven Simple Tenses		The Seven Compound Tenses	
Singular	Plural	Singular	Plural
1 presente de indicativo		8 perfecto de indicativo	
encuentro	encontramos	he encontrado	hemos encontrado
encuentras	encontráis	has encontrado	habéis encontrado
encuentra	encuentran	ha encontrado	han encontrado
2 imperfecto de indicativo		9 pluscuamperfecto de indicativo	
encontraba	encontrábamos	había encontrado	habíamos encontrado
encontrabas	encontrabais	habías encontrado	habíais encontrado
encontraba	encontraban	había encontrado	habían encontrado
3 pretérito		10 pretérito anterior	
encontré	encontramos	hube encontrado	hubimos encontrado
encontraste	encontrasteis	hubiste encontrado	hubisteis encontrado
encontró	encontraron	hubo encontrado	hubieron encontrado
4 futuro		11 futuro perfecto	
encontraré	encontraremos	habré encontrado	habremos encontrado
encontrarás	encontraréis	habrás encontrado	habréis encontrado
encontrará	encontrarán	habrá encontrado	habrán encontrado
5 potencial simple		12 potencial compuesto	
encontraría	encontraríamos	habría encontrado	habríamos encontrado
encontrarías	encontraríais	habrías encontrado	habríais encontrado
encontraría	encontrarían	habría encontrado	habrían encontrado
6 presente de subjuntivo		13 perfecto de subjuntivo	
encuentre	encontremos	haya encontrado	hayamos encontrado
encuentres	encontréis	hayas encontrado	hayáis encontrado
encuentre	encuentren	haya encontrado	hayan encontrado
7 imperfecto de subjuntivo		14 pluscuamperfecto de subjuntivo	
encontrara	encontráramos	hubiera encontrado	hubiéramos encontrado
encontraras	encontrarais	hubieras encontrado	hubierais encontrado
encontrara	encontraran	hubiera encontrado	hubieran encontrado
OR		OR	
encontrase	encontrásemos	hubiese encontrado	hubiésemos encontrado
encontrases	encontraseis	hubieses encontrado	hubieseis encontrado
encontrase	encontrasen	hubiese encontrado	hubiesen encontrado

imperativo	
—	encontremos
encuentra; no encuentres	encontrad; no encontréis
encuentre	encuentren

un encuentro   encounter, meeting
salir al encuentro de   to go to meet

encontrarse con alguien   to meet
  someone, to run across someone
  (pres. part.: encontrándose)

Reflexive regular **-ar** verb

to get sick, to fall sick, to become sick, to fall ill, to become ill

The Seven Simple Tenses		The Seven Compound Tenses	
Singular	Plural	Singular	Plural
1 presente de indicativo		8 perfecto de indicativo	
me enfermo	nos enfermamos	me he enfermado	nos hemos enfermado
te enfermas	os enfermáis	te has enfermado	os habéis enfermado
se enferma	se enferman	se ha enfermado	se han enfermado
2 imperfecto de indicativo		9 pluscuamperfecto de indicativo	
me enfermaba	nos enfermábamos	me había enfermado	nos habíamos enfermado
te enfermabas	os enfermabais	te habías enfermado	os habíais enfermado
se enfermaba	se enfermaban	se había enfermado	se habían enfermado
3 pretérito		10 pretérito anterior	
me enfermé	nos enfermamos	me hube enfermado	nos hubimos enfermado
te enfermaste	os enfermasteis	te hubiste enfermado	os hubisteis enfermado
se enfermó	se enfermaron	se hubo enfermado	se hubieron enfermado
4 futuro		11 futuro perfecto	
me enfermaré	nos enfermaremos	me habré enfermado	nos habremos enfermado
te enfermarás	os enfermaréis	te habrás enfermado	os habréis enfermado
se enfermará	se enfermarán	se habrá enfermado	se habrán enfermado
5 potencial simple		12 potencial compuesto	
me enfermaría	nos enfermaríamos	me habría enfermado	nos habríamos enfermado
te enfermarías	os enfermaríais	te habrías enfermado	os habríais enfermado
se enfermaría	se enfermarían	se habría enfermado	se habrían enfermado
6 presente de subjuntivo		13 perfecto de subjuntivo	
me enferme	nos enfermemos	me haya enfermado	nos hayamos enfermado
te enfermes	os enferméis	te hayas enfermado	os hayáis enfermado
se enferme	se enfermen	se haya enfermado	se hayan enfermado
7 imperfecto de subjuntivo		14 pluscuamperfecto de subjuntivo	
me enfermara	nos enfermáramos	me hubiera enfermado	nos hubiéramos enfermado
te enfermaras	os enfermarais	te hubieras enfermado	os hubierais enfermado
se enfermara	se enfermaran	se hubiera enfermado	se hubieran enfermado
OR		OR	
me enfermase	nos enfermásemos	me hubiese enfermado	nos hubiésemos enfermado
te enfermases	os enfermaseis	te hubieses enfermado	os hubieseis enfermado
se enfermase	se enfermasen	se hubiese enfermado	se hubiesen enfermado

imperativo

—	enfermémonos
enférmate; no te enfermes	enfermaos; no os enferméis
enférmese	enférmense

Afortunadamente, cuando mi madre se enfermó, estaba en el hospital, visitando a una amiga. Fortunately, when my mother fell ill she was in the hospital visiting a friend.	la enfermería infirmary
	un enfermo, una enferma patient
	un enfermero, una enfermera nurse
	caer enfermo (enferma) to fall sick, to get sick
la enfermedad illness, sickness	estar enfermo (enferma) to be sick

enojarse

Gerundio **enojándose**   Part. pas. **enojado**

to become angry, to
get angry, to get cross

Reflexive regular **-ar** verb

The Seven Simple Tenses		The Seven Compound Tenses	
Singular	Plural	Singular	Plural
1 presente de indicativo		8 perfecto de indicativo	
me enojo	nos enojamos	me he enojado	nos hemos enojado
te enojas	os enojáis	te has enojado	os habéis enojado
se enoja	se enojan	se ha enojado	se han enojado
2 imperfecto de indicativo		9 pluscuamperfecto de indicativo	
me enojaba	nos enojábamos	me había enojado	nos habíamos enojado
te enojabas	os enojabais	te habías enojado	os habíais enojado
se enojaba	se enojaban	se había enojado	se habían enojado
3 pretérito		10 pretérito anterior	
me enojé	nos enojamos	me hube enojado	nos hubimos enojado
te enojaste	os enojasteis	te hubiste enojado	os hubisteis enojado
se enojó	se enojaron	se hubo enojado	se hubieron enojado
4 futuro		11 futuro perfecto	
me enojaré	nos enojaremos	me habré enojado	nos habremos enojado
te enojarás	os enojaréis	te habrás enojado	os habréis enojado
se enojará	se enojarán	se habrá enojado	se habrán enojado
5 potencial simple		12 potencial compuesto	
me enojaría	nos enojaríamos	me habría enojado	nos habríamos enojado
te enojarías	os enojaríais	te habrías enojado	os habríais enojado
se enojaría	se enojarían	se habría enojado	se habrían enojado
6 presente de subjuntivo		13 perfecto de subjuntivo	
me enoje	nos enojemos	me haya enojado	nos hayamos enojado
te enojes	os enojéis	te hayas enojado	os hayáis enojado
se enoje	se enojen	se haya enojado	se hayan enojado
7 imperfecto de subjuntivo		14 pluscuamperfecto de subjuntivo	
me enojara	nos enojáramos	me hubiera enojado	nos hubiéramos enojado
te enojaras	os enojarais	te hubieras enojado	os hubierais enojado
se enojara	se enojaran	se hubiera enojado	se hubieran enojado
OR		OR	
me enojase	nos enojásemos	me hubiese enojado	nos hubiésemos enojado
te enojases	os enojaseis	te hubieses enojado	os hubieseis enojado
se enojase	se enojasen	se hubiese enojado	se hubiesen enojado

imperativo	
—	enojémonos
enójate; no te enojes	enojaos; no os enojéis
enójese	enójense

---

enojar   to annoy, to irritate, to make
   angry, to vex; enojarse de   to
   become angry at someone
el enojo   anger, annoyance; enojadizo,
   enojadiza   ill-tempered, irritable

enojoso, enojosa   irritating,
   troublesome; enojosamente   angrily
enojado, enojada   angry; una enojada
   fit of anger
enojarse con (contra) alguien   to
   become angry with someone

Regular **-ar** verb

to teach, to show,
to point out

The Seven Simple Tenses		The Seven Compound Tenses	
Singular	Plural	Singular	Plural

1 presente de indicativo

		8 perfecto de indicativo	
enseño	enseñamos	he enseñado	hemos enseñado
enseñas	enseñáis	has enseñado	habéis enseñado
enseña	enseñan	ha enseñado	han enseñado

2 imperfecto de indicativo

		9 pluscuamperfecto de indicativo	
enseñaba	enseñábamos	había enseñado	habíamos enseñado
enseñabas	enseñabais	habías enseñado	habíais enseñado
enseñaba	enseñaban	había enseñado	habían enseñado

3 pretérito

		10 pretérito anterior	
enseñé	enseñamos	hube enseñado	hubimos enseñado
enseñaste	enseñasteis	hubiste enseñado	hubisteis enseñado
enseñó	enseñaron	hubo enseñado	hubieron enseñado

4 futuro

		11 futuro perfecto	
enseñaré	enseñaremos	habré enseñado	habremos enseñado
enseñarás	enseñaréis	habrás enseñado	habréis enseñado
enseñará	enseñarán	habrá enseñado	habrán enseñado

5 potencial simple

		12 potencial compuesto	
enseñaría	enseñaríamos	habría enseñado	habríamos enseñado
enseñarías	enseñaríais	habrías enseñado	habríais enseñado
enseñaría	enseñarían	habría enseñado	habrían enseñado

6 presente de subjuntivo

		13 perfecto de subjuntivo	
enseñe	enseñemos	haya enseñado	hayamos enseñado
enseñes	enseñéis	hayas enseñado	hayáis enseñado
enseñe	enseñen	haya enseñado	hayan enseñado

7 imperfecto de subjuntivo

		14 pluscuamperfecto de subjuntivo	
enseñara	enseñáramos	hubiera enseñado	hubiéramos enseñado
enseñaras	enseñarais	hubieras enseñado	hubierais enseñado
enseñara	enseñaran	hubiera enseñado	hubieran enseñado
OR		OR	
enseñase	enseñásemos	hubiese enseñado	hubiésemos enseñado
enseñases	enseñaseis	hubieses enseñado	hubieseis enseñado
enseñase	enseñasen	hubiese enseñado	hubiesen enseñado

imperativo

—	enseñemos
enseña; no enseñes	enseñad; no enseñéis
enseñe	enseñen

---

enseñarse to teach oneself
enseñar a + inf. to teach + inf.
la enseñanza primaria primary
  education
la enseñanza secundaria secondary
  (high school) education

la enseñanza superior higher
  education
el enseñador, la enseñadora
  instructor

entender

Gerundio **entendiendo**   Part. pas. **entendido**

to understand

Regular **-er** verb endings with stem
change: Tenses 1, 6, Imperative

The Seven Simple Tenses		The Seven Compound Tenses	
Singular	Plural	Singular	Plural
1 presente de indicativo		8 perfecto de indicativo	
entiendo	**entendemos**	**he entendido**	**hemos entendido**
entiendes	**entendéis**	**has entendido**	**habéis entendido**
entiende	**entienden**	**ha entendido**	**han entendido**
2 imperfecto de indicativo		9 pluscuamperfecto de indicativo	
entendía	**entendíamos**	**había entendido**	**habíamos entendido**
entendías	**entendíais**	**habías entendido**	**habíais entendido**
entendía	**entendían**	**había entendido**	**habían entendido**
3 pretérito		10 pretérito anterior	
entendí	**entendimos**	**hube entendido**	**hubimos entendido**
entendiste	**entendisteis**	**hubiste entendido**	**hubisteis entendido**
entendió	**entendieron**	**hubo entendido**	**hubieron entendido**
4 futuro		11 futuro perfecto	
entenderé	**entenderemos**	**habré entendido**	**habremos entendido**
entenderás	**entenderéis**	**habrás entendido**	**habréis entendido**
entenderá	**entenderán**	**habrá entendido**	**habrán entendido**
5 potencial simple		12 potencial compuesto	
entendería	**entenderíamos**	**habría entendido**	**habríamos entendido**
entenderías	**entenderíais**	**habrías entendido**	**habríais entendido**
entendería	**entenderían**	**habría entendido**	**habrían entendido**
6 presente de subjuntivo		13 perfecto de subjuntivo	
entienda	**entendamos**	**haya entendido**	**hayamos entendido**
entiendas	**entendáis**	**hayas entendido**	**hayáis entendido**
entienda	**entiendan**	**haya entendido**	**hayan entendido**
7 imperfecto de subjuntivo		14 pluscuamperfecto de subjuntivo	
entendiera	**entendiéramos**	**hubiera entendido**	**hubiéramos entendido**
entendieras	**entendierais**	**hubieras entendido**	**hubierais entendido**
entendiera	**entendieran**	**hubiera entendido**	**hubieran entendido**
OR		OR	
entendiese	**entendiésemos**	**hubiese entendido**	**hubiésemos entendido**
entendieses	**entendieseis**	**hubieses entendido**	**hubieseis entendido**
entendiese	**entendiesen**	**hubiese entendido**	**hubiesen entendido**

imperativo	
—	**entendamos**
entiende; no entiendas	**entended; no entendáis**
entienda	**entiendan**

¿Qué entiende Ud. por eso? What do
 you mean by that?
dar a entender to insinuate, to hint
el entender understanding
según mi entender according to my
 understanding

desentenderse de to pay no attention to
el entendimiento comprehension,
 understanding
entenderse bien to get along well with
 each other
entenderse to understand each other

Gerundio **entrando**   Part. pas. **entrado**   **entrar**

Regular **-ar** verb

to enter, to go (in),
to come (in)

The Seven Simple Tenses		The Seven Compound Tenses	
Singular	Plural	Singular	Plural
1 presente de indicativo		**8 perfecto de indicativo**	
entro	entramos	he entrado	hemos entrado
entras	entráis	has entrado	habéis entrado
entra	entran	ha entrado	han entrado
2 imperfecto de indicativo		**9 pluscuamperfecto de indicativo**	
entraba	entrábamos	había entrado	habíamos entrado
entrabas	entrabais	habías entrado	habíais entrado
entraba	entraban	había entrado	habían entrado
3 pretérito		**10 pretérito anterior**	
entré	entramos	hube entrado	hubimos entrado
entraste	entrasteis	hubiste entrado	hubisteis entrado
entró	entraron	hubo entrado	hubieron entrado
4 futuro		**11 futuro perfecto**	
entraré	entraremos	habré entrado	habremos entrado
entrarás	entraréis	habrás entrado	habréis entrado
entrará	entrarán	habrá entrado	habrán entrado
5 potencial simple		**12 potencial compuesto**	
entraría	entraríamos	habría entrado	habríamos entrado
entrarías	entraríais	habrías entrado	habríais entrado
entraría	entrarían	habría entrado	habrían entrado
6 presente de subjuntivo		**13 perfecto de subjuntivo**	
entre	entremos	haya entrado	hayamos entrado
entres	entréis	hayas entrado	hayáis entrado
entre	entren	haya entrado	hayan entrado
7 imperfecto de subjuntivo		**14 pluscuamperfecto de subjuntivo**	
entrara	entráramos	hubiera entrado	hubiéramos entrado
entraras	entrarais	hubieras entrado	hubierais entrado
entrara	entraran	hubiera entrado	hubieran entrado
OR		OR	
entrase	entrásemos	hubiese entrado	hubiésemos entrado
entrases	entraseis	hubieses entrado	hubieseis entrado
entrase	entrasen	hubiese entrado	hubiesen entrado

imperativo	
—	entremos
entra; no entres	entrad; no entréis
entre	entren

Yo estudiaba cuando mi hermana
  entró en mi cuarto.   I was studying
  when my sister entered my room.
En boca cerrada no entran moscas.
  Flies do not enter a closed mouth.
  (Silence is golden.)

la entrada   entrance
entrada general   standing room
  (theater, movies)
entrado (entrada) en años   advanced
  in years

145

enunciar

Gerundio **enunciando**   Part. pas. **enunciado**

to enunciate, to state

Regular **-ar** verb

The Seven Simple Tenses		The Seven Compound Tenses	
Singular	Plural	Singular	Plural
1 presente de indicativo		8 perfecto de indicativo	
enuncio	enunciamos	he enunciado	hemos enunciado
enuncias	enunciáis	has enunciado	habéis enunciado
enuncia	enuncian	ha enunciado	han enunciado
2 imperfecto de indicativo		9 pluscuamperfecto de indicativo	
enunciaba	enunciábamos	había enunciado	habíamos enunciado
enunciabas	enunciabais	habías enunciado	habíais enunciado
enunciaba	enunciaban	había enunciado	habían enunciado
3 pretérito		10 pretérito anterior	
enuncié	enunciamos	hube enunciado	hubimos enunciado
enunciaste	enunciasteis	hubiste enunciado	hubisteis enunciado
enunció	enunciaron	hubo enunciado	hubieron enunciado
4 futuro		11 futuro perfecto	
enunciaré	enunciaremos	habré enunciado	habremos enunciado
enunciarás	enunciaréis	habrás enunciado	habréis enunciado
enunciará	enunciarán	habrá enunciado	habrán enunciado
5 potencial simple		12 potencial compuesto	
enunciaría	enunciaríamos	habría enunciado	habríamos enunciado
enunciarías	enunciaríais	habrías enunciado	habríais enunciado
enunciaría	enunciarían	habría enunciado	habrían enunciado
6 presente de subjuntivo		13 perfecto de subjuntivo	
enuncie	enunciemos	haya enunciado	hayamos enunciado
enuncies	enunciéis	hayas enunciado	hayáis enunciado
enuncie	enuncien	haya enunciado	hayan enunciado
7 imperfecto de subjuntivo		14 pluscuamperfecto de subjuntivo	
enunciara	enunciáramos	hubiera enunciado	hubiéramos enunciado
enunciaras	enunciarais	hubieras enunciado	hubierais enunciado
enunciara	enunciaran	hubiera enunciado	hubieran enunciado
OR		OR	
enunciase	enunciásemos	hubiese enunciado	hubiésemos enunciado
enunciases	enunciaseis	hubieses enunciado	hubieseis enunciado
enunciase	enunciasen	hubiese enunciado	hubiesen enunciado

	imperativo	
—	enunciemos
enuncia; no enuncies	enunciad; no enunciéis
enuncie	enuncien

la enunciación, el enunciado
    enunciation, statement, declaration
enunciativo, enunciativa   enunciative

una oración enunciativa   declarative
    sentence

146

Regular **-ar** verb endings with spelling change: **i** to send
becomes **í** on stressed syllable (Tenses 1, 6, Imperative)

The Seven Simple Tenses		The Seven Compound Tenses	
Singular	Plural	Singular	Plural

1 presente de indicativo		8 perfecto de indicativo	
envío	enviamos	he enviado	hemos enviado
envías	enviáis	has enviado	habéis enviado
envía	envían	ha enviado	han enviado

2 imperfecto de indicativo		9 pluscuamperfecto de indicativo	
enviaba	enviábamos	había enviado	habíamos enviado
enviabas	enviabais	habías enviado	habíais enviado
enviaba	enviaban	había enviado	habían enviado

3 pretérito		10 pretérito anterior	
envié	enviamos	hube enviado	hubimos enviado
enviaste	enviasteis	hubiste enviado	hubisteis enviado
envió	enviaron	hubo enviado	hubieron enviado

4 futuro		11 futuro perfecto	
enviaré	enviaremos	habré enviado	habremos enviado
enviarás	enviaréis	habrás enviado	habréis enviado
enviará	enviarán	habrá enviado	habrán enviado

5 potencial simple		12 potencial compuesto	
enviaría	enviaríamos	habría enviado	habríamos enviado
enviarías	enviaríais	habrías enviado	habríais enviado
enviaría	enviarían	habría enviado	habrían enviado

6 presente de subjuntivo		13 perfecto de subjuntivo	
envíe	enviemos	haya enviado	hayamos enviado
envíes	enviéis	hayas enviado	hayáis enviado
envíe	envíen	haya enviado	hayan enviado

7 imperfecto de subjuntivo		14 pluscuamperfecto de subjuntivo	
enviara	enviáramos	hubiera enviado	hubiéramos enviado
enviaras	enviarais	hubieras enviado	hubierais enviado
enviara	enviaran	hubiera enviado	hubieran enviado
OR		OR	
enviase	enviásemos	hubiese enviado	hubiésemos enviado
enviases	enviaseis	hubieses enviado	hubieseis enviado
enviase	enviasen	hubiese enviado	hubiesen enviado

imperativo	
—	enviemos
envía; no envíes	enviad; no enviéis
envíe	envíen

María me envió un mensaje de texto para invitarme a la fiesta   Mary texted me to invite me to the party.
enviar a alguien a pasear   to send someone to take a walk
enviador, enviadora   sender
un enviado   envoy

la enviada   shipment; reenviar   to send back; to forward
enviar por correo electrónico   to e-mail, send by e-mail
enviar un mensaje de texto   to send a text message, to text

equivocarse

Gerundio **equivocándose**   Part. pas. **equivocado**

to be mistaken, to make a mistake

Regular **-ar** verb endings with spelling
change: **c** becomes **qu** before **e**

The Seven Simple Tenses		The Seven Compound Tenses	
Singular	Plural	Singular	Plural

1 presente de indicativo		8 perfecto de indicativo	
me equivoco	nos equivocamos	me he	nos hemos
te equivocas	os equivocáis	te has	os habéis + equivocado
se equivoca	se equivocan	se ha	se han

2 imperfecto de indicativo		9 pluscuamperfecto de indicativo	
me equivocaba	nos equivocábamos	me había	nos habíamos
te equivocabas	os equivocabais	te habías	os habíais + equivocado
se equivocaba	se equivocaban	se había	se habían

3 pretérito		10 pretérito anterior	
me equivoqué	nos equivocamos	me hube	nos hubimos
te equivocaste	os equivocasteis	te hubiste	os hubisteis + equivocado
se equivocó	se equivocaron	se hubo	se hubieron

4 futuro		11 futuro perfecto	
me equivocaré	nos equivocaremos	me habré	nos habremos
te equivocarás	os equivocaréis	te habrás	os habréis + equivocado
se equivocará	se equivocarán	se habrá	se habrán

5 potencial simple		12 potencial compuesto	
me equivocaría	nos equivocaríamos	me habría	nos habríamos
te equivocarías	os equivocaríais	te habrías	os habríais + equivocado
se equivocaría	se equivocarían	se habría	se habrían

6 presente de subjuntivo		13 perfecto de subjuntivo	
me equivoque	nos equivoquemos	me haya	nos hayamos
te equivoques	os equivoquéis	te hayas	os hayáis + equivocado
se equivoque	se equivoquen	se haya	se hayan

7 imperfecto de subjuntivo		14 pluscuamperfecto de subjuntivo	
me equivocara	nos equivocáramos	me hubiera	nos hubiéramos
te equivocaras	os equivocarais	te hubieras	os hubierais + equivocado
se equivocara	se equivocaran	se hubiera	se hubieran
OR		OR	
me equivocase	nos equivocásemos	me hubiese	nos hubiésemos
te equivocases	os equivocaseis	te hubieses	os hubieseis + equivocado
se equivocase	se equivocasen	se hubiese	se hubiesen

	imperativo	
—		equivoquémonos
equivócate; no te equivoques		equivocaos; no os equivoquéis
equivóquese		equivóquense

equivoquista quibbler	equivocarse de fecha to be mistaken
equivocado, equivocada mistaken	about the date
una equivocación error, mistake,	estar equivocado (equivocada) to be
equivocation	mistaken

148

Regular **-ar** verb endings with stem
change: Tenses 1, 6, Imperative

to err, to wander,
to roam, to miss

The Seven Simple Tenses		The Seven Compound Tenses	
Singular	Plural	Singular	Plural
1 presente de indicativo		8 perfecto de indicativo	
yerro	**erramos**	**he errado**	**hemos errado**
yerras	**erráis**	**has errado**	**habéis errado**
yerra	**yerran**	**ha errado**	**han errado**
2 imperfecto de indicativo		9 pluscuamperfecto de indicativo	
erraba	**errábamos**	**había errado**	**habíamos errado**
errabas	**errabais**	**habías errado**	**habíais errado**
erraba	**erraban**	**había errado**	**habían errado**
3 pretérito		10 pretérito anterior	
erré	**erramos**	**hube errado**	**hubimos errado**
erraste	**errasteis**	**hubiste errado**	**hubisteis errado**
erró	**erraron**	**hubo errado**	**hubieron errado**
4 futuro		11 futuro perfecto	
erraré	**erraremos**	**habré errado**	**habremos errado**
errarás	**erraréis**	**habrás errado**	**habréis errado**
errará	**errarán**	**habrá errado**	**habrán errado**
5 potencial simple		12 potencial compuesto	
erraría	**erraríamos**	**habría errado**	**habríamos errado**
errarías	**erraríais**	**habrías errado**	**habríais errado**
erraría	**errarían**	**habría errado**	**habrían errado**
6 presente de subjuntivo		13 perfecto de subjuntivo	
yerre	**erremos**	**haya errado**	**hayamos errado**
yerres	**erréis**	**hayas errado**	**hayáis errado**
yerre	**yerren**	**haya errado**	**hayan errado**
7 imperfecto de subjuntivo		14 pluscuamperfecto de subjuntivo	
errara	**erráramos**	**hubiera errado**	**hubiéramos errado**
erraras	**errarais**	**hubieras errado**	**hubierais errado**
errara	**erraran**	**hubiera errado**	**hubieran errado**
OR		OR	
errase	**errásemos**	**hubiese errado**	**hubiésemos errado**
errases	**erraseis**	**hubieses errado**	**hubieseis errado**
errase	**errasen**	**hubiese errado**	**hubiesen errado**

imperativo	
—	**erremos**
yerra; no yerres	**errad; no erréis**
yerre	**yerren**

una errata   erratum, typographical
  error
un yerro   error, fault, mistake
errante   errant, wandering
deshacer un yerro   to amend an error

un error   error, mistake
un error de imprenta   misprint
errar el tiro   to miss the mark
errar el blanco   to miss the target

escoger

Gerundio **escogiendo**   Part. pas. **escogido**

to choose, to select

Regular **-er** verb endings with spelling change: **g** becomes **j** before **a** or **o**

The Seven Simple Tenses		The Seven Compound Tenses	
Singular	Plural	Singular	Plural
1 presente de indicativo		8 perfecto de indicativo	
escojo	escogemos	he escogido	hemos escogido
escoges	escogéis	has escogido	habéis escogido
escoge	escogen	ha escogido	han escogido
2 imperfecto de indicativo		9 pluscuamperfecto de indicativo	
escogía	escogíamos	había escogido	habíamos escogido
escogías	escogíais	habías escogido	habíais escogido
escogía	escogían	había escogido	habían escogido
3 pretérito		10 pretérito anterior	
escogí	escogimos	hube escogido	hubimos escogido
escogiste	escogisteis	hubiste escogido	hubisteis escogido
escogió	escogieron	hubo escogido	hubieron escogido
4 futuro		11 futuro perfecto	
escogeré	escogeremos	habré escogido	habremos escogido
escogerás	escogeréis	habrás escogido	habréis escogido
escogerá	escogerán	habrá escogido	habrán escogido
5 potencial simple		12 potencial compuesto	
escogería	escogeríamos	habría escogido	habríamos escogido
escogerías	escogeríais	habrías escogido	habríais escogido
escogería	escogerían	habría escogido	habrían escogido
6 presente de subjuntivo		13 perfecto de subjuntivo	
escoja	escojamos	haya escogido	hayamos escogido
escojas	escojáis	hayas escogido	hayáis escogido
escoja	escojan	haya escogido	hayan escogido
7 imperfecto de subjuntivo		14 pluscuamperfecto de subjuntivo	
escogiera	escogiéramos	hubiera escogido	hubiéramos escogido
escogieras	escogierais	hubieras escogido	hubierais escogido
escogiera	escogieran	hubiera escogido	hubieran escogido
OR		OR	
escogiese	escogiésemos	hubiese escogido	hubiésemos escogido
escogieses	escogieseis	hubieses escogido	hubieseis escogido
escogiese	escogiesen	hubiese escogido	hubiesen escogido

imperativo	
—	escojamos
escoge; no escojas	escoged; no escojáis
escoja	escojan

A quien le dan no escoge.   Whoever is given it (something) doesn't choose. (Beggars can't be choosers.)

un escogimiento   choice, selection
escogido, escogida   chosen
See also coger.

escribir

to write

Regular **-ir** verb endings; note irregular
spelling of past participle: **escrito**

The Seven Simple Tenses		The Seven Compound Tenses	
Singular	Plural	Singular	Plural
1 presente de indicativo		**8 perfecto de indicativo**	
escribo	escribimos	he escrito	hemos escrito
escribes	escribís	has escrito	habéis escrito
escribe	escriben	ha escrito	han escrito
2 imperfecto de indicativo		**9 pluscuamperfecto de indicativo**	
escribía	escribíamos	había escrito	habíamos escrito
escribías	escribíais	habías escrito	habíais escrito
escribía	escribían	había escrito	habían escrito
3 pretérito		**10 pretérito anterior**	
escribí	escribimos	hube escrito	hubimos escrito
escribiste	escribisteis	hubiste escrito	hubisteis escrito
escribió	escribieron	hubo escrito	hubieron escrito
4 futuro		**11 futuro perfecto**	
escribiré	escribiremos	habré escrito	habremos escrito
escribirás	escribiréis	habrás escrito	habréis escrito
escribirá	escribirán	habrá escrito	habrán escrito
5 potencial simple		**12 potencial compuesto**	
escribiría	escribiríamos	habría escrito	habríamos escrito
escribirías	escribiríais	habrías escrito	habríais escrito
escribiría	escribirían	habría escrito	habrían escrito
6 presente de subjuntivo		**13 perfecto de subjuntivo**	
escriba	escribamos	haya escrito	hayamos escrito
escribas	escribáis	hayas escrito	hayáis escrito
escriba	escriban	haya escrito	hayan escrito
7 imperfecto de subjuntivo		**14 pluscuamperfecto de subjuntivo**	
escribiera	escribiéramos	hubiera escrito	hubiéramos escrito
escribieras	escribierais	hubieras escrito	hubierais escrito
escribiera	escribieran	hubiera escrito	hubieran escrito
OR		OR	
escribiese	escribiésemos	hubiese escrito	hubiésemos escrito
escribieses	escribieseis	hubieses escrito	hubieseis escrito
escribiese	escribiesen	hubiese escrito	hubiesen escrito

imperativo	
—	escribamos
escribe; no escribas	escribid; no escribáis
escriba	escriban

Mi padre está escribiendo una novela.
  My father is writing a novel.
una máquina de escribir typewriter
por escrito in writing
escribir a máquina to typewrite
escribir a mano to write by hand

un escritorio writing desk
describir to describe
un escritor, una escritora writer,
  author
la descripción description

escuchar

Gerundio **escuchando**   Part. pas. **escuchado**

to listen (to)

Regular **-ar** verb

The Seven Simple Tenses		The Seven Compound Tenses	
Singular	Plural	Singular	Plural
1 presente de indicativo		8 perfecto de indicativo	
escucho	escuchamos	he escuchado	hemos escuchado
escuchas	escucháis	has escuchado	habéis escuchado
escucha	escuchan	ha escuchado	han escuchado
2 imperfecto de indicativo		9 pluscuamperfecto de indicativo	
escuchaba	escuchábamos	había escuchado	habíamos escuchado
escuchabas	escuchabais	habías escuchado	habíais escuchado
escuchaba	escuchaban	había escuchado	habían escuchado
3 pretérito		10 pretérito anterior	
escuché	escuchamos	hube escuchado	hubimos escuchado
escuchaste	escuchasteis	hubiste escuchado	hubisteis escuchado
escuchó	escucharon	hubo escuchado	hubieron escuchado
4 futuro		11 futuro perfecto	
escucharé	escucharemos	habré escuchado	habremos escuchado
escucharás	escucharéis	habrás escuchado	habréis escuchado
escuchará	escucharán	habrá escuchado	habrán escuchado
5 potencial simple		12 potencial compuesto	
escucharía	escucharíamos	habría escuchado	habríamos escuchado
escucharías	escucharíais	habrías escuchado	habríais escuchado
escucharía	escucharían	habría escuchado	habrían escuchado
6 presente de subjuntivo		13 perfecto de subjuntivo	
escuche	escuchemos	haya escuchado	hayamos escuchado
escuches	escuchéis	hayas escuchado	hayáis escuchado
escuche	escuchen	haya escuchado	hayan escuchado
7 imperfecto de subjuntivo		14 pluscuamperfecto de subjuntivo	
escuchara	escucháramos	hubiera escuchado	hubiéramos escuchado
escucharas	escucharais	hubieras escuchado	hubierais escuchado
escuchara	escucharan	hubiera escuchado	hubieran escuchado
OR		OR	
escuchase	escuchásemos	hubiese escuchado	hubiésemos escuchado
escuchases	escuchaseis	hubieses escuchado	hubieseis escuchado
escuchase	escuchasen	hubiese escuchado	hubiesen escuchado

imperativo	
—	escuchemos
escucha; no escuches	escuchad; no escuchéis
escuche	escuchen

Para saber hablar, hay que saber escuchar. In order to know how to talk, one must know how to listen.	Escucho la música. I'm listening to the music.
escuchar + noun to listen to + noun	escuchador, escuchadora, escuchante listener

152

esparcir

to scatter, to spread

The Seven Simple Tenses		The Seven Compound Tenses	
Singular	Plural	Singular	Plural

1 presente de indicativo

		8 perfecto de indicativo	
esparzo	esparcimos	he esparcido	hemos esparcido
esparces	esparcís	has esparcido	habéis esparcido
esparce	esparcen	ha esparcido	han esparcido

2 imperfecto de indicativo

		9 pluscuamperfecto de indicativo	
esparcía	esparcíamos	había esparcido	habíamos esparcido
esparcías	esparcíais	habías esparcido	habíais esparcido
esparcía	esparcían	había esparcido	habían esparcido

3 pretérito

		10 pretérito anterior	
esparcí	esparcimos	hube esparcido	hubimos esparcido
esparciste	esparcisteis	hubiste esparcido	hubisteis esparcido
esparció	esparcieron	hubo esparcido	hubieron esparcido

4 futuro

		11 futuro perfecto	
esparciré	esparciremos	habré esparcido	habremos esparcido
esparcirás	esparciréis	habrás esparcido	habréis esparcido
esparcirá	esparcirán	habrá esparcido	habrán esparcido

5 potencial simple

		12 potencial compuesto	
esparciría	esparciríamos	habría esparcido	habríamos esparcido
esparcirías	esparciríais	habrías esparcido	habríais esparcido
esparciría	esparcirían	habría esparcido	habrían esparcido

6 presente de subjuntivo

		13 perfecto de subjuntivo	
esparza	esparzamos	haya esparcido	hayamos esparcido
esparzas	esparzáis	hayas esparcido	hayáis esparcido
esparza	esparzan	haya esparcido	hayan esparcido

7 imperfecto de subjuntivo

		14 pluscuamperfecto de subjuntivo	
esparciera	esparciéramos	hubiera esparcido	hubiéramos esparcido
esparcieras	esparcierais	hubieras esparcido	hubierais esparcido
esparciera	esparcieran	hubiera esparcido	hubieran esparcido
OR		OR	
esparciese	esparciésemos	hubiese esparcido	hubiésemos esparcido
esparcieses	esparcieseis	hubieses esparcido	hubieseis esparcido
esparciese	esparciesen	hubiese esparcido	hubiesen esparcido

imperativo	
—	esparzamos
esparce; no esparzas	esparcid; no esparzáis
esparza	esparzan

el esparcimiento scattering, spreading	¡Que lástima! Hay basuras esparcidas
esparcidamente separately, here and there	por las calles. What a pity! There is trash strewn about the streets.
el esparcidor, la esparcidora spreader, scatterer	

esperar

Gerundio **esperando**   Part. pas. **esperado**

to expect, to hope,
to wait (for)

Regular **-ar** verb

The Seven Simple Tenses		The Seven Compound Tenses	
Singular	Plural	Singular	Plural
1 presente de indicativo		8 perfecto de indicativo	
espero	esperamos	he esperado	hemos esperado
esperas	esperáis	has esperado	habéis esperado
espera	esperan	ha esperado	han esperado
2 imperfecto de indicativo		9 pluscuamperfecto de indicativo	
esperaba	esperábamos	había esperado	habíamos esperado
esperabas	esperabais	habías esperado	habíais esperado
esperaba	esperaban	había esperado	habían esperado
3 pretérito		10 pretérito anterior	
esperé	esperamos	hube esperado	hubimos esperado
esperaste	esperasteis	hubiste esperado	hubisteis esperado
esperó	esperaron	hubo esperado	hubieron esperado
4 futuro		11 futuro perfecto	
esperaré	esperaremos	habré esperado	habremos esperado
esperarás	esperaréis	habrás esperado	habréis esperado
esperará	esperarán	habrá esperado	habrán esperado
5 potencial simple		12 potencial compuesto	
esperaría	esperaríamos	habría esperado	habríamos esperado
esperarías	esperaríais	habrías esperado	habríais esperado
esperaría	esperarían	habría esperado	habrían esperado
6 presente de subjuntivo		13 perfecto de subjuntivo	
espere	esperemos	haya esperado	hayamos esperado
esperes	esperéis	hayas esperado	hayáis esperado
espere	esperen	haya esperado	hayan esperado
7 imperfecto de subjuntivo		14 pluscuamperfecto de subjuntivo	
esperara	esperáramos	hubiera esperado	hubiéramos esperado
esperaras	esperarais	hubieras esperado	hubierais esperado
esperara	esperaran	hubiera esperado	hubieran esperado
OR		OR	
esperase	esperásemos	hubiese esperado	hubiésemos esperado
esperases	esperaseis	hubieses esperado	hubieseis esperado
esperase	esperasen	hubiese esperado	hubiesen esperado

imperativo	
—	esperemos
espera; no esperes	esperad; no esperéis
espere	esperen

Mientras hay vida hay esperanza.	**dar esperanzas** to give encouragement
Where there is life there is hope.	**desesperar** to despair
la esperanza hope	**la espera** wait, waiting
No hay esperanza. There is no hope.	**la sala de espera** waiting room

Irregular verb | to be

The Seven Simple Tenses		The Seven Compound Tenses	
Singular	Plural	Singular	Plural
1 presente de indicativo		8 perfecto de indicativo	
estoy	estamos	he estado	hemos estado
estás	estáis	has estado	habéis estado
está	están	ha estado	han estado
2 imperfecto de indicativo		9 pluscuamperfecto de indicativo	
estaba	estábamos	había estado	habíamos estado
estabas	estabais	habías estado	habíais estado
estaba	estaban	había estado	habían estado
3 pretérito		10 pretérito anterior	
estuve	estuvimos	hube estado	hubimos estado
estuviste	estuvisteis	hubiste estado	hubisteis estado
estuvo	estuvieron	hubo estado	hubieron estado
4 futuro		11 futuro perfecto	
estaré	estaremos	habré estado	habremos estado
estarás	estaréis	habrás estado	habréis estado
estará	estarán	habrá estado	habrán estado
5 potencial simple		12 potencial compuesto	
estaría	estaríamos	habría estado	habríamos estado
estarías	estaríais	habrías estado	habríais estado
estaría	estarían	habría estado	habrían estado
6 presente de subjuntivo		13 perfecto de subjuntivo	
esté	estemos	haya estado	hayamos estado
estés	estéis	hayas estado	hayáis estado
esté	estén	haya estado	hayan estado
7 imperfecto de subjuntivo		14 pluscuamperfecto de subjuntivo	
estuviera	estuviéramos	hubiera estado	hubiéramos estado
estuvieras	estuvierais	hubieras estado	hubierais estado
estuviera	estuvieran	hubiera estado	hubieran estado
OR		OR	
estuviese	estuviésemos	hubiese estado	hubiésemos estado
estuvieses	estuvieseis	hubieses estado	hubieseis estado
estuviese	estuviesen	hubiese estado	hubiesen estado

	imperativo
—	estemos
está; no estés	estad; no estéis
esté	estén

—¿Cómo está Ud.?
—Estoy muy bien, gracias. ¿Y usted?
—Estoy enfermo hoy.
estar por   to be in favor of
estar para + inf.   to be about + inf.
estar de acuerdo   to agree

estar listo (lista)   to be ready
está bien   all right, okay
Barcelona está en España.   Barcelona
is (located) in Spain.
Está lloviendo ahora.   It's raining
now.

155

estudiar

Gerundio **estudiando**   Part. pas. **estudiado**

to study

Regular **-ar** verb

The Seven Simple Tenses		The Seven Compound Tenses	
Singular	Plural	Singular	Plural
1 presente de indicativo		**8 perfecto de indicativo**	
estudio	**estudiamos**	**he estudiado**	**hemos estudiado**
estudias	**estudiáis**	**has estudiado**	**habéis estudiado**
estudia	**estudian**	**ha estudiado**	**han estudiado**
2 imperfecto de indicativo		**9 pluscuamperfecto de indicativo**	
estudiaba	**estudiábamos**	**había estudiado**	**habíamos estudiado**
estudiabas	**estudiabais**	**habías estudiado**	**habíais estudiado**
estudiaba	**estudiaban**	**había estudiado**	**habían estudiado**
3 pretérito		**10 pretérito anterior**	
estudié	**estudiamos**	**hube estudiado**	**hubimos estudiado**
estudiaste	**estudiasteis**	**hubiste estudiado**	**hubisteis estudiado**
estudió	**estudiaron**	**hubo estudiado**	**hubieron estudiado**
4 futuro		**11 futuro perfecto**	
estudiaré	**estudiaremos**	**habré estudiado**	**habremos estudiado**
estudiarás	**estudiaréis**	**habrás estudiado**	**habréis estudiado**
estudiará	**estudiarán**	**habrá estudiado**	**habrán estudiado**
5 potencial simple		**12 potencial compuesto**	
estudiaría	**estudiaríamos**	**habría estudiado**	**habríamos estudiado**
estudiarías	**estudiaríais**	**habrías estudiado**	**habríais estudiado**
estudiaría	**estudiarían**	**habría estudiado**	**habrían estudiado**
6 presente de subjuntivo		**13 perfecto de subjuntivo**	
estudie	**estudiemos**	**haya estudiado**	**hayamos estudiado**
estudies	**estudiéis**	**hayas estudiado**	**hayáis estudiado**
estudie	**estudien**	**haya estudiado**	**hayan estudiado**
7 imperfecto de subjuntivo		**14 pluscuamperfecto de subjuntivo**	
estudiara	**estudiáramos**	**hubiera estudiado**	**hubiéramos estudiado**
estudiaras	**estudiarais**	**hubieras estudiado**	**hubierais estudiado**
estudiara	**estudiaran**	**hubiera estudiado**	**hubieran estudiado**
OR		OR	
estudiase	**estudiásemos**	**hubiese estudiado**	**hubiésemos estudiado**
estudiases	**estudiaseis**	**hubieses estudiado**	**hubieseis estudiado**
estudiase	**estudiasen**	**hubiese estudiado**	**hubiesen estudiado**

imperativo	
—	**estudiemos**
estudia; no estudies	**estudiad; no estudiéis**
estudie	**estudien**

Estudio mis lecciones de español todos
  los días.   I study my Spanish lessons
  every day.
Estoy estudiando en mi cuarto y no
  puedo mirar la televisión.   I am
  studying in my room and I cannot
  watch television.

un, una estudiante   student
los altos estudios   advanced studies
el estudio   study, studio, study room
estudiosamente   studiously
estudioso, estudiosa   studious
un (una) estudiante de intercambio
  exchange student

156

Regular **-ir** verb endings with spelling
change: **g** becomes **j** before **a** or **o**

to demand, to urge,
to require

The Seven Simple Tenses		The Seven Compound Tenses	
Singular	Plural	Singular	Plural
1 presente de indicativo		8 perfecto de indicativo	
exijo	**exigimos**	**he exigido**	**hemos exigido**
exiges	**exigís**	**has exigido**	**habéis exigido**
exige	**exigen**	**ha exigido**	**han exigido**
2 imperfecto de indicativo		9 pluscuamperfecto de indicativo	
exigía	**exigíamos**	**había exigido**	**habíamos exigido**
exigías	**exigíais**	**habías exigido**	**habíais exigido**
exigía	**exigían**	**había exigido**	**habían exigido**
3 pretérito		10 pretérito anterior	
exigí	**exigimos**	**hube exigido**	**hubimos exigido**
exigiste	**exigisteis**	**hubiste exigido**	**hubisteis exigido**
exigió	**exigieron**	**hubo exigido**	**hubieron exigido**
4 futuro		11 futuro perfecto	
exigiré	**exigiremos**	**habré exigido**	**habremos exigido**
exigirás	**exigiréis**	**habrás exigido**	**habréis exigido**
exigirá	**exigirán**	**habrá exigido**	**habrán exigido**
5 potencial simple		12 potencial compuesto	
exigiría	**exigiríamos**	**habría exigido**	**habríamos exigido**
exigirías	**exigiríais**	**habrías exigido**	**habríais exigido**
exigiría	**exigirían**	**habría exigido**	**habrían exigido**
6 presente de subjuntivo		13 perfecto de subjuntivo	
exija	**exijamos**	**haya exigido**	**hayamos exigido**
exijas	**exijáis**	**hayas exigido**	**hayáis exigido**
exija	**exijan**	**haya exigido**	**hayan exigido**
7 imperfecto de subjuntivo		14 pluscuamperfecto de subjuntivo	
exigiera	**exigiéramos**	**hubiera exigido**	**hubiéramos exigido**
exigieras	**exigierais**	**hubieras exigido**	**hubierais exigido**
exigiera	**exigieran**	**hubiera exigido**	**hubieran exigido**
OR		OR	
exigiese	**exigiésemos**	**hubiese exigido**	**hubiésemos exigido**
exigieses	**exigieseis**	**hubieses exigido**	**hubieseis exigido**
exigiese	**exigiesen**	**hubiese exigido**	**hubiesen exigido**

	imperativo	
—	**exijamos**	
exige; no exijas	**exigid; no exijáis**	
exija	**exijan**	

exigente exacting, demanding	**exigible** demanding, payable on
la exigencia exigency, requirement	demand
exigir el pago to demand payment	**una persona muy exigente** a very
	demanding person

explicar

Gerundio **explicando**   Part. pas. **explicado**

to explain

Regular **-ar** verb endings with spelling change: **c** becomes **qu** before **e**

The Seven Simple Tenses		The Seven Compound Tenses	
Singular	Plural	Singular	Plural
1 presente de indicativo		8 perfecto de indicativo	
explico	explicamos	he explicado	hemos explicado
explicas	explicáis	has explicado	habéis explicado
explica	explican	ha explicado	han explicado
2 imperfecto de indicativo		9 pluscuamperfecto de indicativo	
explicaba	explicábamos	había explicado	habíamos explicado
explicabas	explicabais	habías explicado	habíais explicado
explicaba	explicaban	había explicado	habían explicado
3 pretérito		10 pretérito anterior	
expliqué	explicamos	hube explicado	hubimos explicado
explicaste	explicasteis	hubiste explicado	hubisteis explicado
explicó	explicaron	hubo explicado	hubieron explicado
4 futuro		11 futuro perfecto	
explicaré	explicaremos	habré explicado	habremos explicado
explicarás	explicaréis	habrás explicado	habréis explicado
explicará	explicarán	habrá explicado	habrán explicado
5 potencial simple		12 potencial compuesto	
explicaría	explicaríamos	habría explicado	habríamos explicado
explicarías	explicaríais	habrías explicado	habríais explicado
explicaría	explicarían	habría explicado	habrían explicado
6 presente de subjuntivo		13 perfecto de subjuntivo	
explique	expliquemos	haya explicado	hayamos explicado
expliques	expliquéis	hayas explicado	hayáis explicado
explique	expliquen	haya explicado	hayan explicado
7 imperfecto de subjuntivo		14 pluscuamperfecto de subjuntivo	
explicara	explicáramos	hubiera explicado	hubiéramos explicado
explicaras	explicarais	hubieras explicado	hubierais explicado
explicara	explicaran	hubiera explicado	hubieran explicado
OR		OR	
explicase	explicásemos	hubiese explicado	hubiésemos explicado
explicases	explicaseis	hubieses explicado	hubieseis explicado
explicase	explicasen	hubiese explicado	hubiesen explicado

imperativo	
—	expliquemos
explica; no expliques	explicad; no expliquéis
explique	expliquen

una explicación explanation	explícitamente explicitly
explícito, explícita explicit	pedir explicaciones to demand an
explicativo, explicativa explanatory	explanation

Regular **-ar** verb   to express

The Seven Simple Tenses		The Seven Compound Tenses	
Singular	Plural	Singular	Plural
1 presente de indicativo		8 perfecto de indicativo	
expreso	expresamos	he expresado	hemos expresado
expresas	expresáis	has expresado	habéis expresado
expresa	expresan	ha expresado	han expresado
2 imperfecto de indicativo		9 pluscuamperfecto de indicativo	
expresaba	expresábamos	había expresado	habíamos expresado
expresabas	expresabais	habías expresado	habíais expresado
expresaba	expresaban	había expresado	habían expresado
3 pretérito		10 pretérito anterior	
expresé	expresamos	hube expresado	hubimos expresado
expresaste	expresasteis	hubiste expresado	hubisteis expresado
expresó	expresaron	hubo expresado	hubieron expresado
4 futuro		11 futuro perfecto	
expresaré	expresaremos	habré expresado	habremos expresado
expresarás	expresaréis	habrás expresado	habréis expresado
expresará	expresarán	habrá expresado	habrán expresado
5 potencial simple		12 potencial compuesto	
expresaría	expresaríamos	habría expresado	habríamos expresado
expresarías	expresaríais	habrías expresado	habríais expresado
expresaría	expresarían	habría expresado	habrían expresado
6 presente de subjuntivo		13 perfecto de subjuntivo	
exprese	expresemos	haya expresado	hayamos expresado
expreses	expreséis	hayas expresado	hayáis expresado
exprese	expresen	haya expresado	hayan expresado
7 imperfecto de subjuntivo		14 pluscuamperfecto de subjuntivo	
expresara	expresáramos	hubiera expresado	hubiéramos expresado
expresaras	expresarais	hubieras expresado	hubierais expresado
expresara	expresaran	hubiera expresado	hubieran expresado
OR		OR	
expresase	expresásemos	hubiese expresado	hubiésemos expresado
expresases	expresaseis	hubieses expresado	hubieseis expresado
expresase	expresasen	hubiese expresado	hubiesen expresado

imperativo	
—	expresemos
expresa; no expreses	expresad; no expreséis
exprese	expresen

expresarse to express oneself	el expresionismo expressionism
expresiones de mi parte kindest	expresamente expressly, on purpose
regards, regards from me	expreso express (train, etc.)
una expresión expression, phrase	expresivamente expressively

faltar

Gerundio **faltando**   Part. pas. **faltado**

to be lacking, to be wanting,
to lack, to miss, to need

Regular **-ar** verb

The Seven Simple Tenses		The Seven Compound Tenses	
Singular	Plural	Singular	Plural
1 presente de indicativo		8 perfecto de indicativo	
falto	faltamos	he faltado	hemos faltado
faltas	faltáis	has faltado	habéis faltado
falta	faltan	ha faltado	han faltado
2 imperfecto de indicativo		9 pluscuamperfecto de indicativo	
faltaba	faltábamos	había faltado	habíamos faltado
faltabas	faltabais	habías faltado	habíais faltado
faltaba	faltaban	había faltado	habían faltado
3 pretérito		10 pretérito anterior	
falté	faltamos	hube faltado	hubimos faltado
faltaste	faltasteis	hubiste faltado	hubisteis faltado
faltó	faltaron	hubo faltado	hubieron faltado
4 futuro		11 futuro perfecto	
faltaré	faltaremos	habré faltado	habremos faltado
faltarás	faltaréis	habrás faltado	habréis faltado
faltará	faltarán	habrá faltado	habrán faltado
5 potencial simple		12 potencial compuesto	
faltaría	faltaríamos	habría faltado	habríamos faltado
faltarías	faltaríais	habrías faltado	habríais faltado
faltaría	faltarían	habría faltado	habrían faltado
6 presente de subjuntivo		13 perfecto de subjuntivo	
falte	faltemos	haya faltado	hayamos faltado
faltes	faltéis	hayas faltado	hayáis faltado
falte	falten	haya faltado	hayan faltado
7 imperfecto de subjuntivo		14 pluscuamperfecto de subjuntivo	
faltara	faltáramos	hubiera faltado	hubiéramos faltado
faltaras	faltarais	hubieras faltado	hubierais faltado
faltara	faltaran	hubiera faltado	hubieran faltado
OR		OR	
faltase	faltásemos	hubiese faltado	hubiésemos faltado
faltases	faltaseis	hubieses faltado	hubieseis faltado
faltase	faltasen	hubiese faltado	hubiesen faltado

imperativo	
—	faltemos
falta; no faltes	faltad; no faltéis
falte	falten

Me falta el tiempo para terminar mi
  trabajo. I need (don't have enough)
  time to finish my work.
a falta de for lack of
poner faltas a to find fault with
sin falta without fail, without fault

¡No faltaba más! That's the limit!
la falta lack, want
hacer falta to be necessary
faltante lacking, wanting
faltar poco para + inf. not to be long
  before

felicitar

Regular **-ar** verb   to congratulate, to felicitate

The Seven Simple Tenses		The Seven Compound Tenses	
Singular	Plural	Singular	Plural
1 presente de indicativo		8 perfecto de indicativo	
felicito	felicitamos	he felicitado	hemos felicitado
felicitas	felicitáis	has felicitado	habéis felicitado
felicita	felicitan	ha felicitado	han felicitado
2 imperfecto de indicativo		9 pluscuamperfecto de indicativo	
felicitaba	felicitábamos	había felicitado	habíamos felicitado
felicitabas	felicitabais	habías felicitado	habíais felicitado
felicitaba	felicitaban	había felicitado	habían felicitado
3 pretérito		10 pretérito anterior	
felicité	felicitamos	hube felicitado	hubimos felicitado
felicitaste	felicitasteis	hubiste felicitado	hubisteis felicitado
felicitó	felicitaron	hubo felicitado	hubieron felicitado
4 futuro		11 futuro perfecto	
felicitaré	felicitaremos	habré felicitado	habremos felicitado
felicitarás	felicitaréis	habrás felicitado	habréis felicitado
felicitará	felicitarán	habrá felicitado	habrán felicitado
5 potencial simple		12 potencial compuesto	
felicitaría	felicitaríamos	habría felicitado	habríamos felicitado
felicitarías	felicitaríais	habrías felicitado	habríais felicitado
felicitaría	felicitarían	habría felicitado	habrían felicitado
6 presente de subjuntivo		13 perfecto de subjuntivo	
felicite	felicitemos	haya felicitado	hayamos felicitado
felicites	felicitéis	hayas felicitado	hayáis felicitado
felicite	feliciten	haya felicitado	hayan felicitado
7 imperfecto de subjuntivo		14 pluscuamperfecto de subjuntivo	
felicitara	felicitáramos	hubiera felicitado	hubiéramos felicitado
felicitaras	felicitarais	hubieras felicitado	hubierais felicitado
felicitara	felicitaran	hubiera felicitado	hubieran felicitado
OR		OR	
felicitase	felicitásemos	hubiese felicitado	hubiésemos felicitado
felicitases	felicitaseis	hubieses felicitado	hubieseis felicitado
felicitase	felicitasen	hubiese felicitado	hubiesen felicitado

	imperativo	
—	felicitemos
felicita; no felicites	felicitad; no felicitéis
felicite	feliciten

---

la felicitación, las felicitaciones
  congratulations
feliz   happy, fortunate, lucky *(pl.* felices)
la felicidad   happiness, good fortune
felizmente   happily, fortunately
¡Felices Fiestas!   Happy Holidays!

felicitar a alguien por...   to
  congratulate someone on/for...
Le felicitamos por su elección al
  senado.   We congratulate you on
  your election to the senate.

fiar

Gerundio **fiando**   Part. pas. **fiado**

to confide, to trust

Regular **-ar** verb endings with spelling change: **i** becomes **í** on stressed syllable (Tenses 1, 6, Imperative)

The Seven Simple Tenses		The Seven Compound Tenses	
Singular	Plural	Singular	Plural
1 presente de indicativo		**8 perfecto de indicativo**	
fío	fiamos	he fiado	hemos fiado
fías	fiáis	has fiado	habéis fiado
fía	fían	ha fiado	han fiado
2 imperfecto de indicativo		**9 pluscuamperfecto de indicativo**	
fiaba	fiábamos	había fiado	habíamos fiado
fiabas	fiabais	habías fiado	habíais fiado
fiaba	fiaban	había fiado	habían fiado
3 pretérito		**10 pretérito anterior**	
fié	fiamos	hube fiado	hubimos fiado
fiaste	fiasteis	hubiste fiado	hubisteis fiado
fió	fiaron	hubo fiado	hubieron fiado
4 futuro		**11 futuro perfecto**	
fiaré	fiaremos	habré fiado	habremos fiado
fiarás	fiaréis	habrás fiado	habréis fiado
fiará	fiarán	habrá fiado	habrán fiado
5 potencial simple		**12 potencial compuesto**	
fiaría	fiaríamos	habría fiado	habríamos fiado
fiarías	fiaríais	habrías fiado	habríais fiado
fiaría	fiarían	habría fiado	habrían fiado
6 presente de subjuntivo		**13 perfecto de subjuntivo**	
fíe	fiemos	haya fiado	hayamos fiado
fíes	fiéis	hayas fiado	hayáis fiado
fíe	fíen	haya fiado	hayan fiado
7 imperfecto de subjuntivo		**14 pluscuamperfecto de subjuntivo**	
fiara	fiáramos	hubiera fiado	hubiéramos fiado
fiaras	fiarais	hubieras fiado	hubierais fiado
fiara	fiaran	hubiera fiado	hubieran fiado
OR		OR	
fiase	fiásemos	hubiese fiado	hubiésemos fiado
fiases	fiaseis	hubieses fiado	hubieseis fiado
fiase	fiasen	hubiese fiado	hubiesen fiado

imperativo	
—	fiemos
fía; no fíes	fiad; no fiéis
fíe	fíen

fiarse de to have confidence in	al fiado on credit, on trust
fiable trustworthy	comprar al fiado to buy on credit
la fianza security, surety, guarantee	desconfiar to distrust, to mistrust
fiar en to trust in	

Regular **-ar** verb   to clinch, to fasten, to fix

The Seven Simple Tenses		The Seven Compound Tenses	
Singular	Plural	Singular	Plural
1 presente de indicativo		**8 perfecto de indicativo**	
fijo	**fijamos**	**he fijado**	**hemos fijado**
fijas	**fijáis**	**has fijado**	**habéis fijado**
fija	**fijan**	**ha fijado**	**han fijado**
2 imperfecto de indicativo		**9 pluscuamperfecto de indicativo**	
fijaba	**fijábamos**	**había fijado**	**habíamos fijado**
fijabas	**fijabais**	**habías fijado**	**habíais fijado**
fijaba	**fijaban**	**había fijado**	**habían fijado**
3 pretérito		**10 pretérito anterior**	
fijé	**fijamos**	**hube fijado**	**hubimos fijado**
fijaste	**fijasteis**	**hubiste fijado**	**hubisteis fijado**
fijó	**fijaron**	**hubo fijado**	**hubieron fijado**
4 futuro		**11 futuro perfecto**	
fijaré	**fijaremos**	**habré fijado**	**habremos fijado**
fijarás	**fijaréis**	**habrás fijado**	**habréis fijado**
fijará	**fijarán**	**habrá fijado**	**habrán fijado**
5 potencial simple		**12 potencial compuesto**	
fijaría	**fijaríamos**	**habría fijado**	**habríamos fijado**
fijarías	**fijaríais**	**habrías fijado**	**habríais fijado**
fijaría	**fijarían**	**habría fijado**	**habrían fijado**
6 presente de subjuntivo		**13 perfecto de subjuntivo**	
fije	**fijemos**	**haya fijado**	**hayamos fijado**
fijes	**fijéis**	**hayas fijado**	**hayáis fijado**
fije	**fijen**	**haya fijado**	**hayan fijado**
7 imperfecto de subjuntivo		**14 pluscuamperfecto de subjuntivo**	
fijara	**fijáramos**	**hubiera fijado**	**hubiéramos fijado**
fijaras	**fijarais**	**hubieras fijado**	**hubierais fijado**
fijara	**fijaran**	**hubiera fijado**	**hubieran fijado**
OR		OR	
fijase	**fijásemos**	**hubiese fijado**	**hubiésemos fijado**
fijases	**fijaseis**	**hubieses fijado**	**hubieseis fijado**
fijase	**fijasen**	**hubiese fijado**	**hubiesen fijado**

imperativo	
—	**fijemos**
fija; no fijes	**fijad; no fijéis**
fije	**fijen**

hora fija set time, set hour, time agreed on	**fijarse en** to take notice of, to pay attention to, to settle in
fijamente fixedly, assuredly	**PROHIBIDO FIJAR CARTELES**
una fija door hinge	**POST NO BILLS**

fijarse

Gerundio **fijándose** Part. pas. **fijado**

to take notice, to pay attention, to settle

Reflexive regular **-ar** verb

The Seven Simple Tenses		The Seven Compound Tenses	
Singular	Plural	Singular	Plural
1 presente de indicativo		**8 perfecto de indicativo**	
me fijo	nos fijamos	me he fijado	nos hemos fijado
te fijas	os fijáis	te has fijado	os habéis fijado
se fija	se fijan	se ha fijado	se han fijado
2 imperfecto de indicativo		**9 pluscuamperfecto de indicativo**	
me fijaba	nos fijábamos	me había fijado	nos habíamos fijado
te fijabas	os fijabais	te habías fijado	os habíais fijado
se fijaba	se fijaban	se había fijado	se habían fijado
3 pretérito		**10 pretérito anterior**	
me fijé	nos fijamos	me hube fijado	nos hubimos fijado
te fijaste	os fijasteis	te hubiste fijado	os hubisteis fijado
se fijó	se fijaron	se hubo fijado	se hubieron fijado
4 futuro		**11 futuro perfecto**	
me fijaré	nos fijaremos	me habré fijado	nos habremos fijado
te fijarás	os fijaréis	te habrás fijado	os habréis fijado
se fijará	se fijarán	se habrá fijado	se habrán fijado
5 potencial simple		**12 potencial compuesto**	
me fijaría	nos fijaríamos	me habría fijado	nos habríamos fijado
te fijarías	os fijaríais	te habrías fijado	os habríais fijado
se fijaría	se fijarían	se habría fijado	se habrían fijado
6 presente de subjuntivo		**13 perfecto de subjuntivo**	
me fije	nos fijemos	me haya fijado	nos hayamos fijado
te fijes	os fijéis	te hayas fijado	os hayáis fijado
se fije	se fijen	se haya fijado	se hayan fijado
7 imperfecto de subjuntivo		**14 pluscuamperfecto de subjuntivo**	
me fijara	nos fijáramos	me hubiera fijado	nos hubiéramos fijado
te fijaras	os fijarais	te hubieras fijado	os hubierais fijado
se fijara	se fijaran	se hubiera fijado	se hubieran fijado
OR		OR	
me fijase	nos fijásemos	me hubiese fijado	nos hubiésemos fijado
te fijases	os fijaseis	te hubieses fijado	os hubieseis fijado
se fijase	se fijasen	se hubiese fijado	se hubiesen fijado

imperativo	
—	fijémonos
fíjate; no te fijes	fijaos; no os fijéis
fíjese	fíjense

---

fijar to clinch, to fasten, to fix; fijo (when used as an adj.)

fijarse en to take notice of, to pay attention to, to settle in

hora fija set time, set hour, time agreed on; de fijo surely

fijamente fixedly, assuredly; fijar el precio to fix the price

la fijación de precios price-fixing

The Seven Simple Tenses		The Seven Compound Tenses	
Singular	Plural	Singular	Plural
1 presente de indicativo		8 perfecto de indicativo	
frío	freímos	he frito	hemos frito
fríes	freís	has frito	habéis frito
fríe	fríen	ha frito	han frito
2 imperfecto de indicativo		9 pluscuamperfecto de indicativo	
freía	freíamos	había frito	habíamos frito
freías	freíais	habías frito	habíais frito
freía	freían	había frito	habían frito
3 pretérito		10 pretérito anterior	
freí	freímos	hube frito	hubimos frito
freíste	freísteis	hubiste frito	hubisteis frito
frió	frieron	hubo frito	hubieron frito
4 futuro		11 futuro perfecto	
freiré	freiremos	habré frito	habremos frito
freirás	freiréis	habrás frito	habréis frito
freirá	freirán	habrá frito	habrán frito
5 potencial simple		12 potencial compuesto	
freiría	freiríamos	habría frito	habríamos frito
freirías	freiríais	habrías frito	habríais frito
freiría	freirían	habría frito	habrían frito
6 presente de subjuntivo		13 perfecto de subjuntivo	
fría	friamos	haya frito	hayamos frito
frías	friáis	hayas frito	hayáis frito
fría	frían	haya frito	hayan frito
7 imperfecto de subjuntivo		14 pluscuamperfecto de subjuntivo	
friera	friéramos	hubiera frito	hubiéramos frito
frieras	frierais	hubieras frito	hubierais frito
friera	frieran	hubiera frito	hubieran frito
OR		OR	
friese	friésemos	hubiese frito	hubiésemos frito
frieses	frieseis	hubieses frito	hubieseis frito
friese	friesen	hubiese frito	hubiesen frito

	imperativo	
—	friamos	
fríe; no frías	freíd; no friáis	
fría	frían	

patatas fritas fried potatoes, french fries	**la fritura** fry
la fritada fried food	**frito, frita** fried
patatas fritas a la inglesa potato chips	**los huevos fritos** fried eggs

ganar

Gerundio **ganando**   Part. pas. **ganado**

to earn, to gain, to win

Regular **-ar** verb

The Seven Simple Tenses		The Seven Compound Tenses	
Singular	Plural	Singular	Plural
1 presente de indicativo		**8 perfecto de indicativo**	
gano	ganamos	he ganado	hemos ganado
ganas	ganáis	has ganado	habéis ganado
gana	ganan	ha ganado	han ganado
2 imperfecto de indicativo		**9 pluscuamperfecto de indicativo**	
ganaba	ganábamos	había ganado	habíamos ganado
ganabas	ganabais	habías ganado	habíais ganado
ganaba	ganaban	había ganado	habían ganado
3 pretérito		**10 pretérito anterior**	
gané	ganamos	hube ganado	hubimos ganado
ganaste	ganasteis	hubiste ganado	hubisteis ganado
ganó	ganaron	hubo ganado	hubieron ganado
4 futuro		**11 futuro perfecto**	
ganaré	ganaremos	habré ganado	habremos ganado
ganarás	ganaréis	habrás ganado	habréis ganado
ganará	ganarán	habrá ganado	habrán ganado
5 potencial simple		**12 potencial compuesto**	
ganaría	ganaríamos	habría ganado	habríamos ganado
ganarías	ganaríais	habrías ganado	habríais ganado
ganaría	ganarían	habría ganado	habrían ganado
6 presente de subjuntivo		**13 perfecto de subjuntivo**	
gane	ganemos	haya ganado	hayamos ganado
ganes	ganéis	hayas ganado	hayáis ganado
gane	ganen	haya ganado	hayan ganado
7 imperfecto de subjuntivo		**14 pluscuamperfecto de subjuntivo**	
ganara	ganáramos	hubiera ganado	hubiéramos ganado
ganaras	ganarais	hubieras ganado	hubierais ganado
ganara	ganaran	hubiera ganado	hubieran ganado
OR		OR	
ganase	ganásemos	hubiese ganado	hubiésemos ganado
ganases	ganaseis	hubieses ganado	hubieseis ganado
ganase	ganasen	hubiese ganado	hubiesen ganado

imperativo	
—	ganemos
gana; no ganes	ganad; no ganéis
gane	ganen

ganar el pan, ganar la vida to earn a living	**ganar dinero** to earn (make) money
la ganancia profit, gain	**ganar el premio gordo** to win first prize, the jackpot
desganarse to lose one's appetite; to be bored	**ir ganando** to be winning, to be in the lead
ganador, ganadora winner	**No se ganó Zamora en una hora.** Rome wasn't built in a day. (Zamora is in northwest Spain.)

Regular **-ir** verb endings with stem change: to grieve, to groan, to moan,
Tenses 1, 3, 6, 7, Imperative, *Gerundio*   to howl

The Seven Simple Tenses		The Seven Compound Tenses	
Singular	Plural	Singular	Plural
1 presente de indicativo		8 perfecto de indicativo	
gimo	gemimos	he gemido	hemos gemido
gimes	gemís	has gemido	habéis gemido
gime	gimen	ha gemido	han gemido
2 imperfecto de indicativo		9 pluscuamperfecto de indicativo	
gemía	gemíamos	había gemido	habíamos gemido
gemías	gemíais	habías gemido	habíais gemido
gemía	gemían	había gemido	habían gemido
3 pretérito		10 pretérito anterior	
gemí	gemimos	hube gemido	hubimos gemido
gemiste	gemisteis	hubiste gemido	hubisteis gemido
gimió	gimieron	hubo gemido	hubieron gemido
4 futuro		11 futuro perfecto	
gemiré	gemiremos	habré gemido	habremos gemido
gemirás	gemiréis	habrás gemido	habréis gemido
gemirá	gemirán	habrá gemido	habrán gemido
5 potencial simple		12 potencial compuesto	
gemiría	gemiríamos	habría gemido	habríamos gemido
gemirías	gemiríais	habrías gemido	habríais gemido
gemiría	gemirían	habría gemido	habrían gemido
6 presente de subjuntivo		13 perfecto de subjuntivo	
gima	gimamos	haya gemido	hayamos gemido
gimas	gimáis	hayas gemido	hayáis gemido
gima	giman	haya gemido	hayan gemido
7 imperfecto de subjuntivo		14 pluscuamperfecto de subjuntivo	
gimiera	gimiéramos	hubiera gemido	hubiéramos gemido
gimieras	gimierais	hubieras gemido	hubierais gemido
gimiera	gimieran	hubiera gemido	hubieran gemido
OR		OR	
gimiese	gimiésemos	hubiese gemido	hubiésemos gemido
gimieses	gimieseis	hubieses gemido	hubieseis gemido
gimiese	gimiesen	hubiese gemido	hubiesen gemido

	imperativo	
—	gimamos	
gime; no gimas	gemid; no gimáis	
gima	giman	

gemidor, gemidora   lamenter, griever   el gemiqueo   whining
gemiquear   to whine
el gemido   lamentation, howl, groan,
   moan

gozar

Gerundio **gozando**   Part. pas. **gozado**

to enjoy

Regular **-ar** verb endings with spelling change: **z** becomes **c** before **e**

The Seven Simple Tenses		The Seven Compound Tenses	
Singular	Plural	Singular	Plural
1 presente de indicativo		8 perfecto de indicativo	
gozo	gozamos	he gozado	hemos gozado
gozas	gozáis	has gozado	habéis gozado
goza	gozan	ha gozado	han gozado
2 imperfecto de indicativo		9 pluscuamperfecto de indicativo	
gozaba	gozábamos	había gozado	habíamos gozado
gozabas	gozabais	habías gozado	habíais gozado
gozaba	gozaban	había gozado	habían gozado
3 pretérito		10 pretérito anterior	
gocé	gozamos	hube gozado	hubimos gozado
gozaste	gozasteis	hubiste gozado	hubisteis gozado
gozó	gozaron	hubo gozado	hubieron gozado
4 futuro		11 futuro perfecto	
gozaré	gozaremos	habré gozado	habremos gozado
gozarás	gozaréis	habrás gozado	habréis gozado
gozará	gozarán	habrá gozado	habrán gozado
5 potencial simple		12 potencial compuesto	
gozaría	gozaríamos	habría gozado	habríamos gozado
gozarías	gozaríais	habrías gozado	habríais gozado
gozaría	gozarían	habría gozado	habrían gozado
6 presente de subjuntivo		13 perfecto de subjuntivo	
goce	gocemos	haya gozado	hayamos gozado
goces	gocéis	hayas gozado	hayáis gozado
goce	gocen	haya gozado	hayan gozado
7 imperfecto de subjuntivo		14 pluscuamperfecto de subjuntivo	
gozara	gozáramos	hubiera gozado	hubiéramos gozado
gozaras	gozarais	hubieras gozado	hubierais gozado
gozara	gozaran	hubiera gozado	hubieran gozado
OR		OR	
gozase	gozásemos	hubiese gozado	hubiésemos gozado
gozases	gozaseis	hubieses gozado	hubieseis gozado
gozase	gozasen	hubiese gozado	hubiesen gozado

imperativo	
—	gocemos
goza; no goces	gozad; no gocéis
goce	gocen

el goce enjoyment	el gozo joy, pleasure
saltar de gozo to jump with joy	gozarla to have a good time
gozador, gozadora, gozante enjoyer	gozar de buena salud to enjoy good
gozosamente joyfully	health

Regular **-ar** verb

to shout, to scream,
to shriek, to cry out

The Seven Simple Tenses		The Seven Compound Tenses	
Singular	Plural	Singular	Plural
1 presente de indicativo		8 perfecto de indicativo	
grito	gritamos	he gritado	hemos gritado
gritas	gritáis	has gritado	habéis gritado
grita	gritan	ha gritado	han gritado
2 imperfecto de indicativo		9 pluscuamperfecto de indicativo	
gritaba	gritábamos	había gritado	habíamos gritado
gritabas	gritabais	habías gritado	habíais gritado
gritaba	gritaban	había gritado	habían gritado
3 pretérito		10 pretérito anterior	
grité	gritamos	hube gritado	hubimos gritado
gritaste	gritasteis	hubiste gritado	hubisteis gritado
gritó	gritaron	hubo gritado	hubieron gritado
4 futuro		11 futuro perfecto	
gritaré	gritaremos	habré gritado	habremos gritado
gritarás	gritaréis	habrás gritado	habréis gritado
gritará	gritarán	habrá gritado	habrán gritado
5 potencial simple		12 potencial compuesto	
gritaría	gritaríamos	habría gritado	habríamos gritado
gritarías	gritaríais	habrías gritado	habríais gritado
gritaría	gritarían	habría gritado	habrían gritado
6 presente de subjuntivo		13 perfecto de subjuntivo	
grite	gritemos	haya gritado	hayamos gritado
grites	gritéis	hayas gritado	hayáis gritado
grite	griten	haya gritado	hayan gritado
7 imperfecto de subjuntivo		14 pluscuamperfecto de subjuntivo	
gritara	gritáramos	hubiera gritado	hubiéramos gritado
gritaras	gritarais	hubieras gritado	hubierais gritado
gritara	gritaran	hubiera gritado	hubieran gritado
OR		OR	
gritase	gritásemos	hubiese gritado	hubiésemos gritado
gritases	gritaseis	hubieses gritado	hubieseis gritado
gritase	gritasen	hubiese gritado	hubiesen gritado

imperativo	
—	gritemos
grita; no grites	gritad; no gritéis
grite	griten

el grito   cry, scream, shout
un gritón, una gritona   screamer
a gritos   at the top of one's voice,
 loudly
dar grita a   to hoot at
la grita, la gritería   outcry, shouting

gritar a un actor   to boo an actor
el Grito de Independencia   the shout,
 or cry for freedom, that celebrates
 Mexico's independence from Spain
 (celebrated September 16)

gruñir

Gerundio **gruñendo** Part. pas. **gruñido**

to grumble, to grunt,
to growl, to creak

Regular **-ir** verb endings with spelling change:
Tenses 3 and 7; note present participle

The Seven Simple Tenses | The Seven Compound Tenses

Singular	Plural	Singular	Plural
1 presente de indicativo		8 perfecto de indicativo	
gruño	gruñimos	he gruñido	hemos gruñido
gruñes	gruñís	has gruñido	habéis gruñido
gruñe	gruñen	ha gruñido	han gruñido
2 imperfecto de indicativo		9 pluscuamperfecto de indicativo	
gruñía	gruñíamos	había gruñido	habíamos gruñido
gruñías	gruñíais	habías gruñido	habíais gruñido
gruñía	gruñían	había gruñido	habían gruñido
3 pretérito		10 pretérito anterior	
gruñí	gruñimos	hube gruñido	hubimos gruñido
gruñiste	gruñisteis	hubiste gruñido	hubisteis gruñido
gruñó	gruñeron	hubo gruñido	hubieron gruñido
4 futuro		11 futuro perfecto	
gruñiré	gruñiremos	habré gruñido	habremos gruñido
gruñirás	gruñiréis	habrás gruñido	habréis gruñido
gruñirá	gruñirán	habrá gruñido	habrán gruñido
5 potencial simple		12 potencial compuesto	
gruñiría	gruñiríamos	habría gruñido	habríamos gruñido
gruñirías	gruñiríais	habrías gruñido	habríais gruñido
gruñiría	gruñirían	habría gruñido	habrían gruñido
6 presente de subjuntivo		13 perfecto de subjuntivo	
gruña	gruñamos	haya gruñido	hayamos gruñido
gruñas	gruñáis	hayas gruñido	hayáis gruñido
gruña	gruñan	haya gruñido	hayan gruñido
7 imperfecto de subjuntivo		14 pluscuamperfecto de subjuntivo	
gruñera	gruñéramos	hubiera gruñido	hubiéramos gruñido
gruñeras	gruñerais	hubieras gruñido	hubierais gruñido
gruñera	gruñeran	hubiera gruñido	hubieran gruñido
OR		OR	
gruñese	gruñésemos	hubiese gruñido	hubiésemos gruñido
gruñeses	gruñeseis	hubieses gruñido	hubieseis gruñido
gruñese	gruñesen	hubiese gruñido	hubiesen gruñido

imperativo

—	gruñamos
gruñe; no gruñas	gruñid; no gruñáis
gruña	gruñan

gruñón, gruñona cranky
el gruñido, el gruñimiento grunting,
  grunt, growling, growl

gruñidor, gruñidora growler,
  grumbler

Regular -ar verb endings with spelling change: i becomes   to lead, to guide
í on stressed syllable (Tenses 1, 6, Imperative)

The Seven Simple Tenses		The Seven Compound Tenses	
Singular	Plural	Singular	Plural
1 presente de indicativo		8 perfecto de indicativo	
guío	guiamos	he guiado	hemos guiado
guías	guiáis	has guiado	habéis guiado
guía	guían	ha guiado	han guiado
2 imperfecto de indicativo		9 pluscuamperfecto de indicativo	
guiaba	guiábamos	había guiado	habíamos guiado
guiabas	guiabais	habías guiado	habíais guiado
guiaba	guiaban	había guiado	habían guiado
3 pretérito		10 pretérito anterior	
guié	guiamos	hube guiado	hubimos guiado
guiaste	guiasteis	hubiste guiado	hubisteis guiado
guió	guiaron	hubo guiado	hubieron guiado
4 futuro		11 futuro perfecto	
guiaré	guiaremos	habré guiado	habremos guiado
guiarás	guiaréis	habrás guiado	habréis guiado
guiará	guiarán	habrá guiado	habrán guiado
5 potencial simple		12 potencial compuesto	
guiaría	guiaríamos	habría guiado	habríamos guiado
guiarías	guiaríais	habrías guiado	habríais guiado
guiaría	guiarían	habría guiado	habrían guiado
6 presente de subjuntivo		13 perfecto de subjuntivo	
guíe	guiemos	haya guiado	hayamos guiado
guíes	guiéis	hayas guiado	hayáis guiado
guíe	guíen	haya guiado	hayan guiado
7 imperfecto de subjuntivo		14 pluscuamperfecto de subjuntivo	
guiara	guiáramos	hubiera guiado	hubiéramos guiado
guiaras	guiarais	hubieras guiado	hubierais guiado
guiara	guiaran	hubiera guiado	hubieran guiado
OR		OR	
guiase	guiásemos	hubiese guiado	hubiésemos guiado
guiases	guiaseis	hubieses guiado	hubieseis guiado
guiase	guiasen	hubiese guiado	hubiesen guiado

imperativo	
—	guiemos
guía; no guíes	guiad; no guiéis
guíe	guíen

el guía guide, leader	la guía de teléfonos telephone
la guía guidebook	directory
guiarse por to be guided by, to be	la guía turística tourist guidebook
governed by	

gustar

Gerundio **gustando**   Part. pas. **gustado**

to be pleasing (to), to like

Regular **-ar** verb

The Seven Simple Tenses		The Seven Compound Tenses	
Singular	Plural	Singular	Plural
1 presente de indicativo		8 perfecto de indicativo	
gusta	**gustan**	**ha gustado**	**han gustado**
2 imperfecto de indicativo		9 pluscuamperfecto de indicativo	
gustaba	**gustaban**	**había gustado**	**habían gustado**
3 pretérito		10 pretérito anterior	
gustó	**gustaron**	**hubo gustado**	**hubieron gustado**
4 futuro		11 futuro perfecto	
gustará	**gustarán**	**habrá gustado**	**habrán gustado**
5 potencial simple		12 potencial compuesto	
gustaría	**gustarían**	**habría gustado**	**habrían gustado**
6 presente de subjuntivo		13 perfecto de subjuntivo	
que guste	**que gusten**	**que haya gustado**	**que hayan gustado**
7 imperfecto de subjuntivo		14 pluscuamperfecto de subjuntivo	
que gustara	**que gustaran**	**que hubiera gustado**	**que hubieran gustado**
OR		OR	
que gustase	**que gustasen**	**que hubiese gustado**	**que hubiesen gustado**

imperativo
¡Que guste!	**¡Que gusten!**

This verb is commonly used in the third person singular or plural:	**Me gustaría un pastel.** I would like a pastry.
Me gusta el café. I like coffee.	**Me gusta leer.** I like to read.
Me gustan la leche y el café. I like milk and coffee.	**el gusto** taste, pleasure, liking
A María le gustan los dulces. Mary likes candy.	**dar gusto** to please
A José y a Elena les gustan los deportes. Joseph and Helen like sports.	**gustoso, gustosa** tasty, pleasing
	tener gusto en to be glad to

172

Irregular verb   to have (as an auxiliary, helping
                                                                                 verb to form the compound tenses)

The Seven Simple Tenses		The Seven Compound Tenses	
Singular	Plural	Singular	Plural
1 presente de indicativo		8 perfecto de indicativo	
he	hemos	he habido	hemos habido
has	habéis	has habido	habéis habido
ha	han	ha habido	han habido
2 imperfecto de indicativo		9 pluscuamperfecto de indicativo	
había	habíamos	había habido	habíamos habido
habías	habíais	habías habido	habíais habido
había	habían	había habido	habían habido
3 pretérito		10 pretérito anterior	
hube	hubimos	hube habido	hubimos habido
hubiste	hubisteis	hubiste habido	hubisteis habido
hubo	hubieron	hubo habido	hubieron habido
4 futuro		11 futuro perfecto	
habré	habremos	habré habido	habremos habido
habrás	habréis	habrás habido	habréis habido
habrá	habrán	habrá habido	habrán habido
5 potencial simple		12 potencial compuesto	
habría	habríamos	habría habido	habríamos habido
habrías	habríais	habrías habido	habríais habido
habría	habrían	habría habido	habrían habido
6 presente de subjuntivo		13 perfecto de subjuntivo	
haya	hayamos	haya habido	hayamos habido
hayas	hayáis	hayas habido	hayáis habido
haya	hayan	haya habido	hayan habido
7 imperfecto de subjuntivo		14 pluscuamperfecto de subjuntivo	
hubiera	hubiéramos	hubiera habido	hubiéramos habido
hubieras	hubierais	hubieras habido	hubierais habido
hubiera	hubieran	hubiera habido	hubieran habido
OR		OR	
hubiese	hubiésemos	hubiese habido	hubiésemos habido
hubieses	hubieseis	hubieses habido	hubieseis habido
hubiese	hubiesen	hubiese habido	hubiesen habido

	imperativo
—	hayamos
hé; no hayas	habed; no hayáis
haya	hayan

Haber is used as an auxiliary (helping)
  verb to form the compound tenses.
  (See pp. xxviii–xxxii.)
He hablado.   I have spoken.
The word **hay** can be seen as an
  impersonal irregular form of **haber**.
  Its English equivalent is *There is...* or
  There are...

Hay muchas personas en el cine.
  There are many people in the theater.
Había veinte alumnos en la clase.
  There were twenty students in the class.
el haber   credit (in bookkeeping); **los
  haberes**   assets, possessions
habérselas con alguien   to have a
  showdown with someone

habitar

Gerundio **habitando**   Part. pas. **habitado**

to inhabit, to dwell,
to live, to reside

Regular **-ar** verb

The Seven Simple Tenses		The Seven Compound Tenses	
Singular	Plural	Singular	Plural
1 presente de indicativo		8 perfecto de indicativo	
habito	**habitamos**	**he habitado**	**hemos habitado**
habitas	**habitáis**	**has habitado**	**habéis habitado**
habita	**habitan**	**ha habitado**	**han habitado**
2 imperfecto de indicativo		9 pluscuamperfecto de indicativo	
habitaba	**habitábamos**	**había habitado**	**habíamos habitado**
habitabas	**habitabais**	**habías habitado**	**habíais habitado**
habitaba	**habitaban**	**había habitado**	**habían habitado**
3 pretérito		10 pretérito anterior	
habité	**habitamos**	**hube habitado**	**hubimos habitado**
habitaste	**habitasteis**	**hubiste habitado**	**hubisteis habitado**
habitó	**habitaron**	**hubo habitado**	**hubieron habitado**
4 futuro		11 futuro perfecto	
habitaré	**habitaremos**	**habré habitado**	**habremos habitado**
habitarás	**habitaréis**	**habrás habitado**	**habréis habitado**
habitará	**habitarán**	**habrá habitado**	**habrán habitado**
5 potencial simple		12 potencial compuesto	
habitaría	**habitaríamos**	**habría habitado**	**habríamos habitado**
habitarías	**habitaríais**	**habrías habitado**	**habríais habitado**
habitaría	**habitarían**	**habría habitado**	**habrían habitado**
6 presente de subjuntivo		13 perfecto de subjuntivo	
habite	**habitemos**	**haya habitado**	**hayamos habitado**
habites	**habitéis**	**hayas habitado**	**hayáis habitado**
habite	**habiten**	**haya habitado**	**hayan habitado**
7 imperfecto de subjuntivo		14 pluscuamperfecto de subjuntivo	
habitara	**habitáramos**	**hubiera habitado**	**hubiéramos habitado**
habitaras	**habitarais**	**hubieras habitado**	**hubierais habitado**
habitara	**habitaran**	**hubiera habitado**	**hubieran habitado**
OR		OR	
habitase	**habitásemos**	**hubiese habitado**	**hubiésemos habitado**
habitases	**habitaseis**	**hubieses habitado**	**hubieseis habitado**
habitase	**habitasen**	**hubiese habitado**	**hubiesen habitado**

imperativo	
—	**habitemos**
habita; no habites	**habitad; no habitéis**
habite	**habiten**

la habitación habitation, residence, dwelling, abode	**el, la habitante** inhabitant
habitador, habitadora inhabitant	**la habitación individual** single room
la habitabilidad habitability	**la habitación doble** double room

The Seven Simple Tenses		The Seven Compound Tenses	
Singular	Plural	Singular	Plural
1 presente de indicativo		8 perfecto de indicativo	
hablo	hablamos	he hablado	hemos hablado
hablas	habláis	has hablado	habéis hablado
habla	hablan	ha hablado	han hablado
2 imperfecto de indicativo		9 pluscuamperfecto de indicativo	
hablaba	hablábamos	había hablado	habíamos hablado
hablabas	hablabais	habías hablado	habíais hablado
hablaba	hablaban	había hablado	habían hablado
3 pretérito		10 pretérito anterior	
hablé	hablamos	hube hablado	hubimos hablado
hablaste	hablasteis	hubiste hablado	hubisteis hablado
habló	hablaron	hubo hablado	hubieron hablado
4 futuro		11 futuro perfecto	
hablaré	hablaremos	habré hablado	habremos hablado
hablarás	hablaréis	habrás hablado	habréis hablado
hablará	hablarán	habrá hablado	habrán hablado
5 potencial simple		12 potencial compuesto	
hablaría	hablaríamos	habría hablado	habríamos hablado
hablarías	hablaríais	habrías hablado	habríais hablado
hablaría	hablarían	habría hablado	habrían hablado
6 presente de subjuntivo		13 perfecto de subjuntivo	
hable	hablemos	haya hablado	hayamos hablado
hables	habléis	hayas hablado	hayáis hablado
hable	hablen	haya hablado	hayan hablado
7 imperfecto de subjuntivo		14 pluscuamperfecto de subjuntivo	
hablara	habláramos	hubiera hablado	hubiéramos hablado
hablaras	hablarais	hubieras hablado	hubierais hablado
hablara	hablaran	hubiera hablado	hubieran hablado
OR		OR	
hablase	hablásemos	hubiese hablado	hubiésemos hablado
hablases	hablaseis	hubieses hablado	hubieseis hablado
hablase	hablasen	hubiese hablado	hubiesen hablado

	imperativo
—	hablemos
habla; no hables	hablad; no habléis
hable	hablen

hispanohablante Spanish-speaking	de habla española Spanish-speaking
hablador, habladora talkative	de habla inglesa English-speaking
hablar al oído to whisper in one's ear	**Aquí se habla español.** Spanish is
hablar a gritos to shout	spoken here.
la habladuría gossip, idle rumor	**Hable más despacio, por favor.**
hablar entre dientes to mumble	Speak more slowly, please.

hacer

Gerundio **haciendo**   Part. pas. **hecho**

to do, to make   Irregular verb

The Seven Simple Tenses		The Seven Compound Tenses	
Singular	Plural	Singular	Plural
1 presente de indicativo		**8 perfecto de indicativo**	
hago	hacemos	he hecho	hemos hecho
haces	hacéis	has hecho	habéis hecho
hace	hacen	ha hecho	han hecho
2 imperfecto de indicativo		**9 pluscuamperfecto de indicativo**	
hacía	hacíamos	había hecho	habíamos hecho
hacías	hacíais	habías hecho	habíais hecho
hacía	hacían	había hecho	habían hecho
3 pretérito		**10 pretérito anterior**	
hice	hicimos	hube hecho	hubimos hecho
hiciste	hicisteis	hubiste hecho	hubisteis hecho
hizo	hicieron	hubo hecho	hubieron hecho
4 futuro		**11 futuro perfecto**	
haré	haremos	habré hecho	habremos hecho
harás	haréis	habrás hecho	habréis hecho
hará	harán	habrá hecho	habrán hecho
5 potencial simple		**12 potencial compuesto**	
haría	haríamos	habría hecho	habríamos hecho
harías	haríais	habrías hecho	habríais hecho
haría	harían	habría hecho	habrían hecho
6 presente de subjuntivo		**13 perfecto de subjuntivo**	
haga	hagamos	haya hecho	hayamos hecho
hagas	hagáis	hayas hecho	hayáis hecho
haga	hagan	haya hecho	hayan hecho
7 imperfecto de subjuntivo		**14 pluscuamperfecto de subjuntivo**	
hiciera	hiciéramos	hubiera hecho	hubiéramos hecho
hicieras	hicierais	hubieras hecho	hubierais hecho
hiciera	hicieran	hubiera hecho	hubieran hecho
OR		OR	
hiciese	hiciésemos	hubiese hecho	hubiésemos hecho
hicieses	hicieseis	hubieses hecho	hubieseis hecho
hiciese	hiciesen	hubiese hecho	hubiesen hecho

imperativo	
—	hagamos
haz; no hagas	haced; no hagáis
haga	hagan

Hace tres años que estudio español.
  I have been studying Spanish for
  three years.
Hace calor.   It's warm/hot.
Se hace tarde.   It's getting late.

Dicho y hecho.   No sooner said than
  done.
La práctica hace maestro al novicio.
  Practice makes perfect.
hace un año   a year ago
hacer un viaje   to take a trip
hacer cara a   to face

Regular **-ar** verb   to find, to come across

The Seven Simple Tenses		The Seven Compound Tenses	
Singular	Plural	Singular	Plural
1 presente de indicativo		**8 perfecto de indicativo**	
hallo	hallamos	he hallado	hemos hallado
hallas	halláis	has hallado	habéis hallado
halla	hallan	ha hallado	han hallado
2 imperfecto de indicativo		**9 pluscuamperfecto de indicativo**	
hallaba	hallábamos	había hallado	habíamos hallado
hallabas	hallabais	habías hallado	habíais hallado
hallaba	hallaban	había hallado	habían hallado
3 pretérito		**10 pretérito anterior**	
hallé	hallamos	hube hallado	hubimos hallado
hallaste	hallasteis	hubiste hallado	hubisteis hallado
halló	hallaron	hubo hallado	hubieron hallado
4 futuro		**11 futuro perfecto**	
hallaré	hallaremos	habré hallado	habremos hallado
hallarás	hallaréis	habrás hallado	habréis hallado
hallará	hallarán	habrá hallado	habrán hallado
5 potencial simple		**12 potencial compuesto**	
hallaría	hallaríamos	habría hallado	habríamos hallado
hallarías	hallaríais	habrías hallado	habríais hallado
hallaría	hallarían	habría hallado	habrían hallado
6 presente de subjuntivo		**13 perfecto de subjuntivo**	
halle	hallemos	haya hallado	hayamos hallado
halles	halléis	hayas hallado	hayáis hallado
halle	hallen	haya hallado	hayan hallado
7 imperfecto de subjuntivo		**14 pluscuamperfecto de subjuntivo**	
hallara	halláramos	hubiera hallado	hubiéramos hallado
hallaras	hallarais	hubieras hallado	hubierais hallado
hallara	hallaran	hubiera hallado	hubieran hallado
OR		OR	
hallase	hallásemos	hubiese hallado	hubiésemos hallado
hallases	hallaseis	hubieses hallado	hubieseis hallado
hallase	hallasen	hubiese hallado	hubiesen hallado

imperativo	
—	hallemos
halla; no halles	hallad; no halléis
halle	hallen

---

hallar bien con to be well pleased
   with
un hallazgo a find, something found
hallador, halladora discoverer, finder

la hallada discovery, find
Cosa hallada no es hurtada. Finders
keepers, losers weepers. (hurtar: to
steal)

herir

Gerundio **hiriendo**   Part. pas. **herido**

to harm, to hurt, to wound

Regular **-ir** verb endings with stem change:
Tenses 1, 3, 6, 7, Imperative, *Gerundio*

The Seven Simple Tenses		The Seven Compound Tenses	
Singular	Plural	Singular	Plural
1 presente de indicativo		**8 perfecto de indicativo**	
hiero	herimos	he herido	hemos herido
hieres	herís	has herido	habéis herido
hiere	hieren	ha herido	han herido
2 imperfecto de indicativo		**9 pluscuamperfecto de indicativo**	
hería	heríamos	había herido	habíamos herido
herías	heríais	habías herido	habíais herido
hería	herían	había herido	habían herido
3 pretérito		**10 pretérito anterior**	
herí	herimos	hube herido	hubimos herido
heriste	heristeis	hubiste herido	hubisteis herido
hirió	hirieron	hubo herido	hubieron herido
4 futuro		**11 futuro perfecto**	
heriré	heriremos	habré herido	habremos herido
herirás	heriréis	habrás herido	habréis herido
herirá	herirán	habrá herido	habrán herido
5 potencial simple		**12 potencial compuesto**	
heriría	heriríamos	habría herido	habríamos herido
herirías	heriríais	habrías herido	habríais herido
heriría	herirían	habría herido	habrían herido
6 presente de subjuntivo		**13 perfecto de subjuntivo**	
hiera	hiramos	haya herido	hayamos herido
hieras	hiráis	hayas herido	hayáis herido
hiera	hieran	haya herido	hayan herido
7 imperfecto de subjuntivo		**14 pluscuamperfecto de subjuntivo**	
hiriera	hiriéramos	hubiera herido	hubiéramos herido
hirieras	hirierais	hubieras herido	hubierais herido
hiriera	hirieran	hubiera herido	hubieran herido
OR		OR	
hiriese	hiriésemos	hubiese herido	hubiésemos herido
hirieses	hirieseis	hubieses herido	hubieseis herido
hiriese	hiriesen	hubiese herido	hubiesen herido

imperativo	
—	hiramos
hiere; no hieras	herid; no hiráis
hiera	hieran

la herida wound	a grito herido in loud cries
una herida abierta open wound	
malherido, malherida seriously wounded	

Regular **-ir** verb endings with spelling
change: add **y** before **a**, **e**, or **o**

to escape, to flee,
to run away, to slip away

The Seven Simple Tenses		The Seven Compound Tenses	
Singular	Plural	Singular	Plural
1 presente de indicativo		8 perfecto de indicativo	
huyo	huimos	he huido	hemos huido
huyes	huís	has huido	habéis huido
huye	huyen	ha huido	han huido
2 imperfecto de indicativo		9 pluscuamperfecto de indicativo	
huía	huíamos	había huido	habíamos huido
huías	huíais	habías huido	habíais huido
huía	huían	había huido	habían huido
3 pretérito		10 pretérito anterior	
huí	huimos	hube huido	hubimos huido
huiste	huisteis	hubiste huido	hubisteis huido
huyó	huyeron	hubo huido	hubieron huido
4 futuro		11 futuro perfecto	
huiré	huiremos	habré huido	habremos huido
huirás	huiréis	habrás huido	habréis huido
huirá	huirán	habrá huido	habrán huido
5 potencial simple		12 potencial compuesto	
huiría	huiríamos	habría huido	habríamos huido
huirías	huiríais	habrías huido	habríais huido
huiría	huirían	habría huido	habrían huido
6 presente de subjuntivo		13 perfecto de subjuntivo	
huya	huyamos	haya huido	hayamos huido
huyas	huyáis	hayas huido	hayáis huido
huya	huyan	haya huido	hayan huido
7 imperfecto de subjuntivo		14 pluscuamperfecto de subjuntivo	
huyera	huyéramos	hubiera huido	hubiéramos huido
huyeras	huyerais	hubieras huido	hubierais huido
huyera	huyeran	hubiera huido	hubieran huido
OR		OR	
huyese	huyésemos	hubiese huido	hubiésemos huido
huyeses	huyeseis	hubieses huido	hubieseis huido
huyese	huyesen	hubiese huido	hubiesen huido

imperativo

—	huyamos
huye; no huyas	huid; no huyáis
huya	huyan

¡Huye! Run! Flee!	la huida escape, flight
¡Cómo huyen las horas! How time	rehuir to avoid, refuse, shun
flies!	huidizo, huidiza fugitive
huir de to keep away from	el huido, la huida fugitive, escaped
huidor, huidora fleeing, fugitive	prisoner

179

importar

Gerundio **importando**   Part. pas. **importado**

to matter, to be important

Regular **-ar** verb

The Seven Simple Tenses		The Seven Compound Tenses	
Singular	Plural	Singular	Plural
1 presente de indicativo		8 perfecto de indicativo	
importa	**importan**	**ha importado**	**han importado**
2 imperfecto de indicativo		9 pluscuamperfecto de indicativo	
importaba	**importaban**	**había importado**	**habían importado**
3 pretérito		10 pretérito anterior	
importó	**importaron**	**hubo importado**	**hubieron importado**
4 futuro		11 futuro perfecto	
importará	**importarán**	**habrá importado**	**habrán importado**
5 potencial simple		12 potencial compuesto	
importaría	**importarían**	**habría importado**	**habrían importado**
6 presente de subjuntivo		13 perfecto de subjuntivo	
que importe	**que importen**	**que haya importado**	**que hayan importado**
7 imperfecto de subjuntivo		14 pluscuamperfecto de subjuntivo	
que importara	**que importaran**	**que hubiera importado**	**que hubieran importado**
OR		OR	
que importase	**que importasen**	**que hubiese importado**	**que hubiesen importado**

imperativo
¡Que importe!   **¡Que importen!**

This verb can be conjugated regularly in all the persons but it is used most commonly as an impersonal verb in the third person.

No importa.   It does not matter.
Eso no importa.   That does not matter.
No me importaría.   It wouldn't matter to me.

la importancia   importance
importante   important
dar importancia a   to value
de gran importancia   of great importance
darse importancia   to be pretentious
¿Qué importa?   What difference does it make?

Regular **-ir** verb endings with spelling change: add **y** before **a**, **e**, or **o**

to include, to enclose

The Seven Simple Tenses		The Seven Compound Tenses	
Singular	Plural	Singular	Plural
1 presente de indicativo		8 perfecto de indicativo	
incluyo	incluimos	he incluido	hemos incluido
incluyes	incluís	has incluido	habéis incluido
incluye	incluyen	ha incluido	han incluido
2 imperfecto de indicativo		9 pluscuamperfecto de indicativo	
incluía	incluíamos	había incluido	habíamos incluido
incluías	incluíais	habías incluido	habíais incluido
incluía	incluían	había incluido	habían incluido
3 pretérito		10 pretérito anterior	
incluí	incluimos	hube incluido	hubimos incluido
incluiste	incluisteis	hubiste incluido	hubisteis incluido
incluyó	incluyeron	hubo incluido	hubieron incluido
4 futuro		11 futuro perfecto	
incluiré	incluiremos	habré incluido	habremos incluido
incluirás	incluiréis	habrás incluido	habréis incluido
incluirá	incluirán	habrá incluido	habrán incluido
5 potencial simple		12 potencial compuesto	
incluiría	incluiríamos	habría incluido	habríamos incluido
incluirías	incluiríais	habrías incluido	habríais incluido
incluiría	incluirían	habría incluido	habrían incluido
6 presente de subjuntivo		13 perfecto de subjuntivo	
incluya	incluyamos	haya incluido	hayamos incluido
incluyas	incluyáis	hayas incluido	hayáis incluido
incluya	incluyan	haya incluido	hayan incluido
7 imperfecto de subjuntivo		14 pluscuamperfecto de subjuntivo	
incluyera	incluyéramos	hubiera incluido	hubiéramos incluido
incluyeras	incluyerais	hubieras incluido	hubierais incluido
incluyera	incluyeran	hubiera incluido	hubieran incluido
OR		OR	
incluyese	incluyésemos	hubiese incluido	hubiésemos incluido
incluyeses	incluyeseis	hubieses incluido	hubieseis incluido
incluyese	incluyesen	hubiese incluido	hubiesen incluido

imperatívo	
—	incluyamos
incluye; no incluyas	incluid; no incluyáis
incluya	incluyan

¿La propina está incluida? Is the tip included?
inclusivo, inclusiva inclusive, including

la inclusión inclusion
una inclusa foundling home
inclusivamente inclusively
todo incluido everything included

indicar

Gerundio **indicando**   Part. pas. **indicado**

to indicate, to point out

Regular **-ar** verb endings with spelling change: **c** becomes **qu** before **e**

The Seven Simple Tenses		The Seven Compound Tenses	
Singular	Plural	Singular	Plural
1 presente de indicativo		**8 perfecto de indicativo**	
indico	indicamos	he indicado	hemos indicado
indicas	indicáis	has indicado	habéis indicado
indica	indican	ha indicado	han indicado
2 imperfecto de indicativo		**9 pluscuamperfecto de indicativo**	
indicaba	indicábamos	había indicado	habíamos indicado
indicabas	indicabais	habías indicado	habíais indicado
indicaba	indicaban	había indicado	habían indicado
3 pretérito		**10 pretérito anterior**	
indiqué	indicamos	hube indicado	hubimos indicado
indicaste	indicasteis	hubiste indicado	hubisteis indicado
indicó	indicaron	hubo indicado	hubieron indicado
4 futuro		**11 futuro perfecto**	
indicaré	indicaremos	habré indicado	habremos indicado
indicarás	indicaréis	habrás indicado	habréis indicado
indicará	indicarán	habrá indicado	habrán indicado
5 potencial simple		**12 potencial compuesto**	
indicaría	indicaríamos	habría indicado	habríamos indicado
indicarías	indicaríais	habrías indicado	habríais indicado
indicaría	indicarían	habría indicado	habrían indicado
6 presente de subjuntivo		**13 perfecto de subjuntivo**	
indique	indiquemos	haya indicado	hayamos indicado
indiques	indiquéis	hayas indicado	hayáis indicado
indique	indiquen	haya indicado	hayan indicado
7 imperfecto de subjuntivo		**14 pluscuamperfecto de subjuntivo**	
indicara	indicáramos	hubiera indicado	hubiéramos indicado
indicaras	indicarais	hubieras indicado	hubierais indicado
indicara	indicaran	hubiera indicado	hubieran indicado
OR		OR	
indicase	indicásemos	hubiese indicado	hubiésemos indicado
indicases	indicaseis	hubieses indicado	hubieseis indicado
indicase	indicasen	hubiese indicado	hubiesen indicado

imperativo	
—	indiquemos
indica; no indiques	indicad; no indiquéis
indique	indiquen

indicativo, indicativa   indicative
el indicador   indicator; el indicador
  de humo   smoke detector

la indicación   indication
el indicador de velocidad
  speedometer

Irregular in Tenses 3 and 7, regular **-ir** verb in all   to induce, to influence,
others; spelling change: **c** becomes **zc** before **a** or **o**   to persuade

The Seven Simple Tenses		The Seven Compound Tenses	
Singular	Plural	Singular	Plural
1 presente de indicativo		8 perfecto de indicativo	
induzco	inducimos	he inducido	hemos inducido
induces	inducís	has inducido	habéis inducido
induce	inducen	ha inducido	han inducido
2 imperfecto de indicativo		9 pluscuamperfecto de indicativo	
inducía	inducíamos	había inducido	habíamos inducido
inducías	inducíais	habías inducido	habíais inducido
inducía	inducían	había inducido	habían inducido
3 pretérito		10 pretérito anterior	
induje	indujimos	hube inducido	hubimos inducido
indujiste	indujisteis	hubiste inducido	hubisteis inducido
indujo	indujeron	hubo inducido	hubieron inducido
4 futuro		11 futuro perfecto	
induciré	induciremos	habré inducido	habremos inducido
inducirás	induciréis	habrás inducido	habréis inducido
inducirá	inducirán	habrá inducido	habrán inducido
5 potencial simple		12 potencial compuesto	
induciría	induciríamos	habría inducido	habríamos inducido
inducirías	induciríais	habrías inducido	habríais inducido
induciría	inducirían	habría inducido	habrían inducido
6 presente de subjuntivo		13 perfecto de subjuntivo	
induzca	induzcamos	haya inducido	hayamos inducido
induzcas	induzcáis	hayas inducido	hayáis inducido
induzca	induzcan	haya inducido	hayan inducido
7 imperfecto de subjuntivo		14 pluscuamperfecto de subjuntivo	
indujera	indujéramos	hubiera inducido	hubiéramos inducido
indujeras	indujerais	hubieras inducido	hubierais inducido
indujera	indujeran	hubiera inducido	hubieran inducido
OR		OR	
indujese	indujésemos	hubiese inducido	hubiésemos inducido
indujeses	indujeseis	hubieses inducido	hubieseis inducido
indujese	indujesen	hubiese inducido	hubiesen inducido

imperativo

—	induzcamos
induce; no induzcas	inducid; no induzcáis
induzca	induzcan

inducidor, inducidora inducer	la inducción inducement, induction
el inducimiento inducement	inducir a + inf. to persuade to + inf.

influir

Gerundio **influyendo** Part. pas. **influido**

to influence, to have influence on

Regular **-ir** verb endings with spelling change: add **y** before **a**, **e**, or **o**

The Seven Simple Tenses		The Seven Compound Tenses	
Singular	Plural	Singular	Plural
1 presente de indicativo		8 perfecto de indicativo	
influyo	**influimos**	**he influido**	**hemos influido**
influyes	**influís**	**has influido**	**habéis influido**
influye	**influyen**	**ha influido**	**han influido**
2 imperfecto de indicativo		9 pluscuamperfecto de indicativo	
influía	**influíamos**	**había influido**	**habíamos influido**
influías	**influíais**	**habías influido**	**habíais influido**
influía	**influían**	**había influido**	**habían influido**
3 pretérito		10 pretérito anterior	
influí	**influimos**	**hube influido**	**hubimos influido**
influiste	**influisteis**	**hubiste influido**	**hubisteis influido**
influyó	**influyeron**	**hubo influido**	**hubieron influido**
4 futuro		11 futuro perfecto	
influiré	**influiremos**	**habré influido**	**habremos influido**
influirás	**influiréis**	**habrás influido**	**habréis influido**
influirá	**influirán**	**habrá influido**	**habrán influido**
5 potencial simple		12 potencial compuesto	
influiría	**influiríamos**	**habría influido**	**habríamos influido**
influirías	**influiríais**	**habrías influido**	**habríais influido**
influiría	**influirían**	**habría influido**	**habrían influido**
6 presente de subjuntivo		13 perfecto de subjuntivo	
influya	**influyamos**	**haya influido**	**hayamos influido**
influyas	**influyáis**	**hayas influido**	**hayáis influido**
influya	**influyan**	**haya influido**	**hayan influido**
7 imperfecto de subjuntivo		14 pluscuamperfecto de subjuntivo	
influyera	**influyéramos**	**hubiera influido**	**hubiéramos influido**
influyeras	**influyerais**	**hubieras influido**	**hubierais influido**
influyera	**influyeran**	**hubiera influido**	**hubieran influido**
OR		OR	
influyese	**influyésemos**	**hubiese influido**	**hubiésemos influido**
influyeses	**influyeseis**	**hubieses influido**	**hubieseis influido**
influyese	**influyesen**	**hubiese influido**	**hubiesen influido**

	imperativo	
—	**influyamos**	
influye; no influyas	**influid; no influyáis**	
influya	**influyan**	

la influencia influence	**influir sobre alguien para que +**
influyente influential, influencing	**subjunctive** to influence someone to
influir en to affect, to have an	**+ inf.**
influence on, upon	

Regular **-ir** verb   to insist, to persist, to stress

The Seven Simple Tenses		The Seven Compound Tenses	
Singular	Plural	Singular	Plural
1 presente de indicativo		**8 perfecto de indicativo**	
insisto	**insistimos**	**he insistido**	**hemos insistido**
insistes	**insistís**	**has insistido**	**habéis insistido**
insiste	**insisten**	**ha insistido**	**han insistido**
2 imperfecto de indicativo		**9 pluscuamperfecto de indicativo**	
insistía	**insistíamos**	**había insistido**	**habíamos insistido**
insistías	**insistíais**	**habías insistido**	**habíais insistido**
insistía	**insistían**	**había insistido**	**habían insistido**
3 pretérito		**10 pretérito anterior**	
insistí	**insistimos**	**hube insistido**	**hubimos insistido**
insististe	**insististeis**	**hubiste insistido**	**hubisteis insistido**
insistió	**insistieron**	**hubo insistido**	**hubieron insistido**
4 futuro		**11 futuro perfecto**	
insistiré	**insistiremos**	**habré insistido**	**habremos insistido**
insistirás	**insistiréis**	**habrás insistido**	**habréis insistido**
insistirá	**insistirán**	**habrá insistido**	**habrán insistido**
5 potencial simple		**12 potencial compuesto**	
insistiría	**insistiríamos**	**habría insistido**	**habríamos insistido**
insistirías	**insistiríais**	**habrías insistido**	**habríais insistido**
insistiría	**insistirían**	**habría insistido**	**habrían insistido**
6 presente de subjuntivo		**13 perfecto de subjuntivo**	
insista	**insistamos**	**haya insistido**	**hayamos insistido**
insistas	**insistáis**	**hayas insistido**	**hayáis insistido**
insista	**insistan**	**haya insistido**	**hayan insistido**
7 imperfecto de subjuntivo		**14 pluscuamperfecto de subjuntivo**	
insistiera	**insistiéramos**	**hubiera insistido**	**hubiéramos insistido**
insistieras	**insistierais**	**hubieras insistido**	**hubierais insistido**
insistiera	**insistieran**	**hubiera insistido**	**hubieran insistido**
OR		OR	
insistiese	**insistiésemos**	**hubiese insistido**	**hubiésemos insistido**
insistieses	**insistieseis**	**hubieses insistido**	**hubieseis insistido**
insistiese	**insistiesen**	**hubiese insistido**	**hubiesen insistido**

imperativo		
—	**insistamos**	
insiste; no insistas	**insistís; no insistáis**	
insista	**insistan**	

Mi madre insistió en que yo haga mis deberes antes de salir con mis amigos. My mother insisted that I do my homework before going out with my friends.	**insistir en** to insist on, to persist in **insistente** insistent **la insistencia** insistence, persistence **insistir en la importancia de** to stress the importance of

introducir

Gerundio **introduciendo**   Part. pas. **introducido**

to introduce

Regular **-ir** verb in all tenses except Tenses 3 and 7; spelling change: **c** becomes **zc** before **a** or **o**

The Seven Simple Tenses		The Seven Compound Tenses	
Singular	Plural	Singular	Plural
1 presente de indicativo		8 perfecto de indicativo	
introduzco	introducimos	he introducido	hemos introducido
introduces	introducís	has introducido	habéis introducido
introduce	introducen	ha introducido	han introducido
2 imperfecto de indicativo		9 pluscuamperfecto de indicativo	
introducía	introducíamos	había introducido	habíamos introducido
introducías	introducíais	habías introducido	habíais introducido
introducía	introducían	había introducido	habían introducido
3 pretérito		10 pretérito anterior	
introduje	introdujimos	hube introducido	hubimos introducido
introdujiste	introdujisteis	hubiste introducido	hubisteis introducido
introdujo	introdujeron	hubo introducido	hubieron introducido
4 futuro		11 futuro perfecto	
introduciré	introduciremos	habré introducido	habremos introducido
introducirás	introduciréis	habrás introducido	habréis introducido
introducirá	introducirán	habrá introducido	habrán introducido
5 potencial simple		12 potencial compuesto	
introduciría	introduciríamos	habría introducido	habríamos introducido
introducirías	introduciríais	habrías introducido	habríais introducido
introduciría	introducirían	habría introducido	habrían introducido
6 presente de subjuntivo		13 perfecto de subjuntivo	
introduzca	introduzcamos	haya introducido	hayamos introducido
introduzcas	introduzcáis	hayas introducido	hayáis introducido
introduzca	introduzcan	haya introducido	hayan introducido
7 imperfecto de subjuntivo		14 pluscuamperfecto de subjuntivo	
introdujera	introdujéramos	hubiera introducido	hubiéramos introducido
introdujeras	introdujerais	hubieras introducido	hubierais introducido
introdujera	introdujeran	hubiera introducido	hubieran introducido
OR		OR	
introdujese	introdujésemos	hubiese introducido	hubiésemos introducido
introdujeses	introdujeseis	hubieses introducido	hubieseis introducido
introdujese	introdujesen	hubiese introducido	hubiesen introducido

imperativo

—	**introduzcamos**
introduce; no introduzcas	**introducid; no introduzcáis**
introduzca	**introduzcan**

la introducción introduction	introductor, introductora introducer
introductivo, introductiva	introducir a una persona en la oficina
introductive, introductory	to show a person into the office

Regular **-ir** verb with stem change: Tenses
1, 3, 6, 7, Imperative, *Gerundio*

to invert, to turn upside
down, to invest money

The Seven Simple Tenses		The Seven Compound Tenses	
Singular	Plural	Singular	Plural

1 presente de indicativo		8 perfecto de indicativo	
invierto	invertimos	he invertido	hemos invertido
inviertes	invertís	has invertido	habéis invertido
invierte	invierten	ha invertido	han invertido

2 imperfecto de indicativo		9 pluscuamperfecto de indicativo	
invertía	invertíamos	había invertido	habíamos invertido
invertías	invertíais	habías invertido	habíais invertido
invertía	invertían	había invertido	habían invertido

3 pretérito		10 pretérito anterior	
invertí	invertimos	hube invertido	hubimos invertido
invertiste	invertisteis	hubiste invertido	hubisteis invertido
invirtió	invirtieron	hubo invertido	hubieron invertido

4 futuro		11 futuro perfecto	
invertiré	invertiremos	habré invertido	habremos invertido
invertirás	invertiréis	habrás invertido	habréis invertido
invertirá	invertirán	habrá invertido	habrán invertido

5 potencial simple		12 potencial compuesto	
invertiría	invertiríamos	habría invertido	habríamos invertido
invertirías	invertiríais	habrías invertido	habríais invertido
invertiría	invertirían	habría invertido	habrían invertido

6 presente de subjuntivo		13 perfecto de subjuntivo	
invierta	invirtamos	haya invertido	hayamos invertido
inviertas	invirtáis	hayas invertido	hayáis invertido
invierta	inviertan	haya invertido	hayan invertido

7 imperfecto de subjuntivo		14 pluscuamperfecto de subjuntivo	
invirtiera	invirtiéramos	hubiera invertido	hubiéramos invertido
invirtieras	invirtierais	hubieras invertido	hubierais invertido
invirtiera	invirtieran	hubiera invertido	hubieran invertido
OR		OR	
invirtiese	invirtiésemos	hubiese invertido	hubiésemos invertido
invirtieses	invirtieseis	hubieses invertido	hubieseis invertido
invirtiese	invirtiesen	hubiese invertido	hubiesen invertido

imperativo	
—	invirtamos
invierte; no inviertas	invertid; no invirtáis
invierta	inviertan

Quiero invertir dinero, pero no tengo ni un duro. I'd like to invest money, but I'm flat broke.	el inversor, la inversora investor
	a la inversa inversely
	y a la inversa and vice versa
invertido, invertida inverted, upside-down	la inversión inversion, investment
	invertir dinero to invest money

ir

Gerundio **yendo**　　　　　　Part. pas. **ido**

to go

Irregular verb

The Seven Simple Tenses		The Seven Compound Tenses	
Singular	Plural	Singular	Plural
1　presente de indicativo		8　perfecto de indicativo	
voy	**vamos**	**he ido**	**hemos ido**
vas	**vais**	**has ido**	**habéis ido**
va	**van**	**ha ido**	**han ido**
2　imperfecto de indicativo		9　pluscuamperfecto de indicativo	
iba	**íbamos**	**había ido**	**habíamos ido**
ibas	**ibais**	**habías ido**	**habíais ido**
iba	**iban**	**había ido**	**habían ido**
3　pretérito		10　pretérito anterior	
fui	**fuimos**	**hube ido**	**hubimos ido**
fuiste	**fuisteis**	**hubiste ido**	**hubisteis ido**
fue	**fueron**	**hubo ido**	**hubieron ido**
4　futuro		11　futuro perfecto	
iré	**iremos**	**habré ido**	**habremos ido**
irás	**iréis**	**habrás ido**	**habréis ido**
irá	**irán**	**habrá ido**	**habrán ido**
5　potencial simple		12　potencial compuesto	
iría	**iríamos**	**habría ido**	**habríamos ido**
irías	**iríais**	**habrías ido**	**habríais ido**
iría	**irían**	**habría ido**	**habrían ido**
6　presente de subjuntivo		13　perfecto de subjuntivo	
vaya	**vayamos**	**haya ido**	**hayamos ido**
vayas	**vayáis**	**hayas ido**	**hayáis ido**
vaya	**vayan**	**haya ido**	**hayan ido**
7　imperfecto de subjuntivo		14　pluscuamperfecto de subjuntivo	
fuera	**fuéramos**	**hubiera ido**	**hubiéramos ido**
fueras	**fuerais**	**hubieras ido**	**hubierais ido**
fuera	**fueran**	**hubiera ido**	**hubieran ido**
OR		OR	
fuese	**fuésemos**	**hubiese ido**	**hubiésemos ido**
fueses	**fueseis**	**hubieses ido**	**hubieseis ido**
fuese	**fuesen**	**hubiese ido**	**hubiesen ido**

imperativo	
—	**vamos (no vayamos)**
ve; no vayas	**id; no vayáis**
vaya	**vayan**

Voy a pagar al contado.　I'm going to
　pay in cash.
ir de compras　to go shopping
ir a caballo　to ride horseback
ir de brazo　to walk arm in arm

un billete de ida y vuelta　return ticket
¿Cómo le va?　How goes it? How
　are you?
¡Qué va!　Nonsense!
ir a pie　to walk (to go on foot)

Reflexive irregular verb   to go away

The Seven Simple Tenses		The Seven Compound Tenses	
Singular	Plural	Singular	Plural
1 presente de indicativo		8 perfecto de indicativo	
me voy	**nos vamos**	**me he ido**	**nos hemos ido**
te vas	**os vais**	**te has ido**	**os habéis ido**
se va	**se van**	**se ha ido**	**se han ido**
2 imperfecto de indicativo		9 pluscuamperfecto de indicativo	
me iba	**nos íbamos**	**me había ido**	**nos habíamos ido**
te ibas	**os ibais**	**te habías ido**	**os habíais ido**
se iba	**se iban**	**se había ido**	**se habían ido**
3 pretérito		10 pretérito anterior	
me fui	**nos fuimos**	**me hube ido**	**nos hubimos ido**
te fuiste	**os fuisteis**	**te hubiste ido**	**os hubisteis ido**
se fue	**se fueron**	**se hubo ido**	**se hubieron ido**
4 futuro		11 futuro perfecto	
me iré	**nos iremos**	**me habré ido**	**nos habremos ido**
te irás	**os iréis**	**te habrás ido**	**os habréis ido**
se irá	**se irán**	**se habrá ido**	**se habrán ido**
5 potencial simple		12 potencial compuesto	
me iría	**nos iríamos**	**me habría ido**	**nos habríamos ido**
te irías	**os iríais**	**te habrías ido**	**os habríais ido**
se iría	**se irían**	**se habría ido**	**se habrían ido**
6 presente de subjuntivo		13 perfecto de subjuntivo	
me vaya	**nos vayamos**	**me haya ido**	**nos hayamos ido**
te vayas	**os vayáis**	**te hayas ido**	**os hayáis ido**
se vaya	**se vayan**	**se haya ido**	**se hayan ido**
7 imperfecto de subjuntivo		14 pluscuamperfecto de subjuntivo	
me fuera	**nos fuéramos**	**me hubiera ido**	**nos hubiéramos ido**
te fueras	**os fuerais**	**te hubieras ido**	**os hubierais ido**
se fuera	**se fueran**	**se hubiera ido**	**se hubieran ido**
OR		OR	
me fuese	**nos fuésemos**	**me hubiese ido**	**nos hubiésemos ido**
te fueses	**os fueseis**	**te hubieses ido**	**os hubieseis ido**
se fuese	**se fuesen**	**se hubiese ido**	**se hubiesen ido**

imperativo

—	**vámonos; no nos vayamos**
vete; no te vayas	**idos; no os vayáis**
váyase; no se vaya	**váyanse; no se vayan**

¡Vámonos! Let's go! Let's leave!
¡Vete! Go away!
¡Váyase! Go away!
Si a Roma fueres, haz como vieres.
    When in Rome do as the Romans do.
    [Note that it is not uncommon to use

the future subjunctive in proverbs, as
in *fueres* (**ir** or **ser**) and *vieres* (**ver**);
see pp. xxxi–xxxii.]
irse de prisa   to rush away

189

jugar

Gerundio jugando   **Part. pas. jugado**

to play (a game, sport)

Regular -ar verb endings with stem change: Tenses 1, 6, Imperative; spelling change: g becomes gu before e

The Seven Simple Tenses		The Seven Compound Tenses	
Singular	Plural	Singular	Plural
1 presente de indicativo		**8 perfecto de indicativo**	
juego	jugamos	he jugado	hemos jugado
juegas	jugáis	has jugado	habéis jugado
juega	juegan	ha jugado	han jugado
2 imperfecto de indicativo		**9 pluscuamperfecto de indicativo**	
jugaba	jubábamos	había jugado	habíamos jugado
jugabas	jugabaís	habías jugado	habíais jugado
jugaba	jugaban	había jugado	habían jugado
3 pretérito		**10 pretérito anterior**	
jugué	jugamos	hube jugado	hubimos jugado
jugaste	jugasteis	hubiste jugado	hubisteis jugado
jugó	jugaron	hubo jugado	hubieron jugado
4 futuro		**11 futuro perfecto**	
jugaré	jugaremos	habré jugado	habremos jugado
jugarás	jugaréis	habrás jugado	habréis jugado
jugará	jugarán	habrá jugado	habrán jugado
5 potencial simple		**12 potencial compuesto**	
jugaría	jugaríamos	habría jugado	habríamos jugado
jugarías	jugaríais	habrías jugado	habríais jugado
jugaría	jugarían	habría jugado	habrían jugado
6 presente de subjuntivo		**13 perfecto de subjuntivo**	
juegue	juguemos	haya jugado	hayamos jugado
juegues	juguéis	hayas jugado	hayáis jugado
juegue	jueguen	haya jugado	hayan jugado
7 imperfecto de subjuntivo		**14 pluscuamperfecto de subjuntivo**	
jugara	jugáramos	hubiera jugado	hubiéramos jugado
jugaras	jugarais	hubieras jugado	hubierais jugado
jugara	jugaran	hubiera jugado	hubieran jugado
OR		OR	
jugase	jugásemos	hubiese jugado	hubiésemos jugado
jugases	jugaseis	hubieses jugado	hubieseis jugado
jugase	jugasen	hubiese jugado	hubiesen jugado

imperativo	
—	juguemos
juega; no juegues	jugad; no juguéis
juegue	jueguen

---

un juguete   toy, plaything
jugar a los naipes, a las cartas   to play cards
jugador, jugadora   player
jugar al tenis   to play tennis
un juego   game

jugar al béisbol   to play baseball
¡Hagan juego!   Place your bets!
el juego de palabras   play on words, pun
Don't confuse jugar with tocar, which can also mean to play.

Regular **-ar** verb endings with spelling
change: **z** becomes **c** before **e**

to throw, to hurl,
to fling, to launch

The Seven Simple Tenses		The Seven Compound Tenses	
Singular	Plural	Singular	Plural
1 presente de indicativo		8 perfecto de indicativo	
lanzo	lanzamos	he lanzado	hemos lanzado
lanzas	lanzáis	has lanzado	habéis lanzado
lanza	lanzan	ha lanzado	han lanzado
2 imperfecto de indicativo		9 pluscuamperfecto de indicativo	
lanzaba	lanzábamos	había lanzado	habíamos lanzado
lanzabas	lanzabais	habías lanzado	habíais lanzado
lanzaba	lanzaban	había lanzado	habían lanzado
3 pretérito		10 pretérito anterior	
lancé	lanzamos	hube lanzado	hubimos lanzado
lanzaste	lanzasteis	hubiste lanzado	hubisteis lanzado
lanzó	lanzaron	hubo lanzado	hubieron lanzado
4 futuro		11 futuro perfecto	
lanzaré	lanzaremos	habré lanzado	habremos lanzado
lanzarás	lanzaréis	habrás lanzado	habréis lanzado
lanzará	lanzarán	habrá lanzado	habrán lanzado
5 potencial simple		12 potencial compuesto	
lanzaría	lanzaríamos	habría lanzado	habríamos lanzado
lanzarías	lanzaríais	habrías lanzado	habríais lanzado
lanzaría	lanzarían	habría lanzado	habrían lanzado
6 presente de subjuntivo		13 perfecto de subjuntivo	
lance	lancemos	haya lanzado	hayamos lanzado
lances	lancéis	hayas lanzado	hayáis lanzado
lance	lancen	haya lanzado	hayan lanzado
7 imperfecto de subjuntivo		14 pluscuamperfecto de subjuntivo	
lanzara	lanzáramos	hubiera lanzado	hubiéramos lanzado
lanzaras	lanzarais	hubieras lanzado	hubierais lanzado
lanzara	lanzaran	hubiera lanzado	hubieran lanzado
OR		OR	
lanzase	lanzásemos	hubiese lanzado	hubiésemos lanzado
lanzases	lanzaseis	hubieses lanzado	hubieseis lanzado
lanzase	lanzasen	hubiese lanzado	hubiesen lanzado

imperativo	
—	lancemos
lanza; no lances	lanzad; no lancéis
lance	lancen

la lanza lance, spear	lanzarse to throw oneself
el lanzamiento casting, throwing, launching	lanzarse al agua to jump into the water
la plataforma de lanzamiento launching pad	

lavar

Gerundio **lavando** Part. pas. **lavado**

to wash

Regular **-ar** verb

The Seven Simple Tenses		The Seven Compound Tenses	
Singular	Plural	Singular	Plural
1 presente de indicativo		8 perfecto de indicativo	
lavo	**lavamos**	**he lavado**	**hemos lavado**
lavas	**laváis**	**has lavado**	**habéis lavado**
lava	**lavan**	**ha lavado**	**han lavado**
2 imperfecto de indicativo		9 pluscuamperfecto de indicativo	
lavaba	**lavábamos**	**había lavado**	**habíamos lavado**
lavabas	**lavabais**	**habías lavado**	**habíais lavado**
lavaba	**lavaban**	**había lavado**	**habían lavado**
3 pretérito		10 pretérito anterior	
lavé	**lavamos**	**hube lavado**	**hubimos lavado**
lavaste	**lavasteis**	**hubiste lavado**	**hubisteis lavado**
lavó	**lavaron**	**hubo lavado**	**hubieron lavado**
4 futuro		11 futuro perfecto	
lavaré	**lavaremos**	**habré lavado**	**habremos lavado**
lavarás	**lavaréis**	**habrás lavado**	**habréis lavado**
lavará	**lavarán**	**habrá lavado**	**habrán lavado**
5 potencial simple		12 potencial compuesto	
lavaría	**lavaríamos**	**habría lavado**	**habríamos lavado**
lavarías	**lavaríais**	**habrías lavado**	**habríais lavado**
lavaría	**lavarían**	**habría lavado**	**habrían lavado**
6 presente de subjuntivo		13 perfecto de subjuntivo	
lave	**lavemos**	**haya lavado**	**hayamos lavado**
laves	**lavéis**	**hayas lavado**	**hayáis lavado**
lave	**laven**	**haya lavado**	**hayan lavado**
7 imperfecto de subjuntivo		14 pluscuamperfecto de subjuntivo	
lavara	**laváramos**	**hubiera lavado**	**hubiéramos lavado**
lavaras	**lavarais**	**hubieras lavado**	**hubierais lavado**
lavara	**lavaran**	**hubiera lavado**	**hubieran lavado**
OR		OR	
lavase	**lavásemos**	**hubiese lavado**	**hubiésemos lavado**
lavases	**lavaseis**	**hubieses lavado**	**hubieseis lavado**
lavase	**lavasen**	**hubiese lavado**	**hubiesen lavado**

imperativo	
—	**lavemos**
lava; no laves	**lavad; no lavéis**
lave	**laven**

---

el lavatorio, el lavabo lavatory,
  washroom, washstand
la lavandería laundry
el lavamanos washstand, washbowl

lavandero, lavandera launderer
lavar en seco to dry clean
la lavadora clothes washing machine
See also lavarse.

192

Reflexive regular **-ar** verb   to wash oneself

The Seven Simple Tenses		The Seven Compound Tenses	
Singular	Plural	Singular	Plural
1 presente de indicativo		8 perfecto de indicativo	
me lavo	nos lavamos	me he lavado	nos hemos lavado
te lavas	os laváis	te has lavado	os habéis lavado
se lava	se lavan	se ha lavado	se han lavado
2 imperfecto de indicativo		9 pluscuamperfecto de indicativo	
me lavaba	nos lavábamos	me había lavado	nos habíamos lavado
te lavabas	os lavabais	te habías lavado	os habíais lavado
se lavaba	se lavaban	se había lavado	se habían lavado
3 pretérito		10 pretérito anterior	
me lavé	nos lavamos	me hube lavado	nos hubimos lavado
te lavaste	os lavasteis	te hubiste lavado	os hubisteis lavado
se lavó	se lavaron	se hubo lavado	se hubieron lavado
4 futuro		11 futuro perfecto	
me lavaré	nos lavaremos	me habré lavado	nos habremos lavado
te lavarás	os lavaréis	te habrás lavado	os habréis lavado
se lavará	se lavarán	se habrá lavado	se habrán lavado
5 potencial simple		12 potencial compuesto	
me lavaría	nos lavaríamos	me habría lavado	nos habríamos lavado
te lavarías	os lavaríais	te habrías lavado	os habríais lavado
se lavaría	se lavarían	se habría lavado	se habrían lavado
6 presente de subjuntivo		13 perfecto de subjuntivo	
me lave	nos lavemos	me haya lavado	nos hayamos lavado
te laves	os lavéis	te hayas lavado	os hayáis lavado
se lave	se laven	se haya lavado	se hayan lavado
7 imperfecto de subjuntivo		14 pluscuamperfecto de subjuntivo	
me lavara	nos laváramos	me hubiera lavado	nos hubiéramos lavado
te lavaras	os lavarais	te hubieras lavado	os hubierais lavado
se lavara	se lavaran	se hubiera lavado	se hubieran lavado
OR		OR	
me lavase	nos lavásemos	me hubiese lavado	nos hubiésemos lavado
te lavases	os lavaseis	te hubieses lavado	os hubieseis lavado
se lavase	se lavasen	se hubiese lavadose hubiesen lavado	

imperativo

—	lavémonos; no nos lavemos
lávate; no te laves	lavaos; no os lavéis
lávese; no se lave	lávense; no se laven

el lavaplatos dishwasher (machine)	**lavandero, lavandera** launderer
el / la lavaplatos dishwasher (person)	**la lavandería** laundry
el lavatorio, el lavabo lavatory, washroom, washstand	See also **lavar**.

leer

Gerundio **leyendo**

Part. pas. **leído**

to read

Irregular verb

The Seven Simple Tenses		The Seven Compound Tenses	
Singular	Plural	Singular	Plural
1 presente de indicativo		**8 perfecto de indicativo**	
leo	leemos	he leído	hemos leído
lees	leéis	has leído	habéis leído
lee	leen	ha leído	han leído
2 imperfecto de indicativo		**9 pluscuamperfecto de indicativo**	
leía	leíamos	había leído	habíamos leído
leías	leíais	habías leído	habíais leído
leía	leían	había leído	habían leído
3 pretérito		**10 pretérito anterior**	
leí	leímos	hube leído	hubimos leído
leíste	leísteis	hubiste leído	hubisteis leído
leyó	leyeron	hubo leído	hubieron leído
4 futuro		**11 futuro perfecto**	
leeré	leeremos	habré leído	habremos leído
leerás	leeréis	habrás leído	habréis leído
leerá	leerán	habrá leído	habrán leído
5 potencial simple		**12 potencial compuesto**	
leería	leeríamos	habría leído	habríamos leído
leerías	leeríais	habrías leído	habríais leído
leería	leerían	habría leído	habrían leído
6 presente de subjuntivo		**13 perfecto de subjuntivo**	
lea	leamos	haya leído	hayamos leído
leas	leáis	hayas leído	hayáis leído
lea	lean	haya leído	hayan leído
7 imperfecto de subjuntivo		**14 pluscuamperfecto de subjuntivo**	
leyera	leyéramos	hubiera leído	hubiéramos leído
leyeras	leyerais	hubieras leído	hubierais leído
leyera	leyeran	hubiera leído	hubieran leído
OR		OR	
leyese	leyésemos	hubiese leído	hubiésemos leído
leyeses	leyeseis	hubieses leído	hubieseis leído
leyese	leyesen	hubiese leído	hubiesen leído

imperativo	
—	leamos
lee; no leas	leed; no leáis
lea	lean

Me gusta leer. I like to read.
Estoy leyendo un libro de Isabel Allende.
  I'm reading a book by Isabel Allende.
la lectura reading
releer to read again, to reread
leer entre líneas to read between the
  lines

la lección lesson
un, una leccionista private tutor
lector, lectora reader
leer para sí to read to oneself
leer mal to misread
leer en voz alta to read aloud
leer en voz baja to read quietly

Gerundio **levantando**   Part. pas. **levantado**

levantar

Regular **-ar** verb

to lift, to raise

The Seven Simple Tenses		The Seven Compound Tenses	
Singular	Plural	Singular	Plural
1 presente de indicativo		8 perfecto de indicativo	
levanto	**levantamos**	**he levantado**	**hemos levantado**
levantas	**levantáis**	**has levantado**	**habéis levantado**
levanta	**levantan**	**ha levantado**	**han levantado**
2 imperfecto de indicativo		9 pluscuamperfecto de indicativo	
levantaba	**levantábamos**	**había levantado**	**habíamos levantado**
levantabas	**levantabais**	**habías levantado**	**habíais levantado**
levantaba	**levantaban**	**había levantado**	**habían levantado**
3 pretérito		10 pretérito anterior	
levanté	**levantamos**	**hube levantado**	**hubimos levantado**
levantaste	**levantasteis**	**hubiste levantado**	**hubisteis levantado**
levantó	**levantaron**	**hubo levantado**	**hubieron levantado**
4 futuro		11 futuro perfecto	
levantaré	**levantaremos**	**habré levantado**	**habremos levantado**
levantarás	**levantaréis**	**habrás levantado**	**habréis levantado**
levantará	**levantarán**	**habrá levantado**	**habrán levantado**
5 potencial simple		12 potencial compuesto	
levantaría	**levantaríamos**	**habría levantado**	**habríamos levantado**
levantarías	**levantaríais**	**habrías levantado**	**habríais levantado**
levantaría	**levantarían**	**habría levantado**	**habrían levantado**
6 presente de subjuntivo		13 perfecto de subjuntivo	
levante	**levantemos**	**haya levantado**	**hayamos levantado**
levantes	**levantéis**	**hayas levantado**	**hayáis levantado**
levante	**levanten**	**haya levantado**	**hayan levantado**
7 imperfecto de subjuntivo		14 pluscuamperfecto de subjuntivo	
levantara	**levantáramos**	**hubiera levantado**	**hubiéramos levantado**
levantaras	**levantarais**	**hubieras levantado**	**hubierais levantado**
levantara	**levantaran**	**hubiera levantado**	**hubieran levantado**
OR		OR	
levantase	**levantásemos**	**hubiese levantado**	**hubiésemos levantado**
levantases	**levantaseis**	**hubieses levantado**	**hubieseis levantado**
levantase	**levantasen**	**hubiese levantado**	**hubiesen levantado**

imperativo	
—	**levantemos**
levanta; no levantes	**levantad; no levantéis**
levante	**levanten**

levantar los manteles to clear the table	el Levante Levant, East
levantar fuego to make a disturbance	el levantamiento elevation, raising
levantar con algo to get away with something	levantar la voz to raise one's voice
levantar la cabeza to take heart (courage)	See also **levantarse**.

levantarse

Gerundio **levantándose**   Part. pas. **levantado**

to get up, to rise

Reflexive regular **-ar** verb

The Seven Simple Tenses		The Seven Compound Tenses	
Singular	Plural	Singular	Plural
1 presente de indicativo		8 perfecto de indicativo	
me levanto	nos levantamos	me he levantado	nos hemos levantado
te levantas	os levantáis	te has levantado	os habéis levantado
se levanta	se levantan	se ha levantado	se han levantado
2 imperfecto de indicativo		9 pluscuamperfecto de indicativo	
me levantaba	nos levantábamos	me había levantado	nos habíamos levantado
te levantabas	os levantabais	te habías levantado	os habíais levantado
se levantaba	se levantaban	se había levantado	se habían levantado
3 pretérito		10 pretérito anterior	
me levanté	nos levantamos	me hube levantado	nos hubimos levantado
te levantaste	os levantasteis	te hubiste levantado	os hubisteis levantado
se levantó	se levantaron	se hubo levantado	se hubieron levantado
4 futuro		11 futuro perfecto	
me levantaré	nos levantaremos	me habré levantado	nos habremos levantado
te levantarás	os levantaréis	te habrás levantado	os habréis levantado
se levantará	se levantarán	se habrá levantado	se habrán levantado
5 potencial simple		12 potencial compuesto	
me levantaría	nos levantaríamos	me habría levantado	nos habríamos levantado
te levantarías	os levantaríais	te habrías levantado	os habríais levantado
se levantaría	se levantarían	se habría levantado	se habrían levantado
6 presente de subjuntivo		13 perfecto de subjuntivo	
me levante	nos levantemos	me haya levantado	nos hayamos levantado
te levantes	os levantéis	te hayas levantado	os hayáis levantado
se levante	se levanten	se haya levantado	se hayan levantado
7 imperfecto de subjuntivo		14 pluscuamperfecto de subjuntivo	
me levantara	nos levantáramos	me hubiera levantado	nos hubiéramos levantado
te levantaras	os levantarais	te hubieras levantado	os hubierais levantado
se levantara	se levantaran	se hubiera levantado	se hubieran levantado
OR		OR	
me levantase	nos levantásemos	me hubiese levantado	nos hubiésemos levantado
te levantases	os levantaseis	te hubieses levantado	os hubieseis levantado
se levantase	se levantasen	se hubiese levantado	se hubiesen levantado

	imperativo	
—	levantémonos; no nos levantemos
levántate; no te levantes	levantaos; no os levantéis
levántese; no se levante	levántense; no se levanten

levantar los manteles to clear the table	levantarse de la cama to get out of bed
levantar la sesión to adjourn	levantarse con el pie izquierdo to get up on the wrong side of bed
levantar con algo to get away with something	See also **levantar**.
el levantamiento elevation, raising	

196

Regular **-ar** verb   to call, to name

The Seven Simple Tenses		The Seven Compound Tenses	
Singular	Plural	Singular	Plural
1 presente de indicativo		8 perfecto de indicativo	
llamo	**llamamos**	**he llamado**	**hemos llamado**
llamas	**llamáis**	**has llamado**	**habéis llamado**
llama	**llaman**	**ha llamado**	**han llamado**
2 imperfecto de indicativo		9 pluscuamperfecto de indicativo	
llamaba	**llamábamos**	**había llamado**	**habíamos llamado**
llamabas	**llamabais**	**habías llamado**	**habíais llamado**
llamaba	**llamaban**	**había llamado**	**habían llamado**
3 pretérito		10 pretérito anterior	
llamé	**llamamos**	**hube llamado**	**hubimos llamado**
llamaste	**llamasteis**	**hubiste llamado**	**hubisteis llamado**
llamó	**llamaron**	**hubo llamado**	**hubieron llamado**
4 futuro		11 futuro perfecto	
llamaré	**llamaremos**	**habré llamado**	**habremos llamado**
llamarás	**llamaréis**	**habrás llamado**	**habréis llamado**
llamará	**llamarán**	**habrá llamado**	**habrán llamado**
5 potencial simple		12 potencial compuesto	
llamaría	**llamaríamos**	**habría llamado**	**habríamos llamado**
llamarías	**llamaríais**	**habrías llamado**	**habríais llamado**
llamaría	**llamarían**	**habría llamado**	**habrían llamado**
6 presente de subjuntivo		13 perfecto de subjuntivo·	
llame	**llamemos**	**haya llamado**	**hayamos llamado**
llames	**llaméis**	**hayas llamado**	**hayáis llamado**
llame	**llamen**	**haya llamado**	**hayan llamado**
7 imperfecto de subjuntivo		14 pluscuamperfecto de subjuntivo	
llamara	**llamáramos**	**hubiera llamado**	**hubiéramos llamado**
llamaras	**llamarais**	**hubieras llamado**	**hubierais llamado**
llamara	**llamaran**	**hubiera llamado**	**hubieran llamado**
OR		OR	
llamase	**llamásemos**	**hubiese llamado**	**hubiésemos llamado**
llamases	**llamaseis**	**hubieses llamado**	**hubieseis llamado**
llamase	**llamasen**	**hubiese llamado**	**hubiesen llamado**

imperativo	
—	**llamemos**
llama; no llames	**llamad; no llaméis**
llame	**llamen**

llamar al doctor to call the doctor	**una llamada** call, knock, ring
llamar por los nombres to call the roll	**una llamada de emergencia** emergency call
llamar por teléfono to telephone	**llamar un taxi** to call a taxi
llamar la atención sobre to call attention to	See also **llamarse**.

llamarse

Gerundio **llamándose**   Part. pas. **llamado**

to be called, to be named

Reflexive regular **-ar** verb

The Seven Simple Tenses		The Seven Compound Tenses	
Singular	Plural	Singular	Plural
1 presente de indicativo		8 perfecto de indicativo	
me llamo	nos llamamos	me he llamado	nos hemos llamado
te llamas	os llamáis	te has llamado	os habéis llamado
se llama	se llaman	se ha llamado	se han llamado
2 imperfecto de indicativo		9 pluscuamperfecto de indicativo	
me llamaba	nos llamábamos	me había llamado	nos habíamos llamado
te llamabas	os llamabais	te habías llamado	os habíais llamado
se llamaba	se llamaban	se había llamado	se habían llamado
3 pretérito		10 pretérito anterior	
me llamé	nos llamamos	me hube llamado	nos hubimos llamado
te llamaste	os llamasteis	te hubiste llamado	os hubisteis llamado
se llamó	se llamaron	se hubo llamado	se hubieron llamado
4 futuro		11 futuro perfecto	
me llamaré	nos llamaremos	me habré llamado	nos habremos llamado
te llamarás	os llamaréis	te habrás llamado	os habréis llamado
se llamará	se llamarán	se habrá llamado	se habrán llamado
5 potencial simple		12 potencial compuesto	
me llamaría	nos llamaríamos	me habría llamado	nos habríamos llamado
te llamarías	os llamaríais	te habrías llamado	os habríais llamado
se llamaría	se llamarían	se habría llamado	se habrían llamado
6 presente de subjuntivo		13 perfecto de subjuntivo	
me llame	nos llamemos	me haya llamado	nos hayamos llamado
te llames	os llaméis	te hayas llamado	os hayáis llamado
se llame	se llamen	se haya llamado	se hayan llamado
7 imperfecto de subjuntivo		14 pluscuamperfecto de subjuntivo	
me llamara	nos llamáramos	me hubiera llamado	nos hubiéramos llamado
te llamaras	os llamarais	te hubieras llamado	os hubierais llamado
se llamara	se llamaran	se hubiera llamado	se hubieran llamado
OR		OR	
me llamase	nos llamásemos	me hubiese llamado	nos hubiésemos llamado
te llamases	os llamaseis	te hubieses llamado	os hubieseis llamado
se llamase	se llamasen	se hubiese llamado	se hubiesen llamado

	imperativo
—	llamémonos; no nos llamemos
llámate; no te llames	llamaos; no os llaméis
llámese; no se llame	llámense; no se llamen

—¿Cómo se llama usted?   What is your name? (How do you call yourself?)
—Me llamo Juan Morales.   My name is John Morales.

—¿Y cómo se llaman sus hermanos? And what are your brothers' names?
—Se llaman Luis y Pedro.   Their names are Louis and Peter.

Regular -**ar** verb endings with spelling
change: **g** becomes **gu** before **e**

to arrive

The Seven Simple Tenses		The Seven Compound Tenses	
Singular	Plural	Singular	Plural
1 presente de indicativo		8 perfecto de indicativo	
llego	llegamos	he llegado	hemos llegado
llegas	llegáis	has llegado	habéis llegado
llega	llegan	ha llegado	han llegado
2 imperfecto de indicativo		9 pluscuamperfecto de indicativo	
llegaba	llegábamos	había llegado	habíamos llegado
llegabas	llegabais	habías llegado	habíais llegado
llegaba	llegaban	había llegado	habían llegado
3 pretérito		10 pretérito anterior	
llegué	llegamos	hube llegado	hubimos llegado
llegaste	llegasteis	hubiste llegado	hubisteis llegado
llegó	llegaron	hubo llegado	hubieron llegado
4 futuro		11 futuro perfecto	
llegaré	llegaremos	habré llegado	habremos llegado
llegarás	llegaréis	habrás llegado	habréis llegado
llegará	llegarán	habrá llegado	habrán llegado
5 potencial simple		12 potencial compuesto	
llegaría	llegaríamos	habría llegado	habríamos llegado
llegarías	llegaríais	habrías llegado	habríais llegado
llegaría	llegarían	habría llegado	habrían llegado
6 presente de subjuntivo		13 perfecto de subjuntivo	
llegue	lleguemos	haya llegado	hayamos llegado
llegues	lleguéis	hayas llegado	hayáis llegado
llegue	lleguen	haya llegado	hayan llegado
7 imperfecto de subjuntivo		14 pluscuamperfecto de subjuntivo	
llegara	llegáramos	hubiera llegado	hubiéramos llegado
llegaras	llegarais	hubieras llegado	hubierais llegado
llegara	llegaran	hubiera llegado	hubieran llegado
OR		OR	
llegase	llegásemos	hubiese llegado	hubiésemos llegado
llegases	llegaseis	hubieses llegado	hubieseis llegado
llegase	llegasen	hubiese llegado	hubiesen llegado

imperativo	
—	lleguemos
llega; no llegues	llegad; no lleguéis
llegue	lleguen

llegar a ser to become	al llegar on arrival, upon arriving
Luis y Luisa quieren llegar a ser	la llegada arrival
médicos. Louis and Louise want to	llegar a saber to find out
become doctors.	llegar tarde to arrive late
llegar a to reach	

llenar

Gerundio **llenando** Part. pas. **llenado**

to fill

Regular **-ar** verb

The Seven Simple Tenses		The Seven Compound Tenses	
Singular	Plural	Singular	Plural
1 presente de indicativo		8 perfecto de indicativo	
lleno	**llenamos**	**he llenado**	**hemos llenado**
llenas	**llenáis**	**has llenado**	**habéis llenado**
llena	**llenan**	**ha llenado**	**han llenado**
2 imperfecto de indicativo		9 pluscuamperfecto de indicativo	
llenaba	**llenábamos**	**había llenado**	**habíamos llenado**
llenabas	**llenabais**	**habías llenado**	**habíais llenado**
llenaba	**llenaban**	**había llenado**	**habían llenado**
3 pretérito		10 pretérito anterior	
llené	**llenamos**	**hube llenado**	**hubimos llenado**
llenaste	**llenasteis**	**hubiste llenado**	**hubisteis llenado**
llenó	**llenaron**	**hubo llenado**	**hubieron llenado**
4 futuro		11 futuro perfecto	
llenaré	**llenaremos**	**habré llenado**	**habremos llenado**
llenarás	**llenaréis**	**habrás llenado**	**habréis llenado**
llenará	**llenarán**	**habrá llenado**	**habrán llenado**
5 potencial simple		12 potencial compuesto	
llenaría	**llenaríamos**	**habría llenado**	**habríamos llenado**
llenarías	**llenaríais**	**habrías llenado**	**habríais llenado**
llenaría	**llenarían**	**habría llenado**	**habrían llenado**
6 presente de subjuntivo		13 perfecto de subjuntivo	
llene	**llenemos**	**haya llenado**	**hayamos llenado**
llenes	**llenéis**	**hayas llenado**	**hayáis llenado**
llene	**llenen**	**haya llenado**	**hayan llenado**
7 imperfecto de subjuntivo		14 pluscuamperfecto de subjuntivo	
llenara	**llenáramos**	**hubiera llenado**	**hubiéramos llenado**
llenaras	**llenarais**	**hubieras llenado**	**hubierais llenado**
llenara	**llenaran**	**hubiera llenado**	**hubieran llenado**
OR		OR	
llenase	**llenásemos**	**hubiese llenado**	**hubiésemos llenado**
llenases	**llenaseis**	**hubieses llenado**	**hubieseis llenado**
llenase	**llenasen**	**hubiese llenado**	**hubiesen llenado**

imperativo	
—	**llenemos**
llena; no llenes	**llenad; no llenéis**
llene	**llenen**

lleno, llena full, filled	**llenamente** fully
lleno de bote en bote full to the brim	**llenar un formulario** to fill out a form
la llenura abundance, fullness	**la luna llena** full moon
llenar un pedido to fill an order	**Es luna llena.** There's a full moon.

Regular **-ar** verb

to carry (away),
to take (away), to wear

The Seven Simple Tenses		The Seven Compound Tenses	
Singular	Plural	Singular	Plural
1 presente de indicativo		8 perfecto de indicativo	
llevo	llevamos	he llevado	hemos llevado
llevas	lleváis	has llevado	habéis llevado
lleva	llevan	ha llevado	han llevado
2 imperfecto de indicativo		9 pluscuamperfecto de indicativo	
llevaba	llevábamos	había llevado	habíamos llevado
llevabas	llevabais	habías llevado	habíais llevado
llevaba	llevaban	había llevado	habían llevado
3 pretérito		10 pretérito anterior	
llevé	llevamos	hube llevado	hubimos llevado
llevaste	llevasteis	hubiste llevado	hubisteis llevado
llevó	llevaron	hubo llevado	hubieron llevado
4 futuro		11 futuro perfecto	
llevaré	llevaremos	habré llevado	habremos llevado
llevarás	llevaréis	habrás llevado	habréis llevado
llevará	llevarán	habrá llevado	habrán llevado
5 potencial simple		12 potencial compuesto	
llevaría	llevaríamos	habría llevado	habríamos llevado
llevarías	llevaríais	habrías llevado	habríais llevado
llevaría	llevarían	habría llevado	habrían llevado
6 presente de subjuntivo		13 perfecto de subjuntivo	
lleve	llevemos	haya llevado	hayamos llevado
lleves	llevéis	hayas llevado	hayáis llevado
lleve	lleven	haya llevado	hayan llevado
7 imperfecto de subjuntivo		14 pluscuamperfecto de subjuntivo	
llevara	lleváramos	hubiera llevado	hubiéramos llevado
llevaras	llevarais	hubieras llevado	hubierais llevado
llevara	llevaran	hubiera llevado	hubieran llevado
OR		OR	
llevase	llevásemos	hubiese llevado	hubiésemos llevado
llevases	llevaseis	hubieses llevado	hubieseis llevado
llevase	llevasen	hubiese llevado	hubiesen llevado

imperativo		
—	llevemos	
lleva; no lleves	llevad; no llevéis	
lleve	lleven	

llevar a cabo   to carry through, to
  accomplish
llevador, llevadora   carrier
llevar puesto   to wear
José llevó la silla de la cocina al
  comedor.   Joseph took the chair
  from the kitchen to the dining room.

María, ¿por qué llevas esa falda?
  Mary, why are you wearing that skirt?
Aquel hombre lleva una vida de
  perros.   That man leads a dog's life.

llorar

Gerundio **llorando**   Part. pas. **llorado**

to weep, to cry, to whine

Regular **-ar** verb

The Seven Simple Tenses		The Seven Compound Tenses	
Singular	Plural	Singular	Plural
1 presente de indicativo		8 perfecto de indicativo	
lloro	lloramos	he llorado	hemos llorado
lloras	lloráis	has llorado	habéis llorado
llora	lloran	ha llorado	han llorado
2 imperfecto de indicativo		9 pluscuamperfecto de indicativo	
lloraba	llorábamos	había llorado	habíamos llorado
llorabas	llorabais	habías llorado	habíais llorado
lloraba	lloraban	había llorado	habían llorado
3 pretérito		10 pretérito anterior	
lloré	lloramos	hube llorado	hubimos llorado
lloraste	llorasteis	hubiste llorado	hubisteis llorado
lloró	lloraron	hubo llorado	hubieron llorado
4 futuro		11 futuro perfecto	
lloraré	lloraremos	habré llorado	habremos llorado
llorarás	lloraréis	habrás llorado	habréis llorado
llorará	llorarán	habrá llorado	habrán llorado
5 potencial simple		12 potencial compuesto	
lloraría	lloraríamos	habría llorado	habríamos llorado
llorarías	lloraríais	habrías llorado	habríais llorado
lloraría	llorarían	habría llorado	habrían llorado
6 presente de subjuntivo		13 perfecto de subjuntivo	
llore	lloremos	haya llorado	hayamos llorado
llores	lloréis	hayas llorado	hayáis llorado
llore	lloren	haya llorado	hayan llorado
7 imperfecto de subjuntivo		14 pluscuamperfecto de subjuntivo	
llorara	lloráramos	hubiera llorado	hubiéramos llorado
lloraras	llorarais	hubieras llorado	hubierais llorado
llorara	lloraran	hubiera llorado	hubieran llorado
OR		OR	
llorase	llorásemos	hubiese llorado	hubiésemos llorado
llorases	lloraseis	hubieses llorado	hubieseis llorado
llorase	llorasen	hubiese llorado	hubiesen llorado

imperativo	
—	lloremos
llora; no llores	llorad; no lloréis
llore	lloren

---

lloroso, llorosa   tearful, sorrowful
llorar con un ojo   to shed crocodile
   tears
el lloro   weeping, crying
llorar por   to weep (cry) for
llorador, lloradora   weeper

llorar por cualquier cosa   to cry about
   anything
lloriquear   to cry constantly, to whine
llorar a lágrima viva   to cry one's
   eyes out
romper a llorar   to burst into tears

llover

Regular **-er** verb endings with stem
change: Tenses 1, 6, Imperative

to rain

The Seven Simple Tenses	The Seven Compound Tenses
Singular Plural	Singular Plural
1 presente de indicativo **llueve** OR **está lloviendo**	8 perfecto de indicativo **ha llovido**
2 imperfecto de indicativo **llovía** OR **estaba lloviendo**	9 pluscuamperfecto de indicativo **había llovido**
3 pretérito **llovió**	10 pretérito anterior **hubo llovido**
4 futuro **lloverá**	11 futuro perfecto **habrá llovido**
5 potencial simple **llovería**	12 potencial compuesto **habría llovido**
6 presente de subjuntivo **llueva**	13 perfecto de subjuntivo **haya llovido**
7 imperfecto de subjuntivo **lloviera** OR **lloviese**	14 pluscuamperfecto de subjuntivo **hubiera llovido** OR **hubiese llovido**

imperativo
¡Que llueva!   Let it rain!

---

la lluvia   rain
llover chuzos   to rain pitchforks (cats and dogs)
lluvioso, lluviosa   rainy
llover a cántaros   to rain in torrents

tiempo lluvioso   rainy weather
llueva o no   rain or shine
lloviznar   to drizzle
la llovizna   drizzle

mandar

Gerundio **mandando**   Part. pas. **mandado**

to command,
to order, to send

Regular **-ar** verb

The Seven Simple Tenses		The Seven Compound Tenses	
Singular	Plural	Singular	Plural
1 presente de indicativo		8 perfecto de indicativo	
mando	mandamos	he mandado	hemos mandado
mandas	mandáis	has mandado	habéis mandado
manda	mandan	ha mandado	han mandado
2 imperfecto de indicativo		9 pluscuamperfecto de indicativo	
mandaba	mandábamos	había mandado	habíamos mandado
mandabas	mandabais	habías mandado	habíais mandado
mandaba	mandaban	había mandado	habían mandado
3 pretérito		10 pretérito anterior	
mandé	mandamos	hube mandado	hubimos mandado
mandaste	mandasteis	hubiste mandado	hubisteis mandado
mandó	mandaron	hubo mandado	hubieron mandado
4 futuro		11 futuro perfecto	
mandaré	mandaremos	habré mandado	habremos mandado
mandarás	mandaréis	habrás mandado	habréis mandado
mandará	mandarán	habrá mandado	habrán mandado
5 potencial simple		12 potencial compuesto	
mandaría	mandaríamos	habría mandado	habríamos mandado
mandarías	mandaríais	habrías mandado	habríais mandado
mandaría	mandarían	habría mandado	habrían mandado
6 presente de subjuntivo		13 perfecto de subjuntivo	
mande	mandemos	haya mandado	hayamos mandado
mandes	mandéis	hayas mandado	hayáis mandado
mande	manden	haya mandado	hayan mandado
7 imperfecto de subjuntivo		14 pluscuamperfecto de subjuntivo	
mandara	mandáramos	hubiera mandado	hubiéramos mandado
mandaras	mandarais	hubieras mandado	hubierais mandado
mandara	mandaran	hubiera mandado	hubieran mandado
OR		OR	
mandase	mandásemos	hubiese mandado	hubiésemos mandado
mandases	mandaseis	hubieses mandado	hubieseis mandado
mandase	mandasen	hubiese mandado	hubiesen mandado

imperativo	
—	mandemos
manda; no mandes	mandad; no mandéis
mande	manden

---

el mandamiento   order
el mandato   order
el mandatorio, la mandatoria   agent
un mandado   an errand; hacer un
    mandado   to run an errand

hacer de un camino dos mandados
    to kill two birds with one stone
mandado / mandada a distancia
    remote-controlled
el mandamiento judicial   court order
mandar un correo electrónico   to
    send an e-mail

Regular **-ar** verb   to walk, to march, to function
                                                  (machine), to run (machine)

The Seven Simple Tenses		The Seven Compound Tenses	
Singular	Plural	Singular	Plural
1 presente de indicativo		**8 perfecto de indicativo**	
marcho	marchamos	he marchado	hemos marchado
marchas	marcháis	has marchado	habéis marchado
marcha	marchan	ha marchado	han marchado
2 imperfecto de indicativo		**9 pluscuamperfecto de indicativo**	
marchaba	marchábamos	había marchado	habíamos marchado
marchabas	marchabais	habías marchado	habíais marchado
marchaba	marchaban	había marchado	habían marchado
3 pretérito		**10 pretérito anterior**	
marché	marchamos	hube marchado	hubimos marchado
marchaste	marchasteis	hubiste marchado	hubisteis marchado
marchó	marcharon	hubo marchado	hubieron marchado
4 futuro		**11 futuro perfecto**	
marcharé	marcharemos	habré marchado	habremos marchado
marcharás	marcharéis	habrás marchado	habréis marchado
marchará	marcharán	habrá marchado	habrán marchado
5 potencial simple		**12 potencial compuesto**	
marcharía	marcharíamos	habría marchado	habríamos marchado
marcharías	marcharíais	habrías marchado	habríais marchado
marcharía	marcharían	habría marchado	habrían marchado
6 presente de subjuntivo		**13 perfecto de subjuntivo**	
marche	marchemos	haya marchado	hayamos marchado
marches	marchéis	hayas marchado	hayáis marchado
marche	marchen	haya marchado	hayan marchado
7 imperfecto de subjuntivo		**14 pluscuamperfecto de subjuntivo**	
marchara	marcháramos	hubiera marchado	hubiéramos marchado
marcharas	marcharais	hubieras marchado	hubierais marchado
marchara	marcharan	hubiera marchado	hubieran marchado
OR		OR	
marchase	marchásemos	hubiese marchado	hubiésemos marchado
marchases	marchaseis	hubieses marchado	hubieseis marchado
marchase	marchasen	hubiese marchado	hubiesen marchado

imperativo	
—	marchemos
marcha; no marches	marchad; no marchéis
marche	marchen

---

la marcha   march
poner en marcha   to put in motion,
  to start
a largas marchas   speedily, with speed
¡En marcha!   Forward march!

Esto no marcha.   That won't work;
  That will not do.
Todo marcha bien.   Everything is
  going okay.

marcharse

Gerundio **marchándose**   Part. pas. **marchado**

to go away, to leave

Reflexive regular **-ar** verb

The Seven Simple Tenses		The Seven Compound Tenses	
Singular	Plural	Singular	Plural

1 presente de indicativo		8 perfecto de indicativo		
me marcho	nos marchamos	me he	nos hemos	
te marchas	os marcháis	te has	os habéis +	marchado
se marcha	se marchan	se ha	se han	

2 imperfecto de indicativo		9 pluscuamperfecto de indicativo		
me marchaba	nos marchábamos	me había	nos habíamos	
te marchabas	os marchabais	te habías	os habíais +	marchado
se marchaba	se marchaban	se había	se habían	

3 pretérito		10 pretérito anterior		
me marché	nos marchamos	me hube	nos hubimos	
te marchaste	os marchasteis	te hubiste	os hubisteis +	marchado
se marchó	se marcharon	se hubo	se hubieron	

4 futuro		11 futuro perfecto		
me marcharé	nos marcharemos	me habré	nos habremos	
te marcharás	os marcharéis	te habrás	os habréis +	marchado
se marchará	se marcharán	se habrá	se habrán	

5 potencial simple		12 potencial compuesto		
me marcharía	nos marcharíamos	me habría	nos habríamos	
te marcharías	os marcharíais	te habrías	os habríais +	marchado
se marcharía	se marcharían	se habría	se habrían	

6 presente de subjuntivo		13 perfecto de subjuntivo		
me marche	nos marchemos	me haya	nos hayamos	
te marches	os marchéis	te hayas	os hayáis +	marchado
se marche	se marchen	se haya	se hayan	

7 imperfecto de subjuntivo		14 pluscuamperfecto de subjuntivo		
me marchara	nos marcháramos	me hubiera	nos hubiéramos	
te marcharas	os marcharais	te hubieras	os hubierais +	marchado
se marchara	se marcharan	se hubiera	se hubieran	
OR		OR		
me marchase	nos marchásemos	me hubiese	nos hubiésemos	
te marchases	os marchaseis	te hubieses	os hubieseis +	marchado
se marchase	se marchasen	se hubiese	se hubiesen	

imperativo	
—	marchémonos
márchate; no te marches	marchaos; no os marchéis
márchese	márchense

¿Por qué te marchas?   Why are you
   leaving?

marcharse por las buenas   to leave
   for good, never to return

See also marchar.

206

Regular **-ar** verb   to kill

The Seven Simple Tenses		The Seven Compound Tenses	
Singular	Plural	Singular	Plural
1 presente de indicativo		8 perfecto de indicativo	
mato	matamos	he matado	hemos matado
matas	matáis	has matado	habéis matado
mata	matan	ha matado	han matado
2 imperfecto de indicativo		9 pluscuamperfecto de indicativo	
mataba	matábamos	había matado	habíamos matado
matabas	matabais	habías matado	habíais matado
mataba	mataban	había matado	habían matado
3 pretérito		10 pretérito anterior	
maté	matamos	hube matado	hubimos matado
mataste	matasteis	hubiste matado	hubisteis matado
mató	mataron	hubo matado	hubieron matado
4 futuro		11 futuro perfecto	
mataré	mataremos	habré matado	habremos matado
matarás	mataréis	habrás matado	habréis matado
matará	matarán	habrá matado	habrán matado
5 potencial simple		12 potencial compuesto	
mataría	mataríamos	habría matado	habríamos matado
matarías	mataríais	habrías matado	habríais matado
mataría	matarían	habría matado	habrían matado
6 presente de subjuntivo		13 perfecto de subjuntivo	
mate	matemos	haya matado	hayamos matado
mates	matéis	hayas matado	hayáis matado
mate	maten	haya matado	hayan matado
7 imperfecto de subjuntivo		14 pluscuamperfecto de subjuntivo	
matara	matáramos	hubiera matado	hubiéramos matado
mataras	matarais	hubieras matado	hubierais matado
matara	mataran	hubiera matado	hubieran matado
OR		OR	
matase	matásemos	hubiese matado	hubiésemos matado
matases	mataseis	hubieses matado	hubieseis matado
matase	matasen	hubiese matado	hubiesen matado

	imperativo	
—	matemos	
mata; no mates	matad; no matéis	
mate	maten	

matar a preguntas to bombard with questions	**matador, matadora** killer; **el matador** bullfighter (kills the bull)
el mate checkmate (chess)	**Quien a hierro mata, a hierro muere.**
matar el tiempo to kill time	Whoever kills by the sword dies by
dar mate a to checkmate (chess)	the sword.
estar a matar con alguien to be angry at someone	

mentir

Gerundio **mintiendo**   Part. pas. **mentido**

to lie, to tell a lie

Regular **-ir** verb endings with stem change:
Tenses 1, 3, 6, 7, Imperative, *Gerundio*

The Seven Simple Tenses		The Seven Compound Tenses	
Singular	Plural	Singular	Plural
1 presente de indicativo		8 perfecto de indicativo	
miento	mentimos	he mentido	hemos mentido
mientes	mentís	has mentido	habéis mentido
miente	mienten	ha mentido	han mentido
2 imperfecto de indicativo		9 pluscuamperfecto de indicativo	
mentía	mentíamos	había mentido	habíamos mentido
mentías	mentíais	habías mentido	habíais mentido
mentía	mentían	había mentido	habían mentido
3 pretérito		10 pretérito anterior	
mentí	mentimos	hube mentido	hubimos mentido
mentiste	mentisteis	hubiste mentido	hubisteis mentido
mintió	mintieron	hubo mentido	hubieron mentido
4 futuro		11 futuro perfecto	
mentiré	mentiremos	habré mentido	habremos mentido
mentirás	mentiréis	habrás mentido	habréis mentido
mentirá	mentirán	habrá mentido	habrán mentido
5 potencial simple		12 potencial compuesto	
mentiría	mentiríamos	habría mentido	habríamos mentido
mentirías	mentiríais	habrías mentido	habríais mentido
mentiría	mentirían	habría mentido	habrían mentido
6 presente de subjuntivo		13 perfecto de subjuntivo	
mienta	mintamos	haya mentido	hayamos mentido
mientas	mintáis	hayas mentido	hayáis mentido
mienta	mientan	haya mentido	hayan mentido
7 imperfecto de subjuntivo		14 pluscuamperfecto de subjuntivo	
mintiera	mintiéramos	hubiera mentido	hubiéramos mentido
mintieras	mintierais	hubieras mentido	hubierais mentido
mintiera	mintieran	hubiera mentido	hubieran mentido
OR		OR	
mintiese	mintiésemos	hubiese mentido	hubiésemos mentido
mintieses	mintieseis	hubieses mentido	hubieseis mentido
mintiese	mintiesen	hubiese mentido	hubiesen mentido

imperativo	
—	mintamos
miente; no mientas	mentid; no mintáis
mienta	mientan

El que una vez mintió, nunca se le
  creyó. Whoever lied once is never
  believed.
una mentira to lie
mentido, mentida deceptive, false

un mentirón a great lie
mentirosamente falsely
una mentirilla a fib
¡Parece mentira¡ I just don't believe
  it!

Regular **-ar** verb   to look, to look at, to watch

The Seven Simple Tenses		The Seven Compound Tenses	
Singular	Plural	Singular	Plural
1 presente de indicativo		8 perfecto de indicativo	
miro	miramos	he mirado	hemos mirado
miras	miráis	has mirado	habéis mirado
mira	miran	ha mirado	han mirado
2 imperfecto de indicativo		9 pluscuamperfecto de indicativo	
miraba	mirábamos	había mirado	habíamos mirado
mirabas	mirabais	habías mirado	habíais mirado
miraba	miraban	había mirado	habían mirado
3 pretérito		10 pretérito anterior	
miré	miramos	hube mirado	hubimos mirado
miraste	mirasteis	hubiste mirado	hubisteis mirado
miró	miraron	hubo mirado	hubieron mirado
4 futuro		11 futuro perfecto	
miraré	miraremos	habré mirado	habremos mirado
mirarás	miraréis	habrás mirado	habréis mirado
mirará	mirarán	habrá mirado	habrán mirado
5 potencial simple		12 potencial compuesto	
miraría	miraríamos	habría mirado	habríamos mirado
mirarías	miraríais	habrías mirado	habríais mirado
miraría	mirarían	habría mirado	habrían mirado
6 presente de subjuntivo		13 perfecto de subjuntivo	
mire	miremos	haya mirado	hayamos mirado
mires	miréis	hayas mirado	hayáis mirado
mire	miren	haya mirado	hayan mirado
7 imperfecto de subjuntivo		14 pluscuamperfecto de subjuntivo	
mirara	miráramos	hubiera mirado	hubiéramos mirado
miraras	mirarais	hubieras mirado	hubierais mirado
mirara	miraran	hubiera mirado	hubieran mirado
OR		OR	
mirase	mirásemos	hubiese mirado	hubiésemos mirado
mirases	miraseis	hubieses mirado	hubieseis mirado
mirase	mirasen	hubiese mirado	hubiesen mirado

imperativo	
—	miremos
mira; no mires	mirad; no miréis
mire	miren

Antes que te cases, mira lo que haces.
  Look before you leap. (Before you get
  married, look at what you're doing.)
mirar la televisión to watch television
mirar por to look after
¡Mira! Look! Look out! See here!
  Listen!

una mirada a look
echar una mirada to take a look at,
  to glance at
mirar alrededor to look around
mirarse to look at oneself, at each other
mirarse en el espejo to look at
  oneself in the mirror

morder

Gerundio **mordiendo**   Part. pas. **mordido**

to bite

Regular **-er** verb endings with stem
change: Tenses 1, 6, Imperative

The Seven Simple Tenses		The Seven Compound Tenses	
Singular	Plural	Singular	Plural
1 presente de indicativo		8 perfecto de indicativo	
muerdo	mordemos	he mordido	hemos mordido
muerdes	mordéis	has mordido	habéis mordido
muerde	muerden	ha mordido	han mordido
2 imperfecto de indicativo		9 pluscuamperfecto de indicativo	
mordía	mordíamos	había mordido	habíamos mordido
mordías	mordíais	habías mordido	habíais mordido
mordía	mordían	había mordido	habían mordido
3 pretérito		10 pretérito anterior	
mordí	mordimos	hube mordido	hubimos mordido
mordiste	mordisteis	hubiste mordido	hubisteis mordido
mordió	mordieron	hubo mordido	hubieron mordido
4 futuro		11 futuro perfecto	
morderé	morderemos	habré mordido	habremos mordido
morderás	morderéis	habrás mordido	habréis mordido
morderá	morderán	habrá mordido	habrán mordido
5 potencial simple		12 potencial compuesto	
mordería	morderíamos	habría mordido	habríamos mordido
morderías	morderíais	habrías mordido	habríais mordido
mordería	morderían	habría mordido	habrían mordido
6 presente de subjuntivo		13 perfecto de subjuntivo	
muerda	mordamos	haya mordido	hayamos mordido
muerdas	mordáis	hayas mordido	hayáis mordido
muerda	muerdan	haya mordido	hayan mordido
7 imperfecto de subjuntivo		14 pluscuamperfecto de subjuntivo	
mordiera	mordiéramos	hubiera mordido	hubiéramos mordido
mordieras	mordierais	hubieras mordido	hubierais mordido
mordiera	mordieran	hubiera mordido	hubieran mordido
OR		OR	
mordiese	mordiésemos	hubiese mordido	hubiésemos mordido
mordieses	mordieseis	hubieses mordido	hubieseis mordido
mordiese	mordiesen	hubiese mordido	hubiesen mordido

imperativo	
—	mordamos
muerde; no muerdas	morded; no mordáis
muerda	muerdan

Perro que ladra no muerde.   A barking
  dog does not bite.
Me mordí el labio.   I bit my lip.
mordazmente   bitingly

la mordacidad   mordancy
una mordedura   a bite
morderse   to bite oneself

Regular **-ir** verb endings with stem change: Tenses   to die
1, 3, 6, 7, Imperative, *Gerundio*, Past Participle

The Seven Simple Tenses		The Seven Compound Tenses	
Singular	Plural	Singular	Plural
1 presente de indicativo		8 perfecto de indicativo	
muero	**morimos**	**he muerto**	**hemos muerto**
mueres	**morís**	**has muerto**	**habéis muerto**
muere	**mueren**	**ha muerto**	**han muerto**
2 imperfecto de indicativo		9 pluscuamperfecto de indicativo	
moría	**moríamos**	**había muerto**	**habíamos muerto**
morías	**moríais**	**habías muerto**	**habíais muerto**
moría	**morían**	**había muerto**	**habían muerto**
3 pretérito		10 pretérito anterior	
morí	**morimos**	**hube muerto**	**hubimos muerto**
moriste	**moristeis**	**hubiste muerto**	**hubisteis muerto**
murió	**murieron**	**hubo muerto**	**hubieron muerto**
4 futuro		11 futuro perfecto	
moriré	**moriremos**	**habré muerto**	**habremos muerto**
morirás	**moriréis**	**habrás muerto**	**habréis muerto**
morirá	**morirán**	**habrá muerto**	**habrán muerto**
5 potencial simple		12 potencial compuesto	
moriría	**moriríamos**	**habría muerto**	**habríamos muerto**
morirías	**moriríais**	**habrías muerto**	**habríais muerto**
moriría	**morirían**	**habría muerto**	**habrían muerto**
6 presente de subjuntivo		13 perfecto de subjuntivo	
muera	**muramos**	**haya muerto**	**hayamos muerto**
mueras	**muráis**	**hayas muerto**	**hayáis muerto**
muera	**mueran**	**haya muerto**	**hayan muerto**
7 imperfecto de subjuntivo		14 pluscuamperfecto de subjuntivo	
muriera	**muriéramos**	**hubiera muerto**	**hubiéramos muerto**
murieras	**murierais**	**hubieras muerto**	**hubierais muerto**
muriera	**murieran**	**hubiera muerto**	**hubieran muerto**
OR		OR	
muriese	**muriésemos**	**hubiese muerto**	**hubiésemos muerto**
murieses	**murieseis**	**hubieses muerto**	**hubieseis muerto**
muriese	**muriesen**	**hubiese muerto**	**hubiesen muerto**

	imperativo	
—	**muramos**	
muere; no mueras	**morid; no muráis**	
muera	**mueran**	

la muerte death	**morir de risa** to die laughing
entremorir to burn out, to flicker	**morirse de miedo** to be scared to
mortal fatal, mortal	death
morir de repente to drop dead	**morirse de hambre** to starve to death
la mortalidad mortality	**morirse de frío** to freeze to death
hasta morir until death	

mostrar

Gerundio **mostrando**   Part. pas. **mostrado**

show, to point out

Regular **-ar** verb endings with stem change: Tenses 1, 6, Imperative

The Seven Simple Tenses		The Seven Compound Tenses	
Singular	Plural	Singular	Plural
1 presente de indicativo		8 perfecto de indicativo	
muestro	mostramos	he mostrado	hemos mostrado
muestras	mostráis	has mostrado	habéis mostrado
muestra	muestran	ha mostrado	han mostrado
2 imperfecto de indicativo		9 pluscuamperfecto de indicativo	
mostraba	mostrábamos	había mostrado	habíamos mostrado
mostrabas	mostrabais	habías mostrado	habíais mostrado
mostraba	mostraban	había mostrado	habían mostrado
3 pretérito		10 pretérito anterior	
mostré	mostramos	hube mostrado	hubimos mostrado
mostraste	mostrasteis	hubiste mostrado	hubisteis mostrado
mostró	mostraron	hubo mostrado	hubieron mostrado
4 futuro		11 futuro perfecto	
mostraré	mostraremos	habré mostrado	habremos mostrado
mostrarás	mostraréis	habrás mostrado	habréis mostrado
mostrará	mostrarán	habrá mostrado	habrán mostrado
5 potencial simple		12 potencial compuesto	
mostraría	mostraríamos	habría mostrado	habríamos mostrado
mostrarías	mostraríais	habrías mostrado	habríais mostrado
mostraría	mostrarían	habría mostrado	habrían mostrado
6 presente de subjuntivo		13 perfecto de subjuntivo	
muestre	mostremos	haya mostrado	hayamos mostrado
muestres	mostréis	hayas mostrado	hayáis mostrado
muestre	muestren	haya mostrado	hayan mostrado
7 imperfecto de subjuntivo		14 pluscuamperfecto de subjuntivo	
mostrara	mostráramos	hubiera mostrado	hubiéramos mostrado
mostraras	mostrarais	hubieras mostrado	hubierais mostrado
mostrara	mostraran	hubiera mostrado	hubieran mostrado
OR		OR	
mostrase	mostrásemos	hubiese mostrado	hubiésemos mostrado
mostrases	mostraseis	hubieses mostrado	hubieseis mostrado
mostrase	mostrasen	hubiese mostrado	hubiesen mostrado

imperativo	
—	mostremos
muestra; no muestres	mostrad; no mostréis
muestre	muestren

Muéstreme. Show me.
mostrador, mostradora counter (in a store where merchandise is displayed under a glass case)

mostrarse to show oneself, to appear
See also **demostrar**.

Regular **-er** verb endings with spelling change: to be born
c becomes **zc** before **a** or **o**

The Seven Simple Tenses		The Seven Compound Tenses	
Singular	Plural	Singular	Plural
1 presente de indicativo		8 perfecto de indicativo	
nazco	nacemos	he nacido	hemos nacido
naces	nacéis	has nacido	habéis nacido
nace	nacen	ha nacido	han nacido
2 imperfecto de indicativo		9 pluscuamperfecto de indicativo	
nacía	nacíamos	había nacido	habíamos nacido
nacías	nacíais	habías nacido	habíais nacido
nacía	nacían	había nacido	habían nacido
3 pretérito		10 pretérito anterior	
nací	nacimos	hube nacido	hubimos nacido
naciste	nacisteis	hubiste nacido	hubisteis nacido
nació	nacieron	hubo nacido	hubieron nacido
4 futuro		11 futuro perfecto	
naceré	naceremos	habré nacido	habremos nacido
nacerás	naceréis	habrás nacido	habréis nacido
nacerá	nacerán	habrá nacido	habrán nacido
5 potencial simple		12 potencial compuesto	
nacería	naceríamos	habría nacido	habríamos nacido
nacerías	naceríais	habrías nacido	habríais nacido
nacería	nacerían	habría nacido	habrían nacido
6 presente de subjuntivo		13 perfecto de subjuntivo	
nazca	nazcamos	haya nacido	hayamos nacido
nazcas	nazcáis	hayas nacido	hayáis nacido
nazca	nazcan	haya nacido	hayan nacido
7 imperfecto de subjuntivo		14 pluscuamperfecto de subjuntivo	
naciera	naciéramos	hubiera nacido	hubiéramos nacido
nacieras	nacierais	hubieras nacido	hubierais nacido
naciera	nacieran	hubiera nacido	hubieran nacido
OR		OR	
naciese	naciésemos	hubiese nacido	hubiésemos nacido
nacieses	nacieseis	hubieses nacido	hubieseis nacido
naciese	naciesen	hubiese nacido	hubiesen nacido

imperativo		
—	nazcamos	
nace; no nazcas	naced; no nazcáis	
nazca	nazcan	

bien nacido (nacida) well-bred	**el nacimiento** birth
mal nacido (nacida) ill-bred	**nacer de pies** to be born with a silver
nacer tarde to be born yesterday (not	spoon in one's mouth
much intelligence)	**renacer** to be born again, to be reborn

nadar

Gerundio **nadando**   Part. pas. **nadado**

to swim

The Seven Simple Tenses		The Seven Compound Tenses	
Singular	Plural	Singular	Plural
1 presente de indicativo		8 perfecto de indicativo	
nado	nadamos	he nadado	hemos nadado
nadas	nadáis	has nadado	habéis nadado
nada	nadan	ha nadado	han nadado
2 imperfecto de indicativo		9 pluscuamperfecto de indicativo	
nadaba	nadábamos	había nadado	habíamos nadado
nadabas	nadabais	habías nadado	habíais nadado
nadaba	nadaban	había nadado	habían nadado
3 pretérito		10 pretérito anterior	
nadé	nadamos	hube nadado	hubimos nadado
nadaste	nadasteis	hubiste nadado	hubisteis nadado
nadó	nadaron	hubo nadado	hubieron nadado
4 futuro		11 futuro perfecto	
nadaré	nadaremos	habré nadado	habremos nadado
nadarás	nadaréis	habrás nadado	habréis nadado
nadará	nadarán	habrá nadado	habrán nadado
5 potencial simple		12 potencial compuesto	
nadaría	nadaríamos	habría nadado	habríamos nadado
nadarías	nadaríais	habrías nadado	habríais nadado
nadaría	nadarían	habría nadado	habrían nadado
6 presente de subjuntivo		13 perfecto de subjuntivo	
nade	nademos	haya nadado	hayamos nadado
nades	nadéis	hayas nadado	hayáis nadado
nade	naden	haya nadado	hayan nadado
7 imperfecto de subjuntivo		14 pluscuamperfecto de subjuntivo	
nadara	nadáramos	hubiera nadado	hubiéramos nadado
nadaras	nadarais	hubieras nadado	hubierais nadado
nadara	nadaran	hubiera nadado	hubieran nadado
OR		OR	
nadase	nadásemos	hubiese nadado	hubiésemos nadado
nadases	nadaseis	hubieses nadado	hubieseis nadado
nadase	nadasen	hubiese nadado	hubiesen nadado

imperativo	
—	nademos
nada; no nades	nadad; no nadéis
nade	naden

Nadar y nadar, y a la orilla ahogar.
  To swim and swim, and drown at the
  shore. (To fail in spite of trying.)
nadador, nadadora swimmer
nadar entre dos aguas to be
  undecided

la natación swimming
nader en to revel in, to delight in, to
  take great pleasure in

The Seven Simple Tenses		The Seven Compound Tenses	
Singular	Plural	Singular	Plural
1 presente de indicativo		**8 perfecto de indicativo**	
necesito	necesitamos	he necesitado	hemos necesitado
necesitas	necesitáis	has necesitado	habéis necesitado
necesita	necesitan	ha necesitado	han necesitado
2 imperfecto de indicativo		**9 pluscuamperfecto de indicativo**	
necesitaba	necesitábamos	había necesitado	habíamos necesitado
necesitabas	necesitabais	habías necesitado	habíais necesitado
necesitaba	necesitaban	había necesitado	habían necesitado
3 pretérito		**10 pretérito anterior**	
necesité	necesitamos	hube necesitado	hubimos necesitado
necesitaste	necesitasteis	hubiste necesitado	hubisteis necesitado
necesitó	necesitaron	hubo necesitado	hubieron necesitado
4 futuro		**11 futuro perfecto**	
necesitaré	necesitaremos	habré necesitado	habremos necesitado
necesitarás	necesitaréis	habrás necesitado	habréis necesitado
necesitará	necesitarán	habrá necesitado	habrán necesitado
5 potencial simple		**12 potencial compuesto**	
necesitaría	necesitaríamos	habría necesitado	habríamos necesitado
necesitarías	necesitaríais	habrías necesitado	habríais necesitado
necesitaría	necesitarían	habría necesitado	habrían necesitado
6 presente de subjuntivo		**13 perfecto de subjuntivo**	
necesite	necesitemos	haya necesitado	hayamos necesitado
necesites	necesitéis	hayas necesitado	hayáis necesitado
necesite	necesiten	haya necesitado	hayan necesitado
7 imperfecto de subjuntivo		**14 pluscuamperfecto de subjuntivo**	
necesitara	necesitáramos	hubiera necesitado	hubiéramos necesitado
necesitaras	necesitarais	hubieras necesitado	hubierais necesitado
necesitara	necesitaran	hubiera necesitado	hubieran necesitado
OR		OR	
necesitase	necesitásemos	hubiese necesitado	hubiésemos necesitado
necesitases	necesitaseis	hubieses necesitado	hubieseis necesitado
necesitase	necesitasen	hubiese necesitado	hubiesen necesitado

	imperativo	
—		necesitemos
necesita; no necesites		necesitad; no necesitéis
necesite		necesiten

Necesito un cuaderno, por favor. I
  need a notebook, please.
La necesidad es la madre de la
  habilidad.   Necessity is the mother
  of invention. (la habilidad: skill)
la necesidad   necessity

necesitar + inf.   to have + inf., to need
  + inf.
por necesidad   from necessity
un necesitado, una necesitada   needy
  person
necesario, necesaria   necessary
necesariamente   necessarily

negar

Gerundio **negando**   Part. pas. **negado**

to deny

Regular **-ar** verb endings with spelling change: **g** becomes **gu** before **e**; stem change: Tenses 1, 6, Imperative

The Seven Simple Tenses		The Seven Compound Tenses	
Singular	Plural	Singular	Plural
1 presente de indicativo		**8 perfecto de indicativo**	
niego	negamos	he negado	hemos negado
niegas	negáis	has negado	habéis negado
niega	niegan	ha negado	han negado
2 imperfecto de indicativo		**9 pluscuamperfecto de indicativo**	
negaba	negábamos	había negado	habíamos negado
negabas	negabais	habías negado	habíais negado
negaba	negaban	había negado	habían negado
3 pretérito		**10 pretérito anterior**	
negué	negamos	hube negado	hubimos negado
negaste	negasteis	hubiste negado	hubisteis negado
negó	negaron	hubo negado	hubieron negado
4 futuro		**11 futuro perfecto**	
negaré	negaremos	habré negado	habremos negado
negarás	negaréis	habrás negado	habréis negado
negará	negarán	habrá negado	habrán negado
5 potencial simple		**12 potencial compuesto**	
negaría	negaríamos	habría negado	habríamos negado
negarías	negaríais	habrías negado	habríais negado
negaría	negarían	habría negado	habrían negado
6 presente de subjuntivo		**13 perfecto de subjuntivo**	
niegue	neguemos	haya negado	hayamos negado
niegues	neguéis	hayas negado	hayáis negado
niegue	nieguen	haya negado	hayan negado
7 imperfecto de subjuntivo		**14 pluscuamperfecto de subjuntivo**	
negara	negáramos	hubiera negado	hubiéramos negado
negaras	negarais	hubieras negado	hubierais negado
negara	negaran	hubiera negado	hubieran negado
OR		OR	
negase	negásemos	hubiese negado	hubiésemos negado
negases	negaseis	hubieses negado	hubieseis negado
negase	negasen	hubiese negado	hubiesen negado

imperativo	
—	neguemos
niega; no niegues	negad; no neguéis
niegue	nieguen

negador, negadora denier	la negación denial, negation
negar haber + past part. to deny having + past part.	negarse a to refuse
	negable deniable
negativo, negativa negative	renegar to abhor, to deny vehemently

Regular **-ar** verb endings with stem change:
Tenses 1, 6, Imperative

to snow

The Seven Simple Tenses	The Seven Compound Tenses
Singular Plural	Singular Plural
1 presente de indicativo **nieva** OR **está nevando**	8 perfecto de indicativo **ha nevado**
2 imperfecto de indicativo **nevaba** OR **estaba nevando**	9 pluscuamperfecto de indicativo **había nevado**
3 pretérito **nevó**	10 pretérito anterior **hubo nevado**
4 futuro **nevará**	11 futuro perfecto **habrá nevado**
5 potencial simple **nevaría**	12 potencial compuesto **habría nevado**
6 presente de subjuntivo **nieve**	13 perfecto de subjuntivo **haya nevado**
7 imperfecto de subjuntivo **nevara** OR **nevase**	14 pluscuamperfecto de subjuntivo **hubiera nevado** OR **hubiese nevado**

imperativo
¡Que nieve!   Let it snow!

---

la nieve   snow
   Me gusta la nieve.   I like snow.
la nevera   refrigerator
un copo de nieve   snowflake
nevado, nevada   snowy, snow covered
una bola de nieve   snowball

la nevada   snowfall
¿Hay mucha nieve aquí en el
   invierno?   Is there much snow here
   in winter?
Sí, nieva mucho aquí en el invierno.
   Yes, it snows a lot here in the winter.

obedecer

Gerundio **obedeciendo**   Part. pas. **obedecido**

to obey

Regular **-er** verb endings with spelling change: **c** becomes **zc** before **a** or **o**

The Seven Simple Tenses		The Seven Compound Tenses	
Singular	Plural	Singular	Plural
1 presente de indicativo		8 perfecto de indicativo	
obedezco	**obedecemos**	**he obedecido**	**hemos obedecido**
obedeces	**obedecéis**	**has obedecido**	**habéis obedecido**
obedece	**obedecen**	**ha obedecido**	**han obedecido**
2 imperfecto de indicativo		9 pluscuamperfecto de indicativo	
obedecía	**obedecíamos**	**había obedecido**	**habíamos obedecido**
obedecías	**obedecíais**	**habías obedecido**	**habíais obedecido**
obedecía	**obedecían**	**había obedecido**	**habían obedecido**
3 pretérito		10 pretérito anterior	
obedecí	**obedecimos**	**hube obedecido**	**hubimos obedecido**
obedeciste	**obedecisteis**	**hubiste obedecido**	**hubisteis obedecido**
obedeció	**obedecieron**	**hubo obedecido**	**hubieron obedecido**
4 futuro		11 futuro perfecto	
obedeceré	**obedeceremos**	**habré obedecido**	**habremos obedecido**
obedecerás	**obedeceréis**	**habrás obedecido**	**habréis obedecido**
obedecerá	**obedecerán**	**habrá obedecido**	**habrán obedecido**
5 potencial simple		12 potencial compuesto	
obedecería	**obedeceríamos**	**habría obedecido**	**habríamos obedecido**
obedecerías	**obedeceríais**	**habrías obedecido**	**habríais obedecido**
obedecería	**obedecerían**	**habría obedecido**	**habrían obedecido**
6 presente de subjuntivo		13 perfecto de subjuntivo	
obedezca	**obedezcamos**	**haya obedecido**	**hayamos obedecido**
obedezcas	**obedezcáis**	**hayas obedecido**	**hayáis obedecido**
obedezca	**obedezcan**	**haya obedecido**	**hayan obedecido**
7 imperfecto de subjuntivo		14 pluscuamperfecto de subjuntivo	
obedeciera	**obedeciéramos**	**hubiera obedecido**	**hubiéramos obedecido**
obedecieras	**obedecierais**	**hubieras obedecido**	**hubierais obedecido**
obedeciera	**obedecieran**	**hubiera obedecido**	**hubieran obedecido**
OR		OR	
obedeciese	**obedeciésemos**	**hubiese obedecido**	**hubiésemos obedecido**
obedecieses	**obedecieseis**	**hubieses obedecido**	**hubieseis obedecido**
obedeciese	**obedeciesen**	**hubiese obedecido**	**hubiesen obedecido**

imperativo	
—	**obedezcamos**
obedece; no obedezcas	**obedeced; no obedezcáis**
obedezca	**obedezcan**

El que no sabe obedecer no sabe mandar.   Whoever doesn't know how to obey doesn't know how to give orders.
el obedecimiento, la obediencia   obedience

obedientemente   obediently
obediente   obedient
desobedecer   to disobey
obedecer las leyes   to obey the law
desobediente   disobedient
obedecer a sus padres   to obey one's parents
la desobediencia   disobedience

The Seven Simple Tenses		The Seven Compound Tenses	
Singular	Plural	Singular	Plural
1 presente de indicativo		8 perfecto de indicativo	
obtengo	**obtenemos**	**he obtenido**	**hemos obtenido**
obtienes	**obtenéis**	**has obtenido**	**habéis obtenido**
obtiene	**obtienen**	**ha obtenido**	**han obtenido**
2 imperfecto de indicativo		9 pluscuamperfecto de indicativo	
obtenía	**obteníamos**	**había obtenido**	**habíamos obtenido**
obtenías	**obteníais**	**habías obtenido**	**habíais obtenido**
obtenía	**obtenían**	**había obtenido**	**habían obtenido**
3 pretérito		10 pretérito anterior	
obtuve	**obtuvimos**	**hube obtenido**	**hubimos obtenido**
obtuviste	**obtuvisteis**	**hubiste obtenido**	**hubisteis obtenido**
obtuvo	**obtuvieron**	**hubo obtenido**	**hubieron obtenido**
4 futuro		11 futuro perfecto	
obtendré	**obtendremos**	**habré obtenido**	**habremos obtenido**
obtendrás	**obtendréis**	**habrás obtenido**	**habréis obtenido**
obtendrá	**obtendrán**	**habrá obtenido**	**habrán obtenido**
5 potencial simple		12 potencial compuesto	
obtendría	**obtendríamos**	**habría obtenido**	**habríamos obtenido**
obtendrías	**obtendríais**	**habrías obtenido**	**habríais obtenido**
obtendría	**obtendrían**	**habría obtenido**	**habrían obtenido**
6 presente de subjuntivo		13 perfecto de subjuntivo	
obtenga	**obtengamos**	**haya obtenido**	**hayamos obtenido**
obtengas	**obtengáis**	**hayas obtenido**	**hayáis obtenido**
obtenga	**obtengan**	**haya obtenido**	**hayan obtenido**
7 imperfecto de subjuntivo		14 pluscuamperfecto de subjuntivo	
obtuviera	**obtuviéramos**	**hubiera obtenido**	**hubiéramos obtenido**
obtuvieras	**obtuvierais**	**hubieras obtenido**	**hubierais obtenido**
obtuviera	**obtuvieran**	**hubiera obtenido**	**hubieran obtenido**
OR		OR	
obtuviese	**obtuviésemos**	**hubiese obtenido**	**hubiésemos obtenido**
obtuvieses	**obtuvieseis**	**hubieses obtenido**	**hubieseis obtenido**
obtuviese	**obtuviesen**	**hubiese obtenido**	**hubiesen obtenido**

imperativo	
—	**obtengamos**
obtén; no obtengas	**obtened; obtengáis**
obtenga	**obtengan**

---

obtenible   obtainable, available
obtener una colocación   to get a job
la obtención   obtainment
obtener buenos resultados   to get

good results
obtener malos resultados   to get bad
results
See also **tener.**

ocupar

Gerundio **ocupando**   Part. pas. **ocupado**

to occupy

Regular **-ar** verb

The Seven Simple Tenses		The Seven Compound Tenses	
Singular	Plural	Singular	Plural
1 presente de indicativo		8 perfecto de indicativo	
ocupo	ocupamos	he ocupado	hemos ocupado
ocupas	ocupáis	has ocupado	habéis ocupado
ocupa	ocupan	ha ocupado	han ocupado
2 imperfecto de indicativo		9 pluscuamperfecto de indicativo	
ocupaba	ocupábamos	había ocupado	habíamos ocupado
ocupabas	ocupabais	habías ocupado	habíais ocupado
ocupaba	ocupaban	había ocupado	habían ocupado
3 pretérito		10 pretérito anterior	
ocupé	ocupamos	hube ocupado	hubimos ocupado
ocupaste	ocupasteis	hubiste ocupado	hubisteis ocupado
ocupó	ocuparon	hubo ocupado	hubieron ocupado
4 futuro		11 futuro perfecto	
ocuparé	ocuparemos	habré ocupado	habremos ocupado
ocuparás	ocuparéis	habrás ocupado	habréis ocupado
ocupará	ocuparán	habrá ocupado	habrán ocupado
5 potencial simple		12 potencial compuesto	
ocuparía	ocuparíamos	habría ocupado	habríamos ocupado
ocuparías	ocuparíais	habrías ocupado	habríais ocupado
ocuparía	ocuparían	habría ocupado	habrían ocupado
6 presente de subjuntivo		13 perfecto de subjuntivo	
ocupe	ocupemos	haya ocupado	hayamos ocupado
ocupes	ocupéis	hayas ocupado	hayáis ocupado
ocupe	ocupen	haya ocupado	hayan ocupado
7 imperfecto de subjuntivo		14 pluscuamperfecto de subjuntivo	
ocupara	ocupáramos	hubiera ocupado	hubiéramos ocupado
ocuparas	ocuparais	hubieras ocupado	hubierais ocupado
ocupara	ocuparan	hubiera ocupado	hubieran ocupado
OR		OR	
ocupase	ocupásemos	hubiese ocupado	hubiésemos ocupado
ocupases	ocupaseis	hubieses ocupado	hubieseis ocupado
ocupase	ocupasen	hubiese ocupado	hubiesen ocupado

imperativo	
—	ocupemos
ocupa; no ocupes	ocupad; no ocupéis
ocupe	ocupen

---

ocupado, ocupada   busy, occupied
  desocupar   to vacate
la ocupación   occupation
ocuparse con algo   to be busy with
  something

ocuparse de (en)   to be busy with, in,
  to be engaged in
un, una ocupante   occupant

ocurrir

Regular **-ir** verb

to occur, to happen

The Seven Simple Tenses		The Seven Compound Tenses	
Singular	Plural	Singular	Plural
1 presente de indicativo		8 perfecto de indicativo	
ocurre	**ocurren**	**ha ocurrido**	**han ocurrido**
2 imperfecto de indicativo		9 pluscuamperfecto de indicativo	
ocurría	**ocurrían**	**había ocurrido**	**habían ocurrido**
3 pretérito		10 pretérito anterior	
ocurrió	**ocurrieron**	**hubo ocurrido**	**hubieron ocurrido**
4 futuro		11 futuro perfecto	
ocurrirá	**ocurrirán**	**habrá ocurrido**	**habrán ocurrido**
5 potencial simple		12 potencial compuesto	
ocurriría	**ocurrirían**	**habría ocurrido**	**habrían ocurrido**
6 presente de subjuntivo		13 perfecto de subjuntivo	
ocurra	**ocurran**	**haya ocurrido**	**hayan ocurrido**
7 imperfecto de subjuntivo		14 pluscuamperfecto de subjuntivo	
ocurriera	**ocurrieran**	**hubiera ocurrido**	**hubieran ocurrido**
OR		OR	
ocurriese	**ocurriesen**	**hubiese ocurrido**	**hubiesen ocurrido**

imperativo
¡Que ocurra! **¡Que ocurran!**
Let it occur! Let them occur!

This verb is generally used in the third person singular and plural.

ocurrente occurring; funny, witty, humorous

la ocurrencia occurrence, happening, event; witticism

ocurra lo que ocurra come what may

ocurrirse to occur

¿Qué ocurre? What's happening? What's going on? What's wrong?

¿Qué ocurrió? What happened?

ofrecer

Gerundio **ofreciendo**   Part. pas. **ofrecido**

to offer

Regular **-er** verb endings with spelling
change: **c** becomes **zc** before **a** or **o**

The Seven Simple Tenses		The Seven Compound Tenses	
Singular	Plural	Singular	Plural
1 presente de indicativo		8 perfecto de indicativo	
ofrezco	**ofrecemos**	**he ofrecido**	**hemos ofrecido**
ofreces	**ofrecéis**	**has ofrecido**	**habéis ofrecido**
ofrece	**ofrecen**	**ha ofrecido**	**han ofrecido**
2 imperfecto de indicativo		9 pluscuamperfecto de indicativo	
ofrecía	**ofrecíamos**	**había ofrecido**	**habíamos ofrecido**
ofrecías	**ofrecíais**	**habías ofrecido**	**habíais ofrecido**
ofrecía	**ofrecían**	**había ofrecido**	**habían ofrecido**
3 pretérito		10 pretérito anterior	
ofrecí	**ofrecimos**	**hube ofrecido**	**hubimos ofrecido**
ofreciste	**ofrecisteis**	**hubiste ofrecido**	**hubisteis ofrecido**
ofreció	**ofrecieron**	**hubo ofrecido**	**hubieron ofrecido**
4 futuro		11 futuro perfecto	
ofreceré	**ofreceremos**	**habré ofrecido**	**habremos ofrecido**
ofrecerás	**ofreceréis**	**habrás ofrecido**	**habréis ofrecido**
ofrecerá	**ofrecerán**	**habrá ofrecido**	**habrán ofrecido**
5 potencial simple		12 potencial compuesto	
ofrecería	**ofreceríamos**	**habría ofrecido**	**habríamos ofrecido**
ofrecerías	**ofreceríais**	**habrías ofrecido**	**habríais ofrecido**
ofrecería	**ofrecerían**	**habría ofrecido**	**habrían ofrecido**
6 presente de subjuntivo		13 perfecto de subjuntivo	
ofrezca	**ofrezcamos**	**haya ofrecido**	**hayamos ofrecido**
ofrezcas	**ofrezcáis**	**hayas ofrecido**	**hayáis ofrecido**
ofrezca	**ofrezcan**	**haya ofrecido**	**hayan ofrecido**
7 imperfecto de subjuntivo		14 pluscuamperfecto de subjuntivo	
ofreciera	**ofreciéramos**	**hubiera ofrecido**	**hubiéramos ofrecido**
ofrecieras	**ofrecierais**	**hubieras ofrecido**	**hubierais ofrecido**
ofreciera	**ofrecieran**	**hubiera ofrecido**	**hubieran ofrecido**
OR		OR	
ofreciese	**ofreciésemos**	**hubiese ofrecido**	**hubiésemos ofrecido**
ofrecieses	**ofrecieseis**	**hubieses ofrecido**	**hubieseis ofrecido**
ofreciese	**ofreciesen**	**hubiese ofrecido**	**hubiesen ofrecido**

imperativo	
—	**ofrezcamos**
ofrece; no ofrezcas	**ofreced; no ofrezcáis**
ofrezca	**ofrezcan**

ofreciente offering	la ofrenda gift, oblation
ofrecer + inf. to offer + inf.	ofrecer el brazo to offer one's arm
el ofrecimiento offer, offering	ofrecer su ayuda to offer your help
el ofrecedor, la ofrecedora offerer	ofrecerse to offer oneself

Irregular verb

to hear

The Seven Simple Tenses		The Seven Compound Tenses	
Singular	Plural	Singular	Plural
1 presente de indicativo		**8 perfecto de indicativo**	
oigo	oímos	he oído	hemos oído
oyes	oís	has oído	habéis oído
oye	oyen	ha oído	han oído
2 imperfecto de indicativo		**9 pluscuamperfecto de indicativo**	
oía	oíamos	había oído	habíamos oído
oías	oíais	habías oído	habíais oído
oía	oían	había oído	habían oído
3 pretérito		**10 pretérito anterior**	
oí	oímos	hube oído	hubimos oído
oíste	oísteis	hubiste oído	hubisteis oído
oyó	oyeron	hubo oído	hubieron oído
4 futuro		**11 futuro perfecto**	
oiré	oiremos	habré oído	habremos oído
oirás	oiréis	habrás oído	habréis oído
oirá	oirán	habrá oído	habrán oído
5 potencial simple		**12 potencial compuesto**	
oiría	oiríamos	habría oído	habríamos oído
oirías	oiríais	habrías oído	habríais oído
oiría	oirían	habría oído	habrían oído
6 presente de subjuntivo		**13 perfecto de subjuntivo**	
oiga	oigamos	haya oído	hayamos oído
oigas	oigáis	hayas oído	hayáis oído
oiga	oigan	haya oído	hayan oído
7 imperfecto de subjuntivo		**14 pluscuamperfecto de subjuntivo**	
oyera	oyéramos	hubiera oído	hubiéramos oído
oyeras	oyerais	hubieras oído	hubierais oído
oyera	oyeran	hubiera oído	hubieran oído
OR		OR	
oyese	oyésemos	hubiese oído	hubiésemos oído
oyeses	oyeseis	hubieses oído	hubieseis oído
oyese	oyesen	hubiese oído	hubiesen oído

imperativo	
—	oigamos
oye; no oigas	oíd; no oigáis
oiga	oigan

Oigo la voz de un amigo. I hear the voice of a friend.	dar oídos to lend an ear
	al oído confidentially
Las paredes oyen. (Las paredes tienen oídos.) The walls have ears.	oír decir to hear tell, to hear say
la oída hearing; de oídas by hearsay	el oído hearing (sense)
por oídos, de oídos by hearing	oír hablar de to hear of, to hear talk of; desoír to ignore, to be deaf to

223

oler

Gerundio **oliendo** Part. pas. **olido**

to smell, to scent

Regular **-er** verb endings with stem change: Tenses 1, 6, Imperative

The Seven Simple Tenses		The Seven Compound Tenses	
Singular	Plural	Singular	Plural
1 presente de indicativo		8 perfecto de indicativo	
huelo	olemos	he olido	hemos olido
hueles	oléis	has olido	habéis olido
huele	huelen	ha olido	han olido
2 imperfecto de indicativo		9 pluscuamperfecto de indicativo	
olía	olíamos	había olido	habíamos olido
olías	olíais	habías olido	habíais olido
olía	olían	había olido	habían olido
3 pretérito		10 pretérito anterior	
olí	olimos	hube olido	hubimos olido
oliste	olisteis	hubiste olido	hubisteis olido
olió	olieron	hubo olido	hubieron olido
4 futuro		11 futuro perfecto	
oleré	oleremos	habré olido	habremos olido
olerás	oleréis	habrás olido	habréis olido
olerá	olerán	habrá olido	habrán olido
5 potencial simple		12 potencial compuesto	
olería	oleríamos	habría olido	habríamos olido
olerías	oleríais	habrías olido	habríais olido
olería	olerían	habría olido	habrían olido
6 presente de subjuntivo		13 perfecto de subjuntivo	
huela	olamos	haya olido	hayamos olido
huelas	oláis	hayas olido	hayáis olido
huela	huelan	haya olido	hayan olido
7 imperfecto de subjuntivo		14 pluscuamperfecto de subjuntivo	
oliera	oliéramos	hubiera olido	hubiéramos olido
olieras	olierais	hubieras olido	hubierais olido
oliera	olieran	hubiera olido	hubieran olido
OR		OR	
oliese	oliésemos	hubiese olido	hubiésemos olido
olieses	olieseis	hubieses olido	hubieseis olido
oliese	oliesen	hubiese olido	hubiesen olido

imperativo	
—	olamos
huele; no huelas	oled; no oláis
huela	huelan

el olfato, la olfacción olfaction (the
 sense of smelling, act of smelling)
olfatear to sniff
oler a to smell of; oler a rosa to
 smell like a rose

No huele bien. It looks fishy. (It
 doesn't smell good.)

224

The Seven Simple Tenses		The Seven Compound Tenses	
Singular	Plural	Singular	Plural
1 presente de indicativo		8 perfecto de indicativo	
olvido	olvidamos	he olvidado	hemos olvidado
olvidas	olvidáis	has olvidado	habéis olvidado
olvida	olvidan	ha olvidado	han olvidado
2 imperfecto de indicativo		9 pluscuamperfecto de indicativo	
olvidaba	olvidábamos	había olvidado	habíamos olvidado
olvidabas	olvidabais	habías olvidado	habíais olvidado
olvidaba	olvidaban	había olvidado	habían olvidado
3 pretérito		10 pretérito anterior	
olvidé	olvidamos	hube olvidado	hubimos olvidado
olvidaste	olvidasteis	hubiste olvidado	hubisteis olvidado
olvidó	olvidaron	hubo olvidado	hubieron olvidado
4 futuro		11 futuro perfecto	
olvidaré	olvidaremos	habré olvidado	habremos olvidado
olvidarás	olvidaréis	habrás olvidado	habréis olvidado
olvidará	olvidarán	habrá olvidado	habrán olvidado
5 potencial simple		12 potencial compuesto	
olvidaría	olvidaríamos	habría olvidado	habríamos olvidado
olvidarías	olvidaríais	habrías olvidado	habríais olvidado
olvidaría	olvidarían	habría olvidado	habrían olvidado
6 presente de subjuntivo		13 perfecto de subjuntivo	
olvide	olvidemos	haya olvidado	hayamos olvidado
olvides	olvidéis	hayas olvidado	hayáis olvidado
olvide	olviden	haya olvidado	hayan olvidado
7 imperfecto de subjuntivo		14 pluscuamperfecto de subjuntivo	
olvidara	olvidáramos	hubiera olvidado	hubiéramos olvidado
olvidaras	olvidarais	hubieras olvidado	hubierais olvidado
olvidara	olvidaran	hubiera olvidado	hubieran olvidado
OR		OR	
olvidase	olvidásemos	hubiese olvidado	hubiésemos olvidado
olvidases	olvidaseis	hubieses olvidado	hubieseis olvidado
olvidase	olvidasen	hubiese olvidado	hubiesen olvidado

imperativo	
—	olvidemos
olvida; no olvides	olvidad; no olvidéis
olvide	olviden

olvidado, olvidada forgotten
olvidar + inf. to forget + inf.
olvidadizo, olvidadiza forgetful
olvidarse de to forget
el olvido forgetfulness, oblivion

olvidarse de + inf. to forget + inf.
Se me olvidó. It slipped my mind.
olvidar la hora to forget the time
¡No te olvides de cerrar la puerta!
Don't forget to close the door!

ordenar
Gerundio **ordenando**
Part. pas. **ordenado**

to order, to command,
to put in order, to arrange

Regular **-ar** verb

The Seven Simple Tenses		The Seven Compound Tenses	
Singular	Plural	Singular	Plural
1 presente de indicativo		**8 perfecto de indicativo**	
ordeno	ordenamos	he ordenado	hemos ordenado
ordenas	ordenáis	has ordenado	habéis ordenado
ordena	ordenan	ha ordenado	han ordenado
2 imperfecto de indicativo		**9 pluscuamperfecto de indicativo**	
ordenaba	ordenábamos	había ordenado	habíamos ordenado
ordenabas	ordenabais	habías ordenado	habíais ordenado
ordenaba	ordenaban	había ordenado	habían ordenado
3 pretérito		**10 pretérito anterior**	
ordené	ordenamos	hube ordenado	hubimos ordenado
ordenaste	ordenasteis	hubiste ordenado	hubisteis ordenado
ordenó	ordenaron	hubo ordenado	hubieron ordenado
4 futuro		**11 futuro perfecto**	
ordenaré	ordenaremos	habré ordenado	habremos ordenado
ordenarás	ordenaréis	habrás ordenado	habréis ordenado
ordenará	ordenarán	habrá ordenado	habrán ordenado
5 potencial simple		**12 potencial compuesto**	
ordenaría	ordenaríamos	habría ordenado	habríamos ordenado
ordenarías	ordenaríais	habrías ordenado	habríais ordenado
ordenaría	ordenarían	habría ordenado	habrían ordenado
6 presente de subjuntivo		**13 perfecto de subjuntivo**	
ordene	ordenemos	haya ordenado	hayamos ordenado
ordenes	ordenéis	hayas ordenado	hayáis ordenado
ordene	ordenen	haya ordenado	hayan ordenado
7 imperfecto de subjuntivo		**14 pluscuamperfecto de subjuntivo**	
ordenara	ordenáramos	hubiera ordenado	hubiéramos ordenado
ordenaras	ordenarais	hubieras ordenado	hubierais ordenado
ordenara	ordenaran	hubiera ordenado	hubieran ordenado
OR		OR	
ordenase	ordenásemos	hubiese ordenado	hubiésemos ordenado
ordenases	ordenaseis	hubieses ordenado	hubieseis ordenado
ordenase	ordenasen	hubiese ordenado	hubiesen ordenado

imperativo	
—	ordenemos
ordena; no ordenes	ordenad; no ordenéis
ordene	ordenen

el orden, los órdenes   order, orders
ordenarse   to become ordained, to take
  orders
el orden del día   order of the day

ordenadamente   in order, orderly,
  methodically
llamar al orden   to call to order

organizar

to organize, to arrange, to set up

The Seven Simple Tenses		The Seven Compound Tenses	
Singular	Plural	Singular	Plural
1 presente de indicativo		**8 perfecto de indicativo**	
organizo	organizamos	he organizado	hemos organizado
organizas	organizáis	has organizado	habéis organizado
organiza	organizan	ha organizado	han organizado
2 imperfecto de indicativo		**9 pluscuamperfecto de indicativo**	
organizaba	organizábamos	había organizado	habíamos organizado
organizabas	organizabais	habías organizado	habíais organizado
organizaba	organizaban	había organizado	habían organizado
3 pretérito		**10 pretérito anterior**	
organicé	organizamos	hube organizado	hubimos organizado
organizaste	organizasteis	hubiste organizado	hubisteis organizado
organizó	organizaron	hubo organizado	hubieron organizado
4 futuro		**11 futuro perfecto**	
organizaré	organizaremos	habré organizado	habremos organizado
organizarás	organizaréis	habrás organizado	habréis organizado
organizará	organizarán	habrá organizado	habrán organizado
5 potencial simple		**12 potencial compuesto**	
organizaría	organizaríamos	habría organizado	habríamos organizado
organizarías	organizaríais	habrías organizado	habríais organizado
organizaría	organizarían	habría organizado	habrían organizado
6 presente de subjuntivo		**13 perfecto de subjuntivo**	
organice	organicemos	haya organizado	hayamos organizado
organices	organicéis	hayas organizado	hayáis organizado
organice	organicen	haya organizado	hayan organizado
7 imperfecto de subjuntivo		**14 pluscuamperfecto de subjuntivo**	
organizara	organizáramos	hubiera organizado	hubiéramos organizado
organizaras	organizarais	hubieras organizado	hubierais organizado
organizara	organizaran	hubiera organizado	hubieran organizado
OR		OR	
organizase	organizásemos	hubiese organizado	hubiésemos organizado
organizases	organizaseis	hubieses organizado	hubieseis organizado
organizase	organizasen	hubiese organizado	hubiesen organizado

imperativo	
—	organicemos
organiza; no organices	organizad; no organicéis
organice	organicen

Marisol organizó una fiesta para su padre.   Marisol organized (planned) a party for her father.
organizado, organizada   organized
el organizador, la organizadora organizer

la organización   organization
organizable   organizable
la Organización de las Naciones Unidas (ONU)   the United Nations Organization (UNO, UN)

osar

Gerundio **osando**   Part. pas. **osado**

to dare, to venture

Regular **-ar** verb

The Seven Simple Tenses		The Seven Compound Tenses	
Singular	Plural	Singular	Plural
1 presente de indicativo		8 perfecto de indicativo	
oso	osamos	he osado	hemos osado
osas	osáis	has osado	habéis osado
osa	osan	ha osado	han osado
2 imperfecto de indicativo		9 pluscuamperfecto de indicativo	
osaba	osábamos	había osado	habíamos osado
osabas	osabais	habías osado	habíais osado
osaba	osaban	había osado	habían osado
3 pretérito		10 pretérito anterior	
osé	osamos	hube osado	hubimos osado
osaste	osasteis	hubiste osado	hubisteis osado
osó	osaron	hubo osado	hubieron osado
4 futuro		11 futuro perfecto	
osaré	osaremos	habré osado	habremos osado
osarás	osaréis	habrás osado	habréis osado
osará	osarán	habrá osado	habrán osado
5 potencial simple		12 potencial compuesto	
osaría	osaríamos	habría osado	habríamos osado
osarías	osaríais	habrías osado	habríais osado
osaría	osarían	habría osado	habrían osado
6 presente de subjuntivo		13 perfecto de subjuntivo	
ose	osemos	haya osado	hayamos osado
oses	oséis	hayas osado	hayáis osado
ose	osen	haya osado	hayan osado
7 imperfecto de subjuntivo		14 pluscuamperfecto de subjuntivo	
osara	osáramos	hubiera osado	hubiéramos osado
osaras	osarais	hubieras osado	hubierais osado
osara	osaran	hubiera osado	hubieran osado
OR		OR	
osase	osásemos	hubiese osado	hubiésemos osado
osases	osaseis	hubieses osado	hubieseis osado
osase	osasen	hubiese osado	hubiesen osado

	imperativo	
—	osemos	
osa; no oses	osad; no oséis	
ose	osen	

osado, osada   audacious, bold, daring   la osadía   audacity, boldness
osadamente   boldly, daring

pagar
to pay (for)

Regular **-ar** verb endings with spelling change: **g** becomes **gu** before **e**

The Seven Simple Tenses		The Seven Compound Tenses	
Singular	Plural	Singular	Plural
1 presente de indicativo		8 perfecto de indicativo	
pago	pagamos	he pagado	hemos pagado
pagas	pagáis	has pagado	habéis pagado
paga	pagan	ha pagado	han pagado
2 imperfecto de indicativo		9 pluscuamperfecto de indicativo	
pagaba	pagábamos	había pagado	habíamos pagado
pagabas	pagabais	habías pagado	habíais pagado
pagaba	pagaban	había pagado	habían pagado
3 pretérito		10 pretérito anterior	
pagué	pagamos	hube pagado	hubimos pagado
pagaste	pagasteis	hubiste pagado	hubisteis pagado
pagó	pagaron	hubo pagado	hubieron pagado
4 futuro		11 futuro perfecto	
pagaré	pagaremos	habré pagado	habremos pagado
pagarás	pagaréis	habrás pagado	habréis pagado
pagará	pagarán	habrá pagado	habrán pagado
5 potencial simple		12 potencial compuesto	
pagaría	pagaríamos	habría pagado	habríamos pagado
pagarías	pagaríais	habrías pagado	habríais pagado
pagaría	pagarían	habría pagado	habrían pagado
6 presente de subjuntivo		13 perfecto de subjuntivo	
pague	paguemos	haya pagado	hayamos pagado
pagues	paguéis	hayas pagado	hayáis pagado
pague	paguen	haya pagado	hayan pagado
7 imperfecto de subjuntivo		14 pluscuamperfecto de subjuntivo	
pagara	pagáramos	hubiera pagado	hubiéramos pagado
pagaras	pagarais	hubieras pagado	hubierais pagado
pagara	pagaran	hubiera pagado	hubieran pagado
OR		OR	
pagase	pagásemos	hubiese pagado	hubiésemos pagado
pagases	pagaseis	hubieses pagado	hubieseis pagado
pagase	pagasen	hubiese pagado	hubiesen pagado

imperativo	
—	paguemos
paga; no pagues	pagad; no paguéis
pague	paguen

¿Dónde se paga la cuenta? Where can one pay the bill?
la paga payment
pagar al contado to pay in cash
pagable payable
pagar contra entrega C.O.D. (Collect on delivery)

pagador, pagadora payer
el pagaré promissory note, I.O.U.
pagar la cuenta to pay the bill
pagar un crimen to pay for a crime
pagar un ojo de la cara to pay an arm and a leg

pararse

Gerundio **parándose**

Part. pas. **parado**

to stop (oneself)

Reflexive regular **-ar** verb

The Seven Simple Tenses		The Seven Compound Tenses	
Singular	Plural	Singular	Plural
1 presente de indicativo		8 perfecto de indicativo	
me paro	nos paramos	me he parado	nos hemos parado
te paras	os paráis	te has parado	os habéis parado
se para	se paran	se ha parado	se han parado
2 imperfecto de indicativo		9 pluscuamperfecto de indicativo	
me paraba	nos parábamos	me había parado	nos habíamos parado
te parabas	os parabais	te habías parado	os habíais parado
se paraba	se paraban	se había parado	se habían parado
3 pretérito		10 pretérito anterior	
me paré	nos paramos	me hube parado	nos hubimos parado
te paraste	os parasteis	te hubiste parado	os hubisteis parado
se paró	se pararon	se hubo parado	se hubieron parado
4 futuro		11 futuro perfecto	
me pararé	nos pararemos	me habré parado	nos habremos parado
te pararás	os pararéis	te habrás parado	os habréis parado
se parará	se pararán	se habrá parado	se habrán parado
5 potencial simple		12 potencial compuesto	
me pararía	nos pararíamos	me habría parado	nos habríamos parado
te pararías	os pararíais	te habrías parado	os habríais parado
se pararía	se pararían	se habría parado	se habrían parado
6 presente de subjuntivo		13 perfecto de subjuntivo	
me pare	nos paremos	me haya parado	nos hayamos parado
te pares	os paréis	te hayas parado	os hayáis parado
se pare	se paren	se haya parado	se hayan parado
7 imperfecto de subjuntivo		14 pluscuamperfecto de subjuntivo	
me parara	nos paráramos	me hubiera parado	nos hubiéramos parado
te pararas	os pararais	te hubieras parado	os hubierais parado
se parara	se pararan	se hubiera parado	se hubieran parado
OR		OR	
me parase	nos parásemos	me hubiese parado	nos hubiésemos parado
te parases	os paraseis	te hubieses parado	os hubieseis parado
se parase	se parasen	se hubiese parado	se hubiesen parado

	imperativo
—	parémonos
párate; no te pares	paraos; no os paréis
párese	párense

la parada stop	parar en mal to end badly
parar to stop (someone or something)	la parada de taxis taxi stand
una paradeta, una paradilla pause	sin parar right away (without
no poder parar to be restless	stopping)
una parada en seco dead stop	

Regular **-er** verb endings with spelling change: to seem, to appear
c becomes **zc** before **a** or **o**

The Seven Simple Tenses		The Seven Compound Tenses	
Singular	Plural	Singular	Plural
1 presente de indicativo		8 perfecto de indicativo	
parezco	parecemos	he parecido	hemos parecido
pareces	parecéis	has parecido	habéis parecido
parece	parecen	ha parecido	han parecido
2 imperfecto de indicativo		9 pluscuamperfecto de indicativo	
parecía	parecíamos	había parecido	habíamos parecido
parecías	parecíais	habías parecido	habíais parecido
parecía	parecían	había parecido	habían parecido
3 pretérito		10 pretérito anterior	
parecí	parecimos	hube parecido	hubimos parecido
pareciste	parecisteis	hubiste parecido	hubisteis parecido
pareció	parecieron	hubo parecido	hubieron parecido
4 futuro		11 futuro perfecto	
pareceré	pareceremos	habré parecido	habremos parecido
parecerás	pareceréis	habrás parecido	habréis parecido
parecerá	parecerán	habrá parecido	habrán parecido
5 potencial simple		12 potencial compuesto	
parecería	pareceríamos	habría parecido	habríamos parecido
parecerías	pareceríais	habrías parecido	habríais parecido
parecería	parecerían	habría parecido	habrían parecido
6 presente de subjuntivo		13 perfecto de subjuntivo	
parezca	parezcamos	haya parecido	hayamos parecido
parezcas	parezcáis	hayas parecido	hayáis parecido
parezca	parezcan	haya parecido	hayan parecido
7 imperfecto de subjuntivo		14 pluscuamperfecto de subjuntivo	
pareciera	pareciéramos	hubiera parecido	hubiéramos parecido
parecieras	parecierais	hubieras parecido	hubierais parecido
pareciera	parecieran	hubiera parecido	hubieran parecido
OR		OR	
pareciese	pareciésemos	hubiese parecido	hubiésemos parecido
parecieses	parecieseis	hubieses parecido	hubieseis parecido
pareciese	pareciesen	hubiese parecido	hubiesen parecido

imperativo	
—	parezcamos
parece; no parezcas	pareced; no parezcáis
parezca	parezcan

María parece contenta. Mary seems happy.	**al parecer** seemingly, apparently
	pareciente similar
a lo que parece according to what it seems	**Me parece ...** It seems to me ...
	por el bien parecer for the sake of appearances
parecerse a to resemble each other, to look alike	See also **aparecer** and **parecerse**.

231

parecerse

Gerundio **pareciéndose**   Part. pas. **parecido**

to resemble each other,
to look alike

Reflexive verb; regular **-er** verb endings with
spelling change: **c** becomes **zc** before **a** or **o**

The Seven Simple Tenses		The Seven Compound Tenses	
Singular	Plural	Singular	Plural

1 presente de indicativo		**8 perfecto de indicativo**	
me parezco	nos parecemos	me he parecido	nos hemos parecido
te pareces	os parecéis	te has parecido	os habéis parecido
se parece	se parecen	se ha parecido	se han parecido
2 imperfecto de indicativo		**9 pluscuamperfecto de indicativo**	
me parecía	nos parecíamos	me había parecido	nos habíamos parecido
te parecías	os parecíais	te habías parecido	os habíais parecido
se parecía	se parecían	se había parecido	se habían parecido
3 pretérito		**10 pretérito anterior**	
me parecí	nos parecimos	me hube parecido	nos hubimos parecido
te pareciste	os parecisteis	te hubiste parecido	os hubisteis parecido
se pareció	se parecieron	se hubo parecido	se hubieron parecido
4 futuro		**11 futuro perfecto**	
me pareceré	nos pareceremos	me habré parecido	nos habremos parecido
te parecerás	os pareceréis	te habrás parecido	os habréis parecido
se parecerá	se parecerán	se habrá parecido	se habrán parecido
5 potencial simple		**12 potencial compuesto**	
me parecería	nos pareceríamos	me habría parecido	nos habríamos parecido
te parecerías	os pareceríais	te habrías parecido	os habríais parecido
se parecería	se parecerían	se habría parecido	se habrían parecido
6 presente de subjuntivo		**13 perfecto de subjuntivo**	
me parezca	nos parezcamos	me haya parecido	nos hayamos parecido
te parezcas	os parezcáis	te hayas parecido	os hayáis parecido
se parezca	se parezcan	se haya parecido	se hayan parecido
7 imperfecto de subjuntivo		**14 pluscuamperfecto de subjuntivo**	
me pareciera	nos pareciéramos	me hubiera parecido	nos hubiéramos parecido
te parecieras	os parecierais	te hubieras parecido	os hubierais parecido
se pareciera	se parecieran	se hubiera parecido	se hubieran parecido
OR		OR	
me pareciese	nos pareciésemos	me hubiese parecido	nos hubiésemos parecido
te parecieses	os parecieseis	te hubieses parecido	os hubieseis parecido
se pareciese	se pareciesen	se hubiese parecido	se hubiesen parecido

imperativo	
—	**parezcámonos**
parécete; no te parezcas	**pareceos; no os parezcáis**
parézcase	**parézcanse**

parecer to seem, to appear	pareciente similar
al parecer seemingly, apparently	See also parecer.
a lo que parece according to what it seems	

232

partir

Regular **-ir** verb

to leave, to depart,
to divide, to split

The Seven Simple Tenses		The Seven Compound Tenses	
Singular	Plural	Singular	Plural
1 presente de indicativo		8 perfecto de indicativo	
parto	partimos	he partido	hemos partido
partes	partís	has partido	habéis partido
parte	parten	ha partido	han partido
2 imperfecto de indicativo		9 pluscuamperfecto de indicativo	
partía	partíamos	había partido	habíamos partido
partías	partíais	habías partido	habíais partido
partía	partían	había partido	habían partido
3 pretérito		10 pretérito anterior	
partí	partimos	hube partido	hubimos partido
partiste	partisteis	hubiste partido	hubisteis partido
partió	partieron	hubo partido	hubieron partido
4 futuro		11 futuro perfecto	
partiré	partiremos	habré partido	habremos partido
partirás	partiréis	habrás partido	habréis partido
partirá	partirán	habrá partido	habrán partido
5 potencial simple		12 potencial compuesto	
partiría	partiríamos	habría partido	habríamos partido
partirías	partiríais	habrías partido	habríais partido
partiría	partirían	habría partido	habrían partido
6 presente de subjuntivo		13 perfecto de subjuntivo	
parta	partamos	haya partido	hayamos partido
partas	partáis	hayas partido	hayáis partido
parta	partan	haya partido	hayan partido
7 imperfecto de subjuntivo		14 pluscuamperfecto de subjuntivo	
partiera	partiéramos	hubiera partido	hubiéramos partido
partieras	partierais	hubieras partido	hubierais partido
partiera	partieran	hubiera partido	hubieran partido
OR		OR	
partiese	partiésemos	hubiese partido	hubiésemos partido
partieses	partieseis	hubieses partido	hubieseis partido
partiese	partiesen	hubiese partido	hubiesen partido

imperativo	
—	partamos
parte; no partas	partid; no partáis
parta	partan

a partir de beginning with, starting from	**partirse** to become divided
la partida departure	**repartir** to distribute
tomar partido to take sides, to make up one's mind	**partir algo en dos** to divide something in two

pasar

Gerundio **pasando**   Part. pas. **pasado**

to pass (by), to happen,
to spend (time)

Regular **-ar** verb

The Seven Simple Tenses		The Seven Compound Tenses	
Singular	Plural	Singular	Plural
1 presente de indicativo		**8 perfecto de indicativo**	
paso	pasamos	he pasado	hemos pasado
pasas	pasáis	has pasado	habéis pasado
pasa	pasan	ha pasado	han pasado
2 imperfecto de indicativo		**9 pluscuamperfecto de indicativo**	
pasaba	pasábamos	había pasado	habíamos pasado
pasabas	pasabais	habías pasado	habíais pasado
pasaba	pasaban	había pasado	habían pasado
3 pretérito		**10 pretérito anterior**	
pasé	pasamos	hube pasado	hubimos pasado
pasaste	pasasteis	hubiste pasado	hubisteis pasado
pasó	pasaron	hubo pasado	hubieron pasado
4 futuro		**11 futuro perfecto**	
pasaré	pasaremos	habré pasado	habremos pasado
pasarás	pasaréis	habrás pasado	habréis pasado
pasará	pasarán	habrá pasado	habrán pasado
5 potencial simple		**12 potencial compuesto**	
pasaría	pasaríamos	habría pasado	habríamos pasado
pasarías	pasaríais	habrías pasado	habríais pasado
pasaría	pasarían	habría pasado	habrían pasado
6 presente de subjuntivo		**13 perfecto de subjuntivo**	
pase	pasemos	haya pasado	hayamos pasado
pases	paséis	hayas pasado	hayáis pasado
pase	pasen	haya pasado	hayan pasado
7 imperfecto de subjuntivo		**14 pluscuamperfecto de subjuntivo**	
pasara	pasáramos	hubiera pasado	hubiéramos pasado
pasaras	pasarais	hubieras pasado	hubierais pasado
pasara	pasaran	hubiera pasado	hubieran pasado
OR		OR	
pasase	pasásemos	hubiese pasado	hubiésemos pasado
pasases	pasaseis	hubieses pasado	hubieseis pasado
pasase	pasasen	hubiese pasado	hubiesen pasado

imperativo	
—	pasemos
pasa; no pases	pasad; no paséis
pase	pasen

¡Pase un buen día! Have a nice day!
pasajero, pasajera   passenger, traveler
¡Que lo pase Ud. bien! Good luck,
  good-bye!
¿Qué pasa? What's happening?
  What's going on?

el pasatiempo amusement, pastime
Use pasar to mean *spend time:* Me
  gustaría pasar un año en Costa
  Rica. I would like to spend a year in
  Costa Rica.

Reflexive regular **-ar** verb   to take a walk, to parade

The Seven Simple Tenses		The Seven Compound Tenses	
Singular	Plural	Singular	Plural
1 presente de indicativo		8 perfecto de indicativo	
me paseo	nos paseamos	me he paseado	nos hemos paseado
te paseas	os paseáis	te has paseado	os habéis paseado
se pasea	se pasean	se ha paseado	se han paseado
2 imperfecto de indicativo		9 pluscuamperfecto de indicativo	
me paseaba	nos paseábamos	me había paseado	nos habíamos paseado
te paseabas	os paseabais	te habías paseado	os habíais paseado
se paseaba	se paseaban	se había paseado	se habían paseado
3 pretérito		10 pretérito anterior	
me paseé	nos paseamos	me hube paseado	nos hubimos paseado
te paseaste	os paseasteis	te hubiste paseado	os hubisteis paseado
se paseó	se pasearon	se hubo paseado	se hubieron paseado
4 futuro		11 futuro perfecto	
me pasearé	nos pasearemos	me habré paseado	nos habremos paseado
te pasearás	os pasearéis	te habrás paseado	os habréis paseado
se paseará	se pasearán	se habrá paseado	se habrán paseado
5 potencial simple		12 potencial compuesto	
me pasearía	nos pasearíamos	me habría paseado	nos habríamos paseado
te pasearías	os pasearíais	te habrías paseado	os habríais paseado
se pasearía	se pasearían	se habría paseado	se habrían paseado
6 presente de subjuntivo		13 perfecto de subjuntivo	
me pasee	nos paseemos	me haya paseado	nos hayamos paseado
te pasees	os paseéis	te hayas paseado	os hayáis paseado
se pasee	se paseen	se haya paseado	se hayan paseado
7 imperfecto de subjuntivo		14 pluscuamperfecto de subjuntivo	
me paseara	nos paseáramos	me hubiera paseado	nos hubiéramos paseado
te pasearas	os pasearais	te hubieras paseado	os hubierais paseado
se paseara	se pasearan	se hubiera paseado	se hubieran paseado
OR		OR	
me pasease	nos paseásemos	me hubiese paseado	nos hubiésemos paseado
te paseases	os paseaseis	te hubieses paseado	os hubieseis paseado
se pasease	se paseasen	se hubiese paseado	se hubiesen paseado

imperativo	
—	paseémonos
paséate; no te pasees	paseaos; no os paseéis
paséese	paséense

Cuando el gato no está, el ratón se pasea. When the cat's away, the mice will play (the mouse takes a walk).	un, una paseante stroller
	un paseo campestre picnic
	un paseo a walk
un pase pass, permit	sacar a paseo to take out for a walk
ir de paseo to go out for a walk	dar un paseo to take a walk
	pasear to walk (a child, a dog, etc.)

pedir

Gerundio **pidiendo**   Part. pas. **pedido**

to ask for, to request

Regular **-ir** verb endings with stem change:
Tenses 1, 3, 6, 7, Imperative, *Gerundio*

The Seven Simple Tenses		The Seven Compound Tenses	
Singular	Plural	Singular	Plural
1 presente de indicativo		8 perfecto de indicativo	
pido	pedimos	he pedido	hemos pedido
pides	pedís	has pedido	habéis pedido
pide	piden	ha pedido	han pedido
2 imperfecto de indicativo		9 pluscuamperfecto de indicativo	
pedía	pedíamos	había pedido	habíamos pedido
pedías	pedíais	habías pedido	habíais pedido
pedía	pedían	había pedido	habían pedido
3 pretérito		10 pretérito anterior	
pedí	pedimos	hube pedido	hubimos pedido
pediste	pedisteis	hubiste pedido	hubisteis pedido
pidió	pidieron	hubo pedido	hubieron pedido
4 futuro		11 futuro perfecto	
pediré	pediremos	habré pedido	habremos pedido
pedirás	pediréis	habrás pedido	habréis pedido
pedirá	pedirán	habrá pedido	habrán pedido
5 potencial simple		12 potencial compuesto	
pediría	pediríamos	habría pedido	habríamos pedido
pedirías	pediríais	habrías pedido	habríais pedido
pediría	pedirían	habría pedido	habrían pedido
6 presente de subjuntivo		13 perfecto de subjuntivo	
pida	pidamos	haya pedido	hayamos pedido
pidas	pidáis	hayas pedido	hayáis pedido
pida	pidan	haya pedido	hayan pedido
7 imperfecto de subjuntivo		14 pluscuamperfecto de subjuntivo	
pidiera	pidiéramos	hubiera pedido	hubiéramos pedido
pidieras	pidierais	hubieras pedido	hubierais pedido
pidiera	pidieran	hubiera pedido	hubieran pedido
OR		OR	
pidiese	pidiésemos	hubiese pedido	hubiésemos pedido
pidieses	pidieseis	hubieses pedido	hubieseis pedido
pidiese	pidiesen	hubiese pedido	hubiesen pedido

imperativo	
—	pidamos
pide; no pidas	pedid; no pidáis
pida	pidan

El alumno pidió un lápiz al profesor.
  The pupil asked the teacher for a
  pencil.
un pedimento petition
un pedido request, order
See also **despedir**.

hacer un pedido to place an order
colocar un pedido to place an order
pedir prestado to borrow
pedir socorro to ask for help

Reflexive regular **-ar** verb   to comb one's hair

The Seven Simple Tenses		The Seven Compound Tenses	
Singular	Plural	Singular	Plural
1 presente de indicativo		8 perfecto de indicativo	
me peino	nos peinamos	me he peinado	nos hemos peinado
te peinas	os peináis	te has peinado	os habéis peinado
se peina	se peinan	se ha peinado	se han peinado
2 imperfecto de indicativo		9 pluscuamperfecto de indicativo	
me peinaba	nos peinábamos	me había peinado	nos habíamos peinado
te peinabas	os peinabais	te habías peinado	os habíais peinado
se peinaba	se peinaban	se había peinado	se habían peinado
3 pretérito		10 pretérito anterior	
me peiné	nos peinamos	me hube peinado	nos hubimos peinado
te peinaste	os peinasteis	te hubiste peinado	os hubisteis peinado
se peinó	se peinaron	se hubo peinado	se hubieron peinado
4 futuro		11 futuro perfecto	
me peinaré	nos peinaremos	me habré peinado	nos habremos peinado
te peinarás	os peinaréis	te habrás peinado	os habréis peinado
se peinará	se peinarán	se habrá peinado	se habrán peinado
5 potencial simple		12 potencial compuesto	
me peinaría	nos peinaríamos	me habría peinado	nos habríamos peinado
te peinarías	os peinaríais	te habrías peinado	os habríais peinado
se peinaría	se peinarían	se habría peinado	se habrían peinado
6 presente de subjuntivo		13 perfecto de subjuntivo	
me peine	nos peinemos	me haya peinado	nos hayamos peinado
te peines	os peinéis	te hayas peinado	os hayáis peinado
se peine	se peinen	se haya peinado	se hayan peinado
7 imperfecto de subjuntivo		14 pluscuamperfecto de subjuntivo	
me peinara	nos peináramos	me hubiera peinado	nos hubiéramos peinado
te peinaras	os peinarais	te hubieras peinado	os hubierais peinado
se peinara	se peinaran	se hubiera peinado	se hubieran peinado
OR		OR	
me peinase	nos peinásemos	me hubiese peinado	nos hubiésemos peinado
te peinases	os peinaseis	te hubieses peinado	os hubieseis peinado
se peinase	se peinasen	se hubiese peinado	se hubiesen peinado

imperativo	
—	peinémonos
péinate; no te peines	peinaos; no os peinéis
péinese	péinense

¡Cómprate un calvo y péinalo! Beat it! (Buy a bald man and comb his hair!)	un peinado hairdo, hairstyle
	despeinarse to dishevel, to take down one's hair
un peine a comb	una peineta shell comb (used by women as an ornament in the hair)
peinar to comb	

237

pensar

Gerundio **pensando**   Part. pas. **pensado**

to think

Regular **-ar** verb endings with stem
change: Tenses 1, 6, Imperative

The Seven Simple Tenses		The Seven Compound Tenses	
Singular	Plural	Singular	Plural
1 presente de indicativo		8 perfecto de indicativo	
pienso	pensamos	he pensado	hemos pensado
piensas	pensáis	has pensado	habéis pensado
piensa	piensan	ha pensado	han pensado
2 imperfecto de indicativo		9 pluscuamperfecto de indicativo	
pensaba	pensábamos	había pensado	habíamos pensado
pensabas	pensabais	habías pensado	habíais pensado
pensaba	pensaban	había pensado	habían pensado
3 pretérito		10 pretérito anterior	
pensé	pensamos	hube pensado	hubimos pensado
pensaste	pensasteis	hubiste pensado	hubisteis pensado
pensó	pensaron	hubo pensado	hubieron pensado
4 futuro		11 futuro perfecto	
pensaré	pensaremos	habré pensado	habremos pensado
pensarás	pensaréis	habrás pensado	habréis pensado
pensará	pensarán	habrá pensado	habrán pensado
5 potencial simple		12 potencial compuesto	
pensaría	pensaríamos	habría pensado	habríamos pensado
pensarías	pensaríais	habrías pensado	habríais pensado
pensaría	pensarían	habría pensado	habrían pensado
6 presente de subjuntivo		13 perfecto de subjuntivo	
piense	pensemos	haya pensado	hayamos pensado
pienses	penséis	hayas pensado	hayáis pensado
piense	piensen	haya pensado	hayan pensado
7 imperfecto de subjuntivo		14 pluscuamperfecto de subjuntivo	
pensara	pensáramos	hubiera pensado	hubiéramos pensado
pensaras	pensarais	hubieras pensado	hubierais pensado
pensara	pensaran	hubiera pensado	hubieran pensado
OR		OR	
pensase	pensásemos	hubiese pensado	hubiésemos pensado
pensases	pensaseis	hubieses pensado	hubieseis pensado
pensase	pensasen	hubiese pensado	hubiesen pensado

imperativo	
—	pensemos
piensa; no pienses	pensad; no penséis
piense	piensen

¿Qué piensa Ud. de eso? What do you think of that?	sin pensar thoughtlessly
pensar + inf. to intend + inf.	pensativo, pensativa thoughtful, pensive
pensar en to think of, about	repensar to think over (again)
¿En qué piensa Ud.? What are you thinking of?	un pensador, una pensadora thinker

perder

to lose

Regular **-er** verb endings with stem
change: Tenses 1, 6, Imperative

The Seven Simple Tenses		The Seven Compound Tenses	
Singular	Plural	Singular	Plural
1 presente de indicativo		8 perfecto de indicativo	
pierdo	perdemos	he perdido	hemos perdido
pierdes	perdéis	has perdido	habéis perdido
pierde	pierden	ha perdido	han perdido
2 imperfecto de indicativo		9 pluscuamperfecto de indicativo	
perdía	perdíamos	había perdido	habíamos perdido
perdías	perdíais	habías perdido	habíais perdido
perdía	perdían	había perdido	habían perdido
3 pretérito		10 pretérito anterior	
perdí	perdimos	hube perdido	hubimos perdido
perdiste	perdisteis	hubiste perdido	hubisteis perdido
perdió	perdieron	hubo perdido	hubieron perdido
4 futuro		11 futuro perfecto	
perderé	perderemos	habré perdido	habremos perdido
perderás	perderéis	habrás perdido	habréis perdido
perderá	perderán	habrá perdido	habrán perdido
5 potencial simple		12 potencial compuesto	
perdería	perderíamos	habría perdido	habríamos perdido
perderías	perderíais	habrías perdido	habríais perdido
perdería	perderían	habría perdido	habrían perdido
6 presente de subjuntivo		13 perfecto de subjuntivo	
pierda	perdamos	haya perdido	hayamos perdido
pierdas	perdáis	hayas perdido	hayáis perdido
pierda	pierdan	haya perdido	hayan perdido
7 imperfecto de subjuntivo		14 pluscuamperfecto de subjuntivo	
perdiera	perdiéramos	hubiera perdido	hubiéramos perdido
perdieras	perdierais	hubieras perdido	hubierais perdido
perdiera	perdieran	hubiera perdido	hubieran perdido
OR		OR	
perdiese	perdiésemos	hubiese perdido	hubiésemos perdido
perdieses	perdieseis	hubieses perdido	hubieseis perdido
perdiese	perdiesen	hubiese perdido	hubiesen perdido

imperativo	
—	perdamos
pierde; no pierdas	perded; no perdáis
pierda	pierdan

El que todo lo quiere, todo lo pierde.
  Whoever wants everything loses
  everything.
un perdedor, una perdedora loser
perder el juicio to go mad (crazy)

la pérdida loss
perder los estribos to lose self control
perder la memoria to lose one's
  memory
perderse to lose one's way, to get lost

permitir

Gerundio **permitiendo**   Part. pas. **permitido**

to permit, to admit,
to allow, to grant

Regular **-ir** verb

The Seven Simple Tenses		The Seven Compound Tenses	
Singular	Plural	Singular	Plural
1 presente de indicativo		8 perfecto de indicativo	
permito	permitimos	he permitido	hemos permitido
permites	permitís	has permitido	habéis permitido
permite	permiten	ha permitido	han permitido
2 imperfecto de indicativo		9 pluscuamperfecto de indicativo	
permitía	permitíamos	había permitido	habíamos permitido
permitías	permitíais	habías permitido	habíais permitido
permitía	permitían	había permitido	habían permitido
3 pretérito		10 pretérito anterior	
permití	permitimos	hube permitido	hubimos permitido
permitiste	permitisteis	hubiste permitido	hubisteis permitido
permitió	permitieron	hubo permitido	hubieron permitido
4 futuro		11 futuro perfecto	
permitiré	permitiremos	habré permitido	habremos permitido
permitirás	permitiréis	habrás permitido	habréis permitido
permitirá	permitirán	habrá permitido	habrán permitido
5 potencial simple		12 potencial compuesto	
permitiría	permitiríamos	habría permitido	habríamos permitido
permitirías	permitiríais	habrías permitido	habríais permitido
permitiría	permitirían	habría permitido	habrían permitido
6 presente de subjuntivo		13 perfecto de subjuntivo	
permita	permitamos	haya permitido	hayamos permitido
permitas	permitáis	hayas permitido	hayáis permitido
permita	permitan	haya permitido	hayan permitido
7 imperfecto de subjuntivo		14 pluscuamperfecto de subjuntivo	
permitiera	permitiéramos	hubiera permitido	hubiéramos permitido
permitieras	permitierais	hubieras permitido	hubierais permitido
permitiera	permitieran	hubiera permitido	hubieran permitido
OR		OR	
permitiese	permitiésemos	hubiese permitido	hubiésemos permitido
permitieses	permitieseis	hubieses permitido	hubieseis permitido
permitiese	permitiesen	hubiese permitido	hubiesen permitido

imperativo	
—	permitamos
permite; no permitas	permitid; no permitáis
permita	permitan

---

el permiso   permit, permission
¡Con permiso!   Excuse me!
permitirse + inf.   to take the liberty
+ inf.
la permisión   permission

el permiso de conducir   driver's license
emitir   to emit
transmitir   to transmit
No se permite + inf.   It is not
permitted to + inf.

Irregular verb   to be able, can

The Seven Simple Tenses		The Seven Compound Tenses	
Singular	Plural	Singular	Plural
1 presente de indicativo		8 perfecto de indicativo	
puedo	podemos	he podido	hemos podido
puedes	podéis	has podido	habéis podido
puede	pueden	ha podido	han podido
2 imperfecto de indicativo		9 pluscuamperfecto de indicativo	
podía	podíamos	había podido	habíamos podido
podías	podíais	habías podido	habíais podido
podía	podían	había podido	habían podido
3 pretérito		10 pretérito anterior	
pude	pudimos	hube podido	hubimos podido
pudiste	pudisteis	hubiste podido	hubisteis podido
pudo	pudieron	hubo podido	hubieron podido
4 futuro		11 futuro perfecto	
podré	podremos	habré podido	habremos podido
podrás	podréis	habrás podido	habréis podido
podrá	podrán	habrá podido	habrán podido
5 potencial simple		12 potencial compuesto	
podría	podríamos	habría podido	habríamos podido
podrías	podríais	habrías podido	habríais podido
podría	podrían	habría podido	habrían podido
6 presente de subjuntivo		13 perfecto de subjuntivo	
pueda	podamos	haya podido	hayamos podido
puedas	podáis	hayas podido	hayáis podido
pueda	puedan	haya podido	hayan podido
7 imperfecto de subjuntivo		14 pluscuamperfecto de subjuntivo	
pudiera	pudiéramos	hubiera podido	hubiéramos podido
pudieras	pudierais	hubieras podido	hubierais podido
pudiera	pudieran	hubiera podido	hubieran podido
OR		OR	
pudiese	pudiésemos	hubiese podido	hubiésemos podido
pudieses	pudieseis	hubieses podido	hubieseis podido
pudiese	pudiesen	hubiese podido	hubiesen podido

imperativo*

—	podamos
puede; no puedas	poded; no podáis
pueda	puedan

No podemos nadar aquí. Es peligroso.
  We can't swim here. It's dangerous.
In the **pretérito**, *poder* has the special
  meaning of *succeeded*: **Juan pudo
  resolver el problema.**   John
  succeeded in solving the problem.
el poder power

No se puede.   It can't be done.
apoderar to empower
estar en el poder   to be in power
*The verb forms in the imperative of
  this verb are grammatically correct but
  they are used rarely these days.

poner

Gerundio **poniendo**　　Part. pas. **puesto**

to put, to place

Irregular verb

The Seven Simple Tenses		The Seven Compound Tenses	
Singular	Plural	Singular	Plural
1　presente de indicativo		8　perfecto de indicativo	
pongo	ponemos	he puesto	hemos puesto
pones	ponéis	has puesto	habéis puesto
pone	ponen	ha puesto	han puesto
2　imperfecto de indicativo		9　pluscuamperfecto de indicativo	
ponía	poníamos	había puesto	habíamos puesto
ponías	poníais	habías puesto	habíais puesto
ponía	ponían	había puesto	habían puesto
3　pretérito		10　pretérito anterior	
puse	pusimos	hube puesto	hubimos puesto
pusiste	pusisteis	hubiste puesto	hubisteis puesto
puso	pusieron	hubo puesto	hubieron puesto
4　futuro		11　futuro perfecto	
pondré	pondremos	habré puesto	habremos puesto
pondrás	pondréis	habrás puesto	habréis puesto
pondrá	pondrán	habrá puesto	habrán puesto
5　potencial simple		12　potencial compuesto	
pondría	pondríamos	habría puesto	habríamos puesto
pondrías	pondríais	habrías puesto	habríais puesto
pondría	pondrían	habría puesto	habrían puesto
6　presente de subjuntivo		13　perfecto de subjuntivo	
ponga	pongamos	haya puesto	hayamos puesto
pongas	pongáis	hayas puesto	hayáis puesto
ponga	pongan	haya puesto	hayan puesto
7　imperfecto de subjuntivo		14　pluscuamperfecto de subjuntivo	
pusiera	pusiéramos	hubiera puesto	hubiéramos puesto
pusieras	pusierais	hubieras puesto	hubierais puesto
pusiera	pusieran	hubiera puesto	hubieran puesto
OR		OR	
pusiese	pusiésemos	hubiese puesto	hubiésemos puesto
pusieses	pusieseis	hubieses puesto	hubieseis puesto
pusiese	pusiesen	hubiese puesto	hubiesen puesto

	imperativo	
—	pongamos	
pon; no pongas	poned; pongáis	
ponga	pongan	

Magdalena puso el papel en la papelera.	poner la mesa　to set the table
Magdalene put the paper in the wastebasket.	poner de acuerdo　to reach an agreement
poner fin a　to put a stop to	reponer　to replace, to put back
la puesta de/del sol　sunset	poner en marcha　to set in motion
	poner por escrito　to put in writing
	See also ponerse and componer.

Reflexive irregular verb

to put on (clothing),
to become, to set (of sun)

The Seven Simple Tenses		The Seven Compound Tenses	
Singular	Plural	Singular	Plural
1 presente de indicativo		8 perfecto de indicativo	
me pongo	**nos ponemos**	**me he puesto**	**nos hemos puesto**
te pones	**os ponéis**	**te has puesto**	**os habéis puesto**
se pone	**se ponen**	**se ha puesto**	**se han puesto**
2 imperfecto de indicativo		9 pluscuamperfecto de indicativo	
me ponía	**nos poníamos**	**me había puesto**	**nos habíamos puesto**
te ponías	**os poníais**	**te habías puesto**	**os habíais puesto**
se ponía	**se ponían**	**se había puesto**	**se habían puesto**
3 pretérito		10 pretérito anterior	
me puse	**nos pusimos**	**me hube puesto**	**nos hubimos puesto**
te pusiste	**os pusisteis**	**te hubiste puesto**	**os hubisteis puesto**
se puso	**se pusieron**	**se hubo puesto**	**se hubieron puesto**
4 futuro		11 futuro perfecto	
me pondré	**nos pondremos**	**me habré puesto**	**nos habremos puesto**
te pondrás	**os pondréis**	**te habrás puesto**	**os habréis puesto**
se pondrá	**se pondrán**	**se habrá puesto**	**se habrán puesto**
5 potencial simple		12 potencial compuesto	
me pondría	**nos pondríamos**	**me habría puesto**	**nos habríamos puesto**
te pondrías	**os pondríais**	**te habrías puesto**	**os habríais puesto**
se pondría	**se pondrían**	**se habría puesto**	**se habrían puesto**
6 presente de subjuntivo		13 perfecto de subjuntivo	
me ponga	**nos pongamos**	**me haya puesto**	**nos hayamos puesto**
te pongas	**os pongáis**	**te hayas puesto**	**os hayáis puesto**
se ponga	**se pongan**	**se haya puesto**	**se hayan puesto**
7 imperfecto de subjuntivo		14 pluscuamperfecto de subjuntivo	
me pusiera	**nos pusiéramos**	**me hubiera puesto**	**nos hubiéramos puesto**
te pusieras	**os pusierais**	**te hubieras puesto**	**os hubierais puesto**
se pusiera	**se pusieran**	**se hubiera puesto**	**se hubieran puesto**
OR		OR	
me pusiese	**nos pusiésemos**	**me hubiese puesto**	**nos hubiésemos puesto**
te pusieses	**os pusieseis**	**te hubieses puesto**	**os hubieseis puesto**
se pusiese	**se pusiesen**	**se hubiese puesto**	**se hubiesen puesto**

imperativo	
—	**pongámonos**
ponte; no te pongas	**poneos; no os pongáis**
póngase	**pónganse**

---

ponerse el abrigo   to put on one's
  overcoat
reponerse   to calm down, to recover
  (one's health)
ponerse a + inf.   to begin, to start + inf.

María se puso pálida.   Mary became
  pale.
indisponerse   to become ill
ponerse de acuerdo   to reach an
  agreement
See also **poner** and **componer**.

practicar

Gerundio **practicando**   Part. pas. **practicado**

to practice

Regular **-ar** verb endings with spelling change: **c** becomes **qu** before **e**

The Seven Simple Tenses		The Seven Compound Tenses	
Singular	Plural	Singular	Plural
1 presente de indicativo		8 perfecto de indicativo	
practico	practicamos	he practicado	hemos practicado
practicas	practicáis	has practicado	habéis practicado
practica	practican	ha practicado	han practicado
2 imperfecto de indicativo		9 pluscuamperfecto de indicativo	
practicaba	practicábamos	había practicado	habíamos practicado
practicabas	practicabais	habías practicado	habíais practicado
practicaba	practicaban	había practicado	habían practicado
3 pretérito		10 pretérito anterior	
practiqué	practicamos	hube practicado	hubimos practicado
practicaste	practicasteis	hubiste practicado	hubisteis practicado
practicó	practicaron	hubo practicado	hubieron practicado
4 futuro		11 futuro perfecto	
practicaré	practicaremos	habré practicado	habremos practicado
practicarás	practicaréis	habrás practicado	habréis practicado
practicará	practicarán	habrá practicado	habrán practicado
5 potencial simple		12 potencial compuesto	
practicaría	practicaríamos	habría practicado	habríamos practicado
practicarías	practicaríais	habrías practicado	habríais practicado
practicaría	practicarían	habría practicado	habrían practicado
6 presente de subjuntivo		13 perfecto de subjuntivo	
practique	practiquemos	haya practicado	hayamos practicado
practiques	practiquéis	hayas practicado	hayáis practicado
practique	practiquen	haya practicado	hayan practicado
7 imperfecto de subjuntivo		14 pluscuamperfecto de subjuntivo	
practicara	practicáramos	hubiera practicado	hubiéramos practicado
practicaras	practicarais	hubieras practicado	hubierais practicado
practicara	practicaran	hubiera practicado	hubieran practicado
OR		OR	
practicase	practicásemos	hubiese practicado	hubiésemos practicado
practicases	practicaseis	hubieses practicado	hubieseis practicado
practicase	practicasen	hubiese practicado	hubiesen practicado

imperativo	
—	practiquemos
practica; no practiques	practicad; no practiquéis
practique	practiquen

---

práctico, práctica practical
practicar investigaciones to look into, to investigate
la práctica practice, habit
en la práctica in practice

practicar un informe to make a report
Hace treinta años que el doctor Martínez practica la medicina. Dr. Martínez has been practicing medicine for thirty years.

Regular **-ir** verb endings with stem change: to prefer
Tenses 1, 3, 6, 7, Imperative, *Gerundio*

The Seven Simple Tenses		The Seven Compound Tenses	
Singular	Plural	Singular	Plural
1 presente de indicativo		8 perfecto de indicativo	
prefiero	**preferimos**	**he preferido**	**hemos preferido**
prefieres	**preferís**	**has preferido**	**habéis preferido**
prefiere	**prefieren**	**ha preferido**	**han preferido**
2 imperfecto de indicativo		9 pluscuamperfecto de indicativo	
prefería	**preferíamos**	**había preferido**	**habíamos preferido**
preferías	**preferíais**	**habías preferido**	**habíais preferido**
prefería	**preferían**	**había preferido**	**habían preferido**
3 pretérito		10 pretérito anterior	
preferí	**preferimos**	**hube preferido**	**hubimos preferido**
preferiste	**preferisteis**	**hubiste preferido**	**hubisteis preferido**
prefirió	**prefirieron**	**hubo preferido**	**hubieron preferido**
4 futuro		11 futuro perfecto	
preferiré	**preferiremos**	**habré preferido**	**habremos preferido**
preferirás	**preferiréis**	**habrás preferido**	**habréis preferido**
preferirá	**preferirán**	**habrá preferido**	**habrán preferido**
5 potencial simple		12 potencial compuesto	
preferiría	**preferiríamos**	**habría preferido**	**habríamos preferido**
preferirías	**preferiríais**	**habrías preferido**	**habríais preferido**
preferiría	**preferirían**	**habría preferido**	**habrían preferido**
6 presente de subjuntivo		13 perfecto de subjuntivo	
prefiera	**prefiramos**	**haya preferido**	**hayamos preferido**
prefieras	**prefiráis**	**hayas preferido**	**hayáis preferido**
prefiera	**prefieran**	**haya preferido**	**hayan preferido**
7 imperfecto de subjuntivo		14 pluscuamperfecto de subjuntivo	
prefiriera	**prefiriéramos**	**hubiera preferido**	**hubiéramos preferido**
prefirieras	**prefirierais**	**hubieras preferido**	**hubierais preferido**
prefiriera	**prefirieran**	**hubiera preferido**	**hubieran preferido**
OR		OR	
prefiriese	**prefiriésemos**	**hubiese preferido**	**hubiésemos preferido**
prefirieses	**prefirieseis**	**hubieses preferido**	**hubieseis preferido**
prefiriese	**prefiriesen**	**hubiese preferido**	**hubiesen preferido**

imperativo	
—	**prefiramos**
prefiere; no prefieras	**preferid; no prefiráis**
prefiera	**prefieran**

**Preferimos una habitación más
  grande, por favor.** We prefer a
  larger room, please.
preferiblemente preferably
de preferencia preferably
preferible preferable

preferentemente preferably
la preferencia preference
referir to refer, to relate
preferido, preferida preferred,
  favorite

245

preguntar

Gerundio **preguntando**   Part. pas. **preguntado**

to ask, to inquire, to question

Regular **-ar** verb

The Seven Simple Tenses		The Seven Compound Tenses	
Singular	Plural	Singular	Plural
1 presente de indicativo		**8 perfecto de indicativo**	
pregunto	preguntamos	he preguntado	hemos preguntado
preguntas	preguntáis	has preguntado	habéis preguntado
pregunta	preguntan	ha preguntado	han preguntado
2 imperfecto de indicativo		**9 pluscuamperfecto de indicativo**	
preguntaba	preguntábamos	había preguntado	habíamos preguntado
preguntabas	preguntabais	habías preguntado	habíais preguntado
preguntaba	preguntaban	había preguntado	habían preguntado
3 pretérito		**10 pretérito anterior**	
pregunté	preguntamos	hube preguntado	hubimos preguntado
preguntaste	preguntasteis	hubiste preguntado	hubisteis preguntado
preguntó	preguntaron	hubo preguntado	hubieron preguntado
4 futuro		**11 futuro perfecto**	
preguntaré	preguntaremos	habré preguntado	habremos preguntado
preguntarás	preguntaréis	habrás preguntado	habréis preguntado
preguntará	preguntarán	habrá preguntado	habrán preguntado
5 potencial simple		**12 potencial compuesto**	
preguntaría	preguntaríamos	habría preguntado	habríamos preguntado
preguntarías	preguntaríais	habrías preguntado	habríais preguntado
preguntaría	preguntarían	habría preguntado	habrían preguntado
6 presente de subjuntivo		**13 perfecto de subjuntivo**	
pregunte	preguntemos	haya preguntado	hayamos preguntado
preguntes	preguntéis	hayas preguntado	hayáis preguntado
pregunte	pregunten	haya preguntado	hayan preguntado
7 imperfecto de subjuntivo		**14 pluscuamperfecto de subjuntivo**	
preguntara	preguntáramos	hubiera preguntado	hubiéramos preguntado
preguntaras	preguntarais	hubieras preguntado	hubierais preguntado
preguntara	preguntaran	hubiera preguntado	hubieran preguntado
OR		OR	
preguntase	preguntásemos	hubiese preguntado	hubiésemos preguntado
preguntases	preguntaseis	hubieses preguntado	hubieseis preguntado
preguntase	preguntasen	hubiese preguntado	hubiesen preguntado

imperativo	
—	preguntemos
pregunta; no preguntes	preguntad; no preguntéis
pregunte	pregunten

una pregunta question	Don't confuse pedir and preguntar.
preguntarse to wonder, to ask oneself	Pedir means *to ask for something*.
hacer una pregunta to ask a question	Preguntar means *to ask a question*.
preguntante inquiring	La alumna preguntó a la profesora
un preguntón, una preguntona	cómo estaba. The pupil asked the
inquisitive individual	teacher how she was.

The Seven Simple Tenses		The Seven Compound Tenses	
Singular	Plural	Singular	Plural
1 presente de indicativo		8 perfecto de indicativo	
preparo	**preparamos**	**he preparado**	**hemos preparado**
preparas	**preparáis**	**has preparado**	**habéis preparado**
prepara	**preparan**	**ha preparado**	**han preparado**
2 imperfecto de indicativo		9 pluscuamperfecto de indicativo	
preparaba	**preparábamos**	**había preparado**	**habíamos preparado**
preparabas	**preparabais**	**habías preparado**	**habíais preparado**
preparaba	**preparaban**	**había preparado**	**habían preparado**
3 pretérito		10 pretérito anterior	
preparé	**preparamos**	**hube preparado**	**hubimos preparado**
preparaste	**preparasteis**	**hubiste preparado**	**hubisteis preparado**
preparó	**prepararon**	**hubo preparado**	**hubieron preparado**
4 futuro		11 futuro perfecto	
prepararé	**prepararemos**	**habré preparado**	**habremos preparado**
prepararás	**prepararéis**	**habrás preparado**	**habréis preparado**
preparará	**prepararán**	**habrá preparado**	**habrán preparado**
5 potencial simple		12 potencial compuesto	
prepararía	**prepararíamos**	**habría preparado**	**habríamos preparado**
prepararías	**prepararíais**	**habrías preparado**	**habríais preparado**
prepararía	**prepararían**	**habría preparado**	**habrían preparado**
6 presente de subjuntivo		13 perfecto de subjuntivo	
prepare	**preparemos**	**haya preparado**	**hayamos preparado**
prepares	**preparéis**	**hayas preparado**	**hayáis preparado**
prepare	**preparen**	**haya preparado**	**hayan preparado**
7 imperfecto de subjuntivo		14 pluscuamperfecto de subjuntivo	
preparara	**preparáramos**	**hubiera preparado**	**hubiéramos preparado**
prepararas	**prepararais**	**hubieras preparado**	**hubierais preparado**
preparara	**prepararan**	**hubiera preparado**	**hubieran preparado**
OR		OR	
preparase	**preparásemos**	**hubiese preparado**	**hubiésemos preparado**
preparases	**preparaseis**	**hubieses preparado**	**hubieseis preparado**
preparase	**preparasen**	**hubiese preparado**	**hubiesen preparado**

	imperativo	
—		**preparemos**
prepara; no prepares		**preparad; no preparéis**
prepare		**preparen**

preparatorio, preparatoria	el **preparativo** preparation,
preparatory	preparative
la **preparación** preparation	**prepararse** to prepare oneself

prestar

Gerundio **prestando**   Part. pas. **prestado**

to lend

Regular **-ar** verb

The Seven Simple Tenses		The Seven Compound Tenses	
Singular	Plural	Singular	Plural
1 presente de indicativo		8 perfecto de indicativo	
presto	**prestamos**	**he prestado**	**hemos prestado**
prestas	**prestáis**	**has prestado**	**habéis prestado**
presta	**prestan**	**ha prestado**	**han prestado**
2 imperfecto de indicativo		9 pluscuamperfecto de indicativo	
prestaba	**prestábamos**	**había prestado**	**habíamos prestado**
prestabas	**prestabais**	**habías prestado**	**habíais prestado**
prestaba	**prestaban**	**había prestado**	**habían prestado**
3 pretérito		10 pretérito anterior	
presté	**prestamos**	**hube prestado**	**hubimos prestado**
prestaste	**prestasteis**	**hubiste prestado**	**hubisteis prestado**
prestó	**prestaron**	**hubo prestado**	**hubieron prestado**
4 futuro		11 futuro perfecto	
prestaré	**prestaremos**	**habré prestado**	**habremos prestado**
prestarás	**prestaréis**	**habrás prestado**	**habréis prestado**
prestará	**prestarán**	**habrá prestado**	**habrán prestado**
5 potencial simple		12 potencial compuesto	
prestaría	**prestaríamos**	**habría prestado**	**habríamos prestado**
prestarías	**prestaríais**	**habrías prestado**	**habríais prestado**
prestaría	**prestarían**	**habría prestado**	**habrían prestado**
6 presente de subjuntivo		13 perfecto de subjuntivo	
preste	**prestemos**	**haya prestado**	**hayamos prestado**
prestes	**prestéis**	**hayas prestado**	**hayáis prestado**
preste	**presten**	**haya prestado**	**hayan prestado**
7 imperfecto de subjuntivo		14 pluscuamperfecto de subjuntivo	
prestara	**prestáramos**	**hubiera prestado**	**hubiéramos prestado**
prestaras	**prestarais**	**hubieras prestado**	**hubierais prestado**
prestara	**prestaran**	**hubiera prestado**	**hubieran prestado**
OR		OR	
prestase	**prestásemos**	**hubiese prestado**	**hubiésemos prestado**
prestases	**prestaseis**	**hubieses prestado**	**hubieseis prestado**
prestase	**prestasen**	**hubiese prestado**	**hubiesen prestado**

imperativo	
—	**prestemos**
presta; no prestes	**prestad; no prestéis**
preste	**presten**

pedir prestado to borrow	**un, una prestamista** money lender
prestar atención to pay attention	**un préstamo** loan
tomar prestado to borrow	**la prestación** benefit, contribution
prestador, prestadora lender	**prestar juramento** to take an oath

248

Regular **-ar** verb endings with stem
change: Tenses 1, 6, Imperative

to test, to prove,
to try, to try on

The Seven Simple Tenses		The Seven Compound Tenses	
Singular	Plural	Singular	Plural
1 presente de indicativo		8 perfecto de indicativo	
pruebo	probamos	he probado	hemos probado
pruebas	probáis	has probado	habéis probado
prueba	prueban	ha probado	han probado
2 imperfecto de indicativo		9 pluscuamperfecto de indicativo	
probaba	probábamos	había probado	habíamos probado
probabas	probabais	habías probado	habíais probado
probaba	probaban	había probado	habían probado
3 pretérito		10 pretérito anterior	
probé	probamos	hube probado	hubimos probado
probaste	probasteis	hubiste probado	hubisteis probado
probó	probaron	hubo probado	hubieron probado
4 futuro		11 futuro perfecto	
probaré	probaremos	habré probado	habremos probado
probarás	probaréis	habrás probado	habréis probado
probará	probarán	habrá probado	habrán probado
5 potencial simple		12 potencial compuesto	
probaría	probaríamos	habría probado	habríamos probado
probarías	probaríais	habrías probado	habríais probado
probaría	probarían	habría probado	habrían probado
6 presente de subjuntivo		13 perfecto de subjuntivo	
pruebe	probemos	haya probado	hayamos probado
pruebes	probéis	hayas probado	hayáis probado
pruebe	prueben	haya probado	hayan probado
7 imperfecto de subjuntivo		14 pluscuamperfecto de subjuntivo	
probara	probáramos	hubiera probado	hubiéramos probado
probaras	probarais	hubieras probado	hubierais probado
probara	probaran	hubiera probado	hubieran probado
OR		OR	
probase	probásemos	hubiese probado	hubiésemos probado
probases	probaseis	hubieses probado	hubieseis probado
probase	probasen	hubiese probado	hubiesen probado

	imperativo	
—		probemos
prueba; no pruebes		probad; no probéis
pruebe		prueben

¿Me puedo probar este traje? May I try on this suit?	probar de to taste, to take a taste of
la prueba proof, evidence, test	la probatura test, experiment
probablemente probably	probable probable
poner a prueba to put to the test, to try out	la probabilidad probability

probarse

Gerundio **probándose**   Part. pas. **probado**

to try on (clothes)

Reflexive verb; regular **-ar** verb endings with
stem change: Tenses 1, 6, Imperative

The Seven Simple Tenses		The Seven Compound Tenses	
Singular	Plural	Singular	Plural
1 presente de indicativo		8 perfecto de indicativo	
me pruebo	nos probamos	me he probado	nos hemos probado
te pruebas	os probáis	te has probado	os habéis probado
se prueba	se prueban	se ha probado	se han probado
2 imperfecto de indicativo		9 pluscuamperfecto de indicativo	
me probaba	nos probábamos	me había probado	nos habíamos probado
te probabas	os probabais	te habías probado	os habíais probado
se probaba	se probaban	se había probado	se habían probado
3 pretérito		10 pretérito anterior	
me probé	nos probamos	me hube probado	nos hubimos probado
te probaste	os probasteis	te hubiste probado	os hubisteis probado
se probó	se probaron	se hubo probado	se hubieron probado
4 futuro		11 futuro perfecto	
me probaré	nos probaremos	me habré probado	nos habremos probado
te probarás	os probaréis	te habrás probado	os habréis probado
se probará	se probarán	se habrá probado	se habrán probado
5 potencial simple		12 potencial compuesto	
me probaría	nos probaríamos	me habría probado	nos habríamos probado
te probarías	os probaríais	te habrías probado	os habríais probado
se probaría	se probarían	se habría probado	se habrían probado
6 presente de subjuntivo		13 perfecto de subjuntivo	
me pruebe	nos probemos	me haya probado	nos hayamos probado
te pruebes	os probéis	te hayas probado	os hayáis probado
se pruebe	se prueben	se haya probado	se hayan probado
7 imperfecto de subjuntivo		14 pluscuamperfecto de subjuntivo	
me probara	nos probáramos	me hubiera probado	nos hubiéramos probado
te probaras	os probarais	te hubieras probado	os hubierais probado
se probara	se probaran	se hubiera probado	se hubieran probado
OR		OR	
me probase	nos probásemos	me hubiese probado	nos hubiésemos probado
te probases	os probaseis	te hubieses probado	os hubieseis probado
se probase	se probasen	se hubiese probado	se hubiesen probado

imperativo	
—	probémonos
pruébate; no te pruebes	probaos; no os probéis
pruébese	pruébense

¿Puedo probarme este traje?   May I
  try on this suit?

See also probar.

Gerundio **pronunciando**   Part. pas. **pronunciado**   **pronunciar**

Regular **-ar** verb   to pronounce

The Seven Simple Tenses		The Seven Compound Tenses	
Singular	Plural	Singular	Plural
1 presente de indicativo		8 perfecto de indicativo	
pronuncio	**pronunciamos**	**he pronunciado**	**hemos pronunciado**
pronuncias	**pronunciáis**	**has pronunciado**	**habéis pronunciado**
pronuncia	**pronuncian**	**ha pronunciado**	**han pronunciado**
2 imperfecto de indicativo		9 pluscuamperfecto de indicativo	
pronunciaba	**pronunciábamos**	**había pronunciado**	**habíamos pronunciado**
pronunciabas	**pronunciabais**	**habías pronunciado**	**habíais pronunciado**
pronunciaba	**pronunciaban**	**había pronunciado**	**habían pronunciado**
3 pretérito		10 pretérito anterior	
pronuncié	**pronunciamos**	**hube pronunciado**	**hubimos pronunciado**
pronunciaste	**pronunciasteis**	**hubiste pronunciado**	**hubisteis pronunciado**
pronunció	**pronunciaron**	**hubo pronunciado**	**hubieron pronunciado**
4 futuro		11 futuro perfecto	
pronunciaré	**pronunciaremos**	**habré pronunciado**	**habremos pronunciado**
pronunciarás	**pronunciaréis**	**habrás pronunciado**	**habréis pronunciado**
pronunciará	**pronunciarán**	**habrá pronunciado**	**habrán pronunciado**
5 potencial simple		12 potencial compuesto	
pronunciaría	**pronunciaríamos**	**habría pronunciado**	**habríamos pronunciado**
pronunciarías	**pronunciaríais**	**habrías pronunciado**	**habríais pronunciado**
pronunciaría	**pronunciarían**	**habría pronunciado**	**habrían pronunciado**
6 presente de subjuntivo		13 perfecto de subjuntivo	
pronuncie	**pronunciemos**	**haya pronunciado**	**hayamos pronunciado**
pronuncies	**pronunciéis**	**hayas pronunciado**	**hayáis pronunciado**
pronuncie	**pronuncien**	**haya pronunciado**	**hayan pronunciado**
7 imperfecto de subjuntivo		14 pluscuamperfecto de subjuntivo	
pronunciara	**pronunciáramos**	**hubiera pronunciado**	**hubiéramos pronunciado**
pronunciaras	**pronunciarais**	**hubieras pronunciado**	**hubierais pronunciado**
pronunciara	**pronunciaran**	**hubiera pronunciado**	**hubieran pronunciado**
OR		OR	
pronunciase	**pronunciásemos**	**hubiese pronunciado**	**hubiésemos pronunciado**
pronunciases	**pronunciaseis**	**hubieses pronunciado**	**hubieseis pronunciado**
pronunciase	**pronunciasen**	**hubiese pronunciado**	**hubiesen pronunciado**

imperativo

—	**pronunciemos**
pronuncia; no pronuncies	**pronunciad; no pronunciéis**
pronuncie	**pronuncien**

la pronunciación pronunciation
enunciar to enunciate
pronunciado, pronunciada pronounced
anunciar to announce
pronunciar un discurso to make a speech

denunciar to denounce
pronunciar una conferencia to deliver a lecture
renunciar to renounce
impronunciable unpronounceable

251

proteger

Gerundio **protegiendo**   Part. pas. **protegido**

to protect

Regular **-er** verb endings with spelling
change: **g** becomes **j** before **a** or **o**

The Seven Simple Tenses		The Seven Compound Tenses	
Singular	Plural	Singular	Plural
1 presente de indicativo		8 perfecto de indicativo	
protejo	**protegemos**	**he protegido**	**hemos protegido**
proteges	**protegéis**	**has protegido**	**habéis protegido**
protege	**protegen**	**ha protegido**	**han protegido**
2 imperfecto de indicativo		9 pluscuamperfecto de indicativo	
protegía	**protegíamos**	**había protegido**	**habíamos protegido**
protegías	**protegíais**	**habías protegido**	**habíais protegido**
protegía	**protegían**	**había protegido**	**habían protegido**
3 pretérito		10 pretérito anterior	
protegí	**protegimos**	**hube protegido**	**hubimos protegido**
protegiste	**protegisteis**	**hubiste protegido**	**hubisteis protegido**
protegió	**protegieron**	**hubo protegido**	**hubieron protegido**
4 futuro		11 futuro perfecto	
protegeré	**protegeremos**	**habré protegido**	**habremos protegido**
protegerás	**protegeréis**	**habrás protegido**	**habréis protegido**
protegerá	**protegerán**	**habrá protegido**	**habrán protegido**
5 potencial simple		12 potencial compuesto	
protegería	**protegeríamos**	**habría protegido**	**habríamos protegido**
protegerías	**protegeríais**	**habrías protegido**	**habríais protegido**
protegería	**protegerían**	**habría protegido**	**habrían protegido**
6 presente de subjuntivo		13 perfecto de subjuntivo	
proteja	**protejamos**	**haya protegido**	**hayamos protegido**
protejas	**protejáis**	**hayas protegido**	**hayáis protegido**
proteja	**protejan**	**haya protegido**	**hayan protegido**
7 imperfecto de subjuntivo		14 pluscuamperfecto de subjuntivo	
protegiera	**protegiéramos**	**hubiera protegido**	**hubiéramos protegido**
protegieras	**protegierais**	**hubieras protegido**	**hubierais protegido**
protegiera	**protegieran**	**hubiera protegido**	**hubieran protegido**
OR		OR	
protegiese	**protegiésemos**	**hubiese protegido**	**hubiésemos protegido**
protegieses	**protegieseis**	**hubieses protegido**	**hubieseis protegido**
protegiese	**protegiesen**	**hubiese protegido**	**hubiesen protegido**

imperativo	
—	**protejamos**
protege; no protejas	**proteged; no protejáis**
proteja	**protejan**

La vacuna antigripal nos protege
   contra la gripe.   The flu vaccine
   protects us from the flu.
la protección   protection
protegido, protegida   protected,
favorite, protégé

el protector, la protectriz   protector,
   protectress
protectorio, protectoria   protective
proteger contra   to protect against
proteger de   to protect from

quedarse

to remain, to stay

The Seven Simple Tenses		The Seven Compound Tenses	
Singular	Plural	Singular	Plural
1 presente de indicativo		8 perfecto de indicativo	
me quedo	nos quedamos	me he quedado	nos hemos quedado
te quedas	os quedáis	te has quedado	os habéis quedado
se queda	se quedan	se ha quedado	se han quedado
2 imperfecto de indicativo		9 pluscuamperfecto de indicativo	
me quedaba	nos quedábamos	me había quedado	nos habíamos quedado
te quedabas	os quedabais	te habías quedado	os habíais quedado
se quedaba	se quedaban	se había quedado	se habían quedado
3 pretérito		10 pretérito anterior	
me quedé	nos quedamos	me hube quedado	nos hubimos quedado
te quedaste	os quedasteis	te hubiste quedado	os hubisteis quedado
se quedó	se quedaron	se hubo quedado	se hubieron quedado
4 futuro		11 futuro perfecto	
me quedaré	nos quedaremos	me habré quedado	nos habremos quedado
te quedarás	os quedaréis	te habrás quedado	os habréis quedado
se quedará	se quedarán	se habrá quedado	se habrán quedado
5 potencial simple		12 potencial compuesto	
me quedaría	nos quedaríamos	me habría quedado	nos habríamos quedado
te quedarías	os quedaríais	te habrías quedado	os habríais quedado
se quedaría	se quedarían	se habría quedado	se habrían quedado
6 presente de subjuntivo		13 perfecto de subjuntivo	
me quede	nos quedemos	me haya quedado	nos hayamos quedado
te quedes	os quedéis	te hayas quedado	os hayáis quedado
se quede	se queden	se haya quedado	se hayan quedado
7 imperfecto de subjuntivo		14 pluscuamperfecto de subjuntivo	
me quedara	nos quedáramos	me hubiera quedado	nos hubiéramos quedado
te quedaras	os quedarais	te hubieras quedado	os hubierais quedado
se quedara	se quedaran	se hubiera quedado	se hubieran quedado
OR		OR	
me quedase	nos quedásemos	me hubiese quedado	nos hubiésemos quedado
te quedases	os quedaseis	te hubieses quedado	os hubieseis quedado
se quedase	se quedasen	se hubiese quedado	se hubiesen quedado

imperativo	
—	quedémonos
quédate; no te quedes	quedaos; no os quedéis
quédese	quédense

El año pasado, me quedé dos semanas en San José.   Last year, I stayed two weeks in San José.
la quedada   residence, stay
quedar   to remain, to be left;
   ¿Cuánto dinero queda?   How much money is left?

Me quedan dos dólares.   I have two dollars left (remaining).
quedarse con la boca abierta   to be left open-mouthed

253

querer

Gerundio **queriendo**   Part. pas. **querido**

to want, to wish

Irregular verb

The Seven Simple Tenses		The Seven Compound Tenses	
Singular	Plural	Singular	Plural
1 presente de indicativo		8 perfecto de indicativo	
quiero	queremos	he querido	hemos querido
quieres	queréis	has querido	habéis querido
quiere	quieren	ha querido	han querido
2 imperfecto de indicativo		9 pluscuamperfecto de indicativo	
quería	queríamos	había querido	habíamos querido
querías	queríais	habías querido	habíais querido
quería	querían	había querido	habían querido
3 pretérito		10 pretérito anterior	
quise	quisimos	hube querido	hubimos querido
quisiste	quisisteis	hubiste querido	hubisteis querido
quiso	quisieron	hubo querido	hubieron querido
4 futuro		11 futuro perfecto	
querré	querremos	habré querido	habremos querido
querrás	querréis	habrás querido	habréis querido
querrá	querrán	habrá querido	habrán querido
5 potencial simple		12 potencial compuesto	
querría	querríamos	habría querido	habríamos querido
querrías	querríais	habrías querido	habríais querido
querría	querrían	habría querido	habrían querido
6 presente de subjuntivo		13 perfecto de subjuntivo	
quiera	queramos	haya querido	hayamos querido
quieras	queráis	hayas querido	hayáis querido
quiera	quieran	haya querido	hayan querido
7 imperfecto de subjuntivo		14 pluscuamperfecto de subjuntivo	
quisiera	quisiéramos	hubiera querido	hubiéramos querido
quisieras	quisierais	hubieras querido	hubierais querido
quisiera	quisieran	hubiera querido	hubieran querido
OR		OR	
quisiese	quisiésemos	hubiese querido	hubiésemos querido
quisieses	quisieseis	hubieses querido	hubieseis querido
quisiese	quisiesen	hubiese querido	hubiesen querido

imperativo	
—	queramos
quiere; no quieras	quered; no queráis
quiera	quieran

Quisiera un café, por favor. I would like a coffee, please.

querer decir to mean;

¿Qué quiere Ud. decir? What do you mean?

¿Qué quiere decir esto? What does this mean?

querido, querida dear

querido amigo, querida amiga dear friend

querido mío, querida mía my dear

querer bien a to love

querer más to prefer

Reflexive regular **-ar** verb

to take off (clothing),
to remove oneself, to withdraw

The Seven Simple Tenses		The Seven Compound Tenses	
Singular	Plural	Singular	Plural
1 presente de indicativo		8 perfecto de indicativo	
me quito	nos quitamos	me he quitado	nos hemos quitado
te quitas	os quitáis	te has quitado	os habéis quitado
se quita	se quitan	se ha quitado	se han quitado
2 imperfecto de indicativo		9 pluscuamperfecto de indicativo	
me quitaba	nos quitábamos	me había quitado	nos habíamos quitado
te quitabas	os quitabais	te habías quitado	os habíais quitado
se quitaba	se quitaban	se había quitado	se habían quitado
3 pretérito		10 pretérito anterior	
me quité	nos quitamos	me hube quitado	nos hubimos quitado
te quitaste	os quitasteis	te hubiste quitado	os hubisteis quitado
se quitó	se quitaron	se hubo quitado	se hubieron quitado
4 futuro		11 futuro perfecto	
me quitaré	nos quitaremos	me habré quitado	nos habremos quitado
te quitarás	os quitaréis	te habrás quitado	os habréis quitado
se quitará	se quitarán	se habrá quitado	se habrán quitado
5 potencial simple		12 potencial compuesto	
me quitaría	nos quitaríamos	me habría quitado	nos habríamos quitado
te quitarías	os quitaríais	te habrías quitado	os habríais quitado
se quitaría	se quitarían	se habría quitado	se habrían quitado
6 presente de subjuntivo		13 perfecto de subjuntivo	
me quite	nos quitemos	me haya quitado	nos hayamos quitado
te quites	os quitéis	te hayas quitado	os hayáis quitado
se quite	se quiten	se haya quitado	se hayan quitado
7 imperfecto de subjuntivo		14 pluscuamperfecto de subjuntivo	
me quitara	nos quitáramos	me hubiera quitado	nos hubiéramos quitado
te quitaras	os quitarais	te hubieras quitado	os hubierais quitado
se quitara	se quitaran	se hubiera quitado	se hubieran quitado
OR		OR	
me quitase	nos quitásemos	me hubiese quitado	nos hubiésemos quitado
te quitases	os quitaseis	te hubieses quitado	os hubieseis quitado
se quitase	se quitasen	se hubiese quitado	se hubiesen quitado

	imperativo	
—		quitémonos
quítate; no te quites		quitaos; no os quitéis
quítese		quítense

---

la quita   release (from owing money),
  acquittance
¡Quita de ahí!   Get away from here!
quitar   to remove, to take away; to rob,
  to strip

el quite   removal; **el quitasol**   parasol
  (sunshade)
una quitanieves   snowplow

recibir

Gerundio **recibiendo**   Part. pas. **recibido**

to receive, to get

Regular **-ir** verb

The Seven Simple Tenses		The Seven Compound Tenses	
Singular	Plural	Singular	Plural
1 presente de indicativo		8 perfecto de indicativo	
recibo	**recibimos**	**he recibido**	**hemos recibido**
recibes	**recibís**	**has recibido**	**habéis recibido**
recibe	**reciben**	**ha recibido**	**han recibido**
2 imperfecto de indicativo		9 pluscuamperfecto de indicativo	
recibía	**recibíamos**	**había recibido**	**habíamos recibido**
recibías	**recibíais**	**habías recibido**	**habíais recibido**
recibía	**recibían**	**había recibido**	**habían recibido**
3 pretérito		10 pretérito anterior	
recibí	**recibimos**	**hube recibido**	**hubimos recibido**
recibiste	**recibisteis**	**hubiste recibido**	**hubisteis recibido**
recibió	**recibieron**	**hubo recibido**	**hubieron recibido**
4 futuro		11 futuro perfecto	
recibiré	**recibiremos**	**habré recibido**	**habremos recibido**
recibirás	**recibiréis**	**habrás recibido**	**habréis recibido**
recibirá	**recibirán**	**habrá recibido**	**habrán recibido**
5 potencial simple		12 potencial compuesto	
recibiría	**recibiríamos**	**habría recibido**	**habríamos recibido**
recibirías	**recibiríais**	**habrías recibido**	**habríais recibido**
recibiría	**recibirían**	**habría recibido**	**habrían recibido**
6 presente de subjuntivo		13 perfecto de subjuntivo	
reciba	**recibamos**	**haya recibido**	**hayamos recibido**
recibas	**recibáis**	**hayas recibido**	**hayáis recibido**
reciba	**reciban**	**haya recibido**	**hayan recibido**
7 imperfecto de subjuntivo		14 pluscuamperfecto de subjuntivo	
recibiera	**recibiéramos**	**hubiera recibido**	**hubiéramos recibido**
recibieras	**recibierais**	**hubieras recibido**	**hubierais recibido**
recibiera	**recibieran**	**hubiera recibido**	**hubieran recibido**
OR		OR	
recibiese	**recibiésemos**	**hubiese recibido**	**hubiésemos recibido**
recibieses	**recibieseis**	**hubieses recibido**	**hubieseis recibido**
recibiese	**recibiesen**	**hubiese recibido**	**hubiesen recibido**

	imperativo	
—		**recibamos**
recibe; no recibas		**recibid; no recibáis**
reciba		**reciban**

un recibo receipt	**la recepción** reception
de recibo acceptable; **ser de recibo**	**recibirse** to be admitted, to be
to be acceptable	received
acusar recibo to acknowledge receipt	**recibir a cuenta** to receive on account

Regular **-ar** verb endings with stem change:
Tenses 1, 6, Imperative

to remember, to recall,
to remind

The Seven Simple Tenses		The Seven Compound Tenses	
Singular	Plural	Singular	Plural
1 presente de indicativo		8 perfecto de indicativo	
recuerdo	recordamos	he recordado	hemos recordado
recuerdas	recordáis	has recordado	habéis recordado
recuerda	recuerdan	ha recordado	han recordado
2 imperfecto de indicativo		9 pluscuamperfecto de indicativo	
recordaba	recordábamos	había recordado	habíamos recordado
recordabas	recordabais	habías recordado	habíais recordado
recordaba	recordaban	había recordado	habían recordado
3 pretérito		10 pretérito anterior	
recordé	recordamos	hube recordado	hubimos recordado
recordaste	recordasteis	hubiste recordado	hubisteis recordado
recordó	recordaron	hubo recordado	hubieron recordado
4 futuro		11 futuro perfecto	
recordaré	recordaremos	habré recordado	habremos recordado
recordarás	recordaréis	habrás recordado	habréis recordado
recordará	recordarán	habrá recordado	habrán recordado
5 potencial simple		12 potencial compuesto	
recordaría	recordaríamos	habría recordado	habríamos recordado
recordarías	recordaríais	habrías recordado	habríais recordado
recordaría	recordarían	habría recordado	habrían recordado
6 presente de subjuntivo		13 perfecto de subjuntivo	
recuerde	recordemos	haya recordado	hayamos recordado
recuerdes	recordéis	hayas recordado	hayáis recordado
recuerde	recuerden	haya recordado	hayan recordado
7 imperfecto de subjuntivo		14 pluscuamperfecto de subjuntivo	
recordara	recordáramos	hubiera recordado	hubiéramos recordado
recordaras	recordarais	hubieras recordado	hubierais recordado
recordara	recordaran	hubiera recordado	hubieran recordado
OR		OR	
recordase	recordásemos	hubiese recordado	hubiésemos recordado
recordases	recordaseis	hubieses recordado	hubieseis recordado
recordase	recordasen	hubiese recordado	hubiesen recordado

imperativo	
—	recordemos
recuerda; no recuerdes	recordad; no recordéis
recuerde	recuerden

El señor Gómez recuerda los nombres
de todos sus alumnos.   Mr. Gomez
remembers the names of all his
students.
el recuerdo   memory, recollection
recordar algo a uno   to remind

someone of something
los recuerdos   regards, compliments
recordable   memorable
un recordatorio   memento, reminder
una tienda de recuerdos   souvenir
shop

referir

Gerundio **refiriendo**   Part. pas. **referido**

to refer, to relate

Regular **-ir** verb endings with stem change:
Tenses 1, 3, 6, 7, Imperative, *Gerundio*

The Seven Simple Tenses		The Seven Compound Tenses	
Singular	Plural	Singular	Plural
1 presente de indicativo		8 perfecto de indicativo	
refiero	**referimos**	**he referido**	**hemos referido**
refieres	**referís**	**has referido**	**habéis referido**
refiere	**refieren**	**ha referido**	**han referido**
2 imperfecto de indicativo		9 pluscuamperfecto de indicativo	
refería	**referíamos**	**había referido**	**habíamos referido**
referías	**referíais**	**habías referido**	**habíais referido**
refería	**referían**	**había referido**	**habían referido**
3 pretérito		10 pretérito anterior	
referí	**referimos**	**hube referido**	**hubimos referido**
referiste	**referisteis**	**hubiste referido**	**hubisteis referido**
refirió	**refirieron**	**hubo referido**	**hubieron referido**
4 futuro		11 futuro perfecto	
referiré	**referiremos**	**habré referido**	**habremos referido**
referirás	**referiréis**	**habrás referido**	**habréis referido**
referirá	**referirán**	**habrá referido**	**habrán referido**
5 potencial simple		12 potencial compuesto	
referiría	**referiríamos**	**habría referido**	**habríamos referido**
referirías	**referiríais**	**habrías referido**	**habríais referido**
referiría	**referirían**	**habría referido**	**habrían referido**
6 presente de subjuntivo		13 perfecto de subjuntivo	
refiera	**refiramos**	**haya referido**	**hayamos referido**
refieras	**refiráis**	**hayas referido**	**hayáis referido**
refiera	**refieran**	**haya referido**	**hayan referido**
7 imperfecto de subjuntivo		14 pluscuamperfecto de subjuntivo	
refiriera	**refiriéramos**	**hubiera referido**	**hubiéramos referido**
refirieras	**refirieras**	**hubieras referido**	**hubierais referido**
refiriera	**refirieran**	**hubiera referido**	**hubieran referido**
OR		OR	
refiriese	**refiriésemos**	**hubiese referido**	**hubiésemos referido**
refirieses	**refirieseis**	**hubieses referido**	**hubieseis referido**
refiriese	**refiriesen**	**hubiese referido**	**hubiesen referido**

imperativo	
—	**refiramos**
refiere; no refieras	**referid; no refiráis**
refiera	**refieran**

la referencia reference, account (narration)	preferir to prefer
referente concerning, referring, relating (to)	el referido, la referida the person referred to
el referéndum referendum	transferir to transfer
	conferir to confer, to grant

to laugh

Regular **-ir** verb endings with stem change:
Tenses 1, 3, 6, 7, Imperative, *Gerundio*

The Seven Simple Tenses		The Seven Compound Tenses	
Singular	Plural	Singular	Plural
1 presente de indicativo		8 perfecto de indicativo	
río	reímos	he reído	hemos reído
ríes	reís	has reído	habéis reído
ríe	ríen	ha reído	han reído
2 imperfecto de indicativo		9 pluscuamperfecto de indicativo	
reía	reíamos	había reído	habíamos reído
reías	reíais	habías reído	habíais reído
reía	reían	había reído	habían reído
3 pretérito		10 pretérito anterior	
reí	reímos	hube reído	hubimos reído
reíste	reísteis	hubiste reído	hubisteis reído
rió	rieron	hubo reído	hubieron reído
4 futuro		11 futuro perfecto	
reiré	reiremos	habré reído	habremos reído
reirás	reiréis	habrás reído	habréis reído
reirá	reirán	habrá reído	habrán reído
5 potencial simple		12 potencial compuesto	
reiría	reiríamos	habría reído	habríamos reído
reirías	reiríais	habrías reído	habríais reído
reiría	reirían	habría reído	habrían reído
6 presente de subjuntivo		13 perfecto de subjuntivo	
ría	riamos	haya reído	hayamos reído
rías	riáis	hayas reído	hayáis reído
ría	rían	haya reído	hayan reído
7 imperfecto de subjuntivo		14 pluscuamperfecto de subjuntivo	
riera	riéramos	hubiera reído	hubiéramos reído
rieras	rierais	hubieras reído	hubierais reído
riera	rieran	hubiera reído	hubieran reído
OR		OR	
riese	riésemos	hubiese reído	hubiésemos reído
rieses	rieseis	hubieses reído	hubieseis reído
riese	riesen	hubiese reído	hubiesen reído

	imperativo	
—	riamos	
ríe; no rías	reíd; no riáis	
ría	rían	

El que ríe al último ríe mejor.
  Whoever laughs last laughs best.
reír a carcajadas   to laugh loudly
risible   laughable

reír de   to laugh at, to make fun of
risueño, risueña   smiling
la risa   laugh, laughter
See also sonreír.

reñir

Gerundio **riñendo**   Part. pas. **reñido**

to scold, to quarrel

Regular **-ir** verb endings in all tenses except Tenses 3 and 7; stem change: Tenses 1, 3, 6, 7, Imperative, *Gerundio*

The Seven Simple Tenses		The Seven Compound Tenses	
Singular	Plural	Singular	Plural
1 presente de indicativo		8 perfecto de indicativo	
riño	reñimos	he reñido	hemos reñido
riñes	reñís	has reñido	habéis reñido
riñe	riñen	ha reñido	han reñido
2 imperfecto de indicativo		9 pluscuamperfecto de indicativo	
reñía	reñíamos	había reñido	habíamos reñido
reñías	reñíais	habías reñido	habíais reñido
reñía	reñían	había reñido	habían reñido
3 pretérito		10 pretérito anterior	
reñí	reñimos	hube reñido	hubimos reñido
reñiste	reñisteis	hubiste reñido	hubisteis reñido
riñó	riñeron	hubo reñido	hubieron reñido
4 futuro		11 futuro perfecto	
reñiré	reñiremos	habré reñido	habremos reñido
reñirás	reñiréis	habrás reñido	habréis reñido
reñirá	reñirán	habrá reñido	habrán reñido
5 potencial simple		12 potencial compuesto	
reñiría	reñiríamos	habría reñido	habríamos reñido
reñirías	reñiríais	habrías reñido	habríais reñido
reñiría	reñirían	habría reñido	habrían reñido
6 presente de subjuntivo		13 perfecto de subjuntivo	
riña	riñamos	haya reñido	hayamos reñido
riñas	riñáis	hayas reñido	hayáis reñido
riña	riñan	haya reñido	hayan reñido
7 imperfecto de subjuntivo		14 pluscuamperfecto de subjuntivo	
riñera	riñéramos	hubiera reñido	hubiéramos reñido
riñeras	riñerais	hubieras reñido	hubierais reñido
riñera	riñeran	hubiera reñido	hubieran reñido
OR		OR	
riñese	riñésemos	hubiese reñido	hubiésemos reñido
riñeses	riñeseis	hubieses reñido	hubieseis reñido
riñese	riñesen	hubiese reñido	hubiesen reñido

	imperativo	
—	riñamos	
riñe; no riñas	reñid; no riñáis	
riña	riñan	

Dos no riñen si uno no quiere.   Two don't quarrel if one of them doesn't want to.
reñidor, reñidora   quarreller
la reñidura   reprimand, scolding

reñidamente   stubbornly
reñir por   to fight over
reñir a alguien   to tell someone off

to repeat

Regular **-ir** verb endings with stem change:
Tenses 1, 3, 6, 7, Imperative, *Gerundio*

The Seven Simple Tenses		The Seven Compound Tenses	
Singular	Plural	Singular	Plural
1 presente de indicativo		8 perfecto de indicativo	
repito	repetimos	he repetido	hemos repetido
repites	repetís	has repetido	habéis repetido
repite	repiten	ha repetido	han repetido
2 imperfecto de indicativo		9 pluscuamperfecto de indicativo	
repetía	repetíamos	había repetido	habíamos repetido
repetías	repetíais	habías repetido	habíais repetido
repetía	repetían	había repetido	habían repetido
3 pretérito		10 pretérito anterior	
repetí	repetimos	hube repetido	hubimos repetido
repetiste	repetisteis	hubiste repetido	hubisteis repetido
repitió	repitieron	hubo repetido	hubieron repetido
4 futuro		11 futuro perfecto	
repetiré	repetiremos	habré repetido	habremos repetido
repetirás	repetiréis	habrás repetido	habréis repetido
repetirá	repetirán	habrá repetido	habrán repetido
5 potencial simple		12 potencial compuesto	
repetiría	repetiríamos	habría repetido	habríamos repetido
repetirías	repetiríais	habrías repetido	habríais repetido
repetiría	repetirían	habría repetido	habrían repetido
6 presente de subjuntivo		13 perfecto de subjuntivo	
repita	repitamos	haya repetido	hayamos repetido
repitas	repitáis	hayas repetido	hayáis repetido
repita	repitan	haya repetido	hayan repetido
7 imperfecto de subjuntivo		14 pluscuamperfecto de subjuntivo	
repitiera	repitiéramos	hubiera repetido	hubiéramos repetido
repitieras	repitierais	hubieras repetido	hubierais repetido
repitiera	repitieran	hubiera repetido	hubieran repetido
OR		OR	
repitiese	repitiésemos	hubiese repetido	hubiésemos repetido
repitieses	repitieseis	hubieses repetido	hubieseis repetido
repitiese	repitiesen	hubiese repetido	hubiesen repetido

imperativo		
—	repitamos	
repite; no repitas	repetid; no repitáis	
repita	repitan	

¡Que se repita! Encore!	repetirse to repeat to oneself
la repetición repetition	repetidas veces over and over again
repitiente *(adj.)* repeating	repetido, repetida repeated
repetidamente repeatedly	

responder

Gerundio **respondiendo** Part. pas. **respondido**

to answer, to reply, to respond

Regular **-er** verb

The Seven Simple Tenses		The Seven Compound Tenses	
Singular	Plural	Singular	Plural
1 presente de indicativo		8 perfecto de indicativo	
respondo	respondemos	he respondido	hemos respondido
respondes	respondéis	has respondido	habéis respondido
responde	responden	ha respondido	han respondido
2 imperfecto de indicativo		9 pluscuamperfecto de indicativo	
respondía	respondíamos	había respondido	habíamos respondido
respondías	respondíais	habías respondido	habíais respondido
respondía	respondían	había respondido	habían respondido
3 pretérito		10 pretérito anterior	
respondí	respondimos	hube respondido	hubimos respondido
respondiste	respondisteis	hubiste respondido	hubisteis respondido
respondió	respondieron	hubo respondido	hubieron respondido
4 futuro		11 futuro perfecto	
responderé	responderemos	habré respondido	habremos respondido
responderás	responderéis	habrás respondido	habréis respondido
responderá	responderán	habrá respondido	habrán respondido
5 potencial simple		12 potencial compuesto	
respondería	responderíamos	habría respondido	habríamos respondido
responderías	responderíais	habrías respondido	habríais respondido
respondería	responderían	habría respondido	habrían respondido
6 presente de subjuntivo		13 perfecto de subjuntivo	
responda	respondamos	haya respondido	hayamos respondido
respondas	respondáis	hayas respondido	hayáis respondido
responda	respondan	haya respondido	hayan respondido
7 imperfecto de subjuntivo		14 pluscuamperfecto de subjuntivo	
respondiera	respondiéramos	hubiera respondido	hubiéramos respondido
respondieras	respondierais	hubieras respondido	hubierais respondido
respondiera	respondieran	hubiera respondido	hubieran respondido
OR		OR	
respondiese	respondiésemos	hubiese respondido	hubiésemos respondido
respondieses	respondieseis	hubieses respondido	hubieseis respondido
respondiese	respondiesen	hubiese respondido	hubiesen respondido

imperativo	
—	respondamos
responde; no respondas	responded; no respondáis
responda	respondan

María respondió inmediatamente a la
 pregunta.   Mary answered the
 question right away.
una respuesta   answer, reply, response
responsivo, responsiva   responsive
respondiente   respondent

corresponder   to correspond
la correspondencia   correspondence
corresponder a   to reciprocate
correspondientemente
  correspondingly

Regular **-er** verb endings with stem change: to revolve, to turn around,
Tenses 1, 6, Imperative, Past Participle   to turn over, to turn upside down

The Seven Simple Tenses		The Seven Compound Tenses	
Singular	Plural	Singular	Plural
1 presente de indicativo		8 perfecto de indicativo	
revuelvo	**revolvemos**	**he revuelto**	**hemos revuelto**
revuelves	**revolvéis**	**has revuelto**	**habéis revuelto**
revuelve	**revuelven**	**ha revuelto**	**han revuelto**
2 imperfecto de indicativo		9 pluscuamperfecto de indicativo	
revolvía	**revolvíamos**	**había revuelto**	**habíamos revuelto**
revolvías	**revolvíais**	**habías revuelto**	**habíais revuelto**
revolvía	**revolvían**	**había revuelto**	**habían revuelto**
3 pretérito		10 pretérito anterior	
revolví	**revolvimos**	**hube revuelto**	**hubimos revuelto**
revolviste	**revolvisteis**	**hubiste revuelto**	**hubisteis revuelto**
revolvió	**revolvieron**	**hubo revuelto**	**hubieron revuelto**
4 futuro		11 futuro perfecto	
revolveré	**revolveremos**	**habré revuelto**	**habremos revuelto**
revolverás	**revolveréis**	**habrás revuelto**	**habréis revuelto**
revolverá	**revolverán**	**habrá revuelto**	**habrán revuelto**
5 potencial simple		12 potencial compuesto	
revolvería	**revolveríamos**	**habría revuelto**	**habríamos revuelto**
revolverías	**revolveríais**	**habrías revuelto**	**habríais revuelto**
revolvería	**revolverían**	**habría revuelto**	**habrían revuelto**
6 presente de subjuntivo		13 perfecto de subjuntivo	
revuelva	**revolvamos**	**haya revuelto**	**hayamos revuelto**
revuelvas	**revolváis**	**hayas revuelto**	**hayáis revuelto**
revuelva	**revuelvan**	**haya revuelto**	**hayan revuelto**
7 imperfecto de subjuntivo		14 pluscuamperfecto de subjuntivo	
revolviera	**revolviéramos**	**hubiera revuelto**	**hubiéramos revuelto**
revolvieras	**revolvierais**	**hubieras revuelto**	**hubierais revuelto**
revolviera	**revolvieran**	**hubiera revuelto**	**hubieran revuelto**
OR		OR	
revolviese	**revolviésemos**	**hubiese revuelto**	**hubiésemos revuelto**
revolvieses	**revolvieseis**	**hubieses revuelto**	**hubieseis revuelto**
revolviese	**revolviesen**	**hubiese revuelto**	**hubiesen revuelto**

imperativo

—	**revolvamos**
revuelve; no revuelvas	**revolved; no revolváis**
revuelva	**revuelvan**

huevos revueltos   scrambled eggs   revueltamente   upside down
el revolvimiento   revolving, revolution   See also **volver**.
la revolución   revolution

rogar

Gerundio **rogando**   Part. pas. **rogado**

to supplicate, to ask, to ask for, to request, to beg, to pray

Regular **-ar** verb endings with stem change: Tenses 1, 6, Imperative; spelling change: **g** becomes **gu** before **e**

The Seven Simple Tenses		The Seven Compound Tenses	
Singular	Plural	Singular	Plural
1 presente de indicativo		**8 perfecto de indicativo**	
ruego	rogamos	he rogado	hemos rogado
ruegas	rogáis	has rogado	habéis rogado
ruega	ruegan	ha rogado	han rogado
2 imperfecto de indicativo		**9 pluscuamperfecto de indicativo**	
rogaba	rogábamos	había rogado	habíamos rogado
rogabas	rogabais	habías rogado	habíais rogado
rogaba	rogaban	había rogado	habían rogado
3 pretérito		**10 pretérito anterior**	
rogué	rogamos	hube rogado	hubimos rogado
rogaste	rogasteis	hubiste rogado	hubisteis rogado
rogó	rogaron	hubo rogado	hubieron rogado
4 futuro		**11 futuro perfecto**	
rogaré	rogaremos	habré rogado	habremos rogado
rogarás	rogaréis	habrás rogado	habréis rogado
rogará	rogarán	habrá rogado	habrán rogado
5 potencial simple		**12 potencial compuesto**	
rogaría	rogaríamos	habría rogado	habríamos rogado
rogarías	rogaríais	habrías rogado	habríais rogado
rogaría	rogarían	habría rogado	habrían rogado
6 presente de subjuntivo		**13 perfecto de subjuntivo**	
ruegue	roguemos	haya rogado	hayamos rogado
ruegues	roguéis	hayas rogado	hayáis rogado
ruegue	rueguen	haya rogado	hayan rogado
7 imperfecto de subjuntivo		**14 pluscuamperfecto de subjuntivo**	
rogara	rogáramos	hubiera rogado	hubiéramos rogado
rogaras	rogarais	hubieras rogado	hubierais rogado
rogara	rogaran	hubiera rogado	hubieran rogado
OR		OR	
rogase	rogásemos	hubiese rogado	hubiésemos rogado
rogases	rogaseis	hubieses rogado	hubieseis rogado
rogase	rogasen	hubiese rogado	hubiesen rogado

imperativo	
—	roguemos
ruega; no ruegues	rogad; no roguéis
ruegue	rueguen

A Dios rogando y con el mazo dando. Put your faith in God and keep your powder dry.

rogador, rogadora supplicant

rogar por to plead for
rogativo, rogativa supplicatory
una prerrogativa prerogative

Regular **-er** verb with spelling change: to break, to shatter, to tear
irregular past participle

The Seven Simple Tenses		The Seven Compound Tenses	
Singular	Plural	Singular	Plural
1 presente de indicativo		8 perfecto de indicativo	
rompo	rompemos	he roto	hemos roto
rompes	rompéis	has roto	habéis roto
rompe	rompen	ha roto	han roto
2 imperfecto de indicativo		9 pluscuamperfecto de indicativo	
rompía	rompíamos	había roto	habíamos roto
rompías	rompíais	habías roto	habíais roto
rompía	rompían	había roto	habían roto
3 pretérito		10 pretérito anterior	
rompí	rompimos	hube roto	hubimos roto
rompiste	rompisteis	hubiste roto	hubisteis roto
rompió	rompieron	hubo roto	hubieron roto
4 futuro		11 futuro perfecto	
romperé	romperemos	habré roto	habremos roto
romperás	romperéis	habrás roto	habréis roto
romperá	romperán	habrá roto	habrán roto
5 potencial simple		12 potencial compuesto	
rompería	romperíamos	habría roto	habríamos roto
romperías	romperíais	habrías roto	habríais roto
rompería	romperían	habría roto	habrían roto
6 presente de subjuntivo		13 perfecto de subjuntivo	
rompa	rompamos	haya roto	hayamos roto
rompas	rompáis	hayas roto	hayáis roto
rompa	rompan	haya roto	hayan roto
7 imperfecto de subjuntivo		14 pluscuamperfecto de subjuntivo	
rompiera	rompiéramos	hubiera roto	hubiéramos roto
rompieras	rompierais	hubieras roto	hubierais roto
rompiera	rompieran	hubiera roto	hubieran roto
OR		OR	
rompiese	rompiésemos	hubiese roto	hubiésemos roto
rompieses	rompieseis	hubieses roto	hubieseis roto
rompiese	rompiesen	hubiese roto	hubiesen roto

imperativo	
—	rompamos
rompe; no rompas	romped; no rompáis
rompa	rompan

un rompenueces nutcracker	romper con to break relations with
romper a + inf. to start suddenly + inf.	romper las relaciones to break off
una rompedura breakage, rupture	relations, an engagement
romper la cabeza to rack one's brains	roto, rota broken
romper a llorar to break into tears	

saber

Gerundio **sabiendo**   Part. pas. **sabido**

to know, to know how

Irregular verb

The Seven Simple Tenses		The Seven Compound Tenses	
Singular	Plural	Singular	Plural
1 presente de indicativo		**8 perfecto de indicativo**	
sé	sabemos	he sabido	hemos sabido
sabes	sabéis	has sabido	habéis sabido
sabe	saben	ha sabido	han sabido
2 imperfecto de indicativo		**9 pluscuamperfecto de indicativo**	
sabía	sabíamos	había sabido	habíamos sabido
sabías	sabíais	habías sabido	habíais sabido
sabía	sabían	había sabido	habían sabido
3 pretérito		**10 pretérito anterior**	
supe	supimos	hube sabido	hubimos sabido
supiste	supisteis	hubiste sabido	hubisteis sabido
supo	supieron	hubo sabido	hubieron sabido
4 futuro		**11 futuro perfecto**	
sabré	sabremos	habré sabido	habremos sabido
sabrás	sabréis	habrás sabido	habréis sabido
sabrá	sabrán	habrá sabido	habrán sabido
5 potencial simple		**12 potencial compuesto**	
sabría	sabríamos	habría sabido	habríamos sabido
sabrías	sabríais	habrías sabido	habríais sabido
sabría	sabrían	habría sabido	habrían sabido
6 presente de subjuntivo		**13 perfecto de subjuntivo**	
sepa	sepamos	haya sabido	hayamos sabido
sepas	sepáis	hayas sabido	hayáis sabido
sepa	sepan	haya sabido	hayan sabido
7 imperfecto de subjuntivo		**14 pluscuamperfecto de subjuntivo**	
supiera	supiéramos	hubiera sabido	hubiéramos sabido
supieras	supierais	hubieras sabido	hubierais sabido
supiera	supieran	hubiera sabido	hubieran sabido
OR		OR	
supiese	supiésemos	hubiese sabido	hubiésemos sabido
supieses	supieseis	hubieses sabido	hubieseis sabido
supiese	supiesen	hubiese sabido	hubiesen sabido

imperativo	
—	sepamos
sabe; no sepas	sabed; no sepáis
sepa	sepan

¿Sabe Ud. nadar? Do you know how to swim?

No sé nada de este asunto. I don't know anything about this matter.

¡Quién sabe! Who knows! Maybe!

Saber es poder. Knowledge is power.

sabio, sabia wise, learned

Que yo sepa ... As far as I know ...

un sabidillo, una sabidilla a know-it-all individual

la sabiduría knowledge, learning, wisdom

Regular **-ar** verb endings with spelling change: to take out, to get
c becomes **qu** before **e**

The Seven Simple Tenses		The Seven Compound Tenses	
Singular	Plural	Singular	Plural
1 presente de indicativo		8 perfecto de indicativo	
saco	sacamos	he sacado	hemos sacado
sacas	sacáis	has sacado	habéis sacado
saca	sacan	ha sacado	han sacado
2 imperfecto de indicativo		9 pluscuamperfecto de indicativo	
sacaba	sacábamos	había sacado	habíamos sacado
sacabas	sacabais	habías sacado	habíais sacado
sacaba	sacaban	había sacado	habían sacado
3 pretérito		10 pretérito anterior	
saqué	sacamos	hube sacado	hubimos sacado
sacaste	sacasteis	hubiste sacado	hubisteis sacado
sacó	sacaron	hubo sacado	hubieron sacado
4 futuro		11 futuro perfecto	
sacaré	sacaremos	habré sacado	habremos sacado
sacarás	sacaréis	habrás sacado	habréis sacado
sacará	sacarán	habrá sacado	habrán sacado
5 potencial simple		12 potencial compuesto	
sacaría	sacaríamos	habría sacado	habríamos sacado
sacarías	sacaríais	habrías sacado	habríais sacado
sacaría	sacarían	habría sacado	habrían sacado
6 presente de subjuntivo		13 perfecto de subjuntivo	
saque	saquemos	haya sacado	hayamos sacado
saques	saquéis	hayas sacado	hayáis sacado
saque	saquen	haya sacado	hayan sacado
7 imperfecto de subjuntivo		14 pluscuamperfecto de subjuntivo	
sacara	sacáramos	hubiera sacado	hubiéramos sacado
sacaras	sacarais	hubieras sacado	hubierais sacado
sacara	sacaran	hubiera sacado	hubieran sacado
OR		OR	
sacase	sacásemos	hubiese sacado	hubiésemos sacado
sacases	sacaseis	hubieses sacado	hubieseis sacado
sacase	sacasen	hubiese sacado	hubiesen sacado

imperativo	
—	saquemos
saca; no saques	sacad; no saquéis
saque	saquen

Mi tío sacó una foto del presidente.
  My uncle took a picture of the
  president.
sacar agua to draw water
sacar fotos to take pictures
sacar a paseo to take out for a walk;
  ensacar to put in a bag, to bag

un saco bag, sack; saco de noche
  overnight bag
un sacapuntas pencil sharpener (un
  afilalápices)

salir

Gerundio **saliendo**   Part. pas. **salido**

to go out, to leave

Irregular verb

The Seven Simple Tenses		The Seven Compound Tenses	
Singular	Plural	Singular	Plural
1 presente de indicativo		8 perfecto de indicativo	
salgo	salimos	he salido	hemos salido
sales	salís	has salido	habéis salido
sale	salen	ha salido	han salido
2 imperfecto de indicativo		9 pluscuamperfecto de indicativo	
salía	salíamos	había salido	habíamos salido
salías	salíais	habías salido	habíais salido
salía	salían	había salido	habían salido
3 pretérito		10 pretérito anterior	
salí	salimos	hube salido	hubimos salido
saliste	salisteis	hubiste salido	hubisteis salido
salió	salieron	hubo salido	hubieron salido
4 futuro		11 futuro perfecto	
saldré	saldremos	habré salido	habremos salido
saldrás	saldréis	habrás salido	habréis salido
saldrá	saldrán	habrá salido	habrán salido
5 potencial simple		12 potencial compuesto	
saldría	saldríamos	habría salido	habríamos salido
saldrías	saldríais	habrías salido	habríais salido
saldría	saldrían	habría salido	habrían salido
6 presente de subjuntivo		13 perfecto de subjuntivo	
salga	salgamos	haya salido	hayamos salido
salgas	salgáis	hayas salido	hayáis salido
salga	salgan	haya salido	hayan salido
7 imperfecto de subjuntivo		14 pluscuamperfecto de subjuntivo	
saliera	saliéramos	hubiera salido	hubiéramos salido
salieras	salierais	hubieras salido	hubierais salido
saliera	salieran	hubiera salido	hubieran salido
OR		OR	
saliese	saliésemos	hubiese salido	hubiésemos salido
salieses	salieseis	hubieses salido	hubieseis salido
saliese	saliesen	hubiese salido	hubiesen salido

imperativo	
—	salgamos
sal; no salgas	salid; no salgáis
salga	salgan

¿A qué hora sale el tren para San
   José?   At what time does the train
   leave for San José?
la salida   exit
salir a   to resemble, to look like
sin salida   no exit, dead-end street

salir al encuentro de   to go to meet
salir de compras   to go out shopping
salir de   to leave from, to get out of
salir mal   to go wrong, to do badly
la salida de emergencia   emergency
   exit

Regular **-ar** verb endings with spelling
change: **c** becomes **qu** before **e**

to dry, to wipe dry

The Seven Simple Tenses		The Seven Compound Tenses	
Singular	Plural	Singular	Plural
1 presente de indicativo		8 perfecto de indicativo	
seco	secamos	he secado	hemos secado
secas	secáis	has secado	habéis secado
seca	secan	ha secado	han secado
2 imperfecto de indicativo		9 pluscuamperfecto de indicativo	
secaba	secábamos	había secado	habíamos secado
secabas	secabais	habías secado	habíais secado
secaba	secaban	había secado	habían secado
3 pretérito		10 pretérito anterior	
sequé	secamos	hube secado	hubimos secado
secaste	secasteis	hubiste secado	hubisteis secado
secó	secaron	hubo secado	hubieron secado
4 futuro		11 futuro perfecto	
secaré	secaremos	habré secado	habremos secado
secarás	secaréis	habrás secado	habréis secado
secará	secarán	habrá secado	habrán secado
5 potencial simple		12 potencial compuesto	
secaría	secaríamos	habría secado	habríamos secado
secarías	secaríais	habrías secado	habríais secado
secaría	secarían	habría secado	habrían secado
6 presente de subjuntivo		13 perfecto de subjuntivo	
seque	sequemos	haya secado	hayamos secado
seques	sequéis	hayas secado	hayáis secado
seque	sequen	haya secado	hayan secado
7 imperfecto de subjuntivo		14 pluscuamperfecto de subjuntivo	
secara	secáramos	hubiera secado	hubiéramos secado
secaras	secarais	hubieras secado	hubierais secado
secara	secaran	hubiera secado	hubieran secado
OR		OR	
secase	secásemos	hubiese secado	hubiésemos secado
secases	secaseis	hubieses secado	hubieseis secado
secase	secasen	hubiese secado	hubiesen secado

	imperativo	
—	sequemos	
seca; no seques	secad; no sequéis	
seque	sequen	

seco, seca dry, dried up	secado al sol sun dried
limpiar en seco to dry-clean	la secadora dryer, clothes dryer
la seca drought	¡Seco y volteado! Bottoms up!
en seco high and dry	

seguir

Gerundio **siguiendo**   Part. pas. **seguido**

to follow, to pursue, to continue

Regular **-ir** verb endings with stem change:
Tenses 1, 3, 6, 7, Imperative, *Gerundio*

The Seven Simple Tenses		The Seven Compound Tenses	
Singular	Plural	Singular	Plural
1 presente de indicativo		8 perfecto de indicativo	
sigo	seguimos	he seguido	hemos seguido
sigues	seguís	has seguido	habéis seguido
sigue	siguen	ha seguido	han seguido
2 imperfecto de indicativo		9 pluscuamperfecto de indicativo	
seguía	seguíamos	había seguido	habíamos seguido
seguías	seguíais	habías seguido	habíais seguido
seguía	seguían	había seguido	habían seguido
3 pretérito		10 pretérito anterior	
seguí	seguimos	hube seguido	hubimos seguido
seguiste	seguisteis	hubiste seguido	hubisteis seguido
siguió	siguieron	hubo seguido	hubieron seguido
4 futuro		11 futuro perfecto	
seguiré	seguiremos	habré seguido	habremos seguido
seguirás	seguiréis	habrás seguido	habréis seguido
seguirá	seguirán	habrá seguido	habrán seguido
5 potencial simple		12 potencial compuesto	
seguiría	seguiríamos	habría seguido	habríamos seguido
seguirías	seguiríais	habrías seguido	habríais seguido
seguiría	seguirían	habría seguido	habrían seguido
6 presente de subjuntivo		13 perfecto de subjuntivo	
siga	sigamos	haya seguido	hayamos seguido
sigas	sigáis	hayas seguido	hayáis seguido
siga	sigan	haya seguido	hayan seguido
7 imperfecto de subjuntivo		14 pluscuamperfecto de subjuntivo	
siguiera	siguiéramos	hubiera seguido	hubiéramos seguido
siguieras	siguierais	hubieras seguido	hubierais seguido
siguiera	siguieran	hubiera seguido	hubieran seguido
OR		OR	
siguiese	siguiésemos	hubiese seguido	hubiésemos seguido
siguieses	siguieseis	hubieses seguido	hubieseis seguido
siguiese	siguiesen	hubiese seguido	hubiesen seguido

imperativo

—	sigamos
sigue; no sigas	seguid; no sigáis
siga	sigan

según according to	seguirle los pasos a uno to keep one's
proseguir to continue, proceed	eye on someone
al día siguiente on the following day	seguir + pres. part. to keep on + pres.
perseguir to pursue	part.; Siga leyendo. Keep on
las frases siguientes the following	reading.
sentences	

sentarse

Reflexive verb; regular **-ar** verb endings with
stem change: Tenses 1, 6, Imperative

to sit down

The Seven Simple Tenses		The Seven Compound Tenses	
Singular	Plural	Singular	Plural

1 presente de indicativo		8 perfecto de indicativo	
me siento	nos sentamos	me he sentado	nos hemos sentado
te sientas	os sentáis	te has sentado	os habéis sentado
se sienta	se sientan	se ha sentado	se han sentado

2 imperfecto de indicativo		9 pluscuamperfecto de indicativo	
me sentaba	nos sentábamos	me había sentado	nos habíamos sentado
te sentabas	os sentabais	te habías sentado	os habíais sentado
se sentaba	se sentaban	se había sentado	se habían sentado

3 pretérito		10 pretérito anterior	
me senté	nos sentamos	me hube sentado	nos hubimos sentado
te sentaste	os sentasteis	te hubiste sentado	os hubisteis sentado
se sentó	se sentaron	se hubo sentado	se hubieron sentado

4 futuro		11 futuro perfecto	
me sentaré	nos sentaremos	me habré sentado	nos habremos sentado
te sentarás	os sentaréis	te habrás sentado	os habréis sentado
se sentará	se sentarán	se habrá sentado	se habrán sentado

5 potencial simple		12 potencial compuesto	
me sentaría	nos sentaríamos	me habría sentado	nos habríamos sentado
te sentarías	os sentaríais	te habrías sentado	os habríais sentado
se sentaría	se sentarían	se habría sentado	se habrían sentado

6 presente de subjuntivo		13 perfecto de subjuntivo	
me siente	nos sentemos	me haya sentado	nos hayamos sentado
te sientes	os sentéis	te hayas sentado	os hayáis sentado
se siente	se sienten	se haya sentado	se hayan sentado

7 imperfecto de subjuntivo		14 pluscuamperfecto de subjuntivo	
me sentara	nos sentáramos	me hubiera sentado	nos hubiéramos sentado
te sentaras	os sentarais	te hubieras sentado	os hubierais sentado
se sentara	se sentaran	se hubiera sentado	se hubieran sentado
OR		OR	
me sentase	nos sentásemos	me hubiese sentado	nos hubiésemos sentado
te sentases	os sentaseis	te hubieses sentado	os hubieseis sentado
se sentase	se sentasen	se hubiese sentado	se hubiesen sentado

imperativo		
—		sentémonos; no nos sentemos
	siéntate; no te sientes	sentaos; no os sentéis
	siéntese; no se siente	siéntense; no se sienten

un asiento a seat	¡Siéntese Ud.! Sit down!
sentar, asentar to seat	¡Vamos a sentarnos! Let's sit down!
sentado, sentada seated	
una sentada a sitting; de una sentada	
in one sitting	

sentir

Gerundio **sintiendo**   Part. pas. **sentido**

to feel sorry, to regret, to feel

Regular **-ir** verb endings with stem change:
Tenses 1, 3, 6, 7, Imperative, *Gerundio*

The Seven Simple Tenses		The Seven Compound Tenses	
Singular	Plural	Singular	Plural
1 presente de indicativo		8 perfecto de indicativo	
siento	**sentimos**	**he sentido**	**hemos sentido**
sientes	**sentís**	**has sentido**	**habéis sentido**
siente	**sienten**	**ha sentido**	**han sentido**
2 imperfecto de indicativo		9 pluscuamperfecto de indicativo	
sentía	**sentíamos**	**había sentido**	**habíamos sentido**
sentías	**sentíais**	**habías sentido**	**habíais sentido**
sentía	**sentían**	**había sentido**	**habían sentido**
3 pretérito		10 pretérito anterior	
sentí	**sentimos**	**hube sentido**	**hubimos sentido**
sentiste	**sentisteis**	**hubiste sentido**	**hubisteis sentido**
sintió	**sintieron**	**hubo sentido**	**hubieron sentido**
4 futuro		11 futuro perfecto	
sentiré	**sentiremos**	**habré sentido**	**habremos sentido**
sentirás	**sentiréis**	**habrás sentido**	**habréis sentido**
sentirá	**sentirán**	**habrá sentido**	**habrán sentido**
5 potencial simple		12 potencial compuesto	
sentiría	**sentiríamos**	**habría sentido**	**habríamos sentido**
sentirías	**sentiríais**	**habrías sentido**	**habríais sentido**
sentiría	**sentirían**	**habría sentido**	**habrían sentido**
6 presente de subjuntivo		13 perfecto de subjuntivo	
sienta	**sintamos**	**haya sentido**	**hayamos sentido**
sientas	**sintáis**	**hayas sentido**	**hayáis sentido**
sienta	**sientan**	**haya sentido**	**hayan sentido**
7 imperfecto de subjuntivo		14 pluscuamperfecto de subjuntivo	
sintiera	**sintiéramos**	**hubiera sentido**	**hubiéramos sentido**
sintieras	**sintierais**	**hubieras sentido**	**hubierais sentido**
sintiera	**sintieran**	**hubiera sentido**	**hubieran sentido**
OR		OR	
sintiese	**sintiésemos**	**hubiese sentido**	**hubiésemos sentido**
sintieses	**sintieseis**	**hubieses sentido**	**hubieseis sentido**
sintiese	**sintiesen**	**hubiese sentido**	**hubiesen sentido**

imperativo	
—	**sintamos**
siente; no sientas	**sentid; no sintáis**
sienta	**sientan**

La semana pasada sentimos un fuerte
  terremoto.   Last week we felt a
  powerful earthquake.
Lo siento.   I regret it; I'm sorry.
el sentir   feeling; judgment

el sentimiento   feeling, sentiment
un, una sentimental   sentimentalist
sentimentalmente   sentimentally
el sentido   sense, meaning, feeling
See also sentirse.

sentirse

Reflexive verb; regular **-ir** verb endings with stem
change: Tenses 1, 3, 6, 7, Imperative, *Gerundio*

to feel (well, ill)

The Seven Simple Tenses		The Seven Compound Tenses	
Singular	Plural	Singular	Plural
1 presente de indicativo		8 perfecto de indicativo	
me siento	nos sentimos	me he sentido	nos hemos sentido
te sientes	os sentís	te has sentido	os habéis sentido
se siente	se sienten	se ha sentido	se han sentido
2 imperfecto de indicativo		9 pluscuamperfecto de indicativo	
me sentía	nos sentíamos	me había sentido	nos habíamos sentido
te sentías	os sentíais	te habías sentido	os habíais sentido
se sentía	se sentían	se había sentido	se habían sentido
3 pretérito		10 pretérito anterior	
me sentí	nos sentimos	me hube sentido	nos hubimos sentido
te sentiste	os sentisteis	te hubiste sentido	os hubisteis sentido
se sintió	se sintieron	se hubo sentido	se hubieron sentido
4 futuro		11 futuro perfecto	
me sentiré	nos sentiremos	me habré sentido	nos habremos sentido
te sentirás	os sentiréis	te habrás sentido	os habréis sentido
se sentirá	se sentirán	se habrá sentido	se habrán sentido
5 potencial simple		12 potencial compuesto	
me sentiría	nos sentiríamos	me habría sentido	nos habríamos sentido
te sentirías	os sentiríais	te habrías sentido	os habríais sentido
se sentiría	se sentirían	se habría sentido	se habrían sentido
6 presente de subjuntivo		13 perfecto de subjuntivo	
me sienta	nos sintamos	me haya sentido	nos hayamos sentido
te sientas	os sintáis	te hayas sentido	os hayáis sentido
se sienta	se sientan	se haya sentido	se hayan sentido
7 imperfecto de subjuntivo		14 pluscuamperfecto de subjuntivo	
me sintiera	nos sintiéramos	me hubiera sentido	nos hubiéramos sentido
te sintieras	os sintierais	te hubieras sentido	os hubierais sentido
se sintiera	se sintieran	se hubiera sentido	se hubieran sentido
OR		OR	
me sintiese	nos sintiésemos	me hubiese sentido	nos hubiésemos sentido
te sintieses	os sintieseis	te hubieses sentido	os hubieseis sentido
se sintiese	se sintiesen	se hubiese sentido	se hubiesen sentido

imperativo	
—	sintámonos; no nos sintamos
siéntete; no te sientas	sentíos; no os sintáis
siéntase; no se sienta	siéntanse; no se sientan

¿**Cómo se siente Ud.?** How do you feel?	**resentirse** to feel the effects
	resentirse de algo to resent something
Me siento mal. I feel sick.	See also **sentir**.
los sentidos the senses	

ser

Gerundio **siendo** Part. pas. **sido**

to be

Irregular verb

The Seven Simple Tenses		The Seven Compound Tenses	
Singular	Plural	Singular	Plural
1 presente de indicativo		8 perfecto de indicativo	
soy	somos	he sido	hemos sido
eres	sois	has sido	habéis sido
es	son	ha sido	han sido
2 imperfecto de indicativo		9 pluscuamperfecto de indicativo	
era	éramos	había sido	habíamos sido
eras	erais	habías sido	habíais sido
era	eran	había sido	habían sido
3 pretérito		10 pretérito anterior	
fui	fuimos	hube sido	hubimos sido
fuiste	fuisteis	hubiste sido	hubisteis sido
fue	fueron	hubo sido	hubieron sido
4 futuro		11 futuro perfecto	
seré	seremos	habré sido	habremos sido
serás	seréis	habrás sido	habréis sido
será	serán	habrá sido	habrán sido
5 potencial simple		12 potencial compuesto	
sería	seríamos	habría sido	habríamos sido
serías	seríais	habrías sido	habríais sido
sería	serían	habría sido	habrían sido
6 presente de subjuntivo		13 perfecto de subjuntivo	
sea	seamos	haya sido	hayamos sido
seas	seáis	hayas sido	hayáis sido
sea	sean	haya sido	hayan sido
7 imperfecto de subjuntivo		14 pluscuamperfecto de subjuntivo	
fuera	fuéramos	hubiera sido	hubiéramos sido
fueras	fuerais	hubieras sido	hubierais sido
fuera	fueran	hubiera sido	hubieran sido
OR		OR	
fuese	fuésemos	hubiese sido	hubiésemos sido
fueses	fueseis	hubieses sido	hubieseis sido
fuese	fuesen	hubiese sido	hubiesen sido

imperativo

—	seamos
sé; no seas	sed; no seáis
sea	sean

Dime con quien andas y te diré quien eres. Tell me who your friends are and I will tell you who you are.
es decir that is, that is to say; **Si yo fuera usted . . .** If I were you . . .
¿Qué hora es? What time is it?

Es la una. It is one o'clock.
Son las dos. It is two o'clock.
Es (una) lástima. It's a pity. It's too bad.
ser aficionado a to be a fan of
ser amable con to be kind to
ser capaz to be able

Regular **-ir** verb endings with stem change: to serve
Tenses 1, 3, 6, 7, Imperative, *Gerundio*

The Seven Simple Tenses		The Seven Compound Tenses	
Singular	Plural	Singular	Plural
1 presente de indicativo		8 perfecto de indicativo	
sirvo	**servimos**	**he servido**	**hemos servido**
sirves	**servís**	**has servido**	**habéis servido**
sirve	**sirven**	**ha servido**	**han servido**
2 imperfecto de indicativo		9 pluscuamperfecto de indicativo	
servía	**servíamos**	**había servido**	**habíamos servido**
servías	**servíais**	**habías servido**	**habíais servido**
servía	**servían**	**había servido**	**habían servido**
3 pretérito		10 pretérito anterior	
serví	**servimos**	**hube servido**	**hubimos servido**
serviste	**servisteis**	**hubiste servido**	**hubisteis servido**
sirvió	**sirvieron**	**hubo servido**	**hubieron servido**
4 futuro		11 futuro perfecto	
serviré	**serviremos**	**habré servido**	**habremos servido**
servirás	**serviréis**	**habrás servido**	**habréis servido**
servirá	**servirán**	**habrá servido**	**habrán servido**
5 potencial simple		12 potencial compuesto	
serviría	**serviríamos**	**habría servido**	**habríamos servido**
servirías	**serviríais**	**habrías servido**	**habríais servido**
serviría	**servirían**	**habría servido**	**habrían servido**
6 presente de subjuntivo		13 perfecto de subjuntivo	
sirva	**sirvamos**	**haya servido**	**hayamos servido**
sirvas	**sirváis**	**hayas servido**	**hayáis servido**
sirva	**sirvan**	**haya servido**	**hayan servido**
7 imperfecto de subjuntivo		14 pluscuamperfecto de subjuntivo	
sirviera	**sirviéramos**	**hubiera servido**	**hubiéramos servido**
sirvieras	**sirvieras**	**hubieras servido**	**hubierais servido**
sirviera	**sirvieran**	**hubiera servido**	**hubieran servido**
OR		OR	
sirviese	**sirviésemos**	**hubiese servido**	**hubiésemos servido**
sirvieses	**sirvieseis**	**hubieses servido**	**hubieseis servido**
sirviese	**sirviesen**	**hubiese servido**	**hubiesen servido**

	imperativo	
—	**sirvamos**
sirve; no sirvas	**servid; no sirváis**
sirva	**sirvan**

servidor, servidora servant, waiter, waitress	**una servilleta** table napkin
¡Sírvase usted! Help yourself!	**servirse** to serve oneself
el servicio service	**servir para** to be good for
Esto no sirve para nada. This serves no purpose.	**el servicio de soporte técnico** technical support service

soler

Gerundio **soliendo**   Part. pas. **solido**

to be accustomed to, to be in
the habit of, to have the custom of

Regular **-er** verb endings with
stem change: Tenses 1 and 6

The Seven Simple Tenses		The Seven Compound Tenses	
Singular	Plural	Singular	Plural
1 presente de indicativo		**8 perfecto de indicativo**	
suelo	solemos	he solido	hemos solido
sueles	soléis	has solido	habéis solido
suele	suelen	ha solido	han solido
2 imperfecto de indicativo			
solía	solíamos		
solías	solíais		
solía	solían		
6 presente de subjuntivo			
suela	solamos		
suelas	soláis		
suela	suelan		

This verb is defective and it is, therefore, used primarily in the tenses given above. When used, it is always followed by an infinitive.

Suelo acostarme a las diez. I am in the habit of going to bed at ten.

Regular **-ar** verb endings with stem change: to dream
Tenses 1, 6, Imperative

The Seven Simple Tenses		The Seven Compound Tenses	
Singular	Plural	Singular	Plural
1 presente de indicativo		8 perfecto de indicativo	
sueño	soñamos	he soñado	hemos soñado
sueñas	soñáis	has soñado	habéis soñado
sueña	sueñan	ha soñado	han soñado
2 imperfecto de indicativo		9 pluscuamperfecto de indicativo	
soñaba	soñábamos	había soñado	habíamos soñado
soñabas	soñabais	habías soñado	habíais soñado
soñaba	soñaban	había soñado	habían soñado
3 pretérito		10 pretérito anterior	
soñé	soñamos	hube soñado	hubimos soñado
soñaste	soñasteis	hubiste soñado	hubisteis soñado
soñó	soñaron	hubo soñado	hubieron soñado
4 futuro		11 futuro perfecto	
soñaré	soñaremos	habré soñado	habremos soñado
soñarás	soñaréis	habrás soñado	habréis soñado
soñará	soñarán	habrá soñado	habrán soñado
5 potencial simple		12 potencial compuesto	
soñaría	soñaríamos	habría soñado	habríamos soñado
soñarías	soñaríais	habrías soñado	habríais soñado
soñaría	soñarían	habría soñado	habrían soñado
6 presente de subjuntivo		13 perfecto de subjuntivo	
sueñe	soñemos	haya soñado	hayamos soñado
sueñes	soñéis	hayas soñado	hayáis soñado
sueñe	sueñen	haya soñado	hayan soñado
7 imperfecto de subjuntivo		14 pluscuamperfecto de subjuntivo	
soñara	soñáramos	hubiera soñado	hubiéramos soñado
soñaras	soñarais	hubieras soñado	hubierais soñado
soñara	soñaran	hubiera soñado	hubieran soñado
OR		OR	
soñase	soñásemos	hubiese soñado	hubiésemos soñado
soñases	soñaseis	hubieses soñado	hubieseis soñado
soñase	soñasen	hubiese soñado	hubiesen soñado

imperativo	
—	soñemos
sueña; no sueñes	soñad; no soñéis
sueñe	sueñen

soñar con, soñar en to dream of	sueño pesado sound sleep
un sueño hecho realidad a dream come true	el sueño sleep, dream
soñar despierto to daydream	echar un sueño to take a nap
soñador, soñadora dreamer	tener sueño to be sleepy

sonreír

Gerundio **sonriendo**   Part. pas. **sonreído**

to smile

Regular **-ir** verb endings with stem change:
Tenses 1, 3, 6, 7, Imperative, *Gerundio*

The Seven Simple Tenses		The Seven Compound Tenses	
Singular	Plural	Singular	Plural
1 presente de indicativo		8 perfecto de indicativo	
sonrío	sonreímos	he sonreído	hemos sonreído
sonríes	sonreís	has sonreído	habéis sonreído
sonríe	sonríen	ha sonreído	han sonreído
2 imperfecto de indicativo		9 pluscuamperfecto de indicativo	
sonreía	sonreíamos	había sonreído	habíamos sonreído
sonreías	sonreíais	habías sonreído	habíais sonreído
sonreía	sonreían	había sonreído	habían sonreído
3 pretérito		10 pretérito anterior	
sonreí	sonreímos	hube sonreído	hubimos sonreído
sonreíste	sonreísteis	hubiste sonreído	hubisteis sonreído
sonrió	sonrieron	hubo sonreído	hubieron sonreído
4 futuro		11 futuro perfecto	
sonreiré	sonreiremos	habré sonreído	habremos sonreído
sonreirás	sonreiréis	habrás sonreído	habréis sonreído
sonreirá	sonreirán	habrá sonreído	habrán sonreído
5 potencial simple		12 potencial compuesto	
sonreiría	sonreiríamos	habría sonreído	habríamos sonreído
sonreirías	sonreiríais	habrías sonreído	habríais sonreído
sonreiría	sonreirían	habría sonreído	habrían sonreído
6 presente de subjuntivo		13 perfecto de subjuntivo	
sonría	sonriamos	haya sonreído	hayamos sonreído
sonrías	sonriáis	hayas sonreído	hayáis sonreído
sonría	sonrían	haya sonreído	hayan sonreído
7 imperfecto de subjuntivo		14 pluscuamperfecto de subjuntivo	
sonriera	sonriéramos	hubiera sonreído	hubiéramos sonreído
sonrieras	sonrierais	hubieras sonreído	hubierais sonreído
sonriera	sonrieran	hubiera sonreído	hubieran sonreído
OR		OR	
sonriese	sonriésemos	hubiese sonreído	hubiésemos sonreído
sonrieses	sonrieseis	hubieses sonreído	hubieseis sonreído
sonriese	sonriesen	hubiese sonreído	hubiesen sonreído

imperativo

—	sonriamos
sonríe; no sonrías	sonreíd; no sonriáis
sonría	sonrían

La Gioconda tiene una sonrisa bonita.
  The Mona Lisa has a pretty smile.
la sonrisa   smile; no perder la sonrisa
  not to lose a smile, to keep smiling

sonriente   smiling
sonreír a alguien   to smile at someone
See also reír.

telefonear

Regular **-ar** verb

to telephone

The Seven Simple Tenses		The Seven Compound Tenses	
Singular	Plural	Singular	Plural
1 presente de indicativo		8 perfecto de indicativo	
telefoneo	telefoneamos	he telefoneado	hemos telefoneado
telefoneas	telefoneáis	has telefoneado	habéis telefoneado
telefonea	telefonean	ha telefoneado	han telefoneado
2 imperfecto de indicativo		9 pluscuamperfecto de indicativo	
telefoneaba	telefoneábamos	había telefoneado	habíamos telefoneado
telefoneabas	telefoneabais	habías telefoneado	habíais telefoneado
telefoneaba	telefoneaban	había telefoneado	habían telefoneado
3 pretérito		10 pretérito anterior	
telefoneé	telefoneamos	hube telefoneado	hubimos telefoneado
telefoneaste	telefoneasteis	hubiste telefoneado	hubisteis telefoneado
telefoneó	telefonearon	hubo telefoneado	hubieron telefoneado
4 futuro		11 futuro perfecto	
telefonearé	telefonearemos	habré telefoneado	habremos telefoneado
telefonearás	telefonearéis	habrás telefoneado	habréis telefoneado
telefoneará	telefonearán	habrá telefoneado	habrán telefoneado
5 potencial simple		12 potencial compuesto	
telefonearía	telefonearíamos	habría telefoneado	habríamos telefoneado
telefonearías	telefonearíais	habrías telefoneado	habríais telefoneado
telefonearía	telefonearían	habría telefoneado	habrían telefoneado
6 presente de subjuntivo		13 perfecto de subjuntivo	
telefonee	telefoneemos	haya telefoneado	hayamos telefoneado
telefonees	telefoneéis	hayas telefoneado	hayáis telefoneado
telefonee	telefoneen	haya telefoneado	hayan telefoneado
7 imperfecto de subjuntivo		14 pluscuamperfecto de subjuntivo	
telefoneara	telefoneáramos	hubiera telefoneado	hubiéramos telefoneado
telefonearas	telefonearais	hubieras telefoneado	hubierais telefoneado
telefoneara	telefonearan	hubiera telefoneado	hubieran telefoneado
OR		OR	
telefonease	telefoneásemos	hubiese telefoneado	hubiésemos telefoneado
telefoneases	telefoneaseis	hubieses telefoneado	hubieseis telefoneado
telefonease	telefoneasen	hubiese telefoneado	hubiesen telefoneado

imperativo	
—	telefoneemos
telefonea; no telefonees	telefonead; no telefoneéis
telefonee	telefoneen

el teléfono telephone	telefónico, telefónica telephonic
la cabina telefónica telephone booth	por teléfono by telephone
telefonista telephone operator	la guía telefónica telephone book
el número de teléfono telephone number	un teléfono celular cell phone

tener

Gerundio **teniendo** Part. pas. **tenido**

to have, to hold Irregular verb

The Seven Simple Tenses		The Seven Compound Tenses	
Singular	Plural	Singular	Plural
1 presente de indicativo		8 perfecto de indicativo	
tengo	tenemos	he tenido	hemos tenido
tienes	tenéis	has tenido	habéis tenido
tiene	tienen	ha tenido	han tenido
2 imperfecto de indicativo		9 pluscuamperfecto de indicativo	
tenía	teníamos	había tenido	habíamos tenido
tenías	teníais	habías tenido	habíais tenido
tenía	tenían	había tenido	habían tenido
3 pretérito		10 pretérito anterior	
tuve	tuvimos	hube tenido	hubimos tenido
tuviste	tuvisteis	hubiste tenido	hubisteis tenido
tuvo	tuvieron	hubo tenido	hubieron tenido
4 futuro		11 futuro perfecto	
tendré	tendremos	habré tenido	habremos tenido
tendrás	tendréis	habrás tenido	habréis tenido
tendrá	tendrán	habrá tenido	habrán tenido
5 potencial simple		12 potencial compuesto	
tendría	tendríamos	habría tenido	habríamos tenido
tendrías	tendríais	habrías tenido	habríais tenido
tendría	tendrían	habría tenido	habrían tenido
6 presente de subjuntivo		13 perfecto de subjuntivo	
tenga	tengamos	haya tenido	hayamos tenido
tengas	tengáis	hayas tenido	hayáis tenido
tenga	tengan	haya tenido	hayan tenido
7 imperfecto de subjuntivo		14 pluscuamperfecto de subjuntivo	
tuviera	tuviéramos	hubiera tenido	hubiéramos tenido
tuvieras	tuvierais	hubieras tenido	hubierais tenido
tuviera	tuvieran	hubiera tenido	hubieran tenido
OR		OR	
tuviese	tuviésemos	hubiese tenido	hubiésemos tenido
tuvieses	tuvieseis	hubieses tenido	hubieseis tenido
tuviese	tuviesen	hubiese tenido	hubiesen tenido

imperativo	
—	tengamos
ten; no tengas	tened; no tengáis
tenga	tengan

¡Tengo mucha hambre! I'm very hungry!
Tienes que estudiar. You have to study.
Anda despacio que tengo prisa.
  Make haste slowly.
tener prisa to be in a hurry

tener frío to be (feel) cold (persons)
tener hambre to be hungry
tener calor to be (feel) warm (persons)
tener sed to be thirsty
retener to retain

Gerundio **terminando**   Part. pas. **terminado**   **terminar**

Regular **-ar** verb   to end, to terminate, to finish

The Seven Simple Tenses		The Seven Compound Tenses	
Singular	Plural	Singular	Plural
1 presente de indicativo		8 perfecto de indicativo	
termino	terminamos	he terminado	hemos terminado
terminas	termináis	has terminado	habéis terminado
termina	terminan	ha terminado	han terminado
2 imperfecto de indicativo		9 pluscuamperfecto de indicativo	
terminaba	terminábamos	había terminado	habíamos terminado
terminabas	terminabais	habías terminado	habíais terminado
terminaba	terminaban	había terminado	habían terminado
3 pretérito		10 pretérito anterior	
terminé	terminamos	hube terminado	hubimos terminado
terminaste	terminasteis	hubiste terminado	hubisteis terminado
terminó	terminaron	hubo terminado	hubieron terminado
4 futuro		11 futuro perfecto	
terminaré	terminaremos	habré terminado	habremos terminado
terminarás	terminaréis	habrás terminado	habréis terminado
terminará	terminarán	habrá terminado	habrán terminado
5 potencial simple		12 potencial compuesto	
terminaría	terminaríamos	habría terminado	habríamos terminado
terminarías	terminaríais	habrías terminado	habríais terminado
terminaría	terminarían	habría terminado	habrían terminado
6 presente de subjuntivo		13 perfecto de subjuntivo	
termine	terminemos	haya terminado	hayamos terminado
termines	terminéis	hayas terminado	hayáis terminado
termine	terminen	haya terminado	hayan terminado
7 imperfecto de subjuntivo		14 pluscuamperfecto de subjuntivo	
terminara	termináramos	hubiera terminado	hubiéramos terminado
terminaras	terminarais	hubieras terminado	hubierais terminado
terminara	terminaran	hubiera terminado	hubieran terminado
OR		OR	
terminase	terminásemos	hubiese terminado	hubiésemos terminado
terminases	terminaseis	hubieses terminado	hubieseis terminado
terminase	terminasen	hubiese terminado	hubiesen terminado

	imperativo	
—	terminemos	
termina; no termines	terminad; no terminéis	
termine	terminen	

la terminación termination, ending, completion	**estar en buenos términos con** to be on good terms with
terminante conclusive	**llevar a término** to complete
el término end, ending; term	**la terminal aérea** air terminal
determinar to determine	
en otros términos in other terms, in other words	

281

tirar

Gerundio **tirando**   Part. pas. **tirado**

to pull, to draw, to pitch (a ball), to shoot (a gun),   Regular **-ar** verb
to throw, to fling, to print (typography)

The Seven Simple Tenses		The Seven Compound Tenses	
Singular	Plural	Singular	Plural
1 presente de indicativo		8 perfecto de indicativo	
tiro	**tiramos**	**he tirado**	**hemos tirado**
tiras	**tiráis**	**has tirado**	**habéis tirado**
tira	**tiran**	**ha tirado**	**han tirado**
2 imperfecto de indicativo		9 pluscuamperfecto de indicativo	
tiraba	**tirábamos**	**había tirado**	**habíamos tirado**
tirabas	**tirabais**	**habías tirado**	**habíais tirado**
tiraba	**tiraban**	**había tirado**	**habían tirado**
3 pretérito		10 pretérito anterior	
tiré	**tiramos**	**hube tirado**	**hubimos tirado**
tiraste	**tirasteis**	**hubiste tirado**	**hubisteis tirado**
tiró	**tiraron**	**hubo tirado**	**hubieron tirado**
4 futuro		11 futuro perfecto	
tiraré	**tiraremos**	**habré tirado**	**habremos tirado**
tirarás	**tiraréis**	**habrás tirado**	**habréis tirado**
tirará	**tirarán**	**habrá tirado**	**habrán tirado**
5 potencial simple		12 potencial compuesto	
tiraría	**tiraríamos**	**habría tirado**	**habríamos tirado**
tirarías	**tiraríais**	**habrías tirado**	**habríais tirado**
tiraría	**tirarían**	**habría tirado**	**habrían tirado**
6 presente de subjuntivo		13 perfecto de subjuntivo	
tire	**tiremos**	**haya tirado**	**hayamos tirado**
tires	**tiréis**	**hayas tirado**	**hayáis tirado**
tire	**tiren**	**haya tirado**	**hayan tirado**
7 imperfecto de subjuntivo		14 pluscuamperfecto de subjuntivo	
tirara	**tiráramos**	**hubiera tirado**	**hubiéramos tirado**
tiraras	**tirarais**	**hubieras tirado**	**hubierais tirado**
tirara	**tiraran**	**hubiera tirado**	**hubieran tirado**
OR		OR	
tirase	**tirásemos**	**hubiese tirado**	**hubiésemos tirado**
tirases	**tiraseis**	**hubieses tirado**	**hubieseis tirado**
tirase	**tirasen**	**hubiese tirado**	**hubiesen tirado**

imperativo	
—	**tiremos**
tira; no tires	**tirad; no tiréis**
tire	**tiren**

tirar a   to shoot at
tirar una línea   to draw a line
a tiro   within reach; a tiro de piedra
   within a stone's throw; ni a tiros   not

for love nor money; al tiro   right
away
tirarse al agua   to jump in the water

282

Regular **-ar** verb endings with spelling
change: **c** becomes **qu** before **e**

to play (music or a musical
instrument), to touch

The Seven Simple Tenses		The Seven Compound Tenses	
Singular	Plural	Singular	Plural
1 presente de indicativo		8 perfecto de indicativo	
toco	tocamos	he tocado	hemos tocado
tocas	tocáis	has tocado	habéis tocado
toca	tocan	ha tocado	han tocado
2 imperfecto de indicativo		9 pluscuamperfecto de indicativo	
tocaba	tocábamos	había tocado	habíamos tocado
tocabas	tocabais	habías tocado	habíais tocado
tocaba	tocaban	había tocado	habían tocado
3 pretérito		10 pretérito anterior	
toqué	tocamos	hube tocado	hubimos tocado
tocaste	tocasteis	hubiste tocado	hubisteis tocado
tocó	tocaron	hubo tocado	hubieron tocado
4 futuro		11 futuro perfecto	
tocaré	tocaremos	habré tocado	habremos tocado
tocarás	tocaréis	habrás tocado	habréis tocado
tocará	tocarán	habrá tocado	habrán tocado
5 potencial simple		12 potencial compuesto	
tocaría	tocaríamos	habría tocado	habríamos tocado
tocarías	tocaríais	habrías tocado	habríais tocado
tocaría	tocarían	habría tocado	habrían tocado
6 presente de subjuntivo		13 perfecto de subjuntivo	
toque	toquemos	haya tocado	hayamos tocado
toques	toquéis	hayas tocado	hayáis tocado
toque	toquen	haya tocado	hayan tocado
7 imperfecto de subjuntivo		14 pluscuamperfecto de subjuntivo	
tocara	tocáramos	hubiera tocado	hubiéramos tocado
tocaras	tocarais	hubieras tocado	hubierais tocado
tocara	tocaran	hubiera tocado	hubieran tocado
OR		OR	
tocase	tocásemos	hubiese tocado	hubiésemos tocado
tocases	tocaseis	hubieses tocado	hubieseis tocado
tocase	tocasen	hubiese tocado	hubiesen tocado

imperativo	
—	toquemos
toca; no toques	tocad; no toquéis
toque	toquen

¿Sabe Ud. tocar el piano?   Do you
 know how to play the piano?
Sí, yo sé tocar el piano.   Yes, I know
 how to play the piano.
tocar a la puerta   to knock on the door

tocar a uno   to be someone's turn; Le
 toca a Juan.   It's John's turn.
Don't confuse tocar with jugar, which
 also means *to play*.

tomar
Gerundio **tomando**   Part. pas. **tomado**

to take , to have   Regular **-ar** verb
(something to eat or drink)

The Seven Simple Tenses		The Seven Compound Tenses	
Singular	Plural	Singular	Plural
1 presente de indicativo		8 perfecto de indicativo	
tomo	tomamos	he tomado	hemos tomado
tomas	tomáis	has tomado	habéis tomado
toma	toman	ha tomado	han tomado
2 imperfecto de indicativo		9 pluscuamperfecto de indicativo	
tomaba	tomábamos	había tomado	habíamos tomado
tomabas	tomabais	habías tomado	habíais tomado
tomaba	tomaban	había tomado	habían tomado
3 pretérito		10 pretérito anterior	
tomé	tomamos	hube tomado	hubimos tomado
tomaste	tomasteis	hubiste tomado	hubisteis tomado
tomó	tomaron	hubo tomado	hubieron tomado
4 futuro		11 futuro perfecto	
tomaré	tomaremos	habré tomado	habremos tomado
tomarás	tomaréis	habrás tomado	habréis tomado
tomará	tomarán	habrá tomado	habrán tomado
5 potencial simple		12 potencial compuesto	
tomaría	tomaríamos	habría tomado	habríamos tomado
tomarías	tomaríais	habrías tomado	habríais tomado
tomaría	tomarían	habría tomado	habrían tomado
6 presente de subjuntivo		13 perfecto de subjuntivo	
tome	tomemos	haya tomado	hayamos tomado
tomes	toméis	hayas tomado	hayáis tomado
tome	tomen	haya tomado	hayan tomado
7 imperfecto de subjuntivo		14 pluscuamperfecto de subjuntivo	
tomara	tomáramos	hubiera tomado	hubiéramos tomado
tomaras	tomarais	hubieras tomado	hubierais tomado
tomara	tomaran	hubiera tomado	hubieran tomado
OR		OR	
tomase	tomásemos	hubiese tomado	hubiésemos tomado
tomases	tomaseis	hubieses tomado	hubieseis tomado
tomase	tomasen	hubiese tomado	hubiesen tomado

imperativo	
—	tomemos
toma; no tomes	tomad; no toméis
tome	tomen

¿A qué hora toma Ud. el desayuno?
  At what time do you have breakfast?
Tomo el desayuno a las siete y media.
  I have breakfast at seven thirty.
¿Qué toma Ud. en el desayuno?
  What do you have for breakfast?

tomar el sol   to take a sun bath
tomar en cuenta   to consider
tomar parte en   to take part in
tomar asiento   to take a seat
tomar nota   to take note (of)

trabajar

Regular **-ar** verb   to work, to labor

The Seven Simple Tenses		The Seven Compound Tenses	
Singular	Plural	Singular	Plural
1 presente de indicativo		8 perfecto de indicativo	
trabajo	**trabajamos**	**he trabajado**	**hemos trabajado**
trabajas	**trabajáis**	**has trabajado**	**habéis trabajado**
trabaja	**trabajan**	**ha trabajado**	**han trabajado**
2 imperfecto de indicativo		9 pluscuamperfecto de indicativo	
trabajaba	**trabajábamos**	**había trabajado**	**habíamos trabajado**
trabajabas	**trabajabais**	**habías trabajado**	**habíais trabajado**
trabajaba	**trabajaban**	**había trabajado**	**habían trabajado**
3 pretérito		10 pretérito anterior	
trabajé	**trabajamos**	**hube trabajado**	**hubimos trabajado**
trabajaste	**trabajasteis**	**hubiste trabajado**	**hubisteis trabajado**
trabajó	**trabajaron**	**hubo trabajado**	**hubieron trabajado**
4 futuro		11 futuro perfecto	
trabajaré	**trabajaremos**	**habré trabajado**	**habremos trabajado**
trabajarás	**trabajaréis**	**habrás trabajado**	**habréis trabajado**
trabajará	**trabajarán**	**habrá trabajado**	**habrán trabajado**
5 potencial simple		12 potencial compuesto	
trabajaría	**trabajaríamos**	**habría trabajado**	**habríamos trabajado**
trabajarías	**trabajaríais**	**habrías trabajado**	**habríais trabajado**
trabajaría	**trabajarían**	**habría trabajado**	**habrían trabajado**
6 presente de subjuntivo		13 perfecto de subjuntivo	
trabaje	**trabajemos**	**haya trabajado**	**hayamos trabajado**
trabajes	**trabajéis**	**hayas trabajado**	**hayáis trabajado**
trabaje	**trabajen**	**haya trabajado**	**hayan trabajado**
7 imperfecto de subjuntivo		14 pluscuamperfecto de subjuntivo	
trabajara	**trabajáramos**	**hubiera trabajado**	**hubiéramos trabajado**
trabajaras	**trabajarais**	**hubieras trabajado**	**hubierais trabajado**
trabajara	**trabajaran**	**hubiera trabajado**	**hubieran trabajado**
OR		OR	
trabajase	**trabajásemos**	**hubiese trabajado**	**hubiésemos trabajado**
trabajases	**trabajaseis**	**hubieses trabajado**	**hubieseis trabajado**
trabajase	**trabajasen**	**hubiese trabajado**	**hubiesen trabajado**

	imperativo	
—	**trabajemos**
trabaja; no trabajes	**trabajad; no trabajéis**
trabaje	**trabajen**

Mi hermana **trabaja** a tiempo parcial para pagar su matrícula. My sister works part-time to pay (for) her tuition.	**trabajador, trabajadora** worker
	trabajar de manos to do manual work
	trabajar en + inf. to strive + inf.
el trabajo work	**tener trabajo que hacer** to have work to do

traducir

Gerundio **traduciendo** Part. pas. **traducido**

to translate

Irregular in Tenses 3 and 7, regular **-ir** endings in all others; spelling change: **c** becomes **zc** before **a** or **o**

The Seven Simple Tenses		The Seven Compound Tenses	
Singular	Plural	Singular	Plural
1 presente de indicativo		**8 perfecto de indicativo**	
traduzco	traducimos	he traducido	hemos traducido
traduces	traducís	has traducido	habéis traducido
traduce	traducen	ha traducido	han traducido
2 imperfecto de indicativo		**9 pluscuamperfecto de indicativo**	
traducía	traducíamos	había traducido	habíamos traducido
traducías	traducíais	habías traducido	habíais traducido
traducía	traducían	había traducido	habían traducido
3 pretérito		**10 pretérito anterior**	
traduje	tradujimos	hube traducido	hubimos traducido
tradujiste	tradujisteis	hubiste traducido	hubisteis traducido
tradujo	tradujeron	hubo traducido	hubieron traducido
4 futuro		**11 futuro perfecto**	
traduciré	traduciremos	habré traducido	habremos traducido
traducirás	traduciréis	habrás traducido	habréis traducido
traducirá	traducirán	habrá traducido	habrán traducido
5 potencial simple		**12 potencial compuesto**	
traduciría	traduciríamos	habría traducido	habríamos traducido
traducirías	traduciríais	habrías traducido	habríais traducido
traduciría	traducirían	habría traducido	habrían traducido
6 presente de subjuntivo		**13 perfecto de subjuntivo**	
traduzca	traduzcamos	haya traducido	hayamos traducido
traduzcas	traduzcáis	hayas traducido	hayáis traducido
traduzca	traduzcan	haya traducido	hayan traducido
7 imperfecto de subjuntivo		**14 pluscuamperfecto de subjuntivo**	
tradujera	tradujéramos	hubiera traducido	hubiéramos traducido
tradujeras	tradujerais	hubieras traducido	hubierais traducido
tradujera	tradujeran	hubiera traducido	hubieran traducido
OR		OR	
tradujese	tradujésemos	hubiese traducido	hubiésemos traducido
tradujeses	tradujeseis	hubieses traducido	hubieseis traducido
tradujese	tradujesen	hubiese traducido	hubiesen traducido

imperativo	
—	traduzcamos
traduce; no traduzcas	traducid; no traduzcáis
traduzca	traduzcan

la traducción translation	traducir del español al inglés to
traducible translatable	translate from Spanish to English
traductor, traductora translator	
traducir del inglés al español to	
translate from English to Spanish	

Irregular verb   to bring

The Seven Simple Tenses		The Seven Compound Tenses	
Singular	Plural	Singular	Plural
1 presente de indicativo		8 perfecto de indicativo	
traigo	traemos	he traído	hemos traído
traes	traéis	has traído	habéis traído
trae	traen	ha traído	han traído
2 imperfecto de indicativo		9 pluscuamperfecto de indicativo	
traía	traíamos	había traído	habíamos traído
traías	traíais	habías traído	habíais traído
traía	traían	había traído	habían traído
3 pretérito		10 pretérito anterior	
traje	trajimos	hube traído	hubimos traído
trajiste	trajisteis	hubiste traído	hubisteis traído
trajo	trajeron	hubo traído	hubieron traído
4 futuro		11 futuro perfecto	
traeré	traeremos	habré traído	habremos traído
traerás	traeréis	habrás traído	habréis traído
traerá	traerán	habrá traído	habrán traído
5 potencial simple		12 potencial compuesto	
traería	traeríamos	habría traído	habríamos traído
traerías	traeríais	habrías traído	habríais traído
traería	traerían	habría traído	habrían traído
6 presente de subjuntivo		13 perfecto de subjuntivo	
traiga	traigamos	haya traído	hayamos traído
traigas	traigáis	hayas traído	hayáis traído
traiga	traigan	haya traído	hayan traído
7 imperfecto de subjuntivo		14 pluscuamperfecto de subjuntivo	
trajera	trajéramos	hubiera traído	hubiéramos traído
trajeras	trajerais	hubieras traído	hubierais traído
trajera	trajeran	hubiera traído	hubieran traído
OR		OR	
trajese	trajésemos	hubiese traído	hubiésemos traído
trajeses	trajeseis	hubieses traído	hubieseis traído
trajese	trajesen	hubiese traído	hubiesen traído

imperativo

—	traigamos
trae; no traigas	traed; no traigáis
traiga	traigan

Tráigame una silla, por favor.   Bring me a chair, please.

¿Qué te trae por aquí?   What brings you here?

el traje   costume, dress, suit

el traje de baño   bathing suit

contraer   to contract

el traje hecho   ready-made suit

traer a la mente   to bring to mind

traer buena suerte   to bring good luck

tropezar

Gerundio **tropezando**   Part. pas. **tropezado**

to stumble, to blunder

Regular **-ar** verb endings with stem change: Tenses 1, 6, Imperative; spelling change: **z** becomes **c** before **e**

The Seven Simple Tenses		The Seven Compound Tenses	
Singular	Plural	Singular	Plural
1 presente de indicativo		8 perfecto de indicativo	
tropiezo	**tropezamos**	**he tropezado**	**hemos tropezado**
tropiezas	**tropezáis**	**has tropezado**	**habéis tropezado**
tropieza	**tropiezan**	**ha tropezado**	**han tropezado**
2 imperfecto de indicativo		9 pluscuamperfecto de indicativo	
tropezaba	**tropezábamos**	**había tropezado**	**habíamos tropezado**
tropezabas	**tropezabais**	**habías tropezado**	**habíais tropezado**
tropezaba	**tropezaban**	**había tropezado**	**habían tropezado**
3 pretérito		10 pretérito anterior	
tropecé	**tropezamos**	**hube tropezado**	**hubimos tropezado**
tropezaste	**tropezasteis**	**hubiste tropezado**	**hubisteis tropezado**
tropezó	**tropezaron**	**hubo tropezado**	**hubieron tropezado**
4 futuro		11 futuro perfecto	
tropezaré	**tropezaremos**	**habré tropezado**	**habremos tropezado**
tropezarás	**tropezaréis**	**habrás tropezado**	**habréis tropezado**
tropezará	**tropezarán**	**habrá tropezado**	**habrán tropezado**
5 potencial simple		12 potencial compuesto	
tropezaría	**tropezaríamos**	**habría tropezado**	**habríamos tropezado**
tropezarías	**tropezaríais**	**habrías tropezado**	**habríais tropezado**
tropezaría	**tropezarían**	**habría tropezado**	**habrían tropezado**
6 presente de subjuntivo		13 perfecto de subjuntivo	
tropiece	**tropecemos**	**haya tropezado**	**hayamos tropezado**
tropieces	**tropecéis**	**hayas tropezado**	**hayáis tropezado**
tropiece	**tropiecen**	**haya tropezado**	**hayan tropezado**
7 imperfecto de subjuntivo		14 pluscuamperfecto de subjuntivo	
tropezara	**tropezáramos**	**hubiera tropezado**	**hubiéramos tropezado**
tropezaras	**tropezarais**	**hubieras tropezado**	**hubierais tropezado**
tropezara	**tropezaran**	**hubiera tropezado**	**hubieran tropezado**
OR		OR	
tropezase	**tropezásemos**	**hubiese tropezado**	**hubiésemos tropezado**
tropezases	**tropezaseis**	**hubieses tropezado**	**hubieseis tropezado**
tropezase	**tropezasen**	**hubiese tropezado**	**hubiesen tropezado**

imperativo	
—	**tropecemos**
tropieza; no tropieces	**tropezad; no tropecéis**
tropiece	**tropiecen**

tropezar con alguien to run across someone, to meet someone unexpectedly	tropezador, tropezadora tripper, stumbler
la tropezadura stumbling	dar un tropezón to trip, to stumble

Regular **-ir** verb

to connect, to unite,
to join, to bind, to attach

The Seven Simple Tenses		The Seven Compound Tenses	
Singular	Plural	Singular	Plural
1 presente de indicativo		8 perfecto de indicativo	
uno	unimos	he unido	hemos unido
unes	unís	has unido	habéis unido
une	unen	ha unido	han unido
2 imperfecto de indicativo		9 pluscuamperfecto de indicativo	
unía	uníamos	había unido	habíamos unido
unías	uníais	habías unido	habíais unido
unía	unían	había unido	habían unido
3 pretérito		10 pretérito anterior	
uní	unimos	hube unido	hubimos unido
uniste	unisteis	hubiste unido	hubisteis unido
unió	unieron	hubo unido	hubieron unido
4 futuro		11 futuro perfecto	
uniré	uniremos	habré unido	habremos unido
unirás	uniréis	habrás unido	habréis unido
unirá	unirán	habrá unido	habrán unido
5 potencial simple		12 potencial compuesto	
uniría	uniríamos	habría unido	habríamos unido
unirías	uniríais	habrías unido	habríais unido
uniría	unirían	habría unido	habrían unido
6 presente de subjuntivo		13 perfecto de subjuntivo	
una	unamos	haya unido	hayamos unido
unas	unáis	hayas unido	hayáis unido
una	unan	haya unido	hayan unido
7 imperfecto de subjuntivo		14 pluscuamperfecto de subjuntivo	
uniera	uniéramos	hubiera unido	hubiéramos unido
unieras	unierais	hubieras unido	hubierais unido
uniera	unieran	hubiera unido	hubieran unido
OR		OR	
uniese	uniésemos	hubiese unido	hubiésemos unido
unieses	unieseis	hubieses unido	hubieseis unido
uniese	uniesen	hubiese unido	hubiesen unido

imperativo	
—	unamos
une; no unas	unid; no unáis
una	unan

unido, unida united	**la unión** union, agreement, harmony
unirse to be united; to get married	**las Naciones Unidas (ONU)** the
los Estados Unidos the United States	United Nations (UN)
La unión hace la fuerza. There is	
strength in unity.	

usar

Gerundio **usando**   Part. pas. **usado**

to use, to employ, to wear

Regular **-ar** verb

The Seven Simple Tenses		The Seven Compound Tenses	
Singular	Plural	Singular	Plural
1 presente de indicativo		8 perfecto de indicativo	
uso	usamos	he usado	hemos usado
usas	usáis	has usado	habéis usado
usa	usan	ha usado	han usado
2 imperfecto de indicativo		9 pluscuamperfecto de indicativo	
usaba	usábamos	había usado	habíamos usado
usabas	usabais	habías usado	habíais usado
usaba	usaban	había usado	habían usado
3 pretérito		10 pretérito anterior	
usé	usamos	hube usado	hubimos usado
usaste	usasteis	hubiste usado	hubisteis usado
usó	usaron	hubo usado	hubieron usado
4 futuro		11 futuro perfecto	
usaré	usaremos	habré usado	habremos usado
usarás	usaréis	habrás usado	habréis usado
usará	usarán	habrá usado	habrán usado
5 potencial simple		12 potencial compuesto	
usaría	usaríamos	habría usado	habríamos usado
usarías	usaríais	habrías usado	habríais usado
usaría	usarían	habría usado	habrían usado
6 presente de subjuntivo		13 perfecto de subjuntivo	
use	usemos	haya usado	hayamos usado
uses	uséis	hayas usado	hayáis usado
use	usen	haya usado	hayan usado
7 imperfecto de subjuntivo		14 pluscuamperfecto de subjuntivo	
usara	usáramos	hubiera usado	hubiéramos usado
usaras	usarais	hubieras usado	hubierais usado
usara	usaran	hubiera usado	hubieran usado
OR		OR	
usase	usásemos	hubiese usado	hubiésemos usado
usases	usaseis	hubieses usado	hubieseis usado
usase	usasen	hubiese usado	hubiesen usado

imperativo	
—	usemos
usa; no uses	usad; no uséis
use	usen

¿Usa usted guantes? Do you wear gloves?
en buen uso in good condition
el uso use, usage
en uso in use, in service

usado, usada used; usar + inf. to be used + inf.
desusar to disuse
desusarse to be no longer in use

Irregular verb   to be worth

The Seven Simple Tenses		The Seven Compound Tenses	
Singular	Plural	Singular	Plural
1 presente de indicativo		8 perfecto de indicativo	
valgo	valemos	he valido	hemos valido
vales	valéis	has valido	habéis valido
vale	valen	ha valido	han valido
2 imperfecto de indicativo		9 pluscuamperfecto de indicativo	
valía	valíamos	había valido	habíamos valido
valías	valíais	habías valido	habíais valido
valía	valían	había valido	habían valido
3 pretérito		10 pretérito anterior	
valí	valimos	hube valido	hubimos valido
valiste	valisteis	hubiste valido	hubisteis valido
valió	valieron	hubo valido	hubieron valido
4 futuro		11 futuro perfecto	
valdré	valdremos	habré valido	habremos valido
valdrás	valdréis	habrás valido	habréis valido
valdrá	valdrán	habrá valido	habrán valido
5 potencial simple		12 potencial compuesto	
valdría	valdríamos	habría valido	habríamos valido
valdrías	valdríais	habrías valido	habríais valido
valdría	valdrían	habría valido	habrían valido
6 presente de subjuntivo		13 perfecto de subjuntivo	
valga	valgamos	haya valido	hayamos valido
valgas	valgáis	hayas valido	hayáis valido
valga	valgan	haya valido	hayan valido
7 imperfecto de subjuntivo		14 pluscuamperfecto de subjuntivo	
valiera	valiéramos	hubiera valido	hubiéramos valido
valieras	valierais	hubieras valido	hubierais valido
valiera	valieran	hubiera valido	hubieran valido
OR		OR	
valiese	valiésemos	hubiese valido	hubiésemos valido
valieses	valieseis	hubieses valido	hubieseis valido
valiese	valiesen	hubiese valido	hubiesen valido

imperativo

	valgamos
val *or* vale; no valgas	valed; no valgáis
valga	valgan

Más vale pájaro en mano que ciento
  volando.   A bird in the hand is worth
  two in the bush.
Más vale tarde que nunca.   Better late
  than never.

No vale la pena.   It's not worth the
  trouble.
el valor   value, price, valor
valorar   to appraise, to increase the
  value

vencer

Gerundio **venciendo**   Part. pas. **vencido**

to conquer, to overcome, to defeat

Regular **-er** verb endings with spelling change: **c** becomes **z** before **a** or **o**

The Seven Simple Tenses		The Seven Compound Tenses	
Singular	Plural	Singular	Plural
1 presente de indicativo		8 perfecto de indicativo	
venzo	vencemos	he vencido	hemos vencido
vences	vencéis	has vencido	habéis vencido
vence	vencen	ha vencido	han vencido
2 imperfecto de indicativo		9 pluscuamperfecto de indicativo	
vencía	vencíamos	había vencido	habíamos vencido
vencías	vencíais	habías vencido	habíais vencido
vencía	vencían	había vencido	habían vencido
3 pretérito		10 pretérito anterior	
vencí	vencimos	hube vencido	hubimos vencido
venciste	vencisteis	hubiste vencido	hubisteis vencido
venció	vencieron	hubo vencido	hubieron vencido
4 futuro		11 futuro perfecto	
venceré	venceremos	habré vencido	habremos vencido
vencerás	venceréis	habrás vencido	habréis vencido
vencerá	vencerán	habrá vencido	habrán vencido
5 potencial simple		12 potencial compuesto	
vencería	venceríamos	habría vencido	habríamos vencido
vencerías	venceríais	habrías vencido	habríais vencido
vencería	vencerían	habría vencido	habrían vencido
6 presente de subjuntivo		13 perfecto de subjuntivo	
venza	venzamos	haya vencido	hayamos vencido
venzas	venzáis	hayas vencido	hayáis vencido
venza	venzan	haya vencido	hayan vencido
7 imperfecto de subjuntivo		14 pluscuamperfecto de subjuntivo	
venciera	venciéramos	hubiera vencido	hubiéramos vencido
vencieras	vencierais	hubieras vencido	hubierais vencido
venciera	vencieran	hubiera vencido	hubieran vencido
OR		OR	
venciese	venciésemos	hubiese vencido	hubiésemos vencido
vencieses	vencieseis	hubieses vencido	hubieseis vencido
venciese	venciesen	hubiese vencido	hubiesen vencido

imperativo	
—	venzamos
vence; no venzas	venced; no venzáis
venza	venzan

La semana pasada, el Real Madrid venció al Valencia en un partido de fútbol muy emocionante. Last week, Royal Madrid defeated Valencia in a very exciting soccer game.

vencedor, vencedora   victor
darse por vencido   to give in
vencible   conquerable
vencerse   to control oneself

Gerundio **vendiendo**   Part. pas. **vendido**   # vender

Regular **-er** verb   to sell

The Seven Simple Tenses		The Seven Compound Tenses	
Singular	Plural	Singular	Plural
1 presente de indicativo		8 perfecto de indicativo	
vendo	vendemos	he vendido	hemos vendido
vendes	vendéis	has vendido	habéis vendido
vende	venden	ha vendido	han vendido
2 imperfecto de indicativo		9 pluscuamperfecto de indicativo	
vendía	vendíamos	había vendido	habíamos vendido
vendías	vendíais	habías vendido	habíais vendido
vendía	vendían	había vendido	habían vendido
3 pretérito		10 pretérito anterior	
vendí	vendimos	hube vendido	hubimos vendido
vendiste	vendisteis	hubiste vendido	hubisteis vendido
vendió	vendieron	hubo vendido	hubieron vendido
4 futuro		11 futuro perfecto	
venderé	venderemos	habré vendido	habremos vendido
venderás	venderéis	habrás vendido	habréis vendido
venderá	venderán	habrá vendido	habrán vendido
5 potencial simple		12 potencial compuesto	
vendería	venderíamos	habría vendido	habríamos vendido
venderías	venderíais	habrías vendido	habríais vendido
vendería	venderían	habría vendido	habrían vendido
6 presente de subjuntivo		13 perfecto de subjuntivo	
venda	vendamos	haya vendido	hayamos vendido
vendas	vendáis	hayas vendido	hayáis vendido
venda	vendan	haya vendido	hayan vendido
7 imperfecto de subjuntivo		14 pluscuamperfecto de subjuntivo	
vendiera	vendiéramos	hubiera vendido	hubiéramos vendido
vendieras	vendierais	hubieras vendido	hubierais vendido
vendiera	vendieran	hubiera vendido	hubieran vendido
OR		OR	
vendiese	vendiésemos	hubiese vendido	hubiésemos vendido
vendieses	vendieseis	hubieses vendido	hubieseis vendido
vendiese	vendiesen	hubiese vendido	hubiesen vendido

imperativo	
—	vendamos
vende; no vendas	vended; no vendáis
venda	vendan

Aquí se venden libros. Books are sold here.
vendedor, vendedora seller, sales person
vender a comisión to sell on commission
la venta sale

venta al mayor, venta por mayor wholesale
vender al peso to sell by weight
venta al menor, venta por menor retail sale
revender to resell
el precio de venta selling price

venir

Gerundio **viniendo**   Part. pas. **venido**

to come

Irregular verb

The Seven Simple Tenses		The Seven Compound Tenses	
Singular	Plural	Singular	Plural
1 presente de indicativo		**8 perfecto de indicativo**	
vengo	venimos	he venido	hemos venido
vienes	venís	has venido	habéis venido
viene	vienen	ha venido	han venido
2 imperfecto de indicativo		**9 pluscuamperfecto de indicativo**	
venía	veníamos	había venido	habíamos venido
venías	veníais	habías venido	habíais venido
venía	venían	había venido	habían venido
3 pretérito		**10 pretérito anterior**	
vine	vinimos	hube venido	hubimos venido
viniste	vinisteis	hubiste venido	hubisteis venido
vino	vinieron	hubo venido	hubieron venido
4 futuro		**11 futuro perfecto**	
vendré	vendremos	habré venido	habremos venido
vendrás	vendréis	habrás venido	habréis venido
vendrá	vendrán	habrá venido	habrán venido
5 potencial simple		**12 potencial compuesto**	
vendría	vendríamos	habría venido	habríamos venido
vendrías	vendríais	habrías venido	habríais venido
vendría	vendrían	habría venido	habrían venido
6 presente de subjuntivo		**13 perfecto de subjuntivo**	
venga	vengamos	haya venido	hayamos venido
vengas	vengáis	hayas venido	hayáis venido
venga	vengan	haya venido	hayan venido
7 imperfecto de subjuntivo		**14 pluscuamperfecto de subjuntivo**	
viniera	viniéramos	hubiera venido	hubiéramos venido
vinieras	vinierais	hubieras venido	hubierais venido
viniera	vinieran	hubiera venido	hubieran venido
OR		OR	
viniese	viniésemos	hubiese venido	hubiésemos venido
vinieses	vinieseis	hubieses venido	hubieseis venido
viniese	viniesen	hubiese venido	hubiesen venido

imperativo	
—	vengamos
ven; no vengas	venid; no vengáis
venga	vengan

La señora González y su marido
vienen de Venezuela. Mrs.
González and her husband come from
(are from) Venezuela.

la semana que viene next week

venir a las manos to come to blows

el mes que viene next month

venir a buscar to come for, to get

el porvenir the future

en el *or* en lo porvenir hereafter

Venga lo que venga. Come what may.

venir a la mente/a la cabeza to come
to mind

Irregular verb   to see

The Seven Simple Tenses		The Seven Compound Tenses	
Singular	Plural	Singular	Plural
1 presente de indicativo		8 perfecto de indicativo	
veo	vemos	he visto	hemos visto
ves	veis	has visto	habéis visto
ve	ven	ha visto	han visto
2 imperfecto de indicativo		9 pluscuamperfecto de indicativo	
veía	veíamos	había visto	habíamos visto
veías	veíais	habías visto	habíais visto
veía	veían	había visto	habían visto
3 pretérito		10 pretérito anterior	
vi	vimos	hube visto	hubimos visto
viste	visteis	hubiste visto	hubisteis visto
vio	vieron	hubo visto	hubieron visto
4 futuro		11 futuro perfecto	
veré	veremos	habré visto	habremos visto
verás	veréis	habrás visto	habréis visto
verá	verán	habrá visto	habrán visto
5 potencial simple		12 potencial compuesto	
vería	veríamos	habría visto	habríamos visto
verías	veríais	habrías visto	habríais visto
vería	verían	habría visto	habrían visto
6 presente de subjuntivo		13 perfecto de subjuntivo	
vea	veamos	haya visto	hayamos visto
veas	veáis	hayas visto	hayáis visto
vea	vean	haya visto	hayan visto
7 imperfecto de subjuntivo		14 pluscuamperfecto de subjuntivo	
viera	viéramos	hubiera visto	hubiéramos visto
vieras	vierais	hubieras visto	hubierais visto
viera	vieran	hubiera visto	hubieran visto
OR		OR	
viese	viésemos	hubiese visto	hubiésemos visto
vieses	vieseis	hubieses visto	hubieseis visto
viese	viesen	hubiese visto	hubiesen visto

	imperativo
—	veamos
ve; no veas	ved; no veáis
vea	vean

Hasta que no lo veas, no lo creas.	**Es de ver.** It is worth seeing.
Don't believe it until you see it.	**Ver es creer.** Seeing is believing.
¡Vamos a ver! Let's see	**ver claro** to see clearly
Está por ver. It remains to be seen.	**la vista** sight, seeing, view, vision
¡A ver! Let's see!	**¡Ya se ve!** Of course! Certainly!

295

vestirse

Gerundio **vistiéndose** Part. pas. **vestido**

to dress oneself,
to get dressed

Reflexive verb; regular **-ir** verb endings with stem
change: Tenses 1, 3, 6, 7, Imperative, *Gerundio*

The Seven Simple Tenses		The Seven Compound Tenses	
Singular	Plural	Singular	Plural
1 presente de indicativo		8 perfecto de indicativo	
me visto	**nos vestimos**	**me he vestido**	**nos hemos vestido**
te vistes	**os vestís**	**te has vestido**	**os habéis vestido**
se viste	**se visten**	**se ha vestido**	**se han vestido**
2 imperfecto de indicativo		9 pluscuamperfecto de indicativo	
me vestía	**nos vestíamos**	**me había vestido**	**nos habíamos vestido**
te vestías	**os vestíais**	**te habías vestido**	**os habíais vestido**
se vestía	**se vestían**	**se había vestido**	**se habían vestido**
3 pretérito		10 pretérito anterior	
me vestí	**nos vestimos**	**me hube vestido**	**nos hubimos vestido**
te vestiste	**os vestisteis**	**te hubiste vestido**	**os hubisteis vestido**
se vistió	**se vistieron**	**se hubo vestido**	**se hubieron vestido**
4 futuro		11 futuro perfecto	
me vestiré	**nos vestiremos**	**me habré vestido**	**nos habremos vestido**
te vestirás	**os vestiréis**	**te habrás vestido**	**os habréis vestido**
se vestirá	**se vestirán**	**se habrá vestido**	**se habrán vestido**
5 potencial simple		12 potencial compuesto	
me vestiría	**nos vestiríamos**	**me habría vestido**	**nos habríamos vestido**
te vestirías	**os vestiríais**	**te habrías vestido**	**os habríais vestido**
se vestiría	**se vestirían**	**se habría vestido**	**se habrían vestido**
6 presente de subjuntivo		13 perfecto de subjuntivo	
me vista	**nos vistamos**	**me haya vestido**	**nos hayamos vestido**
te vistas	**os vistáis**	**te hayas vestido**	**os hayáis vestido**
se vista	**se vistan**	**se haya vestido**	**se hayan vestido**
7 imperfecto de subjuntivo		14 pluscuamperfecto de subjuntivo	
me vistiera	**nos vistiéramos**	**me hubiera vestido**	**nos hubiéramos vestido**
te vistieras	**os vistierais**	**te hubieras vestido**	**os hubierais vestido**
se vistiera	**se vistieran**	**se hubiera vestido**	**se hubieran vestido**
OR		OR	
me vistiese	**nos vistiésemos**	**me hubiese vestido**	**nos hubiésemos vestido**
te vistieses	**os vistieseis**	**te hubieses vestido**	**os hubieseis vestido**
se vistiese	**se vistiesen**	**se hubiese vestido**	**se hubiesen vestido**

imperativo	
—	**vistámonos; no nos vistamos**
vístete; no te vistas	**vestíos; no os vistáis**
vístase; no se vista	**vístanse; no se vistan**

---

vestir to clothe, to dress	**vestir de blanco** to dress in white
bien vestido well dressed	**el vestido** clothing, clothes, dress
desvestirse to undress oneself, to get undressed	**vestidos usados** secondhand clothing
vestir de uniforme to dress in uniform	

Gerundio **viajando**   Part. pas. **viajado**   # viajar

Regular **-ar** verb   to travel

The Seven Simple Tenses		The Seven Compound Tenses	
Singular	Plural	Singular	Plural
1 presente de indicativo		**8 perfecto de indicativo**	
viajo	viajáis	he viajado	hemos viajado
viajas	viajáis	has viajado	habéis viajado
viaja	viajan	ha viajado	han viajado
2 imperfecto de indicativo		**9 pluscuamperfecto de indicativo**	
viajaba	viajábamos	había viajado	habíamos viajado
viajabas	viajabais	habías viajado	habíais viajado
viajaba	viajaban	había viajado	habían viajado
3 pretérito		**10 pretérito anterior**	
viajé	viajamos	hube viajado	hubimos viajado
viajaste	viajasteis	hubiste viajado	hubisteis viajado
viajó	viajaron	hubo viajado	hubieron viajado
4 futuro		**11 futuro perfecto**	
viajaré	viajaremos	habré viajado	habremos viajado
viajarás	viajaréis	habrás viajado	habréis viajado
viajará	viajarán	habrá viajado	habrán viajado
5 potencial simple		**12 potencial compuesto**	
viajaría	viajaríamos	habría viajado	habríamos viajado
viajarías	viajaríais	habrías viajado	habríais viajado
viajaría	viajarían	habría viajado	habrían viajado
6 presente de subjuntivo		**13 perfecto de subjuntivo**	
viaje	viajemos	haya viajado	hayamos viajado
viajes	viajéis	hayas viajado	hayáis viajado
viaje	viajen	haya viajado	hayan viajado
7 imperfecto de subjuntivo		**14 pluscuamperfecto de subjuntivo**	
viajara	viajáramos	hubiera viajado	hubiéramos viajado
viajaras	viajarais	hubieras viajado	hubierais viajado
viajara	viajaran	hubiera viajado	hubieran viajado
OR		OR	
viajase	viajásemos	hubiese viajado	hubiésemos viajado
viajases	viajaseis	hubieses viajado	hubieseis viajado
viajase	viajasen	hubiese viajado	hubiesen viajado

imperativo	
—	viajemos
viaja; no viajes	viajad; no viajéis
viaje	viajen

Cuando viajo a Europa, prefiero ir en avión. When I travel to Europe, I prefer to go by plane.	un viaje de negocios business trip
	un viaje de ida y vuelta round trip
	un viaje redondo round trip
el viaje trip	viajero, viajera traveler
¡Buen viaje! Have a good trip!	viajes espaciales space travel
hacer un viaje to take a trip	

297

visitar

Gerundio **visitando**　　　Part. pas. **visitado**

to visit

Regular **-ar** verb

The Seven Simple Tenses		The Seven Compound Tenses	
Singular	Plural	Singular	Plural
1　presente de indicativo		8　perfecto de indicativo	
visito	visitamos	he visitado	hemos visitado
visitas	visitáis	has visitado	habéis visitado
visita	visitan	ha visitado	han visitado
2　imperfecto de indicativo		9　pluscuamperfecto de indicativo	
visitaba	visitábamos	había visitado	habíamos visitado
visitabas	visitabais	habías visitado	habíais visitado
visitaba	visitaban	había visitado	habían visitado
3　pretérito		10　pretérito anterior	
visité	visitamos	hube visitado	hubimos visitado
visitaste	visitasteis	hubiste visitado	hubisteis visitado
visitó	visitaron	hubo visitado	hubieron visitado
4　futuro		11　futuro perfecto	
visitaré	visitaremos	habré visitado	habremos visitado
visitarás	visitaréis	habrás visitado	habréis visitado
visitará	visitarán	habrá visitado	habrán visitado
5　potencial simple		12　potencial compuesto	
visitaría	visitaríamos	habría visitado	habríamos visitado
visitarías	visitaríais	habrías visitado	habríais visitado
visitaría	visitarían	habría visitado	habrían visitado
6　presente de subjuntivo		13　perfecto de subjuntivo	
visite	visitemos	haya visitado	hayamos visitado
visites	visitéis	hayas visitado	hayáis visitado
visite	visiten	haya visitado	hayan visitado
7　imperfecto de subjuntivo		14　pluscuamperfecto de subjuntivo	
visitara	visitáramos	hubiera visitado	hubiéramos visitado
visitaras	visitarais	hubieras visitado	hubierais visitado
visitara	visitaran	hubiera visitado	hubieran visitado
OR		OR	
visitase	visitásemos	hubiese visitado	hubiésemos visitado
visitases	visitaseis	hubieses visitado	hubieseis visitado
visitase	visitasen	hubiese visitado	hubiesen visitado

imperativo	
—	visitemos
visita; no visites	visitad; no visitéis
visite	visiten

una visita　visit	visitarse　to visit one another
una visitación　visitation	tener visita　to have company
visitante　visitor	hacer una visita　to pay a call, a visit
pagar la visita　to return a visit	una visita acompañada　guided tour

The Seven Simple Tenses		The Seven Compound Tenses	
Singular	Plural	Singular	Plural
1 presente de indicativo		8 perfecto de indicativo	
vivo	vivimos	he vivido	hemos vivido
vives	vivís	has vivido	habéis vivido
vive	viven	ha vivido	han vivido
2 imperfecto de indicativo		9 pluscuamperfecto de indicativo	
vivía	vivíamos	había vivido	habíamos vivido
vivías	vivíais	habías vivido	habíais vivido
vivía	vivían	había vivido	habían vivido
3 pretérito		10 pretérito anterior	
viví	vivimos	hube vivido	hubimos vivido
viviste	vivisteis	hubiste vivido	hubisteis vivido
vivió	vivieron	hubo vivido	hubieron vivido
4 futuro		11 futuro perfecto	
viviré	viviremos	habré vivido	habremos vivido
vivirás	viviréis	habrás vivido	habréis vivido
vivirá	vivirán	habrá vivido	habrán vivido
5 potencial simple		12 potencial compuesto	
viviría	viviríamos	habría vivido	habríamos vivido
vivirías	viviríais	habrías vivido	habríais vivido
viviría	vivirían	habría vivido	habrían vivido
6 presente de subjuntivo		13 perfecto de subjuntivo	
viva	vivamos	haya vivido	hayamos vivido
vivas	viváis	hayas vivido	hayáis vivido
viva	vivan	haya vivido	hayan vivido
7 imperfecto de subjuntivo		14 pluscuamperfecto de subjuntivo	
viviera	viviéramos	hubiera vivido	hubiéramos vivido
vivieras	vivierais	hubieras vivido	hubierais vivido
viviera	vivieran	hubiera vivido	hubieran vivido
OR		OR	
viviese	viviésemos	hubiese vivido	hubiésemos vivido
vivieses	vivieseis	hubieses vivido	hubieseis vivido
viviese	viviesen	hubiese vivido	hubiesen vivido

imperativo	
—	vivamos
vive; no vivas	vivid; no viváis
viva	vivan

Vivimos en esta casa desde veinte años. We have been living in this house for twenty years.	la vida life
	vivir para ver to live and learn
	en vida while living, while alive
¡La vida es así! That's life!	vivir a oscuras to live in ignorance
vivir de to live on	ganarse la vida to earn one's living
vivir del aire to live on thin air	revivir to revive

volar

Gerundio **volando**   Part. pas. **volado**

to fly

Regular **-ar** verb endings with stem
change: Tenses 1, 6, Imperative

The Seven Simple Tenses		The Seven Compound Tenses	
Singular	Plural	Singular	Plural
1 presente de indicativo		8 perfecto de indicativo	
vuelo	volamos	he volado	hemos volado
vuelas	voláis	has volado	habéis volado
vuela	vuelan	ha volado	han volado
2 imperfecto de indicativo		9 pluscuamperfecto de indicativo	
volaba	volábamos	había volado	habíamos volado
volabas	volabais	habías volado	habíais volado
volaba	volaban	había volado	habían volado
3 pretérito		10 pretérito anterior	
volé	volamos	hube volado	hubimos volado
volaste	volasteis	hubiste volado	hubisteis volado
voló	volaron	hubo volado	hubieron volado
4 futuro		11 futuro perfecto	
volaré	volaremos	habré volado	habremos volado
volarás	volaréis	habrás volado	habréis volado
volará	volarán	habrá volado	habrán volado
5 potencial simple		12 potencial compuesto	
volaría	volaríamos	habría volado	habríamos volado
volarías	volaríais	habrías volado	habríais volado
volaría	volarían	habría volado	habrían volado
6 presente de subjuntivo		13 perfecto de subjuntivo	
vuele	volemos	haya volado	hayamos volado
vueles	voléis	hayas volado	hayáis volado
vuele	vuelen	haya volado	hayan volado
7 imperfecto de subjuntivo		14 pluscuamperfecto de subjuntivo	
volara	voláramos	hubiera volado	hubiéramos volado
volaras	volarais	hubieras volado	hubierais volado
volara	volaran	hubiera volado	hubieran volado
OR		OR	
volase	volásemos	hubiese volado	hubiésemos volado
volases	volaseis	hubieses volado	hubieseis volado
volase	volasen	hubiese volado	hubiesen volado

imperativo	
—	volemos
vuela; no vueles	volad; no voléis
vuele	vuelen

¡Como vuela el tiempo! How time
flies!
Más vale pájaro en mano que ciento
volando. A bird in the hand is worth
two in the bush.
el vuelo flight

Las horas vuelan. The hours go flying
by.
el volante steering wheel
volear to volley (a ball); el voleo
volley

Regular **-er** verb endings with stem change: to return, to go back
Tenses 1, 6, Imperative, Past Participle

The Seven Simple Tenses		The Seven Compound Tenses	
Singular	Plural	Singular	Plural
1 presente de indicativo		8 perfecto de indicativo	
vuelvo	**volvemos**	**he vuelto**	**hemos vuelto**
vuelves	**volvéis**	**has vuelto**	**habéis vuelto**
vuelve	**vuelven**	**ha vuelto**	**han vuelto**
2 imperfecto de indicativo		9 pluscuamperfecto de indicativo	
volvía	**volvíamos**	**había vuelto**	**habíamos vuelto**
volvías	**volvíais**	**habías vuelto**	**habíais vuelto**
volvía	**volvían**	**había vuelto**	**habían vuelto**
3 pretérito		10 pretérito anterior	
volví	**volvimos**	**hube vuelto**	**hubimos vuelto**
volviste	**volvisteis**	**hubiste vuelto**	**hubisteis vuelto**
volvió	**volvieron**	**hubo vuelto**	**hubieron vuelto**
4 futuro		11 futuro perfecto	
volveré	**volveremos**	**habré vuelto**	**habremos vuelto**
volverás	**volveréis**	**habrás vuelto**	**habréis vuelto**
volverá	**volverán**	**habrá vuelto**	**habrán vuelto**
5 potencial simple		12 potencial compuesto	
volvería	**volveríamos**	**habría vuelto**	**habríamos vuelto**
volverías	**volveríais**	**habrías vuelto**	**habríais vuelto**
volvería	**volverían**	**habría vuelto**	**habrían vuelto**
6 presente de subjuntivo		13 perfecto de subjuntivo	
vuelva	**volvamos**	**haya vuelto**	**hayamos vuelto**
vuelvas	**volváis**	**hayas vuelto**	**hayáis vuelto**
vuelva	**vuelvan**	**haya vuelto**	**hayan vuelto**
7 imperfecto de subjuntivo		14 pluscuamperfecto de subjuntivo	
volviera	**volviéramos**	**hubiera vuelto**	**hubiéramos vuelto**
volvieras	**volvierais**	**hubieras vuelto**	**hubierais vuelto**
volviera	**volvieran**	**hubiera vuelto**	**hubieran vuelto**
OR		OR	
volviese	**volviésemos**	**hubiese vuelto**	**hubiésemos vuelto**
volvieses	**volvieseis**	**hubieses vuelto**	**hubieseis vuelto**
volviese	**volviesen**	**hubiese vuelto**	**hubiesen vuelto**

	imperativo	
—	**volvamos**	
vuelve; no vuelvas	**volved; no volváis**	
vuelva	**vuelvan**	

¿A qué hora vuelve Ud. a casa?   At
  what time are you returning home?
volver en sí   to regain consciousness,
  to come to
un revólver   revolver, pistol
volver sobre sus pasos   to retrace
  one's steps

revolver   to revolve, to shake (up), to
  turn around
una vuelta   turn, revolution, turning
dar una vuelta   to take a stroll
revolverse   to turn around (oneself)
See also **devolver** and **revolver**.

English-Spanish Verb Index

The purpose of this index is to give you instantly the Spanish verb for the English verb you have in mind to use. This saves you time if you do not have a standard English-Spanish word dictionary at your fingertips.

When you find the Spanish verb you need through the English verb, look up its verb forms in this book where all verbs are listed alphabetically at the top of each page. If it is not listed among the 301 verbs in this book, consult the list of over 1,000 Spanish verbs conjugated like model verbs among the 301 which begins on page 310. If it is not listed there, consult our more comprehensive book, *501 Spanish Verbs fully conjugated in all the tenses*, 7th edition.

be worth **valer**, 291
become **ponerse**, 243
become angry **enojarse**, 142
become ill, sick **enfermarse**, 141
become tired **cansarse**, 68
become weary **cansarse**, 68
beg **rogar**, 264
begin **comenzar**, 81; **empezar**, 138
believe **creer**, 101
bind **unir**, 289
bite **morder**, 210
bless **bendecir**, 57
blunder **tropezar**, 288
boil **bullir**, 60; **cocer**, 76
bore **aburrir**, 4
born, to be **nacer**, 213
break **romper**, 265
break the law **delinquir**, 113
breakfast, to (have)
  desayunarse, 115
breed **criar**, 102
bring **traer**, 287
bring near **acercar**, 8
bring up (breed, rear) **criar**, 102
burden **cargar**, 70
build **construir**, 91
bustle **bullir**, 59
buy **comprar**, 84

C

call **llamar**, 197
called, to be **llamarse**, 198
can **poder**, 241
care for, to take care of **cuidar**, 105
carry (away) **llevar**, 201
cast **echar**, 135
catch **coger**, 77
celebrate **celebrar**, 72
certify **certificar**, 75
change **cambiar**, 65
choose **escoger**, 150; **elegir**, 137
christen **bautizar**, 55
clinch **fijar**, 163
close **cerrar**, 74
clothe onself **vestirse**, 296
collect **colegir**, 78
comb one's hair **peinarse**, 237
come **venir**, 294
come across or upon **hallar**, 177
come down **bajar**, 52
come (in) **entrar**, 145
command **mandar**, 204; **ordenar**,
  226

commence **comenzar**, 81
complete **acabar**, 6
compose **componer**, 83
conduct **conducir**, 86
confess **confesar**, 87
confide **fiar**, 162
congratulate **felicitar**, 161
connect **unir**, 289
conquer **vencer**, 292
consecrate **bendecir**, 57
constitute **constituir**, 90
construct **construir**, 91
contained, to be **caber**, 62
continue **continuar**, 94;
  seguir, 270
contradict **contradecir**, 95
contribute **contribuir**, 96
cook **cocer**, 76
correct **corregir**, 97
cost **costar**, 99
counsel **aconsejar**, 12
count **contar**, 92
cover **cubrir**, 105
creak (as doors, hinges, *etc.*)
  gruñir, 170
cross **atravesar**, 46; **cruzar**, 103
cross out **borrar**, 58
cry out **gritar**, 169
cry (weep) **llorar**, 202
custom, to have the **soler**, 276

D

dance **bailar**, 51
dare **atreverse**, 47; **osar**, 228
decide **decidir**, 109
defend **defender**, 111
delineate **describir**, 117
demand **exigir**, 157
deny **negar**, 216
depart **partir**, 233
descend **bajar**, 52
describe **describir**, 117
desire **desear**, 119
destroy **destruir**, 124
die **morir**, 211
direct **dirigir**, 128
discover **descubrir**, 118
dismiss **despedir**, 120
dispense **dispensar**, 129
distinguish **distinguir**, 130
distribute **dispensar**, 129
divide **partir**, 233
do **hacer**, 176

do (something) right **acertar**, 10
doubt **dudar**, 134
draw near **acercarse**, 9
draw (pull) **tirar**, 282
dream **soñar**, 277
dress oneself **vestirse**, 296
drink **beber**, 56
drive (a car) **conducir**, 86
dry **secar**, 269
dwell **habitar**, 174

E

earn **ganar**, 166
eat **comer**, 82
eat breakfast **desayunarse**, 115
eat lunch **almorzar**, 29
eat supper **cenar**, 73
elect **elegir**, 137
employ **emplear**, 139; **usar**, 290
enclose **incluir**, 181
encounter **encontrar**, 140
end **acabar**, 6; **terminar**, 281
enjoy **gozar**, 168
enjoy oneself **divertirse**, 131
enliven **despertar**, 122
enter **entrar**, 145
enunciate **enunciar**, 146
erase **borrar**, 58
err **errar**, 149
escape **huir**, 179
escort **acompañar**, 11
excuse **dispensar**, 129
exempt **dispensar**, 129
exercise **ejercer**, 136
exert **ejercer**, 136
expect **aguardar**, 26; **esperar**, 154
explain **explicar**, 158
express **expresar**, 159

F

fall **caer**, 63
fall asleep **dormirse**, 133
fall ill **enfermarse,** 141
fasten **fijar**, 163
fatigue **cansar**, 67
feel **sentir(se)**, 272-273
feel sorry **sentir**, 272
felicitate **felicitar**, 161
fill **llenar**, 200
find **encontrar**, 140; **hallar**, 177
find out **averiguar**, 49
finish **acabar**, 6

fit (into) **caber**, 62
fix (fasten) **fijar**, 163
flee **huir**, 179
fling **arrojar**, 40; **echar**, 135;
    lanzar, 191; **tirar**, 282
flow **correr**, 98
fly **volar**, 300
follow **seguir**, 270
forbid **defender**, 111
forget **olvidar**, 225
frightened, to be **asustarse**, 44
fry **freír**, 165
fulfill **cumplir**, 106
fun of, to make **burlarse**, 60
function (machine) **marchar**, 205

G

gain **ganar**, 166
get **adquirir**, 21; **conseguir**, 89;
    obtener, 219; **recibir**, 256;
    sacar, 267
get angry **enojarse**, 142
get cross **enojarse**, 142
get dressed **vestirse**, 296
get married **casarse**, 71
get sick **enfermarse**, 141
get tired **cansarse**, 71
get undressed **desvestirse**, 125
get up **levantarse**, 196
get weary **cansarse**, 68
give **dar**, 107
give back (an object) **devolver**, 127
give notice **advertir**, 22
give warning **advertir**, 22
go **ir**, 188
go away **irse**, 189;
    marcharse, 206
go back **volver**, 301
go down **bajar**, 52
go in **entrar**, 145
go out **salir**, 268
go through **atravesar**, 46
go to bed **acostarse**, 15
go with **acompañar**, 11
good-by, to say **despedirse**, 121
good time, to have a **divertirse**,
    131
grab **coger**, 77
grant **admitir**, 19; **permitir**, 240
grasp **asir**, 42; **coger**, 77
grieve **gemir**, 167
groan **gemir**, 167
grow **crecer**, 100
grow tired **aburrirse**, 5

grow weary **aburrirse**, 5
growl **gruñir**, 170
grumble **gruñir**, 170
grunt **gruñir**, 170
guide **guiar**, 171
guilty, to be **delinquir**, 113

H

habit, to be in the **soler**, 276
hang up **colgar**, 79
happen **pasar**, 234
harm **herir**, 178
hasten **apresurarse**, 38
have (as an auxiliary verb)
  haber, 173
have (hold) **tener**, 280
have a good time **divertirse**, 131
have breakfast **desayunarse**, 115
have lunch **almorzar**, 29
have supper **cenar**, 73
have the custom of **soler**, 276
have to **deber**, 108
hear **oír**, 223
heave **alzar**, 31
help **ayudar**, 50
hire **alquilar**, 30
hit the mark **acertar**, 10
hit upon **acertar**, 10
hold **tener**, 280
hope **esperar**, 154
hurl **arrojar**, 40; **echar**, 135;
  lanzar, 191
hurry **apresurarse**, 38
hurt **herir**, 178
hustle **bullir**, 59

I

ill, to become, to fall **enfermarse**,
  141
include **incluir**, 181
indicate **indicar**, 182
induce **inducir**, 183
influence **inducir**, 183; **influir**, 184
inhabit **habitar**, 174
inquire **averiguar**, 49;
  preguntar, 246
insist **insistir**, 186
insure **asegurar**, 41
introduce **introducir**, 186
invert **invertir**, 187
invest **invertir**, 187
investigate **averiguar**, 49

J

join **unir**, 289

K

keep (a promise) **cumplir**, 106
keep quiet **callarse**, 64
keep still **callarse**, 64
kill **matar**, 207
know **conocer**, 88; **saber**, 266
know how **saber**, 266

L

labor **trabajar**, 285
lack **faltar**, 160
lacking, to be **faltar**, 160
laugh **reír**, 259
launch **lanzar**, 191
lead **conducir**, 86; **guiar**, 171
learn **aprender**, 37
leave **dejar**, 112; **marcharse**, 206;
  partir, 233; **salir**, 268
leave (go out) **salir**, 268
lend **prestar**, 248
let **dejar**, 112
let go **dejar**, 112
lie down **acostarse**, 15
lie (tell a lie) **mentir**, 208
lift **alzar**, 31; **levantar**, 195
like (be pleasing to) **gustar**, 172
listen (to) **escuchar**, 152
live **vivir**, 299
live in (reside) **habitar**, 174
load **cargar**, 70
look **mirar**, 209
look after **cuidar**, 105
look alike **parecerse**, 232
look at **mirar**, 209
look for **buscar**, 61
lose **perder**, 239
love **amar**, 32
lunch **almorzar**, 29

M

make **hacer**, 176
make fun of **burlarse**, 60
make up (constitute) **constituir**, 90
march **marchar**, 205
marry **casarse**, 71

matter **importar**, 180
meet **encontrar**, 140
miss **errar**, 150; **faltar**, 160
mistaken, to be **equivocarse**, 148
moan **gemir**, 167
move along **caminar**, 66
must **deber**, 108

N

name **llamar**, 197
named, to be **llamarse**, 198
need **faltar**, 160; **necesitar**, 215

O

obey **obedecer**, 218
obtain **adquirir**, 21; **conseguir**, 89;
  obtener, 219; **recibir**, 256
occupy **ocupar**, 220
occur **ocurrir**, 221
offense, to commit an **delinquir**, 113
offer **ofrecer**, 222
open **abrir**, 1
order **mandar**, 204; **ordenar**, 226
organize **organizar**, 227
ought **deber**, 108
overcome **vencer**, 292
overtake **alcanzar**, 27
owe **deber**, 108

P

parade **pasearse**, 235
pass (by) **pasar**, 234
pay **pagar**, 229
pay attention **fijarse**, 164
permit **dejar**, 112; **permitir**, 240
persist **insistir**, 185
persuade **inducir**, 183
pick up **alzar**, 31
pitch **echar**, 135
pitch (a ball) **tirar**, 282
place **colocar**, 80; **poner**, 242
place near **acercar**, 8
play (a game) **jugar**, 190
play (music or a musical instrument)
  tocar, 283
play (a sport) **jugar**, 190
please **agradar**, 24
point out **enseñar**, 143; **indicar**,
  182; **mostrar**, 212
poke fun at **burlarse**, 60

possession, to take **apoderarse**, 36
power, to take **apoderarse**, 36
practice **practicar**, 244
prefer **preferir**, 245
prepare **preparar**, 247
prohibit **defender**, 111
pronounce **pronunciar**, 251
protect **proteger**, 252
prove **demostrar**, 114; **probar**, 249
pull **tirar**, 282
purchase **comprar**, 84
pursue **seguir**, 270
put **colocar**, 81; **poner**, 242
put in order **ordenar**, 226
put on **ponerse**, 243

Q

quarrel **reñir**, 260
question **preguntar**, 246
quiet, to keep **callarse**, 64

R

race **correr**, 98
rain **llover**, 203
raise (breed) **criar**, 102
raise (lift) **levantar**, 195
raise (prices) **alzar**, 31
reach one's birthday **cumplir**, 106
read **leer**, 194
rear (bring up, breed) **criar**, 102
recall **recordar**, 257
receive **recibir**, 256
refer **referir**, 258
refund **devolver**, 127
regret **sentir**, 272
register (a letter) **certificar**, 75
rejoice **alegrarse**, 28
relate **contar**, 93; **referir**, 258
remain **quedarse**, 253
remember **acordarse**, 14;
  recordar, 257
remove (oneself) **quitarse**, 255
rent **alquilar**, 30
repeat **repetir**, 261
reply **contestar**, 93; **responder**, 262
request **pedir**, 236; **rogar**, 264
require **exigir**, 157
resemble each other **parecerse**, 232
reside **habitar**, 174
respond **responder**, 262
rest **descansar**, 116
return (an object) **devolver**, 127
return (go back) **volver**, 301

revolve **revolver**, 263
ridicule **burlarse**, 60
rise (get up) **levantarse**, 196
roam **errar**, 149
run **correr**, 98
run away **huir**, 179
run (machine) **marchar**, 205
run through **atravesar**, 46
rush **apresurarse**, 38

V

venture **osar**, 228; **atreverse**, 47
vex **aburrir**, 4
visit **visitar**, 298

W

wait for **aguardar**, 26; **esperar**, 154
wake up (oneself) **despertarse**, 123
walk **andar**, 34; **caminar**, 66;
marchar, 205
walk, to take a **pasearse**, 235
wander **errar**, 149
want **desear**, 119; **querer**, 254

wanting, to be **faltar**, 160
warn **advertir**, 22
wash oneself **lavarse**, 193
watch **mirar**, 209
wear **llevar**, 201; **usar**, 290
weary **cansar**, 67
weep **llorar**, 202
whine **llorar**, 202
win **ganar**, 166
wipe dry **secar**, 269
wish **desear**, 119; **querer**, 254
withdraw **quitarse**, 255
work **trabajar**, 285
worship **adorar**, 20
worth, to be **valer**, 291
wound **herir**, 178
write **escribir**, 151

Index of common irregular Spanish verb forms identified by infinitive

The purpose of this index is to help you identify those verb forms that cannot be readily identified because they are irregular in some way. For example, if you come across the verb form *fui* (which is very common) in your Spanish readings, this index will tell you that *fui* is a form of *ir* or *ser*. Then you look up *ir* and *ser* in this book and you will find that verb form on the page where all the forms of *ir* and *ser* are given.

Verb forms whose first three or four letters are the same as the infinitive have not been included because they can easily be identified by referring to the alphabetical listing of the 301 verbs in this book.

A

abierto **abrir**
acierto, *etc.* **acertar**
acuerdo, *etc.* **acordar**
acuesto, *etc.*
acostarse
alce, *etc.* **alzar**
ase, *etc.* **asir**
asgo, *etc.* **asir**
ate, *etc.* **atar**

C

caí, *etc.* **caer**
caía, *etc.* **caer**
caigo, *etc.* **caer**
cayera, *etc.* **caer**
cierro, *etc.* **cerrar**
cojo, *etc.* **coger**

cuece, *etc.* **cocer**
cuelgo, *etc.* **colgar**
cuento, *etc.* **contar**
cuesta, *etc.* **costar**
cuezo, *etc.* **cocer**
cupiera, *etc.* **caber**

D

da, *etc.* **dar**
dad **dar**
dé **dar**
demos **dar**
des **dar**
di, *etc.* **dar**, **decir**
dice, *etc.* **decir**
dicho **decir**
diciendo **decir**
diera, *etc.* **dar**
diese, *etc.* **dar**

digo, *etc.* **decir**
dije, *etc.* **decir**
dimos, *etc.* **dar**
dio **dar**
diré, *etc.* **decir**
diría, *etc.* **decir**
doy **dar**
duermo, *etc.* **dormir**
durmamos **dormir**
durmiendo **dormir**

E

eliges, *etc.* **elegir**
eligiendo **elegir**
eligiera, *etc.* **elegir**
elijo, *etc.* **elegir**
era, *etc.* **ser**
eres **ser**
es **ser**

F

fíe, *etc.* **fiar**
fío, *etc.* **fiar**
friendo **freír**
friera, *etc.* **freír**
frío, *etc.* **freír**
frito **freír**
fue, *etc.* **ir, ser**
fuera, *etc.* **ir, ser**
fuese, *etc.* **ir, ser**
fui, *etc.* **ir, ser**

G

gima, *etc.* **gemir**
gimiendo **gemir**
gimiera, *etc.* **gemir**
gimiese, *etc.* **gemir**
gimo, *etc.* **gemir**
goce, *etc.* **gozar**
gocé **gozar**

H

ha **haber**
habré, *etc.* **haber**
haga, *etc.* **hacer**
hago, *etc.* **hacer**
han **haber**
haría, *etc.* **hacer**
has **haber**
haya, *etc.* **haber**
haz **hacer**
he **haber**
hé **haber**
hecho **hacer**
hemos **haber**
hice, *etc.* **hacer**
hiciera, *etc.* **hacer**
hiciese, *etc.* **hacer**
hiera, *etc.* **herir**
hiero, *etc.* **herir**
hiramos **herir**
hiriendo **herir**
hiriera, *etc.* **herir**
hiriese, *etc.* **herir**
hizo **hacer**
hube, *etc.* **haber**
hubiera, *etc.* **haber**
hubiese, *etc.* **haber**
huela, *etc.* **oler**
huelo, *etc.* **oler**

huya, *etc.* **huir**
huyendo **huir**
huyera, *etc.* **huir**
huyese, *etc.* **huir**
huyo, *etc.* **huir**

I

iba, *etc.* **ir**
id **ir**
ido **ir**
idos **irse**

J

juego, *etc.* **jugar**
juegue, *etc.* **jugar**

L

lea, *etc.* **leer**
leído **leer**
leo, *etc.* **leer**
leyendo **leer**
leyera, *etc.* **leer**
leyese, *etc.* **leer**
llueva **llover**
llueve **llover**

M

mienta, *etc.* **mentir**
miento, *etc.* **mentir**
mintiendo **mentir**
mintiera, *etc.* **mentir**
mintiese, *etc.* **mentir**
muerda, *etc.* **morder**
muerdo, *etc.* **morder**
muero, *etc.* **morir**
muerto **morir**
muestre, *etc.* **mostrar**
muestro, *etc.* **mostrar**
muramos **morir**
muriendo **morir**
muriera, *etc.* **morir**
muriese, *etc.* **morir**

N

nazca, *etc.* **nacer**
nazco, *etc.* **nacer**
niego, *etc.* **negar**

niegue, *etc.* **negar**
nieva **nevar**
nieve **nevar**

O

oíd, *etc.* **oír**
oiga, *etc.* **oír**
oigo, *etc.* **oír**
oliendo **oler**
oliera, *etc.* **oler**
oliese, *etc.* **oler**
oye, *etc.* **oír**
oyendo **oír**
oyera, *etc.* **oír**
oyese, *etc.* **oír**

P

pida, *etc.* **pedir**
pidamos **pedir**
pidiendo **pedir**
pidiera, *etc.* **pedir**
pidiese, *etc.* **pedir**
pidiese, *etc.* **pedir**
pido, *etc.* **pedir**
pienso, *etc.* **pensar**
pierda, *etc.* **perder**
pierdo, *etc.* **perder**
ponga, *etc.* **poner**
pongámonos
  ponerse
ponte **ponerse**
pruebe, *etc.* **probar**
pruebo, *etc.* **probar**
pude, *etc.* **poder**
pudiendo **poder**
pudiera, *etc.* **poder**
pudiese, *etc.* **poder**
puedo, *etc.* **poder**
puesto **poner**
puse, *etc.* **poner**
pusiera, *etc.* **poner**
pusiese, *etc.* **poner**

Q

quepo, *etc.* **caber**
quiero, *etc.* **querer**
quise, *etc.* **querer**
quisiera, *etc.* **querer**
quisiese, *etc.* **querer**

R

ría, *etc.* **reír**
raimos **reír**
riendo **reír**
riera, *etc.* **reír**
riese, *etc.* **reír**
riña, *etc.* **reñir**
riñendo **reñir**
riñera, *etc.* **reñir**
riñese, *etc.* **reñir**
riño, *etc.* **reñir**
río, *etc.* **reír**
roto **romper**
ruego, *etc.* **rogar**
ruegue, *etc.* **rogar**

S

saque, *etc.* **sacar**
sé **saber, ser**
sea, *etc.* **ser**
sed **ser**
sepa, *etc.* **saber**
seque, *etc.* **secar**
sido **ser**
siendo **ser**
siento, *etc.* **sentar, sentir**
sigo, *etc.* **seguir**
siguiendo **seguir**
siguiera, *etc.* **seguir**
siguiese, *etc.* **segur**
sintiendo **sentir**

sintiera, *etc.* **sentir**
sintiese, *etc.* **sentir**
sintió **sentir**
sirviendo **servir**
sirvo, *etc.* **servir**
sois **ser**
somos **ser**
son **ser**
soy **ser**
suela, *etc.* **soler**
suelo, *etc.* **soler**
sueño, *etc.* **soñar**
supe, *etc.* **saber**
supiera, *etc.* **saber**
supiese, *etc.* **saber**

T

tienes, *etc.* **tener**
toque, *etc.* **tocar**
traigo, *etc.* **traer**
traje, *etc.* **traer**
tuve, *etc.* **tener**

U

uno, *etc.* **unir**

V

va **ir**
vais **ir**
vámonos **irse**

vamos **ir**
van **ir**
vas **ir**
vaya, *etc.* **ir**
ve **ir, ver**
vea, *etc.* **ver**
ved **ver**
vendré, *etc.* **venir**
venga, vengo **venir**
veo, *etc.* **ver**
ves, *etc.* **ver**
vete, *etc.* **irse**
vi, *etc.* **ver**
viendo, *etc.* **ver**
viene, *etc.* **venir**
viera, *etc.* **ver**
viese, *etc.* **ver**
vimos, *etc.* **ver**
vine, *etc.* **venir**
vio **ver**
viste **ver, vestir**
vistiendo **vestir**
vistiese **vestir(se)**
visto **ver, vestir**
voy **ir**
vuelo, *etc.* **volar**
vuelto **volver**
vuelvo, *etc.* **volver**

Y

yendo **ir**
yerro, *etc.* **errar**

Over 1,000 Spanish verbs conjugated like model verbs among the 301

The number after each verb is the page number in this book where a model verb is shown fully conjugated.